The Two Reconstructions

American Politics and Political Economy

A series edited by Benjamin I. Page

The Two Reconstructions

The Struggle for Black Enfranchisement

RICHARD M. VALELLY

The University of Chicago Press · Chicago and London

Richard M. Valelly is professor of political science at Swarthmore College. He is the author of *Radicalism in the States: The Minnesota Farmer-Labor Party and the American Political Economy* (1989), also published by the University of Chicago Press.

The University of Chicago Press, Chicago 60637
The University of Chicago Press, Ltd., London
© 2004 by The University of Chicago
All rights reserved. Published 2004
Printed in the United States of America
13 12 11 10 09 08 07 06 05 04   1 2 3 4 5

ISBN: 0-226-84528-1 (cloth)
ISBN: 0-226-84530-3 (paper)

Library of Congress Cataloging-in-Publication data is available.

♾ The paper used in this publication meets the minimum requirements of the American National Standard for Information Sciences—Permanence of Paper for Printed Library Materials, ANSI Z39.48-1992.

For Jonathan, Peter, and Nanette

Contents

Preface

There is a deep conundrum at the heart of America's development as a political democracy. The first reconstruction of southern politics (1867–1877) is now widely recognized as a quasi-revolutionary era that followed the Civil War. It saw the rise of biracial party politics and the establishment of voting rights for African Americans. Yet toward the end of the nineteenth century its once-massive political and electoral legacies more or less vanished. Between 1893 and 1911, Congress formally abolished about 94 percent of the elections statutes passed during the first reconstruction. In contrast, the second reconstruction of southern electoral politics (also widely appreciated as a thorough revolution in political equality and race relations) has been much more successful. The Voting Rights Act's temporary provisions have indeed been renewed several times.

The historical and social science riddle lies in the contrast between these two reconstructions. No other democracy in the world has ever enfranchised a large group, then disenfranchised it—and then reenfranchised it. Why did the first effort fail? Why has the second succeeded?[1]

Addressing these questions by means of extended comparison between the two eras can tell us why sweeping political reform works or fails when it does. This study therefore identifies and analyzes crucial similarities and differences between the two reconstructions.

Many scholars think that the acquisition of economic resources and status among the disadvantaged eventually makes their greater political equality inevitable. According to this view the first reconstruction would have succeeded if the land belonging to Confederate planters had been distributed to black southerners after the Civil War instead of being given back to the planters by President Andrew Johnson. Others link a democratic polity's successful incorporation of excluded groups to the emergence within that polity of a broad, firm social consensus in favor of such reform. The idea here is that robust equality in political relationships among social groups, be they social classes, genders, or racial groups, depends on moral enlightenment within the dominant group. Because of their norms and aspirations, democracies have a tendency to cultivate such awakenings. Their members eventually agree, on the merits, with the marginal group's demand for equality. The analytical issue therefore becomes specifying the conditions under which members of the dominant group arrive at such agreement.[2]

While not denying the political importance of resources or of shared norms, this book concentrates on the political entrepreneurship that plays out within the context of incentives and tasks created by the presence of political institutions. It tracks the interaction over time among three things. First, it considers the political conditions for biracial coalition-making within the national political parties. Second, it stresses that coalition-making was not simply about people at the top reaching out. It was also about people at the outskirts of the polity reaching in: forceful political exertion by African Americans cemented coalition-making. Third, it traces the ways American political institutions rewarded—or failed to reward—coalition-making and thus shaped its follow-on processes. In particular, I explore how the political parties and the national courts regulated political possibilities *after* coalition formation.

Understanding African American political and electoral inclusion therefore requires a blend of rational choice concepts (which help with understanding coalition formation) and historical and comparative institutionalism (which helps with understanding dynamics after coalition formation). In offering this blend I hope to join the ranks of scholars who have been concerned with understanding American race relations, inequality, and political change. What this book adds to that corpus is an insistence on the centrality of voting, elections, and political parties in determining the evolution of American race relations and social equality.

Besides refining one's understanding of why much of American politics evolved as it did from the first reconstruction onward, this book's approach also illuminates policy choices and debates. Congress must decide, no later than 2007, whether to renew temporary provisions of the 1965 Voting Rights Act. These provide for continuing Justice Department involvement in monitoring elections and for federal screening of state and local proposals for electoral changes that affect voting and officeholding by minority communities.

Since 1965 Congress has several times carried such measures forward. During that time, black reverse migration to the South has enlarged the number of southerners covered by the act. Also, Hispanic voters in the Southwest, Florida, New York, and Chicago, Native Americans (in, for example, Montana and South Dakota), and other minority populations have come under the act's protection.

But depending on which political party controls Congress in 2007, what stance the president takes, and how the Supreme Court reads the Voting Rights Act, Congress may decline to renew the act's special provisions. Such a decision would obviously alter the political opportunities of many millions more Americans than in 1965.

The historical cast of this book's analysis underscores that whatever Congress does, its actions will compose another unit of analysis in a long string of such units. It will be an "nth" case of a quite old—but by now much evolved—politics. Congress will legislate in the shadow of an extraordinary history of conflict over black voting and officeholding. That political drama has influenced the constitutional law and statutory framework under which Americans live, the political and racial attitudes that prevail today among blacks and whites, and the social and economic context of contemporary race relations. My study thus means to frame the institutional relations between past and present in ways that readers might find intellectually useful—and helpful to them as citizens.

Acknowledgments

During the time that I researched and wrote this book, I leaned on many friends, mentors, and professional acquaintances. Martha Derthick steadily communicated her deep interest in my work from the instant I began it. Partway through the project, she gave me a magnificent framed engraving of Abraham Lincoln for my study. Lincoln kept me company during countless hours of writing and revision. Martha also gave me essential compendia of congressional debates and Supreme Court decisions and often offered penetrating observations about the relation between federalism and political change in American history.

At my suggestion, Peyton McCrary of the Voting Section of the U.S. Justice Department's Civil Rights Division joined the Swarthmore College Department of Political Science as Eugene Lang Professor of Social Change for the academic year 1998–1999. During that time, and in the years since, Peyton has freely shared with me his vast knowledge of the Civil War era (including Lincoln's emerging grasp of black suffrage as a central element in any reconstruction settlement) and of twentieth-century American electoral law and history. More than once Peyton provided me with copies of choice primary documents in his valuable personal collection.

Chris Howard not only correctly insisted that I write a single study (as opposed to a two-volume one), but he also carefully read and commented on the book's first draft. Ken Sharpe read grant proposals and several chapters and offered deeply thoughtful comments, which helped me to sustain my momentum. Amy Bridges, Dan Crofts, Dedi Felman, Michael Fitts, Markus Kruezer, Meta Mendel-Reyes, Rob Mickey, Kent Redding, Richard Rubin, and Steve Teles all also read various parts of the book and offered very helpful suggestions and reactions.

Also, J. Morgan Kousser read early chapters and indicated support for the book's conceptualization; given his unmatched expertise, I was very heartened by that signal. He also helped me throughout the life of the project with tips and advice.

My superb student research assistants at Swarthmore College, Robyn Gearey, Jeremy Weinstein, Lauren Basta, and Amelia Hoover, were efficient, enthusiastic, and creative. The circulation staff of McCabe Library at Swarthmore helped me manage several hundred volumes on loan from it and from Haverford College's Magill Library and Bryn Mawr College's Canaday Library. Minda Hart, the interlibrary loan librarian at McCabe for many years, was an indispensable resource, and it saddens me that she did not live to see this book.

At Cal Tech, J. David Hacker kindly sent me an unpublished paper about the overlooked strengths of the Ninth Census. Ron King taught me much about the 1876 election in Louisiana and South Carolina. John Quist kindly supplied me with page proofs from the late Richard Abbott's new book about Republican newspapers in the South during the first reconstruction. Xi Wang gave me offprints of his law review articles about black suffrage and consulted with me about post-Reconstruction party politics. For help with black voter turnout data from that era I thank Kent Redding, who made available to me his then-unpublished ecological regression estimates, along with his commentary on the strengths and limits of the new technique for ecological regression that has been devised by Gary King. Scott James helped me better understand post-Reconstruction voting rights enforcement. Charles Stewart III gave me corrected electoral data for southern House elections in the 1880s. Hanes Walton Jr. provided valuable advice about nineteenth-century Republican investment in statehood politics. Richard Bensel gave me his state party platform data for the late 1880s and 1890s. Fred Harris pointed out the role of the black college fraternities in developing citizenship programs in the South during the 1930s and generously sent me hard-to-find photocopied materials about these organizations. Dan Kryder, Jane Levey, and Suzanne Mettler answered questions about returning black veterans of World War II. Steve Reich helped me understand the ins and outs of researching the NAACP Papers at the Library of Congress. Manfred Berg, the German historian of the NAACP, very generously sent me photocopies of primary documents that he found at the Library of Congress while researching the NAACP. Gudmund Iversen guided me through an OLS analysis of the NAACP's impact on black voter registration in the 1940s and 1950s. Michael Klarman (thanks to a tip I got from Howard Gillman) sent me an offprint of his fine law review piece on the white primary cases. Dan West briefed me on his participation in the great Selma-to-Montgomery march of 1965. Rob Lenz generously gave me private papers from his time as a defense attorney in Freedom Summer and in 1966 in Mississippi and consented to the deposit of these papers at the Peace Collection of the Swarthmore College Libraries. Pamela Karlan gave expert answers to questions about the Voting Rights Act's implementation. Laughlin McDonald gave me an advance copy of his book about voting rights politics in Georgia. Robert Inman generously gave me a copy of his unpublished estimates, co-authored with Michael Fitts, of the fiscal impact of the act on southern states. Phil Klinkner shared his unpublished analysis of racialized electoral administration in Florida in the 2000 election.

Ira Katznelson, Theda Skocpol, and Rogers Smith supported my grant proposals and let me know how important they considered the prospect of the book's completion. Theda also provided essential advice and exhortation by email and in person, and she showed me her valuable personal collection of rare ephemera and documents about black fraternal organizations, sending me several electronic images of them.

Ben Yagoda, a fine writer of the English language, often counseled me during the writing process. My family carefully listened to all of my ideas about how to title the book. Frank Gruber, Larry Hanks, Rich Kazis, Colin Moore, Andy Perrin, Beth Rubenstein, Kay Schlozman, Cathy Shaw, Gigi Simeone, and Charles Stewart III all offered good advice on that matter as well. Desmond King, in the end, coined the book's main title. Jim Shoch was a great listener and probing questioner. Matthew Holden regularly touched base with me over the years to find out how I was doing. Tom Hall and Jeffrey Celebre never tired of taking warm satisfaction in my progress reports. Carol Nackenoff talked with me about American citizenship at the drop of a hat. Keith Reeves taught me much about the political meaning of black officeholding.

When I began the project, the journal *Politics and Society* gave it a critical boost by publishing my first comparison of the two reconstructions in March 1993. Several former MIT colleagues, Suzanne Berger, Joshua Cohen, Willard Johnson, Peter Lemieux, Mike Lipsky, and Charles Stewart III, aided the formulation of that piece, as did Sidney Tarrow and Margaret Weir.

A research fellowship in the spring of 1992 at Harvard University's W. E. B. Du Bois Institute for Afro-American Research enormously expanded my grasp of black history and of African American studies generally. I thank the institute's director, Henry Louis Gates Jr., the W. E. B. Du Bois Professor of the Humanities at Harvard, and Randall Burkett, then the institute's associate director. During that fellowship, Silva Haratounian and Gail Mantelman, who provided secretarial assistance back at MIT, expertly managed my rapidly growing research files. Also, the Mark DeWolfe Howe Civil Liberties Fund of the Harvard Law School generously defrayed research expenses.

Owing to the good offices of Suzanne Berger, then chair of MIT's Department of Political Science, MIT granted me a paid sabbatical leave in the fall of 1992. Kathy Green, then acting librarian at the Dewey Library, gave me my own office in the library stacks, in which I wrote happily and copiously. The interlibrary loan librarians at the MIT Humanities Library cheerfully found many rare publications for me.

I am grateful to Paul E. Peterson for commissioning a study of black disenfranchisement for presentation at a January 1993 conference at Harvard University under the auspices of Harvard's Center for American Political Studies. Gary Orfield (and later H. Douglas Price) provided superb comments on that paper. In subsequent presentations of that study at Northwestern University and at the University of Virginia, I received further useful feedback before its publication. At the Virginia presentation, in particular, Ed Ayers, Brian Balogh, and Charles McCurdy provided valuable expert reactions.

During the summer of 1994, thanks to Martha Derthick and Michael Lacey, then director of the Division of United States Studies at the Woodrow Wilson International Center for Scholars, I received generous funding, a quiet office, and superb staff support for researching the Voting Rights Act's implementation.

In June 1996 the Massachusetts Historical Society awarded me an Andrew W. Mellon Fellowship to work at its Center for the Study of New England History with the papers of Senators George Frisbie Hoar and Henry Cabot Lodge.

In the academic year 1996–1997, while on sabbatical leave from Swarthmore College, I embarked on the task of writing the entire book. Swarthmore paid for the fall semester. The National Endowment for the Humanities replaced my salary for the spring term. I thank its director, Sheldon Hackney, for the Fellowship for College Teachers and Independent Scholars and for selecting my grant to form part of his special initiative, the NEH National Conversation on American Pluralism and Identity.

In the academic year 2000–2001, Swarthmore College again supported my research and writing, awarding me both a regular semester's leave in the fall of 2000 and a Eugene Lang Faculty Research Fellowship for the spring of 2001, thus assuring this book's completion.

These acknowledgements would be incomplete if I failed to thank Dick and Nancy Valelly for taking a deep interest in African American history and for their own contributions to its recovery and celebration.

Toward the end of this book's gestation, I profited greatly from the advice and comments of my editor, John Tryneski. The sensitive, detailed evaluations offered by the manuscript referees for the University of Chicago Press, one anonymous, the other James Morone of Brown University, helped galvanize the final "wrap" of the manuscript. Jane Zanichkowsky, my copyeditor, gave a nice finish of limpidity to the writing and addressed countless items in the text. Leslie Keros was a superb production editor.

I may well have overlooked someone who deserves acknowledgment besides those whom I have identified above. If I have, it results only from a lapse in memory, not any lack of gratitude.

My beloved sons and wife, Jonathan and Peter Valelly and Nanette Tobin, expressed deep and unflagging interest in my book project the entire time. With tender gratitude for their love for me, I dedicate this book to them.

Chapter One

The Strange Career of African American Voting and Office-Holding

African Americans' rights—to vote and to hold office—have had a strange career.[1] A sudden, large increase in rates of black voting and office-holding has taken place *twice* over the course of American political evolution. The meaning of that fact, as we will see, is disturbing. From a social science standpoint it is also deeply interesting.

The first large expansion in African American voting rights took place after the Civil War. It was so sweeping that in 1874, when Congress revised the United States Code, the revisors were able to take forty-seven separate regulatory provisions from the federal elections statutes enacted between 1870 and 1872 and place them in the code. But inclusion eventually gave way to thorough disenfranchisement of African Americans at the state level. In the late 1890s, southern governments set up poll taxes and literacy tests to push blacks out of the voting booth. This process affected federal law as well. Congress threw out the Reconstruction-era elections statutes. A House report from the Fifty-third Congress (1893–1895) demanded that "every trace of reconstruction measures be wiped from the books." By 1911, this goal was effectively met. About 94 percent of a once-elaborate federal electoral-regulatory code was repealed.[2]

A "second reconstruction" was therefore required for America to become fully democratic and for its inegalitarian race relations to again change accordingly. And therein lies the startling nature of America's two reconstructions. *No* major social group in Western history, other than African Americans, ever entered the electorate of an established democracy and then was extruded by nominally democratic means such as constitutional conventions and ballot referenda, forcing that group to start all over again. Disenfranchisements certainly took place in other nations, for example, in France, which experienced several during the nineteenth century. But such events occurred when the type of regime changed, not under formally democratic conditions. In Europe, Latin America, and elsewhere, liberal democracies never sponsored disenfranchisement. Once previously excluded social groups came into any established democratic system, they stayed in.[3]

This is an extraordinary datum about the United States. We often think of America as exceptional—but never in quite this way. Before discussing this phenomenon, it helps to take a closer look at it. Abraham Lincoln's discussion of black suffrage during his last speech is a good place to start. It was the first time a U.S. president brought up black suffrage and posed it as a national issue.

Speaking from a White House balcony on April 11, 1865, Lincoln shared several pregnant thoughts about "the elective franchise for the colored man" with an assembly gathered below him on the White House lawn. He said that he backed suffrage for "the very intelligent" (by which Lincoln probably meant African American men with property and formal education) and for "those who serve our cause as soldiers" (which then referred to about 150,000 black male army veterans).[4]

The "colored man" to whom Lincoln referred was a prominent part of life both in the border states of Delaware, Kentucky, Maryland, and Missouri and in the eleven states of the former Confederacy—altogether about 46 percent of the Union. But African Americans did not have the right to vote in any of these states. Indeed, when Lincoln spoke these words very few black men—and no black women—had the right to vote. When the states joined the Union after ratification of the Constitution in 1789, only three permitted blacks to vote: Maine, Tennessee, and Vermont. As the Union grew, original and new states consciously disenfranchised blacks. By 1865 free African American men voted only in Maine, Massachusetts, New Hampshire, Vermont, and Rhode Island.[5]

Lincoln's plan of extending voting rights to a large number of the recently emancipated black men plainly foretold a new national politics. Listening to Lincoln, his assassin, John Wilkes Booth, swore in fury that he would "put him through." He did just that a few days later.[6]

African American suffrage might at this moment have died stillborn, for President Andrew Johnson, Lincoln's successor, soon revealed a deep hostility to black voting rights, indeed black rights of any sort. Yet Congress moved to establish widespread black suffrage despite Johnson's opposition. Between December 1866 and December 1867, the percentage of all black adult males eligible to vote suddenly shot up from .5 percent to 80.5 percent, with all of the increase in the former Confederacy. By 1870 the Constitution featured two new amendments, the fourteenth and the fifteenth, enshrining the right to vote. The first reconstruction, as it is sometimes called, was well under way.[7]

Black office-holding emerged very rapidly. About half of the lower house of South Carolina's legislature during the first reconstruction was black, 42 percent of Louisiana's lower house and 19 percent of its upper house was black, and Mississippi's house was 29 percent black and its senate 15 percent black. Even Virginia, which did not experience a "radical" phase in its reconstruction, had for a brief period a lower house that was 21 percent black and an upper house that was 6 percent black.[8]

But in the 1890s, a generation after the great expansion in black voting and office-holding, legislatures and constitutional conventions controlled by white southern Democrats disenfranchised the South's black adult males, extinguishing voting rights for the great majority of African Americans. When women's suffrage arrived in 1920, it did not alter black disenfranchisement in the former Confederacy. Black women did not vote. Not until the 1940s did black voter registration drives in the South eventually reemerge and experience some success. And one more generation of fierce struggle was still required before Congress enacted the 1965 Voting Rights Act. That statute was the turning point in the second reconstruction.

The 1965 act fundamentally recast the legal and administrative context for voting in the South. Previously what might be called "wholesale shrinkage" of the electorate had been accomplished with literacy tests, poll taxes, stringent residency requirements, requirements that registration occur months before elections, and inconvenient hours and arrangements for registration. African Americans who sought to participate anyway were met by "retail shrinkage": rejection at the discretion of local electoral administrators.

Simply by ending this older legal and administrative context, the Voting Rights Act created a new, far freer one. Section 4 of the act applied the statute to any state or county that maintained a voting test or device on November 1, 1964, and where the census showed voter registration or turnout for the 1964 presidential election to be below 50 percent of the voting-age population. These tests or devices were now suspended for five years. The act thus covered all of Alabama, Alaska, Georgia, Louisiana, Mississippi, South Carolina, Virginia, twenty-six North Carolina counties, three Arizona counties, one Hawaii county, and one Idaho county. The act also prevented the state of New York from enforcing its English-language competence test against voting-age Puerto Ricans residing in New York. Section 6 of the act authorized appointment of federal examiners in jurisdictions covered under section 4. They reviewed "applicants' qualifications for voting and placed the names of those qualified to vote on a list of eligible voters . . . local officials were then obligated . . . to place the names of those persons listed by federal examiners on the official voting lists."[9] Section 5, creating a mechanism called "preclearance," required the submission of any planned changes in voting rules in the covered jurisdictions to either the attorney general or the three-judge district court of the District of Columbia for prior approval.

After President Lyndon Baines Johnson signed the Voting Rights Act on August 6, 1965, sharp increases in black voter registration occurred where the act was initially applied in the former Confederacy and in states where it stimulated further struggle. For the Peripheral South (Arkansas, Florida, Tennessee, and Texas), black voter registration jumped from about 60 percent in 1964 to about 71.4 percent by 1968, roughly a 19 percent increase that reflected compliance by state and local officials with the Voting Rights Act and the impact of continued black activism. In the Deep South (Alabama, Georgia, Louisiana, Mississippi, North Carolina, South Carolina, and Virginia), where Jim Crow politics had historically tended to mean greater repression, registration jumped from about 33.8 percent of all black adults in 1964 to 56.6 percent in 1968, or a 67 percent increase, again apparently due to compliance by state and local officials with the commands of the act and continued civil rights activism.[10]

Even so, America today is still struggling over black voting rights. Large numbers of African American adults are blocked from voting by state felony disenfranchisement laws. Felony disenfranchisement too often rests on legal provisions that were enacted with racial intent. Further, several southern states—Florida, Virginia, Alabama, Texas, and Mississippi—disenfranchise ex-felons at very high rates. Provisions of these states' criminal codes shrink the number of potential black voters considerably. About 31 percent of all black men in Florida and Alabama, for instance, are permanently barred from voting.[11]

Also, startling episodes occur and recur. The best known of these happened in November 2000, when many of Florida's black voters found that their presidential ballots were rejected or not counted by election officials at disproportionately high rates.[12]

Finally, increases in black office-holding since passage of the Voting Rights Act have critically depended on federal involvement. In the early

1980s, Congress found it necessary to add a new section to the act intended to press state and local legislative bodies to make black and minority office-holding easier. The new section 2 held that there is a "denial or abridgement of the right to vote" if electoral processes are not "equally open to participation" by "members of a protected class" and if such members "have less opportunity . . . to elect representatives of their choice." The policy directive was clear: government should focus on the mechanisms and processes that impede the election of blacks to public office.

By the early 1990s the House of Representatives had the largest number of black legislators it had ever had—thirty-eight. In southern states that were completely covered by the Voting Rights Act (Alabama, Georgia, Louisiana, Mississippi, South Carolina, Texas, and Virginia), the average percentage of all local elected officials who were black was 3.6 percent in 1974 but had grown to 13.3 percent by 1993, a 269 percent increase. Yet black office-holding is not completely normalized, in or outside the South. Subtle signs of white resistance abound. In 2003, the following was reported in an opinion of a federal district court:

> [A]fter the 2000 Charleston County School Board elections, for the first time in the history of the County, five of the nine school board members were African-American persons. After African-American school board members became a majority on that governing body, the Charleston County Legislative Delegation to the South Carolina General Assembly sponsored several pieces of legislation. . . . [L]egislation was introduced to remove control of the budget of the school system from the School Board and place it under the jurisdiction of the County Council.[13]

Such resistance by whites to black office-holding may, indeed, be covertly inscribed on the Fifteenth Amendment (the second of the two Reconstruction-era amendments constitutionally regulating black voting rights). The amendment contains no explicit provision for office-holding. That is because Congress chose to drop such a stipulation so that the amendment could be ratified quickly.

But the 1982 amendment of the Voting Rights Act (stipulating that minorities be free to vote into public office candidates whom they wish to support) openly acknowledges the significance of black office-holding. This is quite correct. The United States is not a direct democracy; it is a representative system. It cannot be anything other than a representative polity, given its size. For that reason, voting in and of itself has not been and is not sufficient to create a fully democratic public sphere in this country. It is necessary. But group access to office-holding is also necessary.

Black office-holding has always been in part a matter of "civic status." Social standing in America, Judith Shklar cogently argued, has two great emblems: the right to vote and the "opportunity to earn." She might well have added that free access to public office, regardless of class, gender, ethnicity, or race, also entitles a group defined by such divisions to general respect. According to Shklar, "to see just how important [civic standing] has always been, one has to listen to those Americans who have been deprived of it through no fault of their own."[14] Listen, then, to Tom McCain, one of the first blacks elected to local office in Edgefield County, South Carolina, in the 1980s, after a century of lily-white government: "There's an inherent value to office-holding. . . . A race of people who are excluded from public office will always be second class."[15] McCain clearly speaks in the language of social standing.

Or listen to Reverend Henry McNeal Turner, a state senator protesting his expulsion from the Georgia legislature in 1868 on the ground that blacks could vote but were not entitled to hold public office: "I am here to demand my rights, and to hurl the thunderbolt at the men who would dare to cross the threshold of my manhood." Later in his speech of protest, Turner exclaimed: "Congress, after assisting Mr. Lincoln to take me out of servile slavery, did not intend to put me and my race into *political* slavery. If they did, let them take away my ballot—I do not want it, and shall not have it. I don't want to be a mere tool of that sort. I have been a slave long enough already."[16] Denial of access to the political good of holding public office was tantamount to slavery; it made the ballot worthless. Worse, it turned the ballot into an instrument of extreme political dependence, Turner suggested.

With characteristic pungency Turner grasped an additional rationale for black office-holding. It is about an equal place at the table in important policy-making settings: "We are told that if black men want to speak, they must speak through white trumpets . . . through white messengers who will quibble and equivocate, and evade as rapidly as the pendulum of the clock."[17] But, Turner said, white trumpets were not good enough. Black citizens had clear policy needs. They needed jury representation to prevent their being "sent to the Penitentiary in perfect caravans," a school bill for "the rising youths of our State," a civil rights law to prevent black passengers on common carriers from being forced to pay first-class fare only "to be thrust into Jim-Crow cars, for white men to insult their wives, and blackguard our daughters, and smoke them to death," and a laborers' lien to prevent their being "driven away penniless."[18]

True, some analysts deny that the "equal place" proposition requires extensive black office-holding. Survey research conducted by Katherine Tate suggests that for most blacks the "equal place" idea is quite compelling. But, say critics of this view, white politicians and judges can and do represent black voters quite well. Of course they can. Yet Kerry Haynie has shown that increased office-holding by African Americans in state legislatures *by itself* changes states' expenditures on health, education, and welfare. Simple change in the number of black legislators, and nothing more, impacts public spending in the states. Although white politicians of the same party can represent black constituents, there seems to be a significant "extra" that comes from racially integrating a major decision-making body such as a legislature, and the same may well be true of the judiciary.[19]

Finally, the making of black office-holding is a matter of democratic fraternity. Amos Akerman—later a U.S. attorney general—put this point well in argument before the Georgia Supreme Court in 1869, closing as follows:

> Counsel says that the Code was made when this was a white man's country. . . . No matter whose the country was when the Code was made, it is now the country of every citizen in it—the country of the white man and of the black man together. They are bound together politically by a common fortune. . . . Here they must both live. Here they must both labor. Here they may both vote. And here, if I am right in this argument, either may hold office when his fellow-citizens choose to trust him with office.[20]

The epic of black electoral inclusion is not simply about black voting; it is a tale of a double dualism: two reconstructions, each with two dimensions: voting and office-holding.

WHAT NEEDS TO BE EXPLAINED AND HOW

With basic facts in hand, the problem of explanation now confronts us. Why did one effort end in disenfranchisement? Why is the second effort, despite its frictions and weak spots, still a relative success?

In what follows I seek answers by systematically comparing the two reconstructions as if they were two independent cases—that is, as if the course of the first case did not determine the dynamics of the second.[21] Is this assumption too strong? Perhaps. Historically inclined political scientists often emphasize "path dependence." The idea refers to the way actual historical sequence will narrow or even determine the range of things that can happen later. There is some truth to this idea. During the second reconstruction, for instance, federal policymakers worried about lessons concerning southern resistance to federal intervention that they took from the first reconstruction.[22]

The case for treating the two reconstructions as effectively independent rests, however, on fully appreciating the disenfranchisement of black southerners around 1900. William A. Dunning, a contemporary historian, foresaw the "completion" of the "undoing of Reconstruction." During the process, as the historian Michael Perman has emphasized, prominent southern politicians and editorialists repeatedly thought and spoke in such terms as "final settlement," "elimination," and acting "to remove the negro as a factor." The chair of the 1900 Democratic state convention in Alabama told the delegates that "the great question of the Elective Franchise must be settled. The white line was formed in 1874 and swept the white men of Alabama into power. The white line has been re-formed in 1900 to keep them in power forever." These ambitions were realized for several decades. Black voting and office-holding were reduced to zero, as we shall see.[23]

Disenfranchisement also had a structural effect on national politics that reinforced the utter reversal of black voting and office-holding. Section 2 of the Fourteenth Amendment reduces congressional representation of states that deny the suffrage on racial grounds, but this section was never enforced. Democrats thus had an Electoral College bonus that they would not have had otherwise. Also, southern Democrats enjoyed about twenty-five extra seats in Congress for each decade between 1903 and 1953. Their added presence, in turn, altered about 15 percent of roll call outcomes in the House during this period. There was little or no representation of black interests in Congress. Instead, white supremacist interests were not only entrenched but overrepresented.[24]

It is rather telling that when government lawyers in the Johnson administration evaluated policy options for black voting rights in the first two months of 1965, they seriously considered recommending to the president that he instead propose a new constitutional amendment—as if the Fourteenth and Fifteenth Amendments inscribed on the Constitution during the first reconstruction were dead letters for the purpose of establishing black voting rights. *They* evidently saw themselves as starting all over. In an important sense they were.[25]

A comparison of the two reconstructions is aided by a wealth of evidence about the American experience. Between 1868 and the present, questions of inclusion were either openly acknowledged issues or the uninvited guests in about two million national, state, and local elections in the United States. Electoral inclusion surfaced in the courts and in law enforcement. Finally, voting rights and the merits of reform or inaction were discussed in Congress, in newspapers appealing to black and white subscribers, in the streets of white and black residential areas, in citizens' homes, in predominantly black and predominantly white churches, in schools, colleges, and universities, in books, and in magazine articles.[26]

Most of what happened in this myriad of moments cannot be straight-forwardly recovered or investigated, to be sure. Also, accurate individual-level data on all of the relevant voter behavior—registration and election-day turnout compiled by race and gender for all of the relevant jurisdictions—are not available. Still, enough aggregate data have been published for enough jurisdictions, and there are enough reliable descriptions in primary and secondary sources of campaign-related events and legislative, administrative, executive, and judicial behavior, to permit in-depth comparison across time. But the matter hardly ends there. Which kind of explanation will get us through the historical comparison in a satisfying, use-ful way?

To aid in understanding African American electoral inclusion, this book takes cues from historical institutionalist scholarship, particularly from the variant that attends to the interplay between political parties and formal insti-tutions. Stephen Skowronek's inspired description of American national gov-ernment as a "state of courts and parties" is especially useful. The concept refers to defining elements of the political order in the United States. The pio-neering work of J. Morgan Kousser concerning black voting rights policy, pol-itics, and law has shown why the notion is apt. Kousser has demonstrated that during both reconstructions the incorporation of African Americans was deeply influenced by the courts and by political parties. My own ideas about courts and parties were greatly stimulated by his research.[27]

But this book also owes much to the literature concerning social move-ments. I consider contentious and nonparty politics—protest movements, broad-based social movements, and voluntary associations—at length. Such extrapartisan forces are generally missing from the work of scholars dealing with parties and formal institutions. Yet protest and contention have always regulated the politics of African American electoral inclusion.[28]

Finally, this book owes a great deal to what "rational choice" political sci-ence advises, which is to concentrate on strategic and goal-defined behavior. It therefore treats party politicians, federal judges, and the leaders of and par-ticipants in social movements as highly entrepreneurial. Such actors often tried to do new things, despite the odds.

In short, I focus on how a national political order—defined by the activi-ties of the federal courts and by national party system structure—influenced the prospects of coalition and movement politics. I prefer this way of address-ing the puzzles of African American electoral inclusion because the alterna-tives to it are insufficiently institutional or place too much weight on broad, impersonal forces. To show what I mean, let me describe these other theories briefly before laying out how my approach works.

One school of thought would draw from the entire story the proposition that race relations are especially troubled arenas of social conflict owing to the great strength and persistence of racial attitudes among a white majority. A society mired in racism cannot avoid taking a lot of time and effort to work out decent race relations. The long struggle for African American electoral inclusion has therefore been fundamentally a case of gradual social change.[29] The first reconstruction failed, this perspective implies, because change in race relations could not take place faster than change in society would naturally occur. Trying to do so only guaranteed white backlash. William Graham Sumner, a founder of American sociology, put the point memorably with his aphorism that "stateways cannot change folkways." The placement of black electoral inclusion on the political agenda at the national, state, and local levels bothered most whites and triggered resistance from many. The violent streak in the South's political culture augmented the reaction. White "veto movements" such as the Ku Klux Klan of 1868 emerged and swept through the American South in response to black enfranchisement or its possibility.[30] White southerners, and ultimately white northerners, simply would not accept the political equality of blacks no matter what the Constitution said. The second reconstruction's greater success with African American voting and office-holding came, therefore, only in the wake of a broad attitudinal change among whites.[31]

Another perspective, however, holds that the crux of the matter was and is not attitudinal change among whites or the South's political culture. What mattered was the entrapment of African Americans in economic backwardness. This view insists on the political importance of economic weakness among largely landless nineteenth-century blacks. They depended on white landholders, "furnish" merchants, and white-controlled railroads for their access to agricultural markets. They therefore lacked the means to prevent white supremacy. But urbanization and labor shortages in manufacturing north of the Mason-Dixon line steadily chipped away at their marginal status. Black southerners came off the land into different, less oppressive economic settings, north and south, and thus acquired greater political sophistication and resources. In using them to press for civil rights they were able finally to force the issue of their electoral inclusion.[32]

A third analysis also treats political economy and sociology but more explicitly emphasizes the skills and history of an elite class. Black electoral inclusion threatened the labor supply of white landholders sitting at the apex of a quasi-feudal system. Voting by blacks would promote black education, freedom of movement, and legal protections against labor exploitation. According to this account the critical factors were therefore the dexterity and unity of purpose among "a relatively small minority," that is, "the whites of the areas of heavy Negro population." Their "extraordinary achievement" was repeated in seminationalist and ethnic mobilization of other whites. They also gained the respect of Northern capitalists and political reformers who distrusted the lower classes. With such tactics they overthrew Reconstruction, triumphed over the threat of agrarian radicalism (which proposed to substitute class antagonism for racial conflict as the South's organizing force), and developed legal disenfranchisement and a one-party system to preempt challenges to white supremacy.[33]

Until these landed economic elites themselves changed, black electoral inclusion was impossible. Scholars have invoked two specific mechanisms of elite transformation. The advent during World War II of new technology for mechanizing the southern cotton harvest undergirds one version of the theory. Another rendition emphasizes the role of crop production control, first instituted during the New Deal. It displaced cotton tenants on a scale that was sufficient to "prime" the plantation owners to want and adopt machine pickers. Either way, the "need" to control black labor vanished. According to this "laborlords-become-modern-farmers" view, African American electoral inclusion sprang from the metamorphosis of an entrenched, landed ruling class into modern commercial farmers.[34]

Yet another analytical approach comes from efforts to make sense of what the international context of a racially divided nation means for its domestic politics. Scholars working in this vein have deemphasized social structure and highlighted "raison d'état" as a variable. For them, fundamental advances in black rights have depended on war and geopolitical threats to the United States that invited national policymakers to forge social unity. African American electoral inclusion has therefore been a case of geopolitical threat requiring internal democracy. The implication of this view is clear: once the United States aspired to offer a political model to the world after World War II, Congress and the executive branch promoted black electoral inclusion.[35]

Finally, it has been proposed, by me and by Anthony Marx, that central governmental control of the means of coercion was a key variable. During the first reconstruction the federal government was unable to control violence against blacks, but it had much more success during the second. Electoral inclusion came from increased federal control of private violence in the United States, the result of a long state-building process.[36]

In short, there are, by my count, five alternatives to this book's rational choice–historical institutional account, and each has much to offer. Indeed, each "explains" the puzzle of African American electoral inclusion. But I have never been quite satisfied with them. Focusing on attitudes, class, modernization, geopolitics, and the like assumes away the real world of political institutions and of people's struggle with the constraints and opportunities created by formal and informal institutions.

Coalitions and Party Crisis

One major emphasis in this book, therefore, is on coalition-making strategy and behavior within the context of a two-party system. I track the actions of national party politicians—of politicians bound by a sense of shared fate to their party's larger interests or, alternatively, yoked to the interests of a faction.

During both reconstructions, one set of party actors was in conflict with another set—either a rival party or a rival faction within the same party. The first set of politicians needed to expand their electoral coalition in order to defeat the second set. In other words, more powerful, established members of the system needed the incorporation of new voters in order to win conflicts that had emerged at some point before they responded to demands for inclusion. *This* aspect of the two reconstructions was a kind of "revolution from above": one set of political actors moved to bring in lots of new people all at once to advance its own interests.

In other words, I borrow—but also adapt—William Riker's notion of the "minimum winning coalition." The sociologist William Gamson independently arrived at a similar formulation, the "cheapest winning coalition." The idea, in Riker's words, is that "[i]n social situations similar to n-person, zero-sum games with side-payments, participants create coalitions just as large as they believe will ensure winning and no larger."[37] In this book, however, Riker's and Gamson's emphasis on a tight linkage between specific change in coalition size and the relative generosity of the side payments is dropped. It is difficult to see how elites can be so masterful as to precisely allocate the side payments and thus fine-tune the optimal coalition size, yet be so in need of allies that they must expand their coalitions in the first place.

"Zero-sumness" is instead the most important feature of the pre-coalition situation. Elites reach out because they are in a crisis. David Waldner has thus recommended attention to the depth and relative intractability of elite conflict as progenitors of coalition formation. As he puts it, coalition formation results if elites believe that "their long-term capacity to reproduce their elite status" is plainly and unmistakably jeopardized, that is, if "the threatened elite feels that it will be unable to compete . . . in the future."[38]

Chapters 2, 7, and 8 further explore this logic. Chapter 2 shows that Republicans pushed for a new coalition in 1867, adding seven hundred thousand new citizens to their existing electoral coalition, because they believed that their future as a party—then only in existence less than two decades— was at stake. If they did nothing, they would be ruined. Chapters 7 and 8 consider analogous cases in 1948 and from 1961 to 1965. In these moments the Democratic Party's survival was hardly on the line. But such party leaders as Harry Truman and his advisors, and later John F. Kennedy and Lyndon Johnson, worried nonetheless about the costs of inaction. If they did not make coalitions, they would experience painful political losses.

BLACK POLITICAL WILL IN COALITION-MAKING

In short, the concept of coalition formation can unravel the reasons why party politicians did what they did during major episodes in the making of African American voting and office-holding. But its emphasis on political agency also requires extension to the full range of relevant actors. In the original formulation, only elites are agential. New coalition partners simply take the deal they are offered. In fact, *both* partners in coalition formation are highly purposive. The outsiders are just as savvy as the insiders.

With respect to the role of African Americans—and the way they seized political opportunities—I generally portray what might be called *black political will*, a term akin to such cognate ideas as Michael Dawson's "black counterpublic" or Taeku Lee's "activated public opinion." My stress on black group agency undoubtedly stylizes the actual history of this group. The new black history (as opposed to the history of race relations) reveals many intellectual, political, social, and economic tensions and divisions among African Americans over time. They have never formed a phalanx or a monolith, all for one and one for all.

Thus, in his compelling autobiography, Reverend John H. Scott often notes his disappointment in his own community during his time as a leader of the NAACP in the 1940s, 1950s, and 1960s in Lake Providence, a small city in northeastern Louisiana that abutted the Mississippi delta. He writes, "We had a group problem that required group action. We didn't have the luxury of exerting our individualism." But he encountered foot-dragging from "the same scared Negroes. 'Scott, now you know I can't get involved in no voting. You know I'll lose my job.' 'Mr. Charlie owns the plantation I live on and he'll put me off the place if I get involved.'" Scott observes philosophically, "I tried to make them see that they had to stand up some time. . . . But I knew it was hard for the people."[39]

Similarly, the civil rights historian J. Mills Thornton III cautions against seeing the civil rights movement as a "mounting crescendo" of forceful collective action. He notes that it "actually proceeded through tiny revelations of possible change" and was distinguished by very modest local demands. Indeed, in communities where there had always been a strong black leader—someone like John H. Scott, in fact—black citizens were perhaps *less* likely to contemplate conflict simply because there was already some white accommodation of a local leader's persistent activism.[40]

Still, the idea of a consequential black political will is within shouting distance of the facts. As Katherine Tate, a leading scholar of African American political behavior, observes, "The majority of Blacks believe that what happens to the group affects them personally." Michael Dawson, who was co-investigator for the 1993–1994 National Black Politics Study, administered by the University of Chicago, reports that 68 percent of African American respondents in the early 1990s saw their individual fates as "linked to that of black people." In a nation famous for its liberal individualism, this is unusual. Strong group consciousness is (and was) a vital constant of black political life—and persistently contentious action.[41]

Thus, in chapter 2 I describe all-black marching companies in the former Confederacy and group travel to the polls in 1866 and 1867. In chapter 4 I describe armed black militia and their actions in several of the states during the first reconstruction. Frequently, I stress the persistence of efforts by ordinary African Americans to vote in the face of frightening personal costs. These sorts of descriptions I take to be prima facie evidence of coordinated, solidaristic behavior. But they constitute, of course, only indirect evidence of a sense of racial group identity and of strong political consciousness. When I can offer survey evidence indicating the existence of such mental states I use it, but that is fairly rare simply because major surveys of African Americans did not begin until late in the twentieth century. I also must draw inferences from aggregate data and from people's own words. I let well-known (and not so well-known) individuals speak in these pages as a way to reveal the way they think about themselves and their place in history and politics. This has the drawback of treating them as stand-ins for large numbers of African Americans, which is obviously risky business. But the voices help convey the role of black political will.

COALITIONAL AFTERMATH: PARTY-BUILDING
AND JURISPRUDENCE-BUILDING

To recapitulate, coalitional *interaction* between threatened party and a useful outgroup was a major mechanism in African American enfranchisement. But it was only an initial dynamic. What followed during both reconstructions was just as critical. The aftermath reinforced African American enfranchisement in the second case but did not reinforce it in the first.

A flaw in the Riker-Gamson formulation of coalition formation is the inarticulate premise that it is a fairly easy way to triumph over those who threaten the partners in a coalition. How do you beat the other side? Simple: make your side bigger. But numbers, though important, are not wholly dispositive in politics. If they were, the first reconstruction would have been an instant and stable success.

Coalitional expansion portended a change in power relations between groups, between parties, and between those who subscribed to competing visions of American politics. Those who opposed coalitional expansion would not sit still, and in a democratic context they acted as effectively as they could to turn the tables. Successfully establishing equality required the architects of reform and democratic change to have good institutional technology, so to speak. To begin with, they needed battle-tested, resilient political party machinery—or the prospect of making it in short order.[42]

Political parties can be potent when they are seasoned, resilient organizations that generate loyalty among their full-time cadres and their electoral followers and when they are animated by socially useful ideas. Parties attract, channel, and harness the ambition of talented political entrepreneurs. Parties mobilize and sustain the participation of ordinary citizens on a regular basis. They thus organize and regularize electoral processes, from which comes the authority to accumulate and use governmental resources. These general properties make parties highly useful to those who wish to reorder power relations without arbitrary coercion and to perpetuate that reordering.

During both reconstructions, the architects of the new racial and political order also needed public policies that were supple and appropriate to the political problems at hand. In the voting rights area that has meant new jurisprudence, often with major implications for federalism and national regulation of electoral processes. A vital aspect of jurisprudence-building during both reconstructions was change in the legal aspects of electoral federalism. Electoral federalism has been the chief instrument for defining the rights to vote and to hold office in the United States. Under the Constitution of 1787, the determination of voting rights fell to state and local governments. But the Civil War and Reconstruction, and the ensuing massive program of African American electoral inclusion, recast the constitutional responsibilities for establishing and protecting voting rights by means of ratification of the Fifteenth Amendment and passage of several implementing statutes. These legal initiatives posed an enormous challenge to widely held conceptions of American federalism. The same thing happened in 1965 with passage of the Voting Rights Act.

The political party (Republicans in the first reconstruction) or the party faction (liberal Democrats in the second) interested in bringing voter blocs into electoral politics preferred to remove responsibility for voting rights to the national government so that national democratic norms could be allowed to influence voting rights policy and law. This resulted in centralized electoral regulation. The opposition, less interested in inclusion, or preferring exclusion, sought instead to place or to keep responsibility for voting rights in state and local government, separating the use of these rights from the influence of national democratic norms. This implied decentralized electoral regulation.

Regulating the division over these two constitutional perspectives were federal judges and Supreme Court justices. Because federalism is a division of policy responsibilities between governmental tiers that do not seek to abolish or overwhelm each other, questions of institutional balance and equipoise were inevitable. American judges often sought to set the balance one way or another. Judicial review of statutory initiatives affecting African American electoral inclusion, and of the Constitution's relevant commands (principally the Fourteenth and Fifteenth Amendments), meant that judges regularly framed electoral inclusion—or exclusion—in terms of its implications for the balance between national norms concerning rights and the requirements of maintaining federalism.

Jurisprudence-building could therefore go in two directions. It had the potential to complement party-building. But jurisprudence-building was not entirely under the control of biracial coalitions. If federal judges or a Supreme Court majority were worried about the dynamic implications of jurisprudence-building for institutional balance, they could weaken the impact of party-building.

Thus institutional enfranchisement could and did vary in strength. I link the grand historical puzzles of African American electoral inclusion—why twice? did the first reconstruction have to fail? why has the second proceeded so differently?—to differences between the reconstructions in their party- and jurisprudence-building processes. During and after the first reconstruction, enfranchisement was not secured by these mechanisms. African Americans were left terribly vulnerable. When northern Republicans finally cut them loose (see chapter 6), their action sealed a shocking, thorough disenfranchisement. During the second reconstruction, in contrast, these processes institutionalized enfranchisement to a greater degree. There are certainly *new* issues concerning inclusion, such as elections administration and felony disenfranchisement. But the biracial coalition is entrenched today in ways that the biracial coalition of the first reconstruction never was.

WHY THE DIFFERENCES IN PARTY- AND JURISPRUDENCE-BUILDING?

But why the differences in these processes? Were they due to differences in skill or political will within the biracial coalitions? To factionalism within these coalitions? Or to external constraints imposed by society or the economy? The essential fact about party- and jurisprudence-building during both reconstructions is that *they took hard work*. The ultimate success of either reconstruction depended—not solely, but significantly—on how hard participants were forced to work. Whether the work was easy or hard, however, was not up to the coalition-makers. Instead, the work depended on historically received circumstances, namely, on the party system's structure and on how the federal courts were likely to be led by a majority of the Supreme Court.[43]

During the first reconstruction, stabilizing the new biracial coalition required the "crash" construction of eleven new Republican parties within the former Confederate states, where the Republican Party had of course never existed. In contrast, during the second reconstruction, the coalition-making between the Democratic Party's New Deal faction and black southerners demanded no more than a takeover of long-standing organizations. The biracial coalition displaced the southern racial reactionaries and conservatives from their ancestral organization. This was a hard job, and doing it took time. But, as a political task, it was easier than building eleven new state-level parties overnight.

Furthermore, party-building during the first reconstruction was strongly resisted by an opposing party. Here, too, the structure of the party system played a key role. As political dissent and competition withered in the South before and during the Civil War, the idea that two-party competition was legitimate also died. The region's white conservatives (essentially the Democratic party's southern wing) therefore regarded competition from Republican interlopers as illegitimate. But southern Democrats, and

Democrats generally, also had a structural incentive to attack their opponents as often and as harshly as they could. They needed to dominate the South in order to remain *nationally* competitive. Picturing their opposition as unnatural and deeply threatening to whites was politically necessary. Thus their inexorable resistance to Republican party-building made such innovation all the more difficult and all the more likely to be flawed. Crash party-building could not be avoided; neither could fierce obstruction and hindrance from Democrats.

In contrast, during the second reconstruction, there was really no opposing party on site, as it were, ready to impede the internal reconstruction of the South's Democratic parties into biracial organizations. White supremacist third parties were attempted, but they were fragile and short-lived. In addition to never facing hampering tactics from an established force, the new coalition actually had help from the opposition. The Republican Party had an inducement to actively support the reconfiguration of the southern Democratic parties. Their increasingly biracial nature also made it easier for the Republican Party to grow in the South as a "white" alternative. It became a home for white conservative voters. These included defectors from the Democratic Party, younger whites entering the electorate, and people who thought of themselves as Independents but often voted Republican.

As for jurisprudence-building during the two reconstructions, the key factor, in my view, was the basic stance toward the political process taken by the Supreme Court when the jurisprudential results of coalition-making *first* received Court scrutiny. But, given the Court's short-term insulation from partisan pressures, there was no guarantee of a confluence between its first ruling and the new biracial coalition's jurisprudence-building needs.[44]

Informed observers at these moments understood very clearly how suspenseful the initial judicial review was. In a telling remark in private correspondence in March 1871, a little more than a year before the first Court test of Reconstruction constitutional jurisprudence, Representative James A. Garfield wrote, "We are working on the very verge of the Constitution . . . exposing us to the . . . danger of having our work overthrown by the Supreme Court."[45]

Consider, too, the letter that an Alabama Democratic Party official, Frank Mizell, wrote to Governor George Wallace to describe a strategy session concerning Supreme Court review of the 1965 Voting Rights Act. "Pursuant to our conversation of October 17, 1965, I went to Washington, D.C., for the purpose of attending a conference relative to coordination of and mutual cooperation in efforts to contest the Voters [sic] Rights Act by judicial means with the ultimate objective of having it declared unconstitutional and void."

The conference included a representative of Judge Leander Perez of Louisiana, the chair of the Louisiana State Sovereignty Commission, the assistant attorney general of Louisiana, representatives of the governor and the attorney general of Mississippi and of Senator James O. Eastland of Mississippi, representatives of the governor of South Carolina, the assistant attorney general of Virginia, and Senator Sam Ervin of North Carolina. Ervin "remarked that bad laws often get through the legislative mills, and that, under our system, bad legislation *must be contested and defeated in the courts.*" Mizell predicted that the Supreme Court would quickly accept review of a challenge to the Voting Rights Act from South Carolina, and he thus proposed a follow-up planning session in Montgomery or Birmingham.[46]

In other words, because biracial coalition-making during both of America's reconstructions generated new, uncertain constitutional and statutory law, a judicial stance in favor of or against the coalition was a resource for one side or the other. All sides worried about the first Supreme Court test. They sought to shape it.

When the Court hears a "case or controversy" under its Article III power, one side has to lose. The Court gives a rationale for its rejection of one of the two parties to a dispute. That there must be a rationale indeed deepens the binary nature of the decision. "Here are all the reasons for why this side is wrong," the opinion necessarily says. Dissenters from the opinion can explain why they think the *per curiam* opinion is incorrect, but their voices of course only heighten the yes-no clarity of the majority's signal. Furthermore, because of the defining weight of precedent, an initial stance commits the time and energy of future Supreme Court majorities, judges in the lower federal courts—and members of Congress. Depending on the upshot, the Court invites either elaboration and strengthening of the new jurisprudence by other actors or further legal and political resistance to the new coalition.

If the first decision or set of decisions is unfavorable, the Court's stance thus becomes a new strategic problem for a biracial coalition. The number and difficulty of political tasks that it has to perform suddenly increases. The Court's unfavorable stance will have to be addressed and solved by the new biracial coalition, either with new litigation strategies that will reframe the issues for the hostile majority in a way that permits favorable decisions or by changing the Court's composition if and when important vacancies appear. The coalition seeking to incorporate itself by means of policy and law faces a near-term future of conflict with the Court. Adjusting to or taming Court opposition takes time and energy, and it requires living uncertainly with other possible setbacks in the courts.

In summary, the central assignment for reformers—coalitional expansion—was intrinsically quite contentious. It portended a major change in power relations. Those who opposed it were certain to react. The question both times became: How easy or hard would it be to institutionalize enfranchisement by means of party-building and jurisprudence-building? During the first reconstruction it was very hard; during the second it was relatively easier.

The time and energy that each of the two great biracial coalitions could spend instituting reform accorded with the relative difficulty of their additional institutional and jurisprudential projects. Yet the level of difficulty was not decided by the two coalitions explored in this book. It depended instead on the options inherent in the particular configuration of the national party system and in the composition and inclinations of the Supreme Court.

INSTITUTIONS, ENFRANCHISEMENT, AND RACE RELATIONS

In arguing this, I do not mean to deny other ways to understanding the two reconstructions. I offer instead a two-part claim. The first part is that an analytical marriage offers good answers to the great historical puzzles that motivate this book, namely, why two reconstructions? why diverging outcomes? The partners being joined are rational choice theorizing—which explains the genesis of the biracial coalitions—and comparative historical institutionalism—which illuminates party- and jurisprudence-building.

The second part of my claim is that the answers provided by this analytical marriage are at least as satisfying as the answers that are furnished by other leading approaches. What social scientists must strive for is an increasingly refined sense of the *weights* that we ought to attach to the different kinds of variables at work in important historical processes and outcomes. No political science theory can fully resolve the causal complexity of the real world of politics. My analysis is meant only to significantly refine our knowledge of the two reconstructions.

But even apparently modest refinement has considerable rewards. The change that I am urging in our understanding of these two epic cycles has striking implications. It recalibrates how one thinks about the course of American race relations since the Civil War. We know that the first reconstruction failed—but for a very long time, of course, the people in its biracial coalition did not know that it would end in the total disenfranchisement of black southerners. Likewise, we now have a fairly firm sense that the second reconstruction is irreversible. But for a time it was far from obvious, as chapters 9 and 10 show, that it would stabilize.

If the second reconstruction's biracial coalition had had the same kinds of daunting political tasks as its predecessor, then perhaps it too would be rather troubled even today. It might be some sort of success. But it would certainly be less of a success than it has actually been. Similarly, if the first reconstruction's biracial coalition had faced the easier sorts of political tasks that occupied its twentieth-century successor, then we would, I firmly believe, be living in a different country today.

The overall course of American race relations has been fundamentally influenced, in short, by the institutional options available to the great biracial coalitions that launched the two reconstructions. Many Americans, black and white, think that the main problem in U.S. race relations has been white attitudes—and they are not wrong that these attitudes have, on the whole, blocked better race relations. But such a view ignores institutions. What if the progress in race relations that has characterized the United States in the past forty years had instead been achieved much earlier, via the first reconstruction? What if, in other words, the first reconstruction had not been smashed to bits by 1900? Black and white Americans would not have been forced to endure our country's colossal and costly delay in achieving political fraternity across the racial divide. Likewise, what if the second reconstruction were in a truly shaky state today? Institutions, in other words, have governed our common political fate—more than we sometimes acknowledge.

Outline of the Book

To appreciate the importance of party- and jurisprudence-building and the institutional foundations of these processes, one has to absorb the remarkable events and dynamics of America's two reconstructions. The upcoming chapters are about verifying the mechanisms and processes for which my coalitional and institutional theory cues us to look. Consequently, only *relevant* aspects of political history are treated. The two reconstructions have generated vast monographic literatures. But to advance our understanding of the reconstructions, their relation to each other, and their impact, I sharply narrow my focus.

Hence chapter 2 considers the coalition formation that occurred between 1865 and 1868 but most particularly between 1867 and 1868. Chapter 3, however, "flashes forward" to the state of the coalition about a decade and a half later. Why was the coalition both resilient and in trouble? We see there that electoral inclusion was not institutionalized, even though both sides of the biracial coalition signaled continuing commitment to each other.

Chapters 4 and 5 therefore consider party- and jurisprudence-building during the first reconstruction.

Chapter 6 carefully traces what happened when northern Republicans
grasped that they really no longer needed the coalition of 1867–1868. The
full drama and stakes of the second reconstruction become much clearer if
the reader also knows something about disenfranchisement itself. The story
is quite stunning. Chapters 7 and 8 then consider coalition formation in the
making of the second reconstruction. Chapter 9 considers how its party- and
jurisprudence-building processes became quite promising. Chapter 10
explores the other chapters' implications for understanding whether and how
new coalitions in a polity entrench themselves.

You will notice that there is necessarily more coverage of black voting
than of office-holding. Periods with high rates of black office-holding have
been briefer than those with black voting. Black enfranchisement has two
dimensions, but one simply takes up less history than the other.

Chapter Two

Forging the Coalition of 1867–1868

During the first and the second reconstructions, the forging of broad new electoral coalitions was a key dynamic. One set of agents in this forging, the leaders of predominantly white political parties, were political "insiders" who needed help. In both reconstructions, these insiders faced some menace to their political status. To meet the peril, the insiders brought in "outsiders" as political and electoral allies.

This chapter focuses on the emergence of a mortal threat to the Republican Party immediately after the Civil War. The party led the war to a successful conclusion on its own terms. But the threat to its political future—and to its multiple policy goals (besides electoral regulatory policy), including high tariffs, sound money, and federal support for higher education—was unmistakable. It was created by a tenacious political entrepreneur, Abraham Lincoln's successor in office, Andrew Johnson.

The narrative shows how the Republican Party acted to beat Johnson by sharply expanding the party's electoral coalition to include southerners. It did so despite the defeat of state-level black suffrage referenda in the North, which suggested considerable white resistance to the idea. But given the hazard to the party's future, congressional Republicans forcefully established a new, politically winning coalition that joined together about seven hundred thousand black southern men and the northern white male Republican electorate.[1]

To be sure, historians have described very diverse motivations for the first reconstruction. This chapter concentrates, however, only on party-saving. It treats securing the party's future as the dominant motivation. The modernizing of American society and economy, which was indeed a part of Republican ideology, could not take place, after all, without a leading role for the Republican Party in national politics. When Johnson sought to spike coalition formation, the Republicans impeached and tried him.[2]

The other part of coalition formation required, of course, the new partners. In December 1866, the percentage of black adult males eligible to vote nationwide was a tiny .5 percent. But only twelve months later, after Congress enacted the Reconstruction Acts, the percentage was 80.5 percent.[3] The Republican Party's action opened the way for a very high level of participation by black southerners. Blacks were hardly the "foot-ball of reconstruction" (to use the coinage of a white Georgia Republican).[4] We shall see that black southerners launched America's first massive black voting rights movement. Their entry into a new coalition promised them policy rewards, passage into and construction of a biracial public sphere, party organizational life, and a vital change in political status.

Although they received political resources from the established party insiders during the initial coalition-making process such as ready-made political organizations and organizers, the new coalition partners did something more important than simply accept these resources. They also provided their own vital political resources to the insiders. They decisively supplied the behavior and the struggle necessary to actually cement the emerging coalition.

Bottom-up struggle was a fundamental element of coalition-making. It featured a sense of racial group identity, a strongly historicist understanding among African Americans of both the black role in American politics and of the regime's most democratic principles, and a range of collective behaviors in public. Rapid activation of black collective action by entrepreneurs located in all-black institutions and associations occurred. This chapter tells, in short, the story of America's great "revolution from above" during the turmoil that followed Lincoln's assassination and of how African Americans cemented the Republican Party's quest for a new political order.

THE JOHNSON FACTOR

Lincoln's vice president, Andrew Johnson, was a remarkably activist president. In his first months in office, he occupied a political vacuum left by the congressional calendar. The Thirty-ninth Congress, elected in 1864, did not convene until December 1865. But Johnson took the oath of office in the late spring of 1865. Between that moment and the arrival of the Congress, he raced to develop a "restoration" policy, rapidly pressing forward with a racially conservative reconciliation of America's two geographic regions.[5]

In doing so Johnson not only created a positive program; he also *reversed* vital elements of reconstruction policy that Congress and Lincoln had developed before Johnson became president. Reconstruction's clock was not set on the day that Robert E. Lee surrendered the Army of Northern Virginia. Lincoln and Congress had set it well before that. Two prongs of Republican policy were *land reform* and *cordoning off access to public office from former Confederates*. Understanding these policies is essential for understanding Johnson's challenge to the Republican Party.

The Promise of Land Reform

Take land reform qua reconstruction policy.[6] The North's military penetration of the Confederacy set the stage. The Union Army's campaigns in the west, in Louisiana, and on the Atlantic seaboard generated wholesale land seizures during the press of war. The army's ensuing provisions for freedmen's use of the seized land (which varied across the different theaters of war) created, in turn, the potential for significant land reform.

The most politically significant of these army initiatives came from General William Tecumseh Sherman, whose notorious drive eastward from Atlanta in late 1864 placed enormous amounts of abandoned land and large numbers of black refugees under his control. After consulting in January 1865 in Savannah with black leaders and Lincoln's secretary of war, Edwin Stanton, Sherman issued Special Field Order No. 15. It set aside a huge swath of land from Charleston to Florida (the Sherman Reservation) and provided for title to forty acres of land and to mules from his army, hence the still-current phrase "forty acres and a mule." Ten thousand families came to work four hundred thousand acres.[7]

Not long afterward, on March 3, 1865, Congress enacted and Lincoln signed a bill establishing a regionwide version of the Sherman Reservation. It authorized formation of a Bureau of Freedmen, Refugees, and Abandoned Lands in the U.S. Army. Its responsibility (besides direct medical, food, and housing relief) was to assign to individual freedmen "not more than forty acres" of abandoned land for a three-year rental containing an option to buy "with such title thereto as the United States can convey."[8] By mid-1865, the possibility of federally sponsored land reform for the freedmen was in the air in many black areas of the South. If they worked the land for three years they would get their piece of the American promise, too, and in the process the South's agrarian economy would be jump-started back to life.

Securing Loyal Government

When Andrew Johnson became president there was a second institution in place by means of which Republicans intended to control postwar politics and administration. This was the Ironclad Test Oath for elective and appointive office. Besides requiring future defense of and allegiance to the Constitution, the Ironclad Test Oath required its taker to affirm that he had never borne arms against the United States, nor given aid to anyone doing so, nor held office in a government hostile to the United States, nor "yielded a voluntary support to any pretended government . . . within the United States, hostile or inimical thereto."[9] False affirmation subjected one to the penalties of perjury and permanent exclusion from any office of the United States. In mid-1862, Congress and Lincoln required this oath of executive administrators, both in loyal states and in occupied areas of the Confederacy, and required a similar oath of federal jurors.

That the test oath was not simply a wartime measure but also a reconstruction measure first became clear in March 1863, when Senators Lyman Trumbull and Charles Sumner insisted that the oath be required of members of the U.S. Senate. Once extended to Congress, the test oath would clearly block the seating of anyone who had been a member of the Confederacy's governments. Congress took several months to weigh the Trumbull-Sumner proposal and its implications against an alternative model, namely, Lincoln's view that amnesty be granted in order to appoint men who could swear to *future* loyalty. Lincoln hoped to sponsor "self-reconstruction" in the former Confederacy, in contrast with the test oath's emphasis on *past* loyalty.[10]

Congress eventually chose the latter approach when it applied the test oath to itself, and it reaffirmed its view in January 1865 when it extended the test oath to attorneys practicing in the federal courts. The test oath, Congress indicated, would be an integral part of the postwar order. Reconstruction would therefore depend on a highly loyal social base of free black farmers and a class of loyal officeholders.

How Johnson Thwarted Congressional Intentions

Johnson wrecked these plans. By means of executive orders and by allowing Lincoln's provisional governments to collapse, Johnson simply cleared away Congress's earlier reconstruction policy. Some of what he did can be explained by administrative necessity, as he often pointed out. But it is hard to escape the conclusion that for Johnson a fundamental purpose of undoing Congress's and Lincoln's plans was assembling an exclusively white coalition of southern Conservatives and northern Democrats for his 1868 election.[11] To be sure, Johnson's plan to make a cross-sectional party was an enormous contribution to political order. These two wings of the old Democratic Party, sundered by war, awaited reunification. But Johnson's plan also invited conflict. Congressional Republicans would never sit still for it.

Johnson first attacked the test oath initiative (setting in motion an intricate politics of southern pardons that would last, in fact, into the 1880s). On May 29 he issued a proclamation granting amnesty for participation in the rebellion. He did except the most important officials and military officers of the Confederacy, but for the excepted classes the proclamation invited "special application" for presidential pardon and noted that "clemency" would be "liberally extended" unless the facts of a case precluded it.[12] On the same day Johnson also established provisional government in North Carolina by proclamation under Article 4 of the Constitution. The proclamation limited the North Carolina franchise to voters eligible on the date of secession (that is, whites only). He issued similar proclamations for Mississippi (June 13), Georgia and Texas (June 17), Alabama (June 21), South Carolina (June 30), and Florida (July 13). None of the provisional governors took the Ironclad Test Oath; they only took the Amnesty Oath. In turn, none of the provisional governors staffed their governments with men able to take the test oath; instead, they commissioned ex-rebels who had received presidential pardons.[13]

Once he understood its operations, Johnson also quickly acted against the Freedmen's Bureau. The bureau's commissioner, General Oliver Otis Howard, had evidently grasped the implications for the freedmen of Johnson's early summer proclamations. Howard thus issued a special directive on July 28, 1865, directing his assistant commissioners to begin dividing land that was under bureau control among freedmen. He hoped to present Johnson with a fait accompli.[14] But in mid-September Johnson forced Howard to withdraw this order, requiring him instead to return to their previous owners the lands that freedmen had already begun to work. Johnson also removed several assistant commissioners whom he considered insubordinate.[15]

Mississippi's Reconstruction of White Supremacy

These twin initiatives by Johnson, directed against the policy earlier established by Congress, had a clear potential for restoring the historic subordination of African Americans. That potential became manifest in Mississippi by late November, when the state legislature passed several statutes establishing labor peonage. One provided for a system of labor apprenticeship for freedmen under the age of eighteen; another established huge fines for freedmen unable to prove that they worked in a labor contract and required that they work off their fines if unable to pay them; a third provided for the recovery by force of freedmen who quit their contracts; a fourth authorized courts to establish heavy fines for freedmen if they "maliciously" sued white persons who had criminally assaulted freedmen, the fines to be worked off by a sheriff's offering the freedman's labor at a public bid; a fifth reenacted all criminal laws that had applied previously to slaves.[16]

This legislation—soon substantially copied by other southern state legislatures—plainly suggested that in the new political economy toward which Johnson seemed headed, the sole role for blacks was a form of reenslavement. But the diffusion of the Black Codes also meant more than a bold bid by the southern conservatives to reassert racial hierarchy. Their establishment of black labor peonage coincided with slavery's formal abolition by the Thirteenth Amendment, which the secretary of state, William Seward, declared ratified on December 18, 1865.

This confluence of sweeping constitutional change and de facto reenslavement in the South had enormous implications for the political parties under the Constitution's apportionment provisions. Earlier, black southerners had counted as only three-fifths of a person in apportionment and in the Electoral College. Thanks to the Thirteenth Amendment, their political weight now jumped by 66 percent. Yet the Black Codes effectively channeled all that increase in national representative strength to their old overlords, who stood on the verge of gaining more strength within the national party system than they had enjoyed before the Civil War.[17]

Reaction of the Republican-Controlled Thirty-ninth Congress

Initially eager to work with Johnson, Republican congressional leaders were soon astounded. It was obvious to them by late 1865 that Johnson had restructured their political situation. Signaling the new context created by Johnson, congressional delegations composed of southern Conservatives streamed into Washington in the fall of 1865, expecting to be seated for the second session of the Thirty-ninth Congress.[18]

Accounts of Republican caucuses and correspondence and of public discussion before the opening of the Congress on December 5 show that there were now two major issues for Republicans. The first was black civil rights.

The trend begun by Mississippi toward "Black Codes" gravely menaced these rights. The second was southern representation.[19] With passage of the Thirteenth Amendment and Johnson's "restoration," southern states now enjoyed a new *bonus* in numbers of representatives. The resulting political problem for Republicans was the advantage conferred on southern Conservatives. They would reap the gain in apportionment from slavery's abolition but block the political representation of a likely Republican constituency: black voters.

Thaddeus Stevens (R-Pa.) soon explained the strategic issue to the assembled House: "The eighty-three southern members with the Democrats that will in the best time be elected from the North will *always* give them a majority in Congress and in the Electoral College. They will at the very first election take possession of the White House and the halls of Congress. I need not depict the ruin that would follow."[20] Or, more bleakly, the "reward of treason will be an increased representation" in the House, as an Illinois Republican put it. A New York Republican noted that "one South Carolinian, whose hands are red with the blood of fallen patriots . . . will have a voice as potential in these Halls as two and a half Vermont soldiers." This analysis was also shared by African American political leaders.[21]

Congressional Republicans therefore decided that on the first day of the session they would not seat the recently elected southerners. When the clerk of the House called the roll he would simply not name them. Objections from the floor would be out of order, furthermore, because the objectors would not be members of Congress.[22]

Republicans also evidently meant to amend the Constitution in order to address their political concerns. To that end the first order of House business was formation of a Joint Committee on Reconstruction; once Senate leaders modified the House resolution, the Senate added its agreement. Proposals of the committee were not subject to floor amendment but only to floor debate and votes. In addition, congressional Republicans planned two federal statutory corrections of the Black Codes, soon fashioning a civil rights bill and a reappropriation to fund the army's Bureau of Freedmen, Refugees, and Abandoned Lands.[23]

In short, a sense of threat pervaded Republican thinking—threat to themselves and to black southerners. A test of President Johnson's good faith soon emerged. Senator Trumbull carefully revised the Freedmen's Bureau Act to make it acceptable to the president, or so he thought. To the consternation of congressional Republicans, the president vetoed the bill on February 19 and denounced it. On March 27 he also vetoed the 1866 civil rights bill. His message insisted that "sound policy" for the "colored population" could not be made without seating the recently elected southern Conservatives, and it went on to catalogue the bill's threats to racial decorum and to federalism.[24]

Congress's epochal overrides of the civil rights veto on April 6 and 9, 1866, symbolized the break between Johnson and House and Senate Republicans. Then, on April 30, the Joint Committee on Reconstruction reported the Fourteenth Amendment, establishing black civil rights, reducing (per section 2) congressional representation for states denying suffrage "in any way" to male twenty-one-year-olds and barring ex-Confederates from public office. Rising in the Senate on May 23, the Joint Committee's acting chair explained section 1. It would curb the states from harming citizens' civil rights and compel respect for the Bill of Rights. Section 2, furthermore, was meant to induce southern states to grant black suffrage. Otherwise they would "lose . . . that balance of power in Congress which has been so long their pride and their boast." On June 8 the Senate approved; on June 13 the House followed suit.[25] Legislative passage of the Fourteenth Amendment provoked a wide and fierce national debate for several months. Republicans plainly considered the amendment a campaign platform for the 1866 elections, an explicit alternative to Johnson's policy. The voters appeared to respond by delivering impressive gains to the Republicans.[26]

MILITARY RECONSTRUCTION

Further stalemate resulted from the elections, however. This was quite significant for the coalition-making process. Recall that "zero-sumness" is a critically important feature of a pre-coalition situation. Elites reach out to outsiders because the insiders believe that (in Waldner's words) "their long-term capacity to reproduce their elite status" is plainly jeopardized. That is, "the threatened elite feels that it will be unable to compete . . . in the future." Such a feeling continued to grow among Republicans as they observed Johnson's behavior after the 1866 election.[27]

Johnson elaborately ignored the policy mandate of the 1866 elections when he forwarded his annual message in December. By early February 1867, every former Confederate state but Tennessee denied its ratification of the Fourteenth Amendment, as had three border states, Delaware, Maryland, and Kentucky. Johnson and northern Democrats were openly involved in encouraging these states' defiance.[28]

Further deepening the crisis were three decisions of the Supreme Court, which announced a strongly libertarian reaction in late 1866 and early 1867 to the Union's test oath program and to military briskness in suppressing anti-war conspiracies in the North during the war. In the context of the times the Court seemed, in effect, to side with Johnson's "restoration" policy.[29]

Among Republicans there was now fierce debate. One faction argued that Congress ought to try a version of the Fourteenth Amendment plan again. A revised amendment would incorporate black suffrage, and Congress would explicitly indicate that its ratification was the ticket back into the Union. Another faction pushed for complete reversal of Johnson's restoration program, the establishment of interim governments based mainly on black suffrage and sweeping white disenfranchisement, and considerable delay in readmission to the Union.[30] Johnson and several of the southern Conservative representatives and senators-elect of the Thirty-ninth Congress, then stationed in Washington, sought to fuel this split. They developed a compromise version of the Fourteenth Amendment that included *partial* black suffrage, and they claimed that the southern legislatures would ratify it.[31]

In the end, of course, Republicans did not split. Congressional Republicans instead forged a program of immediate universal black male suffrage in the former Confederate states to be initiated under army direction. The main elements of the new policy, passed over Johnson's explicit vetoes (except for the Command of the Army Act, which Johnson signed), comprised the Military Reconstruction Act, the Command of the Army Act, the Tenure of Office Act, and the Local Prejudice Act of March 2, 1867, of the Thirty-ninth Congress and a supplementary act of March 23, 1867, passed during the first session of the Fortieth Congress.[32]

The first reconstruction act held that "no legal State governments or adequate protection for life or property" existed in "rebel States." It therefore established five military districts, to remain in existence until the people of each state "formed a constitution of government . . . framed by a convention of delegates elected by the male citizens of said State twenty-one years old and upward, of whatever race, color, or previous condition . . . except such as may be disfranchised for participation in the rebellion." District 1 encompassed Virginia, District 2, the Carolinas, District 3, Alabama, Georgia, and Florida, District 4, Mississippi and Arkansas, and District 5, Texas and Louisiana.

The Tenure of Office Act and the Command of the Army Act prescribed congressional control of the cabinet and the army, and the Supplementary Reconstruction Act provided mechanisms for the new political processes of the former rebel states. The act required military commanders to register voters and to administer loyalty oaths to registrars by September 30. The resulting electorate would then vote on the question of whether to hold a constitutional convention, and it would select the delegates. Elected constitutional delegates would meet within sixty days, and the resulting constitution would then be submitted for voter approval.[33]

Congress retained the discretion to satisfy itself that the balloting for a convention was "without restraint, fear, or the influence of fraud" and to approve a new state constitution before declaring a state to be "entitled to representation." Also, a new state legislature under a new constitution was required (under the first reconstruction act) to adopt the Fourteenth Amendment before a state could regain congressional representation.

Many Republicans saw black suffrage as a way to bring peace, at last, to the South. It would generate the institutions that would both protect civil rights and stop a regionwide wave of antiblack violence in 1866 that had shocked northern opinion. As the governor of Iowa pointed out in his 1866 inaugural address to the Iowa legislature, enfranchisement would provide "an army of occupation . . . in the yet unquiet regions of the South."[34]

Black suffrage also protected the Republican Party's future—something many northern Democrats had openly recognized as early as 1865. Republicans understood this. Writing to a Wisconsin correspondent in December 1866, Horace Greeley stated, "Enfranchise the blacks, and further rebellions at the South are impossible; and we can have a great National party, which can hopefully contest nearly every State in the Union." Otherwise, Greeley feared, "the . . . Democracy will have nearly every one of the 15 ex-Slave States as fixed capital to begin with."[35] Indeed, Republicans sought to combine mobilization of black southerners with partial demobilization of white southerners. About 703,000 black adult men but only 627,000 whites were eventually registered to vote during military reconstruction. In some states white disenfranchisement, to be sure, was self-imposed by alienated whites. But military application of loyalty oaths and loyalty challenges helped assure that five states ended up with black electoral majorities.[36]

BLACK MOBILIZATION: MILITARY RECONSTRUCTION'S SUPPLY SIDE

The above has been meant to clarify the why and the how of the Republicans' epoch-making policy choice. A high level of partisan and legislative-executive conflict placed party necessity in sharp relief for Republicans and for Johnson's coalition. Their conflict was marked by the perception among Republicans that they stood to lose a very great deal as a party. They needed to create a new electoral coalition that would help anchor their success or else face being the out party for many years.

But Johnson and the Republicans were not the only ones acting highly entrepreneurially. *Both* partners in the coalition formation were highly purposive. The outsiders were just as savvy as the insiders. Let us turn next to the emergence of black involvement in national electoral politics. It assured military reconstruction's early success and thus the Republican Party's future.

Military reconstruction's important initial attainment was the rapid emergence of Republican Party organizations in eleven states and the near-total mobilization of a black electorate within a few months. Table 2.1 provides an overview of the voter-registration outcomes. The figures are based in part on the Ninth Census, which has long had a poor reputation. The most recent research has refurbished its reputation, however, and shown that the low esteem in which it was held was part of the general academic reaction in the 1890s against Reconstruction. Still, given census underenumeration, these figures have to be treated with caution, and they may overstate rates of voter registration by about 9 percent.[37]

With this caveat in mind one sees that the registration process was nevertheless probably quite thorough, except in Arkansas. The army generally implemented congressional policy despite presidential resistance to it (on which more soon). Some commanders were more conservative than others, but only one—the commander in Virginia—appears to have frustrated congressional intent. Also, the Republican Party provided an organizational framework: a system of political clubs called the Union Leagues, first developed during the Civil War to promote northern electoral mobilization.[38]

A decisive factor was the policy's "supply side." If a policy is to succeed, its "target population" must supply the behavior that will make the policy work. It must have demands of its own that are met by helping make the policy—in

Table 2.1 Estimates of Black Adult Male Voter Registration, by State, for Military Reconstruction, 1867

Percentage	State
75–79	Arkansas
80–84	
85–89	Florida, Georgia, Mississippi
90–94	North Carolina, South Carolina
95–100	Alabama, Louisiana, Texas, Virginia

Sources: U.S. Bureau of the Census, Ninth Census, 1870 (Washington: D.C.: GPO, 1872), table 23; William C. Harris, *The Day of the Carpetbagger: Republican Reconstruction in Mississippi* (Baton Rouge: Louisiana State University Press, 1979), p. 76n30; William Russ, "Registration and Disfranchisement under Radical Reconstruction," *Mississippi Valley Historical Review* 21 (September 1934): 163–180, at p. 177.

this case, military reconstruction—work. The freedmen supplied exactly that. This book's emphasis on coalition-making during the first and second reconstructions underscores the great importance of group-based participation. Black southerners' role in the implementation of military suffrage was vital to the post–Civil War restabilization of American politics.[39]

They had good reason to join in. Military reconstruction signaled, after all, a manifest change in their political opportunities. Historians have shown that among the freed population could be found clear frustration at the now-obvious limits of emancipation, desire for full political citizenship, and a wish for broad public policies that served their needs. Black southerners' policy preferences included public education, free personal mobility, recognition of the legal status of black families and marriages, homesteads, fair criminal and civil process, impartial law enforcement, a free ballot to sustain such initiatives, and the right to hold public office. Now they could realize these goals.[40]

They also possessed specific resource endowments that are not widely known beyond the community of first reconstruction scholars. These collective assets supported a new black politics "out in the open." Consider, first, the impact of "soldier-citizenship," an experience that was essential to redefining the social and political roles of black Americans and that indeed later helped many black men attain public office.[41]

BLACK SOLDIER-CITIZENSHIP

One factor in the making of black capacity for concerted action was the development of *soldier-citizenship* among tens of thousands of black men and an awareness of it among hundreds of thousands of blacks. Both preceded political citizenship in 1867. References to soldier-citizenship appeared in speeches and political tracts for decades afterward.

Early in the Civil War, abolitionist governors and army generals pressured the War Department and the president to move well beyond the policy of leaving slavery intact. They did this by raising several black regiments in Louisiana, Kansas, and South Carolina. The crisis of the Union military effort in 1862—as the Union teetered on the verge of having to negotiate some diplomatic adjustment with the Confederacy—then helped bring about widespread army recruitment of northern and southern blacks. Abolitionist societies and northern black political organizations aided these efforts.[42]

In all, about 21 percent of the total American population of black men between ages eighteen and forty-five, nearly two hundred thousand, saw military service. This was a group larger than Robert E. Lee's Army of Northern Virginia. Nearly three-quarters of all free black men living in Union free states served, compared to fewer than half of the black men in this age group living in the Union slave states and 14 percent of men living in Confederate slave states.[43]

Black leaders and the black veterans mustered out of 154 regiments soon believed, with considerable justification, that black soldiering tipped the military balance of the Civil War. Probably, too, this belief could be found among many of the approximately 474,000 blacks who took part in some kind of federally sponsored wartime free labor, about a half of these in military labor (construction and sanitation) and the other half in agricultural labor on federally operated plantations.[44]

Black units were likewise critical to the pacification of the South after Appomattox. In June 1865, the average ratio of black to white federal units in the eleven former Confederate states was about .34; in September 1865, however, the figure jumped to 1.4. In January 1866 it was 2.5, in April 1866 it was .85, and in October 1866 it was .82. Rather little is known about their local impact. But black units were probably often a source of wider black assertion of rights and new political status.[45]

Black suffrage became a matter of justice—as often noted in petitions, memorials, and speeches in 1864 and 1865. Frederick Douglass put the point well in April 1872 at meeting of the National Convention of Colored People in New Orleans when he said: "When the very earth was crumbling under the cause of the Union and the armies of the nation were meeting disaster after disaster; when the recruiting sergeant was beating his drum through every hamlet in the land . . . then it was that the North was brought up to the point where it unchained the black man and put the musket in his hands. Then they called; then we came; and we helped to save the country." How often black speakers offered the argument—and variations on it that stressed the Revolutionary War martyrdom of Crispus Attucks and black military service in the War of 1812—is unknown. But of thirty speeches given by Douglass between 1865 and the New Orleans speech, seventeen mention black soldiering.[46]

EDUCATIONAL AND RELIGIOUS EMANCIPATION

Freedmen also brought to their new political environment resources that sprang from the impact of emancipation, an event so important that it is still celebrated in recurring festivals, parades, and other public gatherings in black communities in the South, the Border States, and the Midwest. Direct testimony, happily, was also partly recovered in 3,428 semi-structured "slave narratives" produced between 1936 and 1938 by the Works Progress

Administration's Federal Writers Project. They show that a large majority despised the local circumstances of their enslavement enough to leave them—right away, within a few months, or within the year—in search of family members and something better and different.[47]

Historians have thus chronicled search and travel in the wake of emancipation. Three important elements of this process were (1) the immediate effort at family reconstruction, as black people traveled widely to find their loved ones and to reunite with them, (2) a demand for formal recognition by local pastors or U.S. Army chaplains of family life by means of legal marriage, and (3) assertion of parental responsibility for black children by, for instance, legal struggle against the apprenticing of black children established under the Black Codes of presidential reconstruction.[48]

Education was another vital immediate result of emancipation, for slavery had depended on, among other things, strictly enforced illiteracy. Literacy of one sort or another was a badge of freedom and a necessity in the postemancipation world of the written labor contracts initiated by U.S. Army officers during and after the war in the occupied South. Southern blacks financed and supported several hundred schools in southern cities. A much smaller number of rural schools also emerged. These institutions built on antebellum urban networks for "secret schooling." Also, there had been private schooling for freedmen and freedwomen in southern cities, as well as official wartime stimulation of schooling in areas under Union occupation (in Virginia, Tennessee, Arkansas, Louisiana, Mississippi, northern Alabama, and coastal South Carolina).[49]

Alongside self-education was *religious organization*. Baptists broke away from white churches to found their own congregations. Emissaries from the African Methodist Episcopal Zion Church and the African Methodist Episcopal Church (A.M.E.) quickly moved into the South, detaching black parishioners from white-controlled churches to form their own new networks. These rapidly sprouting black churches also composed a sabbath school system for all those eager to read the word of God and its accounts of Moses and Christ. The sabbath schools contributed considerably to the growth of black literacy.[50]

PARALLEL POLITICS

Yet another resource and skill-building phenomenon might be dubbed *parallel politics*. Blacks used open-air settings, public spaces, and, in some cities, churches for broadly political purposes, even as presidential reconstruction denied freedmen access to the official spaces of capitols and county courthouses. In early 1866 a meeting at the A.M.E. Church in Tallahassee, Florida, elected a freedman to Congress and outfitted him with money for his trip to Washington. In Norfolk, Virginia, as well as in Beaufort, South Carolina, black mock voting emerged in several wards in connection with state legislative elections. Parades and celebrations of holidays were held in cities and military campgrounds, particularly on the Fourth of July or to commemorate the Emancipation Proclamation. On July 4, 1865, in Mobile, Alabama, for instance, "[t]he procession formed as follows: Two regiments of colored troops—Mechanics' and Draymen's Association—Steamboatmen's Association—Firemen's Association, consisting of eight companies—Benevolent Society—Daughters of Zion—Sons of Zion—Missionary Society—Young Men's Association—Sisters of Charity and many others." Sometimes, too, newspaper readings would be held, particularly in towns and cities, as a literate freedman would announce important news to friends and neighbors, often in a church. A little-known fact about this period is that a dozen black-operated newspapers sprang up in the South.[51]

Also, as southern Conservatives gathered at constitutional conventions in the summer of 1865 to establish new state governments, and as state legislatures convened afterwards, freedmen's conventions met in Arkansas, North Carolina, Tennessee, and Virginia to discuss broad strategic questions and to craft petitions and memorials for submission to the constitutional conventions, the new governors and legislatures, and the U.S. Congress and the president. These knit together an emerging black leadership in cities and towns. Statewide associations also formed such as North Carolina's Equal Rights League and the Georgia Equal Rights Association. The Georgia ERA went so far as to employ a lobbyist in Washington, Reverend Henry McNeal Turner (of whom we shall see more soon.)[52]

There was also a far-flung parallel politics involving the Freedman's Bureau. Freedmen constantly sought to draw the bureau into aiding blacks' desire for control over land and their own labor. These efforts achieved considerable success (for a time) in the Georgia Sea Islands, home to a network of semiautonomous black-controlled jurisdictions, including what became known as the Republic of St. Catherine. Elsewhere, where bureau officials were less friendly, local committees organized to pressure the Freedmen's Bureau for stronger efforts on behalf of the freedmen.[53]

The most militant and insurgent form of parallel politics was the establishment of informal armed militia and marching companies in the Georgia Sea Islands, much of South Carolina, and parts of mainland Florida. In South Carolina this phenomenon first appeared on farms near federal garrisons with black units. Work groups would step to precision marches to relieve the tedium of gang labor. Black veterans in some Atlantic Coast areas became informal instructors in marching and drilling. In time, large rural areas were connected together by marching companies, each of which had its own male hierarchy of "captains" and captain's assistants and a system of secret communication with other companies' leaders. By 1866 many of these companies coordinated work stoppages as part of contract negotiations with planters and landholders.[54]

To summarize, when Congress passed the first Military Reconstruction Act in early March 1867, a regionwide network of black male activists already existed, thicker in some places than others in accordance with demography. Republican party and electoral politics had a potential black male staff, as it were, waiting in the wings to make suffrage work. It comprised ordinary teachers, sabbath school teachers, ministers, former military officers (particularly in Louisiana), and Union veterans, as well as barbers, carpenters, shoemakers, and blacksmiths (that is, people whose jobs allowed them to be at the hub of social networks), rural labor organizers, "company captains," and their assistants. The new coalition, in short, could work on both ends. The party insiders in Washington could count on a staff of black activists on the ground in the former Confederacy, and vice-versa.

RESPONDING TO POLITICAL RESOURCE PROVISION

The new coalition's black staff came out of the woodwork in response to the Republican Party's provision of an organizational framework. Political organizational inputs included the funding for a large network of itinerant speakers (a few of whom were established northern politicians) who proposed to contact black men in cities and countryside, and, quite significantly, a "recycling" of the Union League model of political clubs perfected in the North during the Civil War.[55]

The Union Republican Congressional Executive Committee (URCEC) had been active in the 1866 elections. In 1867 it regrouped and established offices in Washington, D.C., for the specific purpose of building a political infrastructure in the South, raising its funds from assessments on Republican officeholders, congressional employees, and state organizations such as the Massachusetts Reconstruction Association. Quickly realizing that its funds needed to be spent on traveling speakers and not, as initially planned, on simply distributing copious amounts of printed matter to a southern mailing list of perhaps twenty thousand names, the URCEC's directors eventually commissioned somewhere between 115 and 135 black and white traveling lecturers and organizers under the direction of the Union Leagues of America and its various state affiliates.[56]

The URCEC and the League concentrated their personnel in Virginia, Georgia, the Carolinas, Florida, Alabama, and Mississippi, though organizers could be found everywhere in the South. A large fraction of the black Union League employees consisted of ministers. Others, black and white, were schoolmasters or Union veterans and in at least one case a Confederate veteran. Central coordination was achieved during two regional tours. The first featured General Thomas Conway, a former assistant commissioner of the Freedmen's Bureau for Louisiana and director of its educational system who became the director of Union League organization in the South. He undertook an eight-state tour between mid-April and July 1867. The second featured John Mercer Langston, a black, Oberlin-educated lawyer (later dean of the Howard University Law School) who traveled as a schools inspector for the Freedmen's Bureau.[57]

By mid-summer the national headquarters of the Union League counted two hundred thousand to three hundred thousand members in the South, the vast majority black, organized into about two thousand to three thousand chapters. In Mississippi a Natchez newspaper rather worriedly noted that rural and urban organizers were working "with that rapidity of action which usually characterizes the movement of revolutionary organizations." In and around Virginia, the Carolinas, Georgia, Florida, Alabama, and Mississippi, League organizers would arrive in a city or town or at some country crossroad and announce a meeting about the rights of the colored man. Word would spread and at the appointed time, a large crowd would gather, most often at an A.M.E. church. Freedmen would be told about the sequence envisioned by the Military Reconstruction Acts: voter registration → election of delegates to a constitutional convention → constitution-making → constitutional ratification → election of new U.S. House and Senate representatives.[58]

The role of churches was central in this process of response to resource provision. Henry M. Turner, a former army chaplain and Civil War recruiter for the First U.S. Colored Infantry, organized the African Methodist Episcopal Church in Georgia in 1865 and 1866. He reported in late July to the URCEC that "[e]very preacher in the African Methodist Episcopal Church in this state is working well in the Republican cause except two." Of a colleague he wrote, "He knows nothing but radical gospel, prays it in every prayer, preaches it in every sermon, talks it in every conversation, and dreams it every night."[59]

Particular organizers showed great creativity. In July 1867 at the Georgia Republican convention, Turner and Tunis Campbell (of a short-lived black island republic off the coast of Georgia) ran what today would be called a "skills workshop" for the black delegates. It was intended to teach them how to go back to their communities and arrange for the staging of short political plays in local churches.[60]

For contemporaries an unusual aspect of the local responses to URCEC and Union League contact was what happened *after* the organizers left. Militia companies emerged in many places, sponsoring drilling and marching for black men. Follow-up League meetings in churches and schools and political rallies often functioned as quasi-work stoppages. When they did, fusing politics and a nascent agricultural trade unionism, they put planters and white employers on notice that black agricultural labor could not be taken for granted. Republican clubs were organized. In a few of the larger cities the Leagues became trade unions or they organized protests of streetcar segregation.[61]

Alongside League activity were parallel efforts on a smaller scale. In Georgia, the weekly organ of the Georgia Equal Rights Association was read out loud every Sunday for several months after church services in 50 of the state's 131 counties. A black Baptist minister calling himself Professor J. W. Toer traveled in Georgia and Florida with "a magic lantern to exhibit . . . the progress of reconstruction." Many such itinerant lecturers—"political circuit riders" in the apt phrase of Jeffrey Kerr-Ritchie—crisscrossed the South: John V. Given, Henry Jerome Brown, James W. Hunnicutt, James D. Barrett, Joseph R. Holmes, and John Robinson, among others. In Alabama and Mississippi local black notables competed with the Union Leagues and organized their own Republican clubs and organizations, for example, the "Party of Lincoln."[62]

REGIONAL MOBILIZATION

In summary, the coalition-making process on the ground was a broad-based affair. It was, to use Julie Saville's apt phrase, a "registration summer."[63] Saville describes a typical event during registration summer:

> On the first day in which newly eligible ex-slave voters in South Carolina
> were to be registered . . . a party of some 1,000 black men marched to a
> registration site in a rice-growing parish north of Charleston, arriving well
> before the board of registrars had assembled. . . . Two hundred of the marchers,
> armed with guns or muskets, served as a kind of guard for the plantation
> laborers who formed the largest portion of the party . . . virtually every man
> among three or four hundred eligible black voters in St. Thomas Parish must
> have participated . . . along with several hundred men younger than 21 years
> of age.

Table 2.2 Aspects of Registration Summer, 1867

- 115–135 Republican Party–sponsored organizers toured Virginia, Georgia, the Carolinas, Florida, Alabama, and Mississippi
- Military-appointed registrars—a third of whom were black in some states—traveled in every county in 10 former Confederate states over a 10–14 week period enrolling eligible voters
- Former Confederate states experienced a 50 percent rise in number of civilian Freedmen's Bureau personnel
- Local entrepreneurs toured and/or called meetings
- Local associations in certain cities and counties arranged for dissemination of information by black churches
- In a few southern cities white northern Republican politicians spoke publicly
- Contentious collective action formed along emerging black-controlled institutional foundations: marching companies, political clubs, churches, and schools

Registration involved men moving in groups out of doors. But women were part of it, too. They exhorted their menfolk and made sure that the men did what they were supposed to.[64]

The political ferment in the South is captured in table 2.2. During this period, URCEC, the Union League, and a variety of smaller associations and political entrepreneurs spread word of the Reconstruction Acts, using the black institutions then emerging. In the process they encountered a vast raft of potential activists located within black institutions and networks. And these activists responded to the encounter and to their reading of the situation. They and other black southerners supplied the behavior needed to make suffrage extension work. They were already organized into new institutions that were largely unknown to most contemporary white observers.

RETROSPECT AND PROSPECT

At this point in the chapter we are close to finishing the characterization of the coalition-forging that launched the first reconstruction. Threatened by Andrew Johnson's political strategies, the Republican Party responded, as we have seen, by expanding its electoral coalition and building a cross-sectional organization. African American southerners decisively seized the political opportunity. But Johnson *continued* to threaten the Republican Party. Having already responded to earlier threats by greatly expanding its electoral base, the party ran out of electoral options for coping with the renewed menace. In order to protect itself, and in the process protect their new coalition, the Republicans impeached and tried Johnson. The rest of this chapter sketches this final act in the formation of the new coalition. A key player, of course, was the army.

Johnson did not passively accept the Republican strategy of coalition expansion. He tried to somehow stop the suffrage extension already under way and triggered the most severe constitutional emergency America has ever experienced.[65] No sooner had Congress passed the Reconstruction Acts than Johnson sought to weaken their implementation. Yet he did not really control the country's one competent, centralized, command-and-control agency: the U.S. Army. This would seem curious, because the president is formally the commander-in-chief. But Republicans, not the president, enjoyed the loyalty of the army's top command. By early 1867 Secretary of War Edwin Stanton and General-in-Chief Ulysses S. Grant considered the president's restoration of rebels to positions of local and state (and potentially congressional) power a threat to the army. They turned to covert cooperation with congressional Republicans in planning military reconstruction of the South.[66]

Generally speaking, the army promoted suffrage extension as intended. For instance, military commanders and Freedmen's Bureau officials in the reconstruction districts organized the communication of information about the policy change among a largely illiterate population. There was a temporary but sharp increase in the number of army Freedmen's Bureau agents and officials, whose main purpose probably was distribution of voter registration information. In March 1867 the average number of civilian employees of the bureau was about thirty per state, but this figure shot up by August 1867, during the height of the military registration process, to about forty-four per state, almost a 50 percent increase, while a similar (but much smaller and less rapid) increase occurred for military officers attached to the bureau.[67]

A bureau official in Alabama highlighted the value of reliable political information when he reported to his superior that after "whites had left" a meeting that he had convened, the freedmen in attendance crowded around him with "expressions of unbounded delight . . . the inference was too plain that a despotic influence is habitually over them."[68] In Mississippi, after some white planters discouraged black voter registration by telling freedmen that registrars were actually recruiters intent on pressing freedmen into military service, the military commander arranged for registrars to visit every plantation in the state.[69] In other words, the army afforded a crucial degree of protection to southern blacks. During a period of ten to fourteen weeks in mid-1867, it helped shield acts of public assembly in connection with voter registration, election, gathering for a constitutional convention, and ratification of a constitution.[70]

Finally, the military registration process mobilized associational resources among the civilian population that could make the process work on the ground. In several states military commanders chose to appoint two white members and one freedman to the boards of registrars. The Third Military District's commander did so specifically to encourage black registration, and he paid registrars rather well. Given the number of boards, the registrar appointment process had a vital role in triggering helpful political action. Alabama had 44 registrars, Georgia 44, South Carolina 109, North Carolina 170, and Texas somewhere between 90 and 165, for instance. All board members were required to swear the Ironclad Test Oath. In recruiting registrars, military officers could not help but tap and activate helpful associational networks among both blacks and "loyal" whites.[71] In short, Congress's alliance with the army was an asset in the "revolution from above" launched by the Republicans in order to protect their position.

But toward the end of "registration summer," 1867, Johnson sought to wrest control of the army away from Congress, even though political mobilization of African Americans was already far advanced. In mid-August he suspended Edwin Stanton, appointed Ulysses S. Grant to the cabinet post, and then reshuffled the commands of the military districts.

Johnson's campaign to assert his control of the army took on a darker hue in late 1867, when the president sent his annual message to Congress. Johnson denounced black suffrage as an evil actually greater than the Civil War: "Of all the dangers which our nation has yet encountered, *none are equal* to those which must result from the success of the effort now making to Africanize the half of our country." Johnson then told Congress that he had contemplated precipitating a new civil war! He had decided against it, however, because happily "[t]he people were not wholly disarmed in the power of self-defense" via the electoral process.[72]

A few days later he complied with the Tenure of Office Act (an early instance of the legislative veto) and formally advised the Senate of his removal of the secretary of war. Under the terms of the statute, the Senate then voted its disapproval in early January 1868; Grant vacated the office and Stanton reentered the position. But Johnson upped the ante again. In early February 1868 he recommended a new Department of the Atlantic, based in Washington, D.C., and ordered Grant to promote General William Tecumseh Sherman to the exact same rank as Grant's so that he could assume the new department's command. Johnson told his secretary of the navy that this was in preparation for a crisis. Sherman, however, refused both the promotion and the command. The general telegraphed his brother, Ohio senator John Sherman, that "the President would make use of me to beget violence."[73]

The struggle to control the army came to a head on February 21, 1868, when the president dismissed the secretary of war. By again dismissing Stanton after previously informing the Senate of his first dismissal and then apparently acquiescing in the Senate's disapproval by reinstating Stanton, Johnson kicked the trip wire written into the Tenure of Office Act. Borrowing the Constitution's language, the act labeled any violation a "high misdemeanor." It also established severe criminal sanctions.[74]

In short, the rules of the constitutional game gave Congress a decisive advantage in blocking Johnson's effort to claim the army's institutional resources for his own political purposes. Under the Constitution, Congress can remove the officer who functions as commander-in-chief of the armed forces. In that sense, as impeachment and trial of the president beckoned following Stanton's second ouster, the Constitution sealed a new coalition in American politics.

If Congress had not called Johnson's bluff, black suffrage and congressional reconstruction might have faced further presidential attack. As it happened, impeachment and trial reduced Johnson to merely rhetorical resistance. To close off all incentive for further resistance, in late July 1868, Congress passed, over Johnson's veto, a joint resolution holding that no state failing to comply with the Reconstruction Acts would have its votes counted in the Electoral College in 1868 and 1869. With these actions in the first half of 1868, the Republican Party reasserted the resolve to govern that it had shown all along in proposing and pursuing black suffrage.

CONCLUSION

This chapter has shown that party politicians brought new voters in when those politicians faced a threat. William Riker famously suggested that "[i]n . . . situations similar to n-person, zero-sum games . . . participants create coalitions" that "they believe will ensure winning." I underscored the depth and relative intractability of elite conflict as a progenitor of coalition formation. As Waldner puts it, coalition formation results if elites believe that "their long-term capacity to reproduce their elite status" is plainly and unmistakably jeopardized, that is, if "the threatened elite feels that it will be unable to compete . . . in the future." This formulation nicely captures the mindset of the congressional Republicans in the face of Andrew Johnson's party-building ambition and his exceptional intransigence.[75]

But the fact that Republicans needed a coalition hardly guaranteed that they would get one. Bottom-up struggle and initiative by the freedmen cemented the coalition. Such action featured a sense of racial group identity and a range of collective behaviors in public. The promotion of black collective action by entrepreneurs located in generally all-black institutions and associations was crucial. A key role was played, in particular, by black marching companies, by black registrars, and by the Union Leagues. The overall result was a party- and movement-generated transformation of the very context for national party politics.

But how resilient was that change? What about *consolidation* of the new coalition? Chapter 3 "flashes forward" to what is known as the Compromise of 1877 and to the years after this moment in American political development. It sketches a curious mix: a partial reversal of African American electoral incorporation about a decade and a half after the remarkable process of coalition formation and yet a coalition that also possessed resilience.

Chapter Three

Incomplete Institutionalization

After the biracial coalition of 1867–1868 emerged and set a new course in political democracy, it experienced a reversal of fortune. Despite the coalition's success at putting Ulysses S. Grant in the White House in 1868 and also holding onto Congress, it began to unravel. First, in the 1872 presidential elections, the Republican Party split into two factions. "Liberal Republicans" fought the reelection of Grant and accepted the southern conservatives' argument that Reconstruction was a policy mistake. Then, in 1874, the Republican Party suffered crushing defeat in the congressional elections, losing ninety-six seats in the House. A sharp contraction of the national economy and Republican sponsorship of the Civil Rights Bill of 1874 (later the 1875 Civil Rights Act) helped the Democrats enormously.

By 1875 Democrats had acquired control of the state governments of Tennessee, Georgia, Texas, Virginia, Alabama, Arkansas, and Mississippi, as well as the North Carolina legislature. They relied on force and intimidation, but they also profited enormously from the economic recession that began in 1873, which gave them a strong argument with many white voters.[1] By 1876, the crisis was palpable. Only Florida, Louisiana, and South Carolina remained under the control of the great coalition of 1867–1868. Addressing the Republican National Convention in 1876, Frederick Douglass asked, "The question now is, do you mean to make good the promises in your Constitution? You say you have emancipated us. . . . But what is your emancipation? . . . your enfranchisement? What does it all amount to, if the black man, after having been made free by the letter of your law, is unable to exercise that freedom?"[2]

Then, as if in mocking response to Douglass's interrogatories, came the Compromise of 1877, which resolved the greatest election crisis in American history, save for the 2000 presidential election. On election night, Samuel Tilden seemed to have won the presidency on the basis of a solid vote in the South, the West, and several large northern states. The Republican candidate, Rutherford B. Hayes, carried none of the southern states that were run by Democrats. But, in the wee hours of the morning, Hayes campaign managers in New York noticed that if the three remaining Republican states in the South—Florida, Louisiana, and South Carolina—reported Hayes the winner, then Hayes would win the Electoral College by one vote. Given the chaos and violence of their elections, these three reports were still pending. Campaign headquarters urgently telegraphed the news to the southern Republicans, telling them to hold their states for Hayes.

In Louisiana and South Carolina rival and heavily armed governments emerged, and each sent disputed certificates to Washington. Florida's certification that Tilden had won was tainted, in addition, by the new Democratic governor's defiance of the Florida Supreme Court's decision that Hayes had won in that state. The Constitution did not clearly show how such a crisis ended. The president of the Senate, a reliable Connecticut Republican, was empowered to count the certificates—but which certificates? Many of Tilden's supporters declared themselves ready to fight a civil war.

Tilden dropped out of view, causing tempers to cool. Grant and Hayes both tilted toward a policy of letting trustworthy southern white leaders fix the situation on the ground. The president indeed told the cabinet that the Fifteenth Amendment "had done the Negro no good."[3]

Congressional Republicans were not, however, willing to back off. They instead pushed a Twelfth Amendment scenario in which the president of the Senate counted the disputed Republican certificates and rejected the disputed Democratic certificates after all. The way out of the deadlock then appeared to be a specially created Electoral Commission, established by both parties. But the commission ruled for Hayes by one vote, that of Justice Joseph Bradley of the Supreme Court. Somehow, this surprised the House Democrats, who expected victory. They organized to block agreement with the vote. But on March 2, 1877, Democrats in control of the House of Representatives ended their obstruction of the Electoral College count. If continued through March 4, it would have blocked the swearing in of a new president. The Democrats finally accepted the 8–7 recommendation of the commission awarding the disputed vote to Rutherford B. Hayes. Some sort of deal had been struck. Its elements included a reduction in federal troop presence in the South, withdrawal to barracks of the federal troops guarding officials of the remaining Republican governments in the black-majority states of Louisiana and South Carolina, federal funding for rivers and harbors construction, and Democratic access to the federal patronage. As the chair of the Kansas Republican committee put it in February, the policy seemed to be, "Carpetbaggers to the rear, and [Negroes] take care of yourselves."[4]

In 1877 Hayes repeatedly stressed, perhaps sincerely, that the South's leading men would guarantee black voting rights. The showcase effort in this connection occurred in South Carolina, where the new governor, Wade Hampton, appointed many African Americans to office. But Hayes, if he meant what he said, should have known better. In short order, Democrats at the state and local levels weakened black voting in the South by means of gerrymandering, violence, and intimidation.[5]

A MIX OF WEAKNESS AND PERSISTENCE

In short, only a decade after its triumphant formation, the great coalition of 1867–1868 was shipwrecked in the South's political storms. Terrible political stresses continued to beset it after 1877. Many fewer blacks voted and held public office than had previously. The southern Republican parties generally broke into competing racial factions, precursors of the "Black and Tan" and "Lily White" factions of the early twentieth century. Often white elites tightly controlled what voting and office-holding there was by African Americans. Persistent vote fraud diluted the impact of black participation. Various kinds of laws sought to tie black labor to the land.[6]

On the other hand, we shall also see that the coalition was hardly broken altogether. Indeed, its simple existence and survival, despite its weak state, created a political context that favored repeated efforts of various sorts to sustain and revitalize it. In different places the coalition was, at different times, jolted back to strength—or it simply had never fallen apart as badly as elsewhere.

This chapter outlines the continuing involvement of the Republican Party's northern wing in southern party politics and its support for black electoral inclusion. A considerable degree of electoral insecurity for the Republicans outside the South created an incentive for northern Republicans to sustain the party's historic southern policy. Their stances and initiatives interacted with black southerners' continuing mobilization of their political resources. There was, in other words, a *mix*—a mix of weakness *and* persistence. Portraying it is essential for understanding the long and puzzling course of African American electoral inclusion. It reveals incomplete institutionalization.

Exploring the state of the coalition after the Compromise of 1877 will, at chapter's end, require us to turn back in time to focus on party- and jurisprudence-building between 1867 and 1877. To what degree did these processes help institutionalize the great coalition? Why was there not greater institutionalization? These are the issues that will concern us in chapters 4 and 5. By assembling conflicting pieces of evidence, this chapter characterizes the coalition of 1867–1868 in its troubled middle age. I begin by sketching the state and local strategies and tactics of Democrats for attacking the coalition.

CONSERVATIVE DEMOCRATIC STRATEGIES AND TACTICS AFTER REDEMPTION

After the Compromise of 1877, Democrats controlled the "redeemer" governments, that is, the state governments that Democrats had "redeemed" from the biracial coalition (to use their slogan.) They used their advantage to gerrymander state legislative districts, to impose new charters on cities with large numbers of black voters in order to make black voter registration or office-holding difficult (as in Virginia and North Carolina), to establish two-box and then eight-box balloting intended to confuse illiterates (as in South Carolina), and to regulate the color, size, and lettering of ballots in order to deprive illiterate black voters of visual cues. The 1877 cumulative poll tax voting requirement in Georgia sharply diminished black voting in that state. Also common were attacks on black office-holding by means of reapportionment, contesting of elections in Democratic-controlled legislatures, prevention of offers of bond credit, and the removal of local public offices from the electoral process. Local offices became appointive, and appointments were usually made by the governor.[7]

Extralegal subversion was, however, the principal way in which southern Conservatives and Democrats attacked African American incorporation. It sometimes took mild forms. Black voters might, for example, find themselves in a separate line on election day, one that moved so slowly that only a very few voted. But Democrats also often resorted to violence and intimidation.[8] Consider the 1882 congressional election in Alabama's First District, which contained Mobile. A cache of apparently secret documents was "discovered" one hot summer day on a Choctaw County road. They "revealed" a horrible plot: a prosperous black farmer and Republican leader, Jack Turner, intended an uprising against whites! The county sheriff jailed Turner at the county courthouse. This frame-up played out as intended when a white mob lynched Turner on August 19. Alabama was awash with stories of similar plots by blacks. On election day, Democrats won all their congressional, state, and local elections.[9]

It is, of course, very hard to say where, when, and how many such attacks on black electoral inclusion took place. Much of what we know is due to the U.S. Senate, which investigated the violence (see table 3.6 below), and to federal elections observers and U.S. marshals, who were themselves intimidated on election day; these events were generally noted at the national level.[10]

A third kind of extralegal attack was fraud. Fraud was extensive and often centrally directed. In Louisiana, for instance, the legislature gave the governor complete authority over elections administration in 1881. As one post-Reconstruction Louisiana governor stated, "The law shall be silent." Local elections boards were generally stacked with more Democrats than non-Democrats, if they had non-Democrats at all. Elections commissioners would allocate Republican ballots to Democrats or, if they did not "count out" votes cast by African Americans, they would instead "count in" false Democratic ballots that had been stuffed into the box. Alternatively, a party of armed men might steal the ballots from black areas after the election was over and destroy them.[11]

THE STATE OF BLACK ELECTORAL INCLUSION (I)

Given such pressures, how broad was African American electoral inclusion, really? Consider office-holding. Table 3.1 shows a sharp drop in the number of black state legislators and members of the U.S. House of Representatives.

The fates of several black congressmen underscore the way the bottom dropped out for black politicians. Alonzo Ransier, who served in the U.S. House from South Carolina between 1873 and 1875, died in 1880 while employed as a day laborer for the city of Charleston. James T. Rapier of Alabama, who served along with Ransier, also died penniless, having spent much of his once-considerable fortune on black schools and churches and schemes for black emigration from the South. Benjamin S. Turner, who served from Alabama from 1871 to 1873, died in 1894 near Selma as a poor farmer. John Hyman of North Carolina, who served in the House from 1874 to 1877, worked in Maryland as a mail clerk from 1879 to 1889 and died in Washington, D.C., in 1891 while working as a clerk in the Department of Agriculture. South Carolina's Robert B. Elliott, who delivered a famous speech to the House in favor of the 1875 Civil Rights Act, died penniless in

Table 3.1 Post-Reconstruction Black Office-Holding

Year	1876	1878	1880	1882	1884	1886	1888	1890
Number	162	74	75	71	66	56	45	35
Percentage change		−54.3	+1.3	−5.3	−7	−15	−19.6	−22

Source: J. Morgan Kousser, "The Voting Rights Act and the Two Reconstructions," in *Controversies in Minority Voting: The Voting Rights Act in Perspective,* ed. Bernard Grofman and Chandler Davidson (Washington, D.C.: Brookings Institution, 1992), pp. 135–76, table 1.

New Orleans in 1884 after losing a job in the U.S. Treasury Department and failing as a lawyer.[12]

What about voting? Here, too, the picture is disquieting, as table 3.2 illustrates. It shows estimates derived by two sociologists using the latest improvement in a statistical technique known as ecological regression (ER).[13] The ER estimates reported in table 3.2 indicate that by 1890 white supremacy had emerged in Georgia, Louisiana, Mississippi, and South Carolina (though, in a little-known biracial revolt, Louisiana's version of white supremacy faced a serious challenge in the late 1890s.) What makes this bad news is that *45 percent* of all African Americans in the United States lived in these four states.[14]

Table 3.2 Relative Persistence of Black Voting

State	Redding-James Ecological Regression Estimates of Black Voter Turnout in Presidential Elections, 1880–1892 (percentage)	
	1880	1892
Alabama	55	55
Arkansas	57	36
Florida	84	**14**
Georgia	42	33
Louisiana	44	30
Mississippi	45	**1**
North Carolina	81	63
South Carolina	77	17
Tennessee	70	**31**
Texas	59	53
Virginia	59	58

Source: Kent Redding and David R. James, "Estimating Levels and Modeling Determinants of Black and White Voter Turnout in the South: 1880 to 1912," *Historical Methods* 34.4 (2001): 141–158.
Note: Cell entries for 1892 in boldface denote *legal disenfranchisement* already under way.

Indeed, tables 3.1 and 3.2 show that white Democrats' attacks on the coalition of 1867–1868 inflicted real damage. Such injury also was manifest in public policy. Many southern states officially segregated schools and forbade interracial marriage. They passed laws designed to curtail the free mobility of black labor. These included contract enforcement provisions, laws fining emigrant agents, laws permitting criminal surety payments by local landlords for prisoners in local jails (a form of debt peonage), and anti-vagrancy laws (making it easy for black men, if they could not prove they had gainful employment, to end up in jail, whence, of course, they could be sprung by a landlord willing to put up the criminal surety).[15]

THE STATE OF BLACK ELECTORAL INCLUSION (II)

On the other hand, African American inclusion clearly persisted to some extent. The question is, how much? Here we can turn to J. Morgan Kousser's pioneering ER estimates of black electoral turnout. In particular, I exploit what I consider a very useful anomaly in his findings. One of the more striking things about Kousser's estimates is that they show large numbers of African Americans voting for Democrats in the 1880s. For instance, in 1882, at the height of "Jack Turnerism," the campaign of intimidation that began in the Mobile area, Kousser's data show a curious result. Of blacks in Alabama who turned out to vote, 36 percent cast their ballots for the Democratic candidate for governor, Edward O'Neal, while only 16 percent cast their ballots for the Republican gubernatorial candidate, James Sheffield, for an overall turnout rate for Alabama's black voters of 52 percent in that election (which O'Neal handily won, 69 percent to 31 percent).[16]

It is possible that large numbers of black Alabama men willingly and freely voted for the Democrat—but not likely. Indeed, if there really had been such high rates of black voting *for* Democrats then it is hard to grasp why they eventually sought to disenfranchise black voters in the 1890s or engaged in election fraud in the 1880s.

Consider, too, the social reinforcement of partisan identity. Black men typically went to the polls in groups, after weeks of often contentious outdoor displays of their partisanship. On election day they asked for their party-strip ballot, voted the full ticket, and then deposited it in full view of others. Their voting was closely monitored by local party leaders and their co-partisans—and often by their spouses. An observation from a white British traveler in South Carolina in the late 1870s seems apt: "Most people . . . admit that, while the blacks will do almost anything else for them, when it comes to voting they cannot be influenced, and insist on voting with their party."[17]

To be sure, black political leaders were often impatient with the Republicans. Black voters sometimes abandoned the Republican Party for independent, third-party politics, as with the Virginia Readjusters (on which more below). Rather than insist on a separate, non-Democratic organization, black voters in some one-party southern cities played Democratic factions against one another. But the only major instance of black voting for Democrats occurred in South Carolina, mainly in 1876, at a rate of about 10 percent, in the context of quite intensive efforts to appeal to black voters and promises that public education would be protected. Widespread, authentic black support for Democrats did not yet exist in the South.[18]

What, then, to make of Kousser's estimates showing substantial pro-Democratic voting among blacks? They show, I believe, the effects of fraud. In other words, in Alabama in 1882, fifty-two of one hundred black male voters actually voted, but only sixteen were counted by Democratic-controlled elections commissioners as they wished and intended to be counted, that is, as voting for the Republican candidate.[19] The other thirty-six black voters showed up and voted but then had their votes fraudulently allocated to the Democratic total in order to guarantee a Democratic victory. Thus, 52 percent was probably the true black turnout figure. But officials were diluting the black vote at a very high rate of 70 percent (36/52). The *efficiency* of black voting, in a sense, was therefore only about 30 percent (16/52). As a result of Democratic fraud, it took fifty-two blacks voting Republican in order for sixteen to be counted for the Republicans. Fraudulent elections administration required blacks to vote at high rates to have even a small impact.

Keeping these points in mind, one sees in table 3.3 a selection of Kousser's estimates of black voter turnout for Republicans in selected southern elections during the 1880s. This is the *first* figure in each pair of columns. The *second* figure shows the efficiency of that turnout, per the arithmetic described above. With the exception of the figures for South Carolina, which represent presidential election turnout, the figures are for gubernatorial elections. That fact is important because determining black turnout in gubernatorial elections rather strongly tests the actual degree of black electoral inclusion. Southern Democrats needed to control this office because the governor controlled or strongly influenced elections administration. The office was indeed the institutional foundation for vote fraud. Also, the governor certified or controlled certification of election results to the U.S. House. To the extent that black voting for gubernatorial elections was not fully controlled by the Democrats, their political position was insecure.

What one sees in scanning table 3.3 are rates of black turnout and voting efficiency that vary across states. Therefore, in table 3.4, the results from

Table 3.3 Relative Efficiency of African American Voting in Selected Elections, 1880–1890

State	1880		1881		1882		1884		1885		1888		1889		1890	
	T	E	T	E	T	E	T	E	T	E	T	E	T	E	T	E
Alabama					52%	30%										
Arkansas													69%	67%	71%	16%
Florida							87%	69%								
Georgia	57%	21%														
Louisiana							51%	57%								
Mississippi			38%	66%												
North Carolina	86%	81%					94%	79%			68%	73%				
South Carolina*					30%	30%					29%	52%				
Tennessee	89%	57%					67%	62%								
Texas					72%†	86%					86%†	67%				
Virginia	90%	70%	60%	81%					97%	73%			85%	65%		

Source: Author's calculations using figures in J. Morgan Kousser, *The Shaping of Southern Politics: Suffrage Restriction and the Establishment of the One-Party South, 1880–1910* (New Haven: Yale University Press, 1974), pp. 28, 102, 106, 174, 183, 199.

Note: No figures are available for 1883, 1886, 1887. T = turnout; E = efficiency.

* presidential contest.

† Greenbacker/Farmers Alliance vote.

Table 3.4 A Typology of Black Electoral Incorporation

	High Efficiency (above 50%)	Low Efficiency (50% or lower)
High turnout (above 50%)	Arkansas North Carolina Tennessee Texas Virginia	Alabama Georgia (1880)
Low turnout (50% or lower)	Mississippi Louisiana	South Carolina Probably Georgia after 1880

table 3.3 are grouped according to whether states had high or low black voter turnout for the Republican Party and according to whether the efficiency of such turnout was high or low. If most states were in the high turnout–high efficiency cell, that would suggest a fairly high degree of actual electoral inclusion. If most states were in the low turnout–low efficiency cell, that would suggest a dismally low degree of actual electoral inclusion.

The surprise in table 3.4 is the location of most former Confederate states. If most states were grouped in the lower right-hand cell of the table, the post-Reconstruction situation would be very disappointing. But most states are instead located on the upper tier and in the left-hand column. In short, the figures reported in tables 3.1 and 3.2 show the setbacks experienced by the coalition of 1867–1868 after the Compromise of 1877. The evidence presented in tables 3.3 and 3.4 captures another part of a complex reality, namely, the genuine resilience of the great coalition.

Looking briefly at the insurgencies and the fiercely defended enclaves that dotted the former Confederacy after the Compromise of 1877 also underscores the coalition's staying power. Imagine a broad aerial view of the South. Surveying the region, one would see something like a checkerboard of sustained and even *new* political mobilizations by black southerners. In the next section, I "zoom in" on two particularly interesting spots on the southern checkerboard: the State of Tennessee and the Commonwealth of Virginia.

MOBILIZATION, INSURGENCIES, AND ENCLAVES

In Tennessee and Virginia, a major issue after the Compromise of 1877 was what to do about Civil War and state debt. Reconstruction did not occur in either state. Fiscal disorder could not therefore be blamed on the Republicans and their biracial coalition. The issue instead split the conservative Democrats.

Thus in 1880, when Tennessee Democrats split over the issue of state funding and credit, the biracial Tennessee Republican Party elected a governor and three members of Congress, sent four black officeholders to the state's General Assembly (a major change in Tennessee's public life), and gained working control of the House. Although riven with racial factionalism, the Tennessee Republican Party also proved capable of the unusual symbolic act in 1885 of uniting around a black legislator as its candidate for speaker of the General Assembly. To put the point differently, in Tennessee the state-level wing of the coalition of 1867–1868 grew stronger after the Compromise of 1877 for a period of several years.[20]

The Readjusters

The same happened in Virginia. Indeed, the Virginia coalition was considerably more powerful than the Tennessee mobilization. In the late 1870s its national Republican partners provided an enormous investment in terms of direct cash inputs for campaign finance and access to federal patronage.[21] On their side of the equation, the Virginia wing of the coalition of 1867–1868 supplied extraordinary talent based in a rich set of social networks, grouped within a third party that was Virginia's de facto Republican Party. In the 1870s the Virginia Conservative Party divided into two factions with clashing fiscal policies. "Funders" were Virginia Conservatives committed to repaying Virginia's antebellum debt (and its growing interest). They did so at the expense of the public school system established by the state's Reconstruction constitution. "Readjusters" were moderate Conservatives who wanted to readjust state debt service to the state's new postwar policy commitments.

In 1879, unable to resolve their differences, both sides adopted the unusual measure of mobilizing and appealing to Virginia's black voters (then about one-third of the state's electorate). This was an interesting instance of both sides simultaneously attempting a Riker-Gamson coalition. The appeal to black voters was actually remobilization. In 1875 both wings of the Conservative Party had backed a suffrage restriction program that was approved by referendum in 1876—on the eve of the 1877–1878 legislative session. By increasing poll taxes and making their payment a prerequisite for voting, and by making conviction of petty larceny a basis for disenfranchisement, both Conservative factions sought to shrink the black and poor white electorates, which had a vested interest in the school system. But the Conservatives then proved unable to resolve the festering funding issue in the legislature. Out of this schism came the Readjusters. They unexpectedly outflanked their opponents by mobilizing a poll-tax payment campaign, thus bringing back in the voters whom the legislature had just pushed out.[22]

In the 1879 statewide elections the Readjusters captured control of the legislature with the help of black voters and a fresh cohort of black legislators. They also gained control of important city governments. They then chose William Mahone, a railroad executive and a renowned former Confederate general, as U.S. senator. In 1881 the Readjuster Party elected the governor, retained its control of the state legislature, and selected a second United States senator, Harrison Riddleberger.

With two Readjusters in the Senate, the party now had enormous patronage resources in the Norfolk and Portsmouth Navy Yards, in customhouses, lighthouses, and postmasterships. Mahone personally added 379 postmasterships while he served as a senator. In turn, such patronage jobs were a rich source of funds for party assessments at 5 percent, which then went to pay for traveling lecturers and campaign materials.[23]

In addition to these institutional foundations were African American militia companies, churches, glee clubs, masonic societies, trade unions, secret clubs based on workplace affiliations (at, for instance, Richmond tobacco factories and warehouses) with such names as the First Star of Jacob and Combination No. 14, and reading and literary societies, such as Petersburg's Chorranesee Literary Society and its James G. Blaine Lyceum and Library Association.[24]

From such networks came a party organization that sponsored key electoral changes (until Conservative-Democratic violence weakened the Readjusters in 1883 and brought partial reversal.) The Readjusters readjusted the size of the electorate. They kept detailed records of poll-tax payments—a difficult logistical task made easier after the 1879–1880 legislature chose a Readjuster state auditor—and paid poll taxes for likely Readjuster voters in arrears. Under state law this method of voter mobilization was legal. Money for poll tax payments came from funds funneled into Virginia by northern Republicans and from the party tax on the wages of patronage appointments and elected officeholders, including national officeholders. The party capped off its program of voter mobilization by legislating the poll tax's abolition (which also, of course, saved it money).[25]

These actions helped increase the total number of voters participating in state legislative races between 1879 and 1881 by about 47 percent, led to a *further* increase between 1881 and 1883 of about 30 percent, an increase of about 30 percent for elections to the U.S. House of Representatives between 1880 (a presidential election year) and 1882 (an off-year), and a smaller but still significant increase of about 5.3 percent in the total number of voters participating in gubernatorial elections between 1873 and 1881.[26]

The number of black state legislators and local officeholders increased very sharply. Sixteen black legislators served in the Virginia General Assembly in the session of 1881–1882. One of these, William Stevens, successfully guided the establishment of an asylum for mentally ill African Americans. Another secured funding for the Virginia Normal and Collegiate Institute, a black college that taught a classical, not an industrial, curriculum. Both of these new institutions were staffed by African American professionals.[27]

Indeed, the Readjusters provided "an honest shuffle and a new deal," as their newspaper called it.[28] They made broad changes in fiscal, revenue, health, educational, agricultural, and penal policy. By 1883 they had brought about a surplus in Virginia's public finances, both by repudiating the commonwealth's previous sixteen-year commitment to pay the part of the public debt attributable to West Virginia and by refunding the remaining debt with new eighteen-to-fifty-year notes bearing one-half the interest rate previously paid by the commonwealth. State revenues went up because state coupons were no longer receivable for taxes and railroads no longer performed their own tax assessments.[29]

The change in debt service and the enlargement of the revenue base in turn led to a *doubling* of the state's involvement in primary and secondary education, a capital improvement program at the University of Virginia, and the funding for the Virginia Normal and Collegiate Institute (now Virginia State University). The number of black schools increased from 675 to 1,256, the number of black pupils from thirty-six thousand to sixty-nine thousand. Black teachers were hired at salaries equal to white teachers' salaries, and black principals were appointed in some of the new schools, particularly in Richmond, whose board of education acquired two black Readjuster members. Besides the new black mental hospital built to house black patients formerly kept in jails, counties were authorized to provide free vaccines, and doctors on the public payroll had their salaries increased. The whipping of convicts was abolished. White Readjuster judges recruited blacks for state juries.[30]

For a time, then, Virginia witnessed a remarkable biracial experiment. After the Readjusters lost control of state government, they formally merged with the Republican Party. Until William Mahone's death, the Virginia Republican Party continued to strongly challenge the state's Democrats. Black voter participation in the twenty-five predominantly black Tidewater counties in eastern Virginia appears, in particular, to have stayed high.[31]

Political Enclaves

The evidence described so far does two things: it highlights the weakening of the 1867–1868 coalition and it suggests how the simple existence of the coalition created a regional political context within which pockets of resurgence could occur. The Tennessee Republican Party bounced back in the early 1880s. In Virginia, a strong, state-level version of the national Riker-Gamson coalition, the Readjuster Party, emerged.

There is yet another way in which the continuation of the coalition created a context in which struggle for inclusion could smolder and sometimes burst forth. It can be seen in the politics of the black congressional district. Such districts resulted from a type of gerrymandering known as "packing," that is, an effort to drain off enough black voters from enough adjacent districts to guarantee majority Democratic delegations to the House. But given the demographic concentrations of African American southerners, such packing generated districts so overwhelmingly black that they could become—despite white violence and fraud—politically safe for black politicians. Three such havens of national-level black political activity were South Carolina's Seventh District, North Carolina's Second District, and Virginia's Fourth District. They sent a total of seven different African American representatives to the House in the post-Reconstruction period.[32]

A cognate sort of politics could be found in exceptionally well-organized, black-controlled counties. Scholars have studied examples in South Carolina and Texas and noted the fair treatment of blacks in the local courts. Several in Arkansas were also black-controlled. The sugar parishes of southern Louisiana were another such enclave. In McIntosh County, Georgia, the law enforcement machinery remained black-controlled despite the best efforts of the state Democratic party.[33]

Third, there were biracial municipal bastions. In Jackson, Mississippi, for instance, the white Republican machine that dominated the city's politics in the 1880s mobilized black voters and ran an integrated city police force, a policy benefit that did not reappear there for a long time once it was dissolved by white Democrats toward the end of the decade. Similar political organizations, often with assertive black involvement, could be found in Little Rock, Chattanooga, Memphis, Nashville, Charlotte and other North Carolina cities, and Jacksonville, Florida. Also in Florida, black office-holding in general collapsed after 1876, but in twenty-three cities *it increased 123 percent* between 1876 and 1889, as blacks were elected to city councils and such posts as mayor, clerk, tax assessor, tax collector, treasurer, and marshal.[34]

To summarize, African American electoral incorporation suffered after the Compromise of 1877. But the black southern wing of the coalition of 1867–1868 persisted in voting, in seeking office, and in making the most of political opportunities that presented themselves. Two places in particular where black southerners made real gains were Tennessee and Virginia, where deep splits among Conservatives and Democrats occurred. Also, we see persistence in places where the possibility of winning election to the U.S. House was substantial, such as districts with very large black majorities.

That the great coalition continued to have life after 1877 is plain enough. The next questions: Did the Republican Party's northern wing contribute to coalition maintenance? Why? How? First the why, then the how.

THE LOGIC OF REPUBLICAN SUPPORT

An important vignette from 1880 illustrates the views that politically successful (and, within their party, dominant) northern Republicans had of the 1867–1868 coalition. Shortly after the 1880 nominating convention, the Republican nominees, James Garfield and Chester Arthur, formalized a renewed voting rights commitment. They did this in two letters to the 1880 convention chair, Massachusetts senator George Frisbie Hoar.[35]

Garfield connected vigorous national enforcement to true sectional reconciliation: "the wounds of the war cannot be completely healed . . . until every citizen, rich or poor, white or black, is secure in the free and equal enjoyment of every civil and political right guaranteed by the Constitution and the laws." Indeed, "[t]he prosperity which is made possible in the South by its great advantages of soil and climate, will never be realized until every voter can freely and safely support any party he pleases."[36]

For his part, Arthur held that "[t]he right and duty to secure honesty and order in popular elections is a matter so vital *that it must stand in front*. The authority of the National Government to preserve from fraud and force elections at which its own officers are chosen is a chief point on which the two parties are *plainly and intensely opposed*." Reviewing the efforts by the Forty-sixth Congress to repeal the federal elections laws, Arthur continued, "the Republican party holds, as a cardinal point . . . that the Government should by every means known to the Constitution, protect all American Citizens everywhere in the full enjoyment of their civil and political rights."[37]

Arthur's language was categorical. He and other leading Republicans thought that protecting African American electoral inclusion was urgent and vitally important. As Arthur put it, the explanation for northern Republicans' focus on the 1867–1868 coalition was "the increased power" that southern Democrats ("those who lately sought the overthrow of the Government") now "derived from the enfranchisement of a race . . . denied its share in governing the country." That power was "now the sole reliance to defeat" the Republican Party. He sketched, in other words, a strategic dilemma facing the Republicans. What they did during Reconstruction, Arthur suggested, paradoxically undercut Republican strength. The only way to transcend the problem was a return to a strong southern policy.[38]

This was a period of partisan stalemate, and Garfield and Arthur had already seen several years of it since the 1874 House elections. Indeed, this period in American political history provides an extreme case of such stalemate: fourteen consecutive years of divided government.[39] The average percentage of all House seats held by Republicans dropped from 61 percent during the 1860–1874 period to 46 percent during the period from 1876 to 1894. The average percentage of all Republican Senate seats decreased from 71 percent to 51 percent; the average Republican electoral (not popular) vote decreased from 75 percent to 49 percent.

Consider table 3.5, which contrasts party competitiveness in presidential elections during and after Reconstruction. It shows the Democrats getting stronger and the Republicans getting weaker. The average change in the percentage of safely Democratic states (states where the Democratic lead was more than 5 percent) was *4.4 percent*, and the average change in the percentage of population that fell into this combined category of "safely Democratic" was *3.7 percent*. But the average change in the percentage of states that were safely Republican (that is, having a lead of more than 5 percent) was *−6.7 percent*, and the average change in the percentage of population that fell into this category was *−6.2 percent*.

These shifts had a clear implication for the Republican Party's southern policy: keep it going. Although Garfield and Arthur only saw the opening years of this trend (and neither lived long enough to experience the entire period of stalemate), they understood black voting rights as a fundamental Republican interest.[40] While president, Arthur soon saw that even very slight shifts for Republicans in their southern strongholds due to black voting made the difference between unified or divided government. In this connection, it is worth quickly revisiting the alliance between northern Republicans and the Virginia Readjusters.

During the Forty-seventh Congress Republicans enjoyed unified government for the first time since Grant's second term. This position resulted from a policy of alliance with independent anti-Conservative movements that pursued black votes and defended black voting and office-holding. The most important of these was the coalition with the biracial Virginia Readjusters. Garfield encouraged it; Arthur openly pursued it.

A major policy reward of the compact proved to be the 1883 tariff. Without southern independents who represented a biracial base and who were willing to vote with the Republicans, there might have been no tariff at all. Indeed, a Readjuster played a key role in the House-Senate conference

Table 3.5 Declining Republican Competitiveness

Partisan Lead Categories	% of States		Change in Percentage Points	Average of Change in Percentage Points for 3 Safest Categories	% of Population		Change in Percentage Points	Average of Change in Percentage Points for 3 Safest Categories
	1856–72	1876–92			1856–72	1876–92		
20.0% + D	5.5	21.6	+16.1		5.7	17.6	+11.9	
10–19.9 D	5.5	16.2	+10.7	+4.4	5.8	15.2	+9.4	+3.7
5–9.9 D	19.1	5.4	–13.7		14.0	3.9	–10.1	
0–4.9 D	5.5	10.8	+5.3		5.7	17.2	+11.5	
0–4.9 R	13.8	16.2	+2.4		30.7	26.6	–4.1	
5–9.9 R	19.4	13.5	–5.9		18.1	10.9	–7.2	
10–19.9 R	8.3	13.5	+5.2	–6.7	7.1	7.9	+.8	–6.2
20.0%+ R	22.2	2.7	–19.5		12.7	0.5	–12.2	

Source: Paul Kleppner, *The Third Electoral System, 1853–1892* (Chapel Hill: University of North Carolina Press, 1979), table 2.7.B.

that forged the tariff. It was the first tariff legislation since 1875 and in many ways the first serious rethinking by Congress of national tariff policy since the landmark 1861 Morrill Tariff.[41]

Republicans continued to need the South—just as they had in 1867—and they needed alliances with such formations as the Readjusters. Men such as William Mahone were valuable partners because they had local legitimacy. Mahone, for instance, was a former Confederate general who fought at Gettysburg and the Battle of the Crater at Petersburg, Virginia. Arthur once reportedly confided to a Readjuster congressman, "We must hunt for Republican leaders in the South, *for the future,* somewhere else than among the scalawags or the Bourbons. There must be other kinds of people there."[42]

In summary, the why of continuing Republican involvement in southern electoral politics has three parts. First, Republicans had a far more insecure electoral environment in which important elections and legislative majorities were made at the margin. Second, they had clear policy goals. Third, they needed voters wherever they could get them, both to address electoral insecurity and to address policy goals.[43] One should therefore expect to find several indicators of the Republican Party's continuing involvement.

INDICATORS OF CONTINUING INVOLVEMENT

Focusing on the "retreat from Reconstruction" of about 1877, many scholars have inferred that black voting rights dropped off as a national issue until the 1960s.[44] But consider table 3.6, offering evidence from the national party platforms. It displays scores for the major parties on salience to them of their struggle over enforcement of equal suffrage in the South and (after 1870) of the Fifteenth Amendment. The critical assumption is that the earlier an issue appears in a party platform, the more important it probably is. Importance of the equal suffrage issue is measured by 1.0 minus the ratio of the number of the paragraph containing the first explicit reference to black suffrage rights and the total number of paragraphs. The higher the number, the greater the importance, and vice versa. The maximum value is 1.0, the lowest 0. By this

Table 3.6 Priority Index of Equal Suffrage for Major Party Platforms

	1868	1872	1876	1880	1884	1888	1892
Republicans	.93	1.0	0.89	0.14	0.04	0.85	0.76
Democrats	0.37	0.93	1.0	0.72	0.45	0.00	0.96

Source: Kirk H. Porter and Donald Bruce Johnson, comps., *National Party Platforms, 1840–1956* (Urbana: University of Illinois Press, 1956).

Table 3.7 Congressional Investigations of Southern Election Fraud

	40–44th Congresses	45th–54th Congresses
House investigations		
Republican control	5	0
Democratic control	2	2
Senate investigations		
Republican control	14	7
Democratic control	0	0

Sources: Congressional Information Service, US Congressional Committee Hearings Index Part I, 23rd Congress–64th Congress, Dec. 1833–Mar. 1917, Reference Bibliography, H1-1-(63-3) S. Doc. v. 7 n.981 (Bethesda, Md.: Congressional Information Service, 1985); Robert Goldman, "'A Free Ballot and a Fair Count:' The Department of Justice and the Enforcement of Voting Rights in the South, 1877–1893," Ph.D. diss., Michigan State University, 1976.

measure Republican involvement initially dropped but then grew substantially for much of the post-Reconstruction period. In other words, one vital contribution that the Republican Party's northern wing made to sustaining the coalition of 1867–1868 was simply continuing to commit itself to the issue of black voting rights in the party's presidential campaign platform.

Yet another indicator is the number of congressional investigations of southern election fraud and violence up to and including the Fifty-fourth Congress (see table 3.7). The table is broken into two periods, before and after 1876. It arrays investigations according to which chamber conducted the investigation and which party sponsored or managed it. This matters because the Republicans continuously controlled the Senate across both time periods. The table shows a Republican Party very busy during Reconstruction and still significantly preoccupied with investigation of southern election violence after the Compromise of 1877.

Consider, as well, table 3.8, presenting data concerning contested elections in the House during the Congresses between the end of Reconstruction and the election of McKinley. Table 3.8 indicates, first, that Republican control of the House produced more contested elections (seventeen cases) than did Democratic control (fifteen cases), even though Republicans controlled only two of the eight Houses organized between 1877 and 1893. Second, such politics was primarily southern contested elections politics. If one considers a fact not represented in the table—that the southern seats made up, on average, slightly fewer than 20 percent of all House seats—then the parenthetical percentage figures in the middle column show that contested elections politics was disproportionately southern. Third, the party in control tended to rule in its favor. In the Fifty-first Congress, Republicans allied with an Arkansas independent who figured in

Table 3.8 Contested House Elections, 45th–52nd Congresses

Congress	Total Cases	Southern Cases (% of total)	Disposition of All Cases
45th (1877–79) *Democratic majority*	5	2 (40%)	100% for Democrats
46th (1879–81) *Democratic majority*	2	2 (100%)	50% for Republicans 50% for Democrats
47th (1881–83) *Republican majority*	8	6 (75%)	75% for Republicans 25% for Democrats
48th (1883–85) *Democratic majority*	7	3 (43%)	100% for Democrats
49th (1885–87) *Democratic majority*	0	0 (0%)	N.A.
50th (1887–89) *Democratic majority*	0	0 (0%)	N.A.
51st (1889–91) *Republican majority*	9	6 (67%)	89% for Republicans 11% for Independents
52d (1891–93) *Democratic majority*	1	0 (0%)	100% for Democrats

Source: Kenneth C. Martis, *The Historical Atlas of Political Parties in the United States Congress, 1789–1989* (New York: Macmillan, 1989).

that state's farmer-labor politics. Republicans thus carried forward the policy of cross-party alliances.

THE PERSISTENCE OF ENFORCEMENT

Consider, in addition to the above, the evidence presented in table 3.9. It shows, by region, cases prosecuted by the Justice Department under federal elections laws. The figures for convictions, given in the last column, suggest the effort's "bite" in any particular region and year. The absolute numbers are not large (as can be seen by using the right-most column to derive the number of southern cases per year resulting in convictions).[45] Still, occasionally a serious fine would be imposed. For instance, an eight-thousand-dollar fine was levied in 1880 against the Democrats of Harrison County, Texas, an amount equivalent to one million dollars today. Also, the presence of U.S. elections officials could influence black voter strategy.[46]

The data in the table come from annual reports of the attorney general's office showing the disposition of its cases as of the first day of the fiscal year, July 1. Thus the data for 1877 show the second Grant administration continuing to do its work in 1876. Though initially the Hayes administration did

Table 3.9 Post-Reconstruction Election Enforcement

Year in Which Attorney General Reported Data	Number of Cases in Southern States*	Number of Cases in Northern States	Number of Cases in Other States†	Total Cases	Percentage of All Cases That Were Southern	Percentage of All National Convictions That Were Southern Cases	Percentage of All Southern Cases That Ended in Conviction
1877	133	40	61	234	57	15	4.5
1878	23	1	2	26	88	0	0
1879	93	15	38	146	64	35	15
1880	53	1	16	70	76	0	0
1881	177	132	33	342	51	57	54
1882	154	72	31	257	60	71	15
1883	201	66	20	287	70	24	6
1884	160	8	22	190	84	65	11
1885	107	173	3	283	38	1	.9

Source: Xi Wang, *The Trial of Democracy: Black Suffrage and Northern Republicans, 1860–1910* (Athens: University of Georgia Press, 1997): 300–301, appendix 7.
*Includes Alabama, Arkansas, Florida, Georgia, Louisiana, Mississippi, North Carolina, South Carolina, Texas, and Virginia (Tennessee was a self-reconstructed state).
†Includes Tennessee, border, and western states.

little, by its last year in office, as the data reported in 1881 (covering the period up to June 30, 1880) suggest, it had swung rather substantially toward enforcement. The Garfield-Arthur administration continued this thrust for several years.[47]

Why could there be any election law enforcement at all? At this point, some background is helpful. The answer is that federal electoral regulation still had statutory life after the Compromise of 1877. In the mid-1870s, the Forty-third Congress authorized a revision of the federal statutes. The revision commissioners seemed to behave curiously. They tore apart various federal elections statutes (among other statutes) and placed their pieces all around the United States Code. Congress then enacted the Revised Statutes with the proviso that the revision supersede all previous statutes.[48]

The confusion of the revision, which has perplexed scholars, may have been quite cunning. In *United States v. Harris* (1883), a Tennessee case stemming from the 1876 elections, the Supreme Court explicitly declared that section 5519 of the code (formerly section 2 of a major federal elections statute, the Ku Klux Act of April 20, 1871) had no basis in the Constitution.[49] However, *Harris* still left section 5508 in place. And 5508, based on section 6 of the first Federal Elections Act, was substantially the same as the relevant portion of the Ku Klux Act invalidated in *Harris*.

In other words, as this little detail of section 5508 implies, by issuing the Revised Statutes Congress may have taken out something like an insurance policy on the federal elections statutes. By creating Title 26 and Title 70, chapter 7 in the United States Code, Congress created a stronger structure. Not an entire *statute* but only a piece of *code* would be called into question. One piece could fall; others would still stand.[50]

Only Democratic-controlled unified government, with a Democratic president who would sign legislation systematically repealing the elections statutes, could create the legislative context for undoing the handiwork of the Forty-third Congress. In time that would happen. In the meantime, as Senator William Frye of Maine told his Democratic counterparts during debate about their 1879 attempt to repeal the enforcement laws, "Do not laugh till you have won. . . . You have not repealed the election laws yet, and you will not repeal them until you have removed the present Executive."[51]

JUDICIAL SUPPORT FOR VOTING ENFORCEMENT

There is further evidence that suggests how even a weak coalition still created its own favorable politics simply by surviving. Not only did the federal election laws continue on the books, but they also were strengthened—by the

Supreme Court, and in response to a new litigation approach devised by government lawyers. During the Arthur administration a ground-breaking, and this time positive, alteration in Supreme Court electoral jurisprudence occurred in *Ex parte Yarbrough*.[52]

The facts were familiar. Yarbrough, several kin, and other white males were involved in a klanlike conspiracy to intimidate black voters. Their defense argued that there was no valid indictment or process under two former pieces of the federal elections acts (now placed in the Revised Statutes of 1874). One section criminalized any conspiracy against a citizen's enjoyment of any right under the Constitution; the other criminalized conspiracy to obstruct voting in national elections. These sections, the defense claimed, were unconstitutional.[53]

The defense's claim was auspicious. The Court had just attacked the 1875 Civil Rights Act. Its ruling in the 1883 *Civil Rights Cases* went a long way toward undermining civil rights. Denials of service to African Americans in hotels, theaters, and railroads cars were permitted by the Fourteenth Amendment because the Constitution only reached explicit state action. Justice Joseph Bradley, writing for the Court, rebuked the African American participants in the cases and, by implication, all African Americans who were concerned about discrimination. He said, in effect, that they should stop complaining. They could no longer be "a special favorite of the laws."[54]

The Court's rollback was one more nail in the coffin of civil rights. In 1879 Justice Bradley also assaulted the robust removal provisions that Congress had placed in the 1875 Judiciary Act (*Virginia v. Rives*).[55] A federal judge, Alexander Rives, issued a writ of habeas corpus for two black defendants who filed removal petitions in which they argued that their trial was unfair because Virginia jury selection discriminated against African Americans. The Supreme Court sided, however, with Virginia because no state statute explicitly forbade blacks to serve on juries. After 1879, civil rights cases could no longer be fought by removal to federal courts but instead required Supreme Court litigation—at a time when the Court increasingly opposed the federal protection of civil rights.[56]

But in *Yarbrough* the Court actually *widened* the scope of the Fifteenth Amendment. Writing for a unanimous Court, Justice Miller denied the defense's petition for a writ of habeas corpus. At stake was whether Congress could constitutionally protect the national electoral processes that selected representatives to Congress. Article 1 of the Constitution gave it ample authority to do so, and it was power that Congress had repeatedly exercised. The Fifteenth Amendment was itself part of that pattern of exercise. The amendment showed that "the right of suffrage was considered to be of supreme importance to the national government, and was not intended to be left within the exclusive control of the states."[57]

Miller's opinion briefly considered whether a seemingly devastating precedent (*Reese*, to be described in chapter 5) applied in this instance, but then he simply asserted that it did not. The defense claimed that *Reese* prevented federal protection of the right to vote from private violence. Indeed, the conservative understanding of the Fifteenth Amendment held that it gave the United States little more than the right to tell state and local officials to stop discriminating against blacks, and that it certainly did not give the United States any right to interfere with what ordinary citizens did. But Miller announced that in many instances the Fifteenth Amendment actually directly conferred a right to vote—which was (and is) a stance typically taken in the most robust interpretations of the Fifteenth Amendment's meaning. Since the United States conferred a right, it could proactively protect the right. The case for direct federal protection of the right to vote from private white violence was sealed, Miller thought, by article I, section 4, which gave Congress the authority to regulate federal elections in any reasonable way that it deemed fit. In effect, Miller fused the Fifteenth Amendment and article I, section 4 to come up with a bold, highly nationalist approach to black voting rights.

The decision in *Yarbrough* suggests that the Justice Department found a new way to present voting rights issues to the Court. If the elections statutes generated endless interventions against the states and private individuals, as in earlier federal elections cases, then the Court stood by a doctrine known as "state action," first articulated in the 1873 *Slaughterhouse Cases* (described more fully in chapter 5). If, on the other hand, violence and fraud in southern electoral processes appeared before the Court in a quite different guise, that of a threat to the integrity of national electoral and policymaking processes, then the Court stood against such a threat.

To recapitulate, the coalition of 1867–1868 plainly continued to have life after the Compromise of 1877. Republicans maintained an active southern policy, as indicated by (1) the Republican platforms' emphasis on voting rights, (2) Republican-led Senate investigations of southern electoral fraud and intimidation, (3) the processing of contested southern elections cases, (4) the fostering of a new constitutional basis in Article 1 for federal electoral regulation, and (5) agreements and cooperation with biracial insurgencies such as the Virginia Readjusters—which, for a time, was an extraordinary experiment in biracial democracy. Indeed, the coalition's continuing existence generated a surprising turn in the Supreme Court's jurisprudence.

But should there not have been more to the picture? Many promising new institutions emerged after 1868. Could not such institutional change have set black electoral incorporation on a better pathway into the future? Plainly, there was *incomplete institutionalization*.

Riker-Gamson coalition-making, as chapter 2 showed, was a very forceful, even revolutionary process. But, as this chapter showed, coalition-making by itself was not enough. The new partners of 1867–1868 clearly won that battle—but the war for coalitional survival evolved into a war of attrition. Why?

Two parts of coalition formation's aftermath were vital. The first was the development or recasting of party organizations and party competition, often generating significant national, state, and local public policy benefits. The second was the development of new jurisprudence, often with major implications for federalism and national regulation of electoral processes. Call these follow-on processes *party-building* and *jurisprudence-building*. Together they define enfranchisement as a deeply institutional process. Chapter 4 considers party-building during the first reconstruction, and chapter 5 treats jurisprudence-building. Together, these chapters clarify why a war of attrition between the coalition of 1867–1868 and its opponents set in by the 1880s.

Chapter Four

Party-Building during the First Reconstruction

oalition formation on the large scale that occurred in 1867–1868 had several immediate concomitants. These included party-building and—with it—both a new biracial public sphere and policy change. Tracing these products of the coalition will illuminate the question that punctuated chapter 3's conclusion: Could the new coalition have become better institutionalized?

The first reconstruction generated the first biracial democratic public sphere in world history. Adapting David Mayhew's language, I conceive of a biracial public sphere as a "realm of public affairs" filled with "public moves and countermoves by politicians and other actors," white *and* black, and "an attentive and sometimes participating audience of large numbers of citizens," again, white and black. About two thousand black men served as federal, state, and local officeholders in the former Confederate states. Nearly a million new black voters entered the electorate.[1]

Between the voting and the office-holding, black Americans cultivated effective citizenship. During the 1868 presidential campaign, maids and cooks reported for work in the homes of Yazoo, Mississippi, wearing buttons that sported the likeness of Ulysses S. Grant. In 1873 a Mississippi plantation manager condescendingly (but for the historian usefully) noted in a letter that "Negroes all crazy on politics again. . . . Every tenth negro a candidate for office."

African Americans attended public rallies and met in political clubs or marched in militia companies on election day.[2]

Symbols of the new public sphere could be found in the nation's capital, Washington, D.C. During a little-known period of home rule (1867–1871) Washington's city government enacted civil rights legislation forbidding racial segregation of theaters, bars, restaurants, and hotels. In a subsequent period of mixed federal and local control (the "territorial" period, May 1871 to June 1878), blacks held office both on a presidentially appointed governor's council and in an elected lower house. The earlier civil rights legislation was reenacted in 1872 and 1873 (and happily so, because eighty years later it was the basis for the final desegregation of District restaurants).[3]

African American members of Congress caused a great stir when they arrived to take their seats. Sometimes their speeches about policy questions packed the galleries, such as South Carolina congressman Robert Elliott's argument for the 1875 Civil Rights Act or Mississippi senator Hiram Revels's maiden speech attacking the idea of rushing to readmit Georgia into the Union and thereby ignoring the Georgia legislature's expulsion of all its black members. A telling incident that captured the extent of change in congressional life came in May 1874 when Speaker of the House James Blaine arranged for Congressman Joseph Rainey of South Carolina to have the honor of briefly presiding over the House.[4]

Finally, there was the Fifteenth Amendment to the federal Constitution. The amendment announced that the "right of citizens of the United States to vote shall not be denied or abridged by the United States or by any state on account of race, color, or previous condition of servitude." Speaking of the amendment's passage and ratification (which was complete by March 30, 1870), Henry McNeal Turner, the Georgia Equal Rights League activist, told an audience in Macon that it was "the finish of our national fabric . . . the crowning achievement of the nineteenth century." Viewing the amendment as the completion of "the majestic achievements of the last seven years," which began with the emancipation, Turner said that he could "only define" the "[e]vents just completed . . . as . . . *inexpressible.*" For his part, Grant issued a special message calling the Fifteenth Amendment "a measure of grander importance than any other one act of the kind from the foundation of our free government to the present day."[5]

On the ground, in mid-May 1870, a South Carolina planter complained that those who worked for him went to town to celebrate the Fifteenth Amendment "with processions, drums, and a barbecue." Robert Elliott, a black emigre from Liverpool, England, who practiced law and was soon to be a U.S. representative, read the amendment aloud to a crowd comprising fire companies, bands, and militias from many quarters and then spoke for three hours.[6]

All of this stands in sharp contrast to what we know about subsequent events. As we saw in chapter 3, the process of electoral inclusion did not "take." Why?

Several factors have been noted by scholars: white racism; the related weakness of any moderate tendency within the southern Democratic parties; the failure of land reform for African Americans; the lack of support for black electoral inclusion from the women's suffrage movement (brought about by the gendering of the Fourteenth Amendment, which for a generation focused suffragists' energy on achieving a gender-neutral suffrage policy); the sharp recession in the early 1870s, while Republicans ran the country; and divisions between rural and urban blacks in the South.[7]

These explanations are, however, surprisingly noninstitutional. This chapter therefore considers an essential component of coalitional strengthening: party-building. It uncovers the mix of success and weakness that characterized the party-building process. Its flaws did not directly cause disenfranchisement several decades later. But they did engender many of the problems that chapter 3 treated.

Had party-building worked out well, the coalition of 1867–1868 would have become better institutionalized. Political parties are potent voluntary organizations that mobilize the loyalty and participation of ordinary citizens on a regular basis. By organizing the electoral process, they gain popular authority to accumulate and use governmental resources to solve public problems and address public needs. Parties therefore channel and harness the ambition of talented political entrepreneurs. Such general properties of party politics suggest that party-building during the first reconstruction might have anchored African American electoral inclusion—enough to help forestall the total reversal that eventually occurred.

The coalition in fact tried something too demanding—namely, "crash" party-building in a war-torn land that was riddled with a historically violent political culture with a strong tendency toward one-partyism. Yet the coalition had no choice. Building a new regional wing of the Republican Party from the ground up as fast as possible was the only option for the coalition if it wished to stabilize and guide the process of black electoral inclusion. Andrew Johnson's intransigence made that clear. Nonetheless, genuinely resilient political parties simply cannot be made to grow on an expedited basis. *Partial* gains were possible; so were flaws

To communicate the gains of crash party-building, this chapter sketches the extent of electoral, office-holding, and policy change. To underscore the difficulties and weaknesses, the chapter then follows the tripartite image of the political party. That is, I consider the new parties-in-government, the new parties-as-organizations, and the new parties-in-the-electorate.

ESTIMATING THE EXTENT OF ELECTORAL INCORPORATION

During the first reconstruction, there was very widespread voting by African American men. Most black adult males were illiterate, true. But illiteracy actually did not block participation because of "party-strip balloting." The parties printed the ballots, sometimes in distinctive colors or with special symbols—say, a likeness of Abraham Lincoln, to take an actual example from the Reconstruction. They supplied equal numbers of poll watchers, and then got their voters to the polls on election day. Once at the polls, voters could easily and quickly choose the ballot provided by their party of choice because it was impossible to mistake which ballot went with which party.

Precisely stating how extensive black voting was in each of the states in the former Confederacy is rather hard to do. Studying the Mississippi election of 1868 for ratifying the proposed new state constitution, Lawrence Powell plausibly calculated a turnout of 80 percent. Two fairly precise estimates have also been offered for Louisiana and South Carolina in 1876. They are available because voters in Louisiana were registered by race and voters in South Carolina recorded their race when they voted. Using these data, Ronald King has provided calculations of black voter turnout in the presidential election of 1876 in those two states. His assessments reveal a rate so high that it greatly exceeds contemporary rates of black voter participation. The 1876 election came, moreover, at the end of Reconstruction, when African American voting was under severe stress.

In 1875 and 1876 about 55 percent of Louisiana's registered voters were African American, and all eligible black men were registered. About 75 percent to 78 percent of black registrants voted in 1876, King estimates. In South Carolina, state census and voter sign-in data suggest that African American men voted at a rate of at least 78 percent and probably higher.[8]

In addition to knowing something about African American *turnout,* it is helpful to know something systematic about the nature of black voters' *partisanship*. It appears, at least for the 1876 elections in Louisiana and South Carolina, that black men voted overwhelmingly for Republican presidential electors (although a small percentage of black men, about 5 percent in Louisiana and about 10 percent in South Carolina, voted for Democratic electors—quite possibly under pressure).[9] The figure also suggests the strength of partisanship among African American men. It is a scatterplot; each black dot registers the joint values for 1872 of (1) the Republican presidential vote in each former Confederate county and (2) the percentage of that county's population that was black. Strictly speaking, the scatterplot proves very little about black partisanship because it is a statistical fallacy to infer individual behavior from aggregate data. Nonetheless, the figure does show quite a strong *association* between Republican voting and racial demography— consistent with the overwhelming qualitative evidence of African Americans' support for the Republican Party.

In addition to extensive voting by blacks, there was extensive office-holding. For all concerned, the issue was highly symbolic. It triggered turgid declamations among white Conservatives about what "Almighty God" intended for the "Saxon race" and "the African." Southern Conservative and Democratic leaders unhesitatingly portrayed black office-holding with maximum hyperbole, treating it as unnatural tyranny, pure and simple. It was a claim that eventually echoed among white northern journalists who sought to capitalize on the mid-1870s disenchantment with Reconstruction by portraying black office-holding as a horrifying experiment.[10]

A somewhat different symbolism prevailed among white northern Republicans indebted to radical Protestant interpretations of America's great social struggle. They saw black office-holding as the next phase in America's providential redemption from slavery's many sins. So Senator Henry Wilson

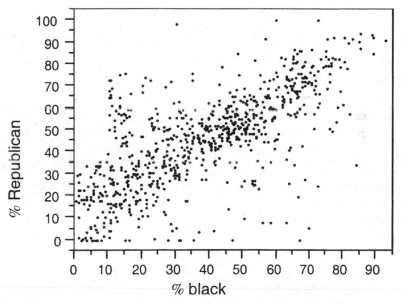

1872 Republican Vote for President, by County in the Former Confederacy, by Race

of Massachusetts put the matter during the Senate's three-day debate in late February 1870 about the credentials of Hiram Revels, a distinguished minister from Natchez chosen by the Mississippi legislature to complete Jefferson Davis's unexpired term in the Senate.[11]

African American leaders often also saw the Reconstruction in religious and historicist terms. The extraordinary transformation of American politics between 1863 and the ratification of the Fifteenth Amendment in 1870 could easily seem to be clear evidence of God's purpose working in human history.[12] When speaking before a largely white audience, black Republican politicians would also put the matter in more prosaic terms. For them, office-holding completed citizenship. Though many were painfully aware of their relative lack of "culture," they did not see office-holding as a concession from whites that necessarily merited gratitude. Some saw it as inherent in the Reconstruction process of restoring blacks' natural rights and equality, which the custom and law of prejudice and slavery had artificially abridged. Others saw it as simply doing what had to be done. As James K. Green, an Alabama state politician, told Congress, "the tocsin of freedom sounded and knocked at the door and we walked out like free men and met the exigencies as they grew up, and shouldered the responsibilities."[13]

Black office-holding ran the gamut. There were black U.S. senators and U.S. representatives. African American men were also superintendants of education in several states, and one was an associate justice of the state supreme court in South Carolina. The black lieutenant governor of Louisiana in 1871 and 1872, P. B. S. Pinchback, moved to the governorship during a temporary vacancy (December 1872 to mid-January 1873) following the governor's impeachment. The vast majority, however, 78 percent, were local officeholders, occupying offices as diverse as boards of education, city councils, mayoralties, county commissions, magistracies, and streetcar commissions. They were concentrated in the Deep South states with majority black or significant black populations: South Carolina, Mississippi, Louisiana, North Carolina, Alabama, and Georgia, in that order. In all, Eric Foner found fifty-six kinds of local office-holding. About 20 percent of the officers were justices of the peace, 11 percent were city council members, 9 percent were county commissioners, 7 percent were registrars, 6 percent were members of boards of education, 5 percent were police officers, and 4 percent were local election officials.[14]

Some sense of the relative scale of black male office-holding can be gained by comparison with female office-holding after ratification of the Nineteenth Amendment. Between 1868 and 1876 an average of 268 black men served during the sessions of the state legislatures in ten southern states, ranging from a high of 96 for the 1872 session of the South Carolina legislature to a low of 1 for the 1875 Texas legislature. In 1868–1869 there were 277 black state legislators in ten southern states; in the closing years of the Reconstruction period there were 249. By contrast, in 1921, 37 women served in twenty-six state legislatures, and ten years later 146 women served in thirty-nine state legislatures.[15]

To summarize, blacks voted heavily, and they were deeply partisan. They held state and local public office in very large numbers. Indeed, they "integrated" the United States Congress. There were two black senators, both from Mississippi. Fourteen black men served in the House of Representatives. In this connection there is a startling detail: two of these congressmen had once been enslaved, sold at auction. Their later success says much about how Reconstruction, as with all egalitarian revolutions, made way for new men, for talented and ambitious individuals eager to serve their constituents.[16]

THE NEW PARTY COMPETITION AND POLICY CHANGE

Did the new biracial public sphere have *policy* consequences? It is a commonplace that Reconstruction had only a few noteworthy policy repercussions. It has often been noted, as well, that national Republican leaders provided little material aid to the southern parties or to their constituents.[17] In fact, however, policy change was substantial during the Reconstruction. It helps to remember what happened during presidential reconstruction, when blacks could not vote. Then the legislatures of former Confederate states produced the Black Codes. But when black ballots counted, policy proposals and outcomes became more egalitarian.

The New Constitutions

Turn first to state-level constitutional change. The military reconstruction program of the Thirty-ninth and Fortieth Congresses called for state-level constitutional conventions. From mid-1867 onward, new coalitions of incorporationist politicians, activists, and notables flocked to Republican Party conventions—as did Conservatives to their own meetings. Both sides hammered out plans for running constitutional delegates. Because Congress also provided for voter ratification of the new constitutions, parties and party factions sought to govern the postconvention phase of constitutional change.[18]

The new constitutions were substantially more democratic documents than the "presidential reconstruction constitutions" of 1865–1866. They

Table 4.1 Types of State-Level Policy During Reconstruction

	Provisions for Public Education		Civil Rights			Labor Law	
	Primary & Secondary	College & University	Civil Enforcement	Criminal Enforcement	Land Reform	Priority of Laborer's Lien	Other
Arkansas	1873: "like and equal" facilities for black children in public schools	1873: separate college		1868: integration of first-class accommodations, conveyances; 1873: integration of all accommodations and conveyances		1868: claims for wages = a superior lien; property under lien required to stay in Arkansas	
Georgia		1870: establishment of Atlanta University					
Florida			1870: integration of first-class rail cars	1873: integration of inns, public schools, common carriers, theaters, and juries		1872: claims for wages = a lien	1873: 10-hr. day law; no garnishing of wages
Louisiana	1869–70: integration launched in New Orleans	1870: legislative aid to Straight University, now Dillard University	1869: ban on discrimination in public resorts 1873: integration of public conveyances and interstate carriers				1874: legislature incorporates a longshoremen's union and outlaws sailor unloading at docks

Mississippi	1871: Revels (later Alcorn) University established	1870: integration of public conveyances	1873: equal treatment of customers required by any publicly licensed business		1872: workers' "first lien" law	
South Carolina	1873: integration of University of South Carolina		1870: equal treatment of customers by any publicly licensed business	1869: South Carolina Land Commission created	1869: workers' "first lien" law	1872, 1875: antiscrip laws; 1874: convict leasing ended; planters' lien restricted to 1/3 of crop; July 1876: state support for large rice workers' strike
Tennessee		1868: integration of common carriers				
Texas	1871: establishment of Agricultural and Mechanical College of Texas (now Texas A&M)				1870: laborer's lien on property improved by him	

Note: Besides support for universal public education and restoration of capital plant of government in all states, there was no legislation of note in Alabama, North Carolina, and Virginia.

contained, among other things, forthright declarations of the natural, civil, and political equality of man (though not of men and women) and provisions for unencumbered voting and office-holding, for popular election of state judges, for charitable institutions for the poor, the aged, the blind, the insane, and the infirm, for the abolition of coerced apprenticeships of black children to white masters (a practice that had sprung up in 1865 and 1866), for egalitarian oaths of voter eligibility and of office, for rights of free speech, expression, and assembly, and for elaborate criminal due process safeguards.[19]

Education

Black suffrage also generated public education, a policy commitment inscribed in the new constitutions. Every reconstructed state provided for universal public education, a major step for the South. As David Tyack and Robert Lowe have noted, "[s]ix constitutions stated that local districts would forfeit state aid if they did not keep schools open for a minimum number of months; several prescribed sources and minimal levels of taxation; and almost all specified precise systems of governance."[20] The regional enrollment of black school-age children increased from 91,000 in 1866 to 150,000 in 1870 and 572,000 by 1877. The increase was quite inadequate, relative to a mammoth need. But the states made a start.

In addition, as table 4.1 suggests, in at least one state, Louisiana, there was modest but real success in addressing one of the most difficult and enduring policy problems of American history—educational integration in the primary and secondary schools. Up to this time no school integration effort had succeeded anywhere in the United States. Although it failed beyond New Orleans, the integration effort did work in that city for three to four years, if sometimes with real difficulty.

In Louisiana, Mississippi, South Carolina, and Texas, the Reconstruction governments also provided for higher education for blacks, fostering new and separate universities in Louisiana and Mississippi. Finally, Palmetto State Republicans briefly integrated the University of South Carolina and set up an integrated law school. It graduated biracial classes of lawyers in 1874, 1875, and 1876.[21]

Civil Rights Laws

Looking at table 4.1, one further notices several civil rights statutes. The most sustained effort occurred in Louisiana, where the segregation struggle lasted for decades, until the Supreme Court finally fully legitimated segregation in *Plessy v. Ferguson* (1896). But during Reconstruction, at least, publicly licensed establishments in New Orleans were substantially in compliance with the state's ban on segregation in such places as theaters, saloons, and restaurants. The Louisiana legislature also enforced nondiscrimination in railway travel to the city.[22]

These laws formed part of a campaign for another national civil rights statute beyond the 1866 Civil Rights Act, an effort led by Senator Charles Sumner and by black Republican Congressmen. Black members of the House were, indeed, more racially "liberal" in their roll-call voting than everyone else in the chamber. Their exertions helped generate the 1875 Civil Rights Act, which regulated common carriers and provided for enforcement in state courts.[23]

Land Reform

Another policy strongly preferred by black southerners was *land reform*, that is, the promise of guaranteed land ownership for people whose enslaved labor had already intimately acquainted them with that land. President Johnson closed off this possibility (as noted in chapter 2), pardoning former Confederate landholders and returning their land. Congress did renew the legislative charter of the Freedmen's Bureau, providing for three-year leases of forty acres of confiscated land at a low interest rate, after which lands could be sold to their leaseholders. Congress also passed the Southern Homestead Act, setting aside forty-six million acres of unsold public lands for freedmen and loyal white refugees until January, 1867, after which anyone was eligible. But as commander-in-chief the president soon ousted bureau officers who obstructed his own land restoration plan, adopted a policy of replacing military agents of the bureau with local civil agents, and neglected staffing the federal land offices in the South. The Southern Homestead Act of 1866 thus eventually only opened up land in Arkansas, Florida, Louisiana, and Mississippi to about four thousand black families.[24]

If land reform was to take place at all, the states would have to see to it. In the end, despite discussion at some state constitutional conventions of tax policies designed to break up plantation agriculture, only one state—South Carolina—seriously promoted black settlement on publicly purchased lands. As it happened, initially South Carolina's land reform was, sadly, corrupt. Yet there is more to the story. Later in South Carolina's reconstruction, land reform became something of a genuine success. In that sense, the policy promise of Reconstruction party-building bore some fruit. After the early frauds were exposed, the state legislature transferred custody of the policy to competent black officials. They eventually assured settlement of about 15 to 17 percent of the state's black population.[25]

Labor Law

As table 4.1 also indicates, other outcomes related to the struggle on the land were regulatory decisions, and just as important, "nondecisions," with regard to agricultural labor.[26]

A bit of economic history is in order. War and emancipation transformed two factors of the southern economy: capital and labor. War created acute capital scarcity, and emancipation abruptly recast and sharpened the region's historic labor scarcity (which, after all, was the initial reason for enslavement of humans for purposes of cash crop labor). There was a potential for labor costs to move up toward a relatively high equilibrium (a happy result that supporters of "free labor" perhaps intuitively anticipated).[27]

Forestalling any such results of acute labor scarcity, Conservatives established the Black Codes in 1865 and 1866. And, to address capital scarcity, the Conservative state legislatures encouraged credit liens on expected crop production in order to capitalize quickly the anticipated returns from tying the black labor force down with Black Codes. The basic liens that came into existence were: (1) the lien on the proceeds of the future crop given by white tenants to the white landlord in the expectation that the crop would be full enough to satisfy the lien and to provide a surplus to the white tenant big enough to let him pay off other claims on the crop as well as retain a profit for himself; (2) the lien given by the tenant to the merchant in order to obtain supplies and equipment (seed, fertilizer, plows, and so on); and (3) the lien on the proceeds from the crop given by the workers to the tenant or the planter, if either hired workers.

But given agriculture's natural uncertainties and conflicts among multiple lien-holders, planters soon wanted legislatures and courts to guarantee that *they* got paid first when crops were liquidated. Such a guarantee would assure their hegemony. What if nothing or very little was left over for merchants and black laborers, and what if new laws blocked these other principals from clearing their debt when crops disappointed everyone's expectations? Undercapitalized merchants might go broke and tenants might soon sink into debt servitude. As for laborers, they would go hungry and would certainly consider moderating wage demands.

Military reconstruction ousted the Conservatives before they could fully settle the legal priority of the various kinds of liens. Reconstruction governors and legislators—in some cases simply by doing nothing for several years—

obstructed planters' and landlords' desires for the priority of the landlord's lien. By perpetuating the legal ambiguity of this lien, Reconstruction officials provided some measure of relative autonomy for black tenants and workers.[28]

Further (again see table 4.1, under "Labor Law, Other"), Republican officials sometimes informally encouraged collective bargaining in agricultural labor. Several states also legislated the priority of the *laborer's* wage lien, that is, guarantees of payment to laborers based on sales of the crop, even if the landlord and merchants did not receive the profit they expected.

South Carolina Republicans went furthest in anticipating more modern labor relations. Besides establishing the priority of the laborer's lien they also attacked landlords' efforts to recompense laborers in scrip, as opposed to real currency. They abolished convict leasing, the only southern officials to do so after first establishing it. In 1876 the Republican governor militarily protected black rice plantation workers in the low country on strike against lower wages and payment in scrip.[29]

In sum, the extent of policy change was greater than many think today. Left out of this chapter, I should note, is any full discussion of *local* policy effects. Black suffrage in some localities required extremely skillful leaders in order to have any effect. Yet in other places it led to (1) strong biracial juries that insisted on tough and equal criminal enforcement, (2) extensive black involvement in schools, (3) the provision of public employment, (4) racially integrated police forces, (5) black sheriffs (or white sheriffs, such as Mississippi's famous carpetbagger sheriff, Albert Morgan) who were genuinely motivated to work on behalf of their constituents, (6) cash relief for the poor (as opposed to forcing paupers onto residential "poor farms"), and (7) black local magistracies.[30]

Party-building—the construction of an institutional framework for controlling and defending the process of African American electoral inclusion—obviously facilitated creative attention, at the state and local levels, to a wide range of policy issues. Seen this way, the first reconstruction had the earmarks of strong, successful electoral inclusion. But something—several things, really—went wrong. The eventual disenfranchisement of black southerners at the end of the nineteenth century clearly indicates that something did *not* happen during the first reconstruction. The rest of this chapter traces the sharp imperfections in the development of an institutional basis for guiding the process of black electoral inclusion. To do this, I follow a classic trichotomy for understanding party-building, considering, in order, the making of *parties-in-government*, the making of *parties-as-organizations*, and the making of *parties-in-the-electorate*.[31]

FISCAL CRISIS AND PARTIES-IN-GOVERNMENT

The first aspect of the way party-building proved inherently incomplete and flawed has to do with the biracial coalition's sudden elevation to "party-in-government" position. Congress wanted the new southern parties to be parties-in-government, but it did not help the new parties with federal resources to accomplish this goal. Republican parties of the South therefore committed themselves to rapid infrastructural development and economic growth, particularly by means of "railroadization." This was a shrewd way to exploit necessity, given the ruin of the regional economy. But the strategy was vulnerable to fluctuations in the macroeconomy, as we shall see.[32]

Ultimately, they had little choice. Southern Republicans had pressed in Congress for federal aid for a railroad system, levee reconstruction, rivers and harbors, education, redistribution of bank note circulation, greenback expansion, reimbursement of war damage to southern Unionist property, and land distribution. In other words, they had pressed for a postwar national plan of southern economic reconstruction.[33]

That the Republican Party had both a small new wing and a large old wing mattered greatly. The history and structure of the party system meant that there were more nonsouthern than southern Republicans in Congress. Northern Republicans had been running Congress their way for several years. Southern Republicans in both the House and the Senate had uncertain electoral bases and were focusing most of their energy on stabilizing their political careers, thus diminishing intrachamber influence.

State-level growth policies were thus inevitably attractive for southern Republicans. By pushing an agenda of modernizing the South by means of a railroad boom, Republicans mounted a program that would allow them, they hoped, to make inroads among white elites and voters.[34] The resulting railroad fever contained a hidden structural weakness, however: no jurisdiction had an incentive to say no. Thus all seeking to join the bandwagon of public aid got it. The state legislatures, county commissions, and municipal governments that rushed to provide the government bonds behind the railroad ventures ended up rapidly "overstocking" the South with railroad start-ups.

Many roads were simply bound to fail. When they did, moreover, they took the recovery-and-growth agenda with them. Fiscal problems brought on by the railroad boom's inevitable shakeout were in turn exacerbated by the regional impact of the 1873 nationwide recession. Republican rule eventually seemed a recipe for economic ruin and political corruption.[35]

Southern Republican rule coincided, in other words, with the necessary task of rebuilding the South's infrastructure. But the South had little governmental capacity, and Congress did not fill the gap. Further, the inter-governmental competition for railroads had no internal institutional brake; it had only the market restraint that eventually kicked in as roads failed. Governments thus "oversupplied"; Republicans got the blame for waste of resources.[36] Indeed, the southern governments were certain to experience a fiscal crisis at the first postwar economic downturn. This problem was built into the activism described above and summarized in table 4.1. Southern governments had to tax at higher real rates than they had before the Civil War in order to supply even the modest level of public education that the new governments established. They also took on the task of rebuilding public infrastructure—asylums, public buildings, and the like. They had more personnel and many more elected officials who made a living from politics. The recession of 1873 inevitably generated an acute fiscal crisis everywhere in the South and a fierce hostility among whites to taxation and public finance.[37]

To summarize, being the South's parties-in-government proved a mixed blessing for the Republican parties. The coalition of 1867–1868 needed the southern parties to function in this manner right away. But its northern congressional wing did precious little to back up the policy and spending needs of the southern counterpart. This is hardly surprising. Members of Congress generally get what they can, while they can, for *their* districts and states, not other districts and states. But the inherent lack of planning within the national party also mortgaged the future of the southern parties.

PARTIES-AS-ORGANIZATIONS AND REPUBLICAN FACTIONALISM

Organizationally speaking, the new Republican parties were remarkably vital. Until southern Conservative violence shattered this base (on which more below), the Republican parties also had a movement infrastructure, the Union Leagues, and that gave the parties a considerable advantage. After the Union Leagues' collapse came other associations, notably the Prince Hall Freemasons, which spread rapidly in the South during Reconstruction, knitting together the former Confederacy's black elites.[38]

Alabama, Florida, Georgia, Louisiana, South Carolina, and Texas Republicans also encouraged trade unionism, masonry, and other kinds of political clubs. Another vital substitute for the Union Leagues that eventually emerged was the black militia movement, discussed below. The militia movement was aided in Arkansas, Louisiana, and South Carolina by the establishment of official state militias with black officers and black recruits.[39]

In addition, there was a vast infrastructure of Republican newspapers—a fact that has just come to light. Richard Abbott identified 478 pro-Republican newspapers for the period 1861–1877 with names such as *Southern Republican* (Demopolis, Alabama), *Mountain Echo* (Fayetteville, Arkansas), *El Republicano* (Key West, Florida), *Savannah Daily Republican* (Georgia), *Terrebonne Republican* (Houma, Louisiana), *Colored Citizen* (Jackson, Mississippi), *Union Republican* (Winston, North Carolina), *Spartanburg Republican* (South Carolina), *National True Republican* (Nashville, Tennessee), *West Texas Republican* (Blanco City), and *State Journal* (Richmond, Virginia). Of these, the great majority emerged during congressional reconstruction. In Louisiana and South Carolina, furthermore, African American editors and publishers played prominent roles. Republican dailies had circulations ranging from about 500 to 2,000 copies; weeklies ranged between 450 and 750. Most of these lasted two years or less. But that rate resembled the mortality rate of Democratic newspapers. About 19 percent of Republican newspapers, in fact, lasted five or more years.

Table 4.2 summarizes aspects of Abbott's laboriously collected data. In every state except Virginia, which never experienced a "radical" phase, the Republicans promoted a party press. Louisiana's policy was the most elaborate, featuring a special commission; accordingly, it had the strongest party press. Elsewhere, state legislators or party-appointed judges were authorized to select newspapers according to congressional districts, counties, or judicial circuits for the purpose of printing state laws and other pieces of official business. Besides advertising the results of Republican government, the existence of papers beyond the capital city sheets also meant that there was a broad, party-controlled network for printing ballots.[40]

But factionalism badly weakened Republican organizational accomplishments. The organizations were developed just enough to spawn fierce rivalries; they were not mature enough for all the rivals to have learned how to tame their factionalism. In at least two states, Arkansas and Louisiana, factionalism evolved into conditions that approximated civil war as one side made common cause with Democrats who were eager to oust the Republicans altogether.

Until the fiscal crisis brought on by the recession of 1873, patronage squabbles, federal, state, and local, all richly fueled several varieties of factionalism. Once southern governments entered a fiscal crisis, furthermore, a new factional division emerged between fiscal reformers and stand-pat politicians.[41] Contests for federal positions or favors such as revenue commissions, the hundreds of fourth-class postmasterships in each state, statewide postal positions, printing contracts (see table 4.2), and appointment as a United States Marshal also generated factionalism. The biggest, most lucrative prize of all was appointment as collector of customs at the major ports. The federal

Table 4.2 The Role of Newspapers in Party-Building

State	Number of Papers Operating, 1865–1877 (total)	Number Active in Presidential Reconstruction	Policy for Planting "Loyal" Papers beyond Capital	Number Awarded Federal Contracts	Number of Republican Dailies, 1867–1877	Most Productive Year (number of papers operating)	Number of Papers Operating in 1876	Ratio of All Republican to All Democratic Newspapers 1865–1877
Alabama	36	1	Yes (1868–1872)	3	3	1869 (13)	4	68%
Arkansas	52	2	Yes (1868–1874)	2	5	1869 (22)	5	N.A.
Florida	22	4	Yes (1868–1877)	2	1	1874 (13)	6	100%
Georgia	19	8	Yes (1868–1870)		2	1870 (6)	1	15%
Louisiana	73	1	Yes (1868–1877)		3	1871 (35)	22	126%
Mississippi	61	0	Yes (1874–1875)	4	4	1869 (16)	10	54%
North Carolina	37	5	Yes (1868–1870)	3	5	1871 (15)	11	N.A.
South Carolina	46	5	Yes (1871–1877)	2	8	1873 (15)	9	88%
Tennessee	51	13	Yes (1868)		5	1869 (19)	10	N.A.
Texas	57	2	Yes (1870)	3	8	1871 (25)	9	34%
Virginia	24	6	No	3	3	1868 (7)	4	28%

Source: My calculations based on Richard Abbott, ed. John W. Quist *For Free Press and Equal Rights: Republican Newspapers in the Reconstruction South* (Athens: University of Georgia Press, 2004), chap. 5 and appendix: Republican Newspapers by State, 1865–1877.

customhouses in southern port cities were big operations, and the collector received a large salary.[42]

Further, a strong material factor drove Republicans into fierce fights with each other. Holders of federal jobs were paid in U.S. currency, but state workers were paid in state scrip, essentially paper IOUs that traded in local markets at a discount. Patronage scrambles could not therefore be easily resolved by buying off contenders for federal jobs with state jobs. One faction inevitably got the short end of the deal. This may be part of why U.S. Senate and House elections regularly featured factionalized contested elections cases. Their frequency, of course, prevented a forceful southern Republican presence in national councils.[43]

There were yet other sources of division. Carpetbaggers (whites of northern provenance) and scalawags (native whites) fought with each other. In Louisiana, not one but *two* generations of carpetbaggers, those from the original Civil War government and those associated with the post-1867 phase, competed. Native blacks competed with blacks who had traveled to the South from the North, many of them highly educated and with experience living abroad.[44]

Also, some scalawag politicians (though by no means all) had particularly thin loyalty to Republicanism and black interests. Thus Arkansas Conservatives covertly redeemed the state in 1873 by quietly converting a scalawag after he was sworn in as governor. In Georgia, scalawags were central to the destruction of the Republican Party, as well. "Moderate" whites tried to hold onto a particularly large white farmer vote for Republicans in the 1867–1868 elections by agreeing to a Conservative plan of throwing black officials out of the state legislature. Pressured by Conservatives, who controlled the Georgia House and who threatened further violence after the spectacular assassination of a leading white radical, "moderates" followed conservatives in expelling three black senators and twenty-nine black representatives from the reconstructed 1868 state legislature. In Texas, "Conservative" Republican scalawags repeatedly sought to split the Republican Party or to fuse with conciliatory Democrats, arguing that the party could not treat seriously demands from black politicians for a significant voice in party campaign strategies. Unusually strong black political organization at the local level and the support of German immigrants steadied the party. But constant Conservative Republican maneuvering contributed to the Texas party's gradual weakening.[45]

Far and away the most damaging source of factionalism was the politics of racial symbolism. Pro-Republican whites generally insisted that blacks adopt a junior position in governing while simultaneously delivering the electoral base. In doing that they guaranteed internal tensions, frustration, and weakness.[46]

In Louisiana, this kind of factionalism was exceptionally destructive. Black politicians eventually coalesced against Governor Henry Clay Warmoth, a capable but racially conservative carpetbagger who blocked their policy agenda and kept rates of black office-holding low. Anxious to avoid impeachment, Warmoth allied himself with Democrats in 1872, taking some anti-Grant Republicans with him. Warmoth's opposition in 1872 comprised a staunchly pro-Grant faction of carpetbaggers teamed up with black Republicans who were led by the black lieutenant governor, P. B. S. Pinchback. In the aftermath of the 1872 election two shadow governments—consisting of legislatures, executives, and militias—emerged, one led by former Republican U.S. senator William Pitt Kellogg, the other by Warmoth's Democratic ally, the "Fusionist" gubernatorial candidate John McEnery. Warmoth played no part in the armed phase of the McEnery-Kellogg conflict in 1873–1874. Yet his maneuvering in 1872–1873 helped make Louisiana violently ungovernable.[47]

To review, rapid party-building meant certain rapid successes. But it also meant an equally rapid growth of problems. Building new party structures was not, by its nature, a seamless process, especially if it was being done on a crash basis from point zero. But, given the structure of the party system in 1867—a cross-regional Democratic Party pitted against a regional Republican Party with no southern presence—there was little alternative. A key result was kaleidoscopic factionalism.

Violence in Electoral Politics and "Parties-in-the-Electorate"

Hardest of all in the crash party-building process was the white-on-black violence that racked southern electoral politics. As the *Nation* put it in March 1871, "Going to the polls should be as safe as going to church." But it was not.[48]

The overall situation was ripe for armed disorder. The South was very violent. Indeed, among American regions, the South was (and is) *uniquely* violent. The postbellum civil disorder added greatly to the region's historic violence. Between full emancipation in 1865 and military reconstruction in 1867, brutal white-on-black atrocities occurred continually all over the South. About 1 percent of all black males in Texas between the ages of fifteen and forty-nine were killed by whites between 1865 and 1868, for instance. Furthermore, thousands of demobilized war veterans were available to be pulled into white paramilitary violence after military reconstruction.[49]

Much of the white-on-black violence and intimidation became organized during Reconstruction. A wave of such violence surged through the region in 1868–1869, when the Ku Klux Klan and klanlike conspiracies emerged in about 25 percent of the South's counties. Often the initial leaders were loose groupings of young former Confederate brigadiers working with newspaper editors who published glowing editorials concerning Klan activity and notices of upcoming organizational meetings. These attracted other local notables (doctors, lawyers, Masons) who in turn recruited young Confederate veterans, idle or unemployed men, county sheriffs, railroad agents, postal clerks, telegraph operators—even college students.[50]

Sheer aggression and pathology among white men were at work. Conspiracies by white landowners seeking to terrorize African Americans into working on terms desired by the landowners were also sources of violence. But much of the literature stresses, in addition, that violence was politically useful to the Conservatives (as the Democratic Party in the South called itself.)[51]

The new militarization of electoral politics placed great pressure on the Republican parties in several ways. First, violence was sometimes strategically directed against white Republican leaders. Georgia's governor was forced to flee his state, for instance. A white U.S. congressman was assassinated in 1868. This kind of pinpoint violence caused parties-in-government to weaken. Second, violence caused a number of voters to flee or to stay away from campaign rallies and the polls, costing the Republican parties electoral victories they would have had otherwise. Third, it threatened the black secondary associations that were crucial for sustained mobilization of the black electorate. The Union Leagues' general death by about 1868–1869 largely resulted from electoral violence. As a regionwide network of associations, the Union Leagues were invaluable for the development of political skills among black and white Republicans. In short, the political violence shattered families and communities and stunted the development of a robust associationalism in the South that could aid party-building.[52]

Worse, the Democrats' insistence on violence carried its own victory. It is often noted that there was no "northern will" or that it faded steadily. But this idea overlooks the structural, institutional, and symbolic limits to central control from Washington. These were put in place *before* Ulysses S. Grant became president.[53]

Responding to public opinion, Congress rapidly shrank the army between 1865 and 1868. Thus during Reconstruction troops were thinly stretched. Restoring the 1865 troop levels was impossible in the sense that the northern public almost certainly would not tolerate a *second* military mobilization after the bloodiest conflict in Western history. Grant's interventions triggered strong libertarian criticism and deeply divided his cabinet. Here, also, the Grant administration was undoubtedly imprisoned by Grant's own 1868 slogan, "Let us have peace."[54]

Furthermore, the central government faced an internal military challenge, namely, pacification of Native American tribes in the Northern Plains and in the Southwest. Thus, the army usually relied on slow-moving infantry in the South, because cavalry were badly needed in lower Texas and on the Plains. It deployed cavalry in the South only when absolutely necessary (it occasionally did so at the direction of the president). Finally, the recapture of the House by the Democratic Party as a result of the 1874 elections sharply constrained a strong central response to the violence of the 1875–1876 Redemption (the name white southern elites devised for subverting Reconstruction).

Thus it was impossible for Republicans to suppress entirely the violence directed against them. Between 1875 and 1876, a Democratic-controlled House, popular protest in the North against Grant's supposedly high-handed methods, indecision within the Grant administration, and the conservatism of the Supreme Court all encouraged a truly vast renewal of organized paramilitary electoral intimidation in Louisiana, Mississippi, and South Carolina. In that sense, the Redemption was completed "legally" because it was the *threat* of massive violence that disorganized local Republicans, in contrast to the savage whippings and murders of the earlier klan period.[55]

The role of violence can be overstated, however. During much of Reconstruction there was relatively free campaigning in probably a majority of locales. In his autobiography, Mifflin Gibbs, a prominent black judge and Republican leader in Arkansas, described campaigning in a state that was known nationally for its civil disturbances. He wrote: "The speakers, with teams and literature and other ammunition of political warfare . . . would start at early morn from their respective headquarters on a tour of one or two hundred miles, filling ten or twenty appointments. . . . The meetings, often in the woods, adjoining church or schoolhouse, were generally at a late hour, the men having to care for their stock, get supper, and come often several miles; hence it was not unusual for proceedings to be at their height at midnight." Caution was necessary, for armed whites did show up at such meetings. But, Gibbs pointed out, the church setting was ideal, for the participants could present themselves as busy at prayer.[56]

Consider, also, that a very rough estimate for the average number of voters per polling station on election day in 1872 is somewhere between fifteen hundred and seventeen hundred adult males, arriving singly or in groups over the course of the day. In most county seats, then numbering about 930, this was a manageable number for state and local law enforcement officials and for militia forces.[57]

Republican governments also consciously devised their electoral procedures in order to protect their electorates from white-on-black violence. That not only made elections manageable; equally important, it encouraged a strong fusion of group and political identity among African American men. Two incidents from the Redemption are particularly revealing. One concerns South Carolina, the other Texas.[58]

South Carolina allowed voters to vote at any polling place within their county of residence. In 1877, when the South Carolina presidential vote was contested and investigated by Congress, Republicans defended this practice. They noted that it helped black men to travel in groups for "mutual protection and safety." Their election law facilitated a disciplined and armed approach to electoral politics.[59] In Texas, county-seat voting occurred over a four-day period. The point of this was to protect Republican voters, which is why Democrats changed voting to precinct-based voting on *one* day, both dispersing and concentrating Republican voters so that one spasm of violence would do the trick.[60]

In addition, between 1870 and 1873, there was a *federal* response that also helped protect and define the Republican party-in-the-electorate. At one point, in fact, Grant, acting against the Ku Klux Klan in South Carolina in order to set an example, suspended the writ of habeas corpus in nine counties, the first (and the last) such suspension in American history.[61]

In this connection, consult table 4.3. Notice, first, that there was a general drop in troop levels from 1868 to 1870, as the state readmission process wound down. Also, after 1870, force levels continued a gradual decline, and during the Compromise of 1877 there was, of course, a huge drop in force levels. Yet there are other interesting patterns in the table. After 1870 one sees something like an electoral cycle in force levels for several states in congressional off-year elections in 1874 and in presidential elections in 1872 and 1876. Notice, too, South Carolina's large increases in force levels in 1871 and 1872; these were part of the federal anti-Klan offensive. In addition, Mississippi experienced an increase in force level from 1874 to 1875 during the crisis of its Republican regime.[62]

Finally, there is a very interesting wrinkle in the story that has only recently received attention. White-on-black violence was intentionally party-destroying. But it was also *un*intentionally party-building. This was because both sides had plenty of guns. Electoral campaigns saw the intimidating movement of large bodies of men moving in disciplined unison, in a

Table 4.3 U.S. Troop Levels in Southern States, 1868–1877

State	1868*	1869*	1870†	1871†	1872†	1873‡	1874†	1875†	1876†	1877‡
Alabama	588	798	623	194	242	187	420	260	201	5
Arkansas	1,562	605	124	63	58	63	124	86	102	13
Florida	1,131	354	317	442	423	352	178	267	294	184
Georgia	983	755	889	524	351	468	97	305	290	70
Louisiana	1,944	953	598	595	421	515	1,143	551	575	123
Mississippi	1,851	978	198	269	337	144	45	596	305	0
North Carolina	939	366	277	303	383	331	139	215	114	18
South Carolina	881	417	427	1,019	947	627	634	605	668	165
Tennessee	370	311	430	326	315	227	191	203	46	38
Texas*	5,765	4,612	4,740	3,853	3,944	N.A.	4,271	N.A.	3,042	N.A.
Virginia	1,733	1,088	426	315	303	432	379	449	384	268
Totals	17,657	11,237	9,049	7,903	7,724	—	7,621	—	6,021	—

Sources: James E. Sefton, *The United States Army and Reconstruction 1865–1877* (Baton Rouge: Louisiana State University Press, 1967), appendix B; Everette Swinney, *Suppressing the Ku Klux Klan: The Enforcement of the Reconstruction Amendments 1870–1877* (New York: Garland, 1987), p. 190.
*Figures in this column or row are from Sefton only.
†Figures in this column are averages of Sefton's figure and Swinney's figure; both figures were close in all cases.
‡Figures in this column are from Swinney only.
Total not computed due to entry of "N.A." for Texas.

threatening manner or under arms. Such display was certainly not for whites only.[63]

By means of a black militia movement that coursed through the region, black men often checked or responded to white violence in many cities and counties. In several places in the South the black militias were tenacious, well-organized, and effective. Indeed, Republicans in command of the southern states did much that fostered a Republican party-in-the-electorate in this way. Governors Powell Clayton of Arkansas (1868–1871), Robert Scott of South Carolina (1868–1872), Edmund Davis of Texas (1870–1873), Henry Warmoth of Louisiana (1868–1872), and Ossian Hart of Florida (1873–1874) all developed partly effective state policies in response to violence, deploying biracial militias to protect black voters. Warmoth, in particular, built a vast police and militia establishment consisting of three separate forces.[64]

Of these regimes, the South Carolina Republican Party went furthest in fostering a militia movement. In March 1869 the first Republican governor organized the National Guard Service of South Carolina, open to all males. Whites boycotted it, but "black Carolinians greeted the formation of the militia with unbridled enthusiasm." In little more than a year about ninety thousand black men enrolled in the service—or about *106 percent* of the actual Republican electorate. In February 1874 the state legislature also authorized county governments to charter private gun clubs, thus spawning a parallel militia.[65]

These militia movements went very far toward building deep partisan identities. George S. Houston, an Alabama state representative who was driven from his home county in 1869 by the Ku Klux Klan, captured the fierce psychology of attachment that worked on many men. Testifying before Congress, he declared, "I say the Republican party freed me, and I will die on top of it. I don't care who is pleased. I vote every time. I was register of my county, and my master sent in and lent me his pistols to carry around my waist when I was register to protect myself against my enemies. I am a Republican today, and if the Republican party can't do me any good, I will never turn against it. . . . I will stick to the Republican party and die in it."[66] George Houston's fierce partisanship suggested that political violence was double-edged in its effect.

But—overall—the net effect of the violent environment was plainly deleterious. From the perspective of party-system development, the first reconstruction represented a sustained, widespread, but never-repeated instance in American party politics of armed electoral competition. No other advanced liberal democracy, with the exception of Germany during the Weimar Republic or Italy immediately before the fascist march on Rome, ever had similar politics.

In the end, the Republican effort to build parties-in-the electorate was decisively shaped and weakened by the defection of southern Democrats from basic norms of democratic party competition. In particular, the cost to black leadership was stupefying. In Louisiana, probably the extreme case, 25 percent of the African Americans who were killed by whites during Reconstruction were officeholders or Republican Party officials.[67]

RECAPITULATING PARTY RECONSTRUCTION

To summarize, during the first reconstruction, black southern voters became central to American politics in a way that would have been impossible to imagine in 1860. They played a key role during the 1865–1867 interregnum in saving the civic future for which Republicans thought they had fought. The new coalition that came out of that moment in turn generated the world's first biracial democratic public sphere—distinctive, recurring, ongoing public occasions featuring political actions by African American citizens and politicians. Black citizens attended public rallies, met in political clubs, and marched in militia companies on election day. Voting rights were used, lived, and experienced by ordinary black Americans on a vast scale. African American members of Congress worked on civil rights legislation and focused on bringing home the bacon. Although the rate of congressional office-holding was quite low, in percentage terms, Congress was in fact "integrated" (between 1873 and 1875) to a degree that did not recur until 1969—ninety-six years later. The same was true for state and local governments. Finally, the Reconstruction governments were more policy-activist and muscular than is generally known.[68]

Yet despite the extraordinary will shown by the coalition of 1867–1868, the party system's structure at that time limited the impact of such will. An infrastructure for the process of electoral inclusion had to be made, and making it as fast as possible in a hostile environment was very hard. In northern states, in contrast, such institution-building took several decades between the 1820s and the early 1850s.

This chapter's use of the classic trichotomy for understanding parties—in government, as organizations, and in the electorate—has highlighted the extent to which party-building during the first reconstruction was jammed into the span of a few short years. There was little alternative to such a crash course. It was the only way to readmit the former Confederate states to the Union and simultaneously address the political threat posed by Andrew Johnson and the Conservatives to both the Republicans and the freedmen. But there was a price to be paid. The possibility of relatively stable democracy, brought about by channeling social conflict into strong, legitimate, competitive party politics, was not quite realized.

During the second reconstruction (as we will see later), the party system's structure placed much less pressure on that period's biracial coalition. Rather than build new parties quickly and from scratch, the coalition needed only to take over existing party organizations—which it did in steps from the 1940s into the 1970s.

What about first reconstruction jurisprudence-building—promoting black electoral inclusion by means of policy and law? Just as there was sweeping change in the party system, there was also great innovation in the legal system. How did such jurisprudence-building turn out? Did it counteract or reinforce the weaknesses of crash party-building? Let us turn now to those vital questions.

Chapter Five

The Limits of Jurisprudence-Building

In addition to party-building and a reconstruction of America's public sphere, another remarkable set of efforts—jurisprudence-building—followed formation of the 1867–1868 coalition. Jurisprudence-building resulted in the Fifteenth Amendment. Coupled to that achievement were elections statutes that implemented both it and the Fourteenth Amendment. These made it a crime for public officials and private parties "to obstruct exercise of the right to vote" and established "detailed federal supervision of the electoral process, from registration to the certification of returns."[1]

In turn, a new generation of federal judges and government lawyers worked feverishly in Washington and in the federal judicial districts and circuits to make the new array of powers work. They included Attorney General Amos Akerman, a native Georgian, and Solicitor General Benjamin Bristow, a native Kentuckian. Both began their federal careers as vigorous United States attorneys. Both served President Grant.[2]

Such men took the view that the federal government could directly protect individual voting rights. The United States could punish individuals who violently and criminally attacked these rights. They wanted therefore to shift to the federal government some of the responsibility for operating electoral processes in the former Confederacy and for the law enforcement that was associated with elections administration. Since ratification of the Constitution of 1787 such powers had resided with the states and local governments. But Akerman and Bristow, among many others, sought supervisory responsibility for the national government.

An imposing private "states' rights" bar stood ready, however, to defend the older constitutional vision barring federal participation in (and regulation of) not only state and local elections but national elections. Prominent southern lawyers such as Mississippi's L. Q. C. Lamar, later a Supreme Court justice, appeared on behalf of federal criminal defendants charged with violating the civil and voting rights of black citizens. Four other constitutional lawyers—Jeremiah S. Black (former president James Buchanan's attorney general), Henry Stanbery (former president Andrew Johnson's attorney general), John Campbell (former associate justice of the Supreme Court, part of the majority in *Dred Scott* and later assistant secretary of war for the Confederacy), and Maryland senator Reverdy Johnson (former president Zachary Taylor's attorney general and later a defense counsel in *Dred Scott*)— also involved themselves in major Reconstruction Amendment cases.[3]

In the end, the states' rights bar got pretty much what it wanted. In 1873—in cases that did not apparently involve voting rights—a Supreme Court majority fashioned a reading of the Reconstruction Amendments that clearly had the potential to subvert the previous effort to establish and enforce black voting rights. The Court held that these amendments were not intended to disturb American federalism. Three years later another Court majority let the other shoe drop. This happened in two elections cases that, unlike the 1873 case, directly raised questions about how to construe the federal statutes passed to enforce the Fourteenth and Fifteenth Amendments. The Court agreed very reluctantly with the idea that black voting rights could be nationally protected. But it also suggested that the elections statutes could easily be abused or poorly implemented by federal prosecutors. Politically, this was a major defeat for the coalition of 1867–1868. After all, by 1876 it did not control Congress and therefore could hardly revise the statutes.

The first critical tests of jurisprudence-building before the Supreme Court went badly, in short. The Court tamed the nationalist, muscular view of the Fourteenth and Fifteenth Amendments that Grant, Congress, and several federal circuit judges and government lawyers had spent several years trying to develop.

Had the nationalizers succeeded in obtaining a favorable stance from the Court, all actors in the polity would have received a powerful signal about the status of the new biracial coalition. A victory for the coalition would have generated further pressure for compliance with a new and evolving constitutional and statutory law. It would have clarified what the relevant actors could expect in the future from the Court and the lower federal courts. Finally, a set-back for the states' rights bar would have committed the time and energy of future Supreme Courts as well as the lower federal courts.

Because the first set of decisions was unfavorable, however, the Court's stance weakened the coalition, first, by lowering political pressure for its opponents to comply with the new constitutional and statutory law, and second, by creating a bulky political problem for it. A coalition that already was much weaker than it was in 1867–1868 now faced the task of finding effective ways around the Court's opposition.

This chapter's purposes, then, are to trace the voting rights jurisprudence that the Republicans initially sought to construct—and to depict its deterioration by the mid-1870s. Doing so offers essential contrast, as we shall see, with the second reconstruction. The best place to begin is with the Fifteenth Amendment.

PARSING THE FIFTEENTH AMENDMENT

Section 1 of the Fifteenth Amendment reads, "The rights of citizens of the United States to vote shall not be denied or abridged by the United States or by any State on account of race, color, or previous condition of servitude." Section 2 reads, "The Congress shall have power to enforce this article by appropriate legislation." Black suffrage was thus incorporated into America's fundamental law.[4]

Many congressional Republicans held that nationwide black suffrage was both just and urgently needed but that it could not easily be achieved by statute. As a series of failed suffrage referenda indicated, the state-level Republican parties outside the South varied widely in their openness to the idea, making it hard to proceed state by state. Also, black suffrage statutes, federal or state, could always be repealed by Democrats, which would both wreak havoc on the Republican Party as an organization and threaten the goal of perfecting American democracy that was sincerely held by key Republican leaders. The third lame-duck session of the Fortieth Congress thus drafted and passed the Fifteenth Amendment and sent it to the states for ratification—all before Grant's call in his first inaugural address for such an amendment, which was actually an exhortation to the state legislatures.[5]

Several strategic considerations account for the amendment's oft-noted imprecision. These include the need for passage while the Fortieth Congress sat (given doubts about passage in the Forty-first Congress), the need for sending it to the states while a majority of the still-sitting legislatures were open for business and controlled by Republicans, and the need for wording it simply and innocuously enough to assure quick state legislative passage.

Ratifying the Fifteenth Amendment would address vital political requirements of the Republican Party. In light of local threats to black suffrage during the 1868 elections, the amendment would alleviate southern party-building problems. It also would help strengthen northern parties by compensating for white defections from the Republican Party in the 1867 elections. Finally, it would help build up Republicanism in border states.

There is scholarly disagreement, however, as to whether the Fifteenth Amendment was meant to lodge suffrage rights for black Americans at the top, within the national government. A striking feature of the amendment is its apparent narrowness. Missing are provisions for universal (as distinct from impartial) suffrage (though this was debated) and any proscription of property, educational, or other apparently neutral but substantively discriminatory restrictions that states could make (again, an issue that Congress discussed.) Also conspicuous is the absence of a provision for black officeholding, which was debated but dropped.

On the other hand, it is plausible to regard the amendment as *covertly* rather powerful. Section 2's statement that "Congress shall have power to enforce this article by appropriate legislation" copied the Thirteenth and the Fourteenth Amendments, and Republicans generally took such language as ample warrant for statutory enforcement (as with the 1866 Civil Rights Act, which turned the Thirteenth Amendment into a positive grant of rights and prefigured the Fourteenth.) In other words, Republicans quite possibly wrote the Fifteenth Amendment in such a way as to get it through Congress and the state legislatures quickly, knowing that they could beef it up later by statute.[6] But it is impossible to know for sure. The debate in the Fortieth Congress focused entirely on section 1. Neither Senator William Stewart (R-Nev.) nor Representative George Boutwell (R-Mass.)—who managed the Fifteenth Amendment in the Senate and the House, respectively—mentioned section 2 at all in their memoirs, and their scant surviving papers are evidently uninformative.[7]

Yet in the succeeding Congress, Senator Oliver Morton (R-Ind.), among others, did argue that section 2 endowed the amendment with a great deal of authority for congressional regulation of the suffrage:

> Now, sir, what is the spirit and true intent of the fifteenth amendment, as
> we all remember it when it passed in this Chamber, as will be shown by
> the *Congressional Globe* . . . ? It is that the colored man, so far as voting is
> concerned, shall be placed upon the same level and footing with the white

> man, *and that Congress shall have the power to secure him that right.* . . . We know
> that the second section was put there for the purpose of enabling Congress
> itself to carry out the provision. It was not to be left to state legislation . . . it
> was put there for the purpose of enabling Congress to take every step that might
> be necessary to secure the colored man in the enjoyment of these rights.[8]

Morton's repeated insistence that the record of debate in the Senate during
the third session of the Fortieth Congress would show extensive discussion of
section 2 was an exaggeration. On the other hand, Morton's faulty *memory*
that there was a rich debate on the subject is suggestive, and it is certainly
true that section 2 was much debated during the ratification process. Also,
both Boutwell and Stewart supported the enforcement legislation that came
afterward.[9]

In short, a perhaps sensible way to think of the Fifteenth Amendment is
that its framers thought that the Republican Party would make up what the
amendment meant as they went along. It would give them a general commission to make detailed statutes. The "originalists" who picture the amendment
as limited and limiting, with little impact on American federalism, surely capture the genuinely conservative elements of the framers' approach. But neither were the framers simply cautious restorationists.[10]

The Uncharted Terrain of Federal Protection

All of this is critical for assessing what happened later. It is commonly
believed that the main intention of the Reconstruction Congresses was to
prohibit racially discriminatory "state action"—but really no more. If so, then
the Supreme Court faithfully elaborated congressional intent in the 1873
Slaughterhouse Cases when it held that the new constitutional amendments
did not alter pre-war federalism.

The Reconstruction Congresses did in fact deeply respect federalism.
They sought quickly to reanimate it. This was, after all, an essential purpose
of military reconstruction. Republicans rejected the idea of imposing a military protectorate on the former Confederacy or turning the former southern
states into territories. Congress intended to rebuild a polity of states coexist-
ing with a national government.[11] The idea that "state action" doctrine was
originally intended is thus only a short step away. According to this view,
Congress meant only to prevent states and their officials from giving certain
rights to some people but not to others on the basis of racial criteria. These
civil and political rights—rights to contract, marry, give testimony, vote,
and so on—were not federally conferred rights; rather, they inhered in the

citizenship of state and local government. All that Congress meant was a prohibition of overt racial discrimination in state allocation of civil and political rights. With regard to harms visited by white private individuals on black citizens, the federal government was not in the business of attempting to prevent or punish these. Rather, such harms were properly subject to sanction by state officials under the police powers of states and localities.

Underlying the restrictive "state action" understanding of the Reconstruction Amendments, particularly the Fourteenth and the Fifteenth, is the position, therefore, that there were very few national civil or political rights. This may seem strange to the contemporary ear because today Americans often have the correct impression that they do enjoy such national rights. But in the nineteenth century, it is often suggested, national civil and political rights per se did not exist.

But the alternative conceptualization is obvious: the Reconstruction Amendments *did* create—and more important, they *presupposed*—national rights. It is true that for the period up to 1866 national rights were seemingly sparse—but only if one overlooks slaveholders' presumption of such rights in their successful agitation for the 1850 Fugitive Slave Act. Nonetheless, in 1862 the secretary of the treasury, Salmon Chase, inquired of the attorney general what national rights existed, an inquiry that led to a reply that, for its time, suggested inclusive, broad understandings of national rights.[12]

Chase could hardly have conceived of such rights or had such an exchange with the attorney general if they were not in some important sense already perceived to exist. A wide array of activist measures forged during the Civil War implied broad change in what it meant to be an American citizen. They included the Homestead Act, the Morrill Land Grant College Act, the Legal Tender Act, and the Freedmen's Bureau. The Civil War and Reconstruction also led to what was actually the world's first old-age income insurance system, a broad veteran's pensions system encompassing blacks and whites. A national citizenship, furthermore, was clearly implied by such phenomena as the oaths of loyalty to the Union and the Constitution that were imposed by Congress on federal military and civil officers, federal jurors, and those conducting business with the federal government.[13]

Finally, a new national citizenship was implied by new uses of the so-called removal power established in the Judiciary Act of 1789. That statute created a framework by which defendants in a state court could remove their litigation to a federal court if it involved a matter or controversy between citizens of different states, per article 3 of the Constitution. The Civil Rights Act of 1866 established the right of removal of civil rights cases to the federal courts. The Judiciary Act of 1875 further amplified civil rights removal. It conferred "federal question" jurisdiction on federal courts for the first time. These were, per article 3, cases "arising under" the Constitution. Such cases now, of course, would include issues touching on the Reconstruction Amendments. The 1875 Judiciary Act elaborately safeguarded a highly robust removal right by allowing federal courts and the United States to sanction state courts for any obstructionism.[14]

All of this meant that most of the time citizens would perforce encounter issues concerning American citizenship at the state and local levels. But adherents of a nationalist sensibility envisioned a potent *reserve power* in the U.S. government for protecting the nationally conferred rights that had been instituted for the purpose of perfecting American democracy. This would explain why section 1 of the Fifteenth Amendment refers to "citizens of the United States" and not merely to "citizens of the States" and why it prohibits denial or abridgement of the right to vote "by the United States" in addition to the prohibition on the states.

Such a nationalist view I shall call Reconstruction constitutionalism. It held that the constitution was not simply a set of limits on government but a source of sovereign, positive, regulatory government able to establish and enforce national rights.[15]

Reconstruction constitutionalism did not inherently mean discontinuity. Rather, it meant building on such elements of the 1787 Constitution as its preamble, the "necessary and proper" clause of article 1, section 8, the document's explicit procedures for amendment, and the guarantee clause of article 4, section 4, assuring each state a republican form of government. The Constitution's own stately reconstruction was made possible, in other words, by its fundamental adequacy for the exigencies of American political development. By means of this reconstructed Constitution federal officials could (sparingly, to be sure) give substance to constitutional commands that there be national political freedom and equality.[16]

Nonetheless, certain complexities engendered by American federalism quickly emerged. Some parts of the Constitution, such as article 1, section 2, seem to assign the establishment and protection of the suffrage to the states. Yet article 1, section 4, and article 4, section 4, to say nothing of the Fourteenth and Fifteenth Amendments, establish a central governmental role for the establishment and protection of voting rights.[17]

Law enforcement was also uncertain. The first reconstruction was in large measure a law enforcement drama, as the U. S. Marshals Service and the U.S. Army took over state and local law enforcement. The second reconstruction, particularly during the Kennedy administration, was likewise filled with similar tensions, as we shall see.[18]

Did the right to vote come from the United States or from the states? Or both? If both, then who was responsible for what part of the right? Public officials—and the citizens whom they sought to protect or to control—wrestled with these new questions. Much of Reconstruction was therefore a clash in the federal courts about which understanding would be entrenched in judicial precedent. The new biracial coalition in American politics thus stimulated fundamental conflict about American institutions and their purposes.

THE ELECTIONS STATUTES

After the Fifteenth Amendment's ratification (March 30, 1870), Reconstruction constitutionalism truly burst forth, as congressional Republicans passed major enforcement and civil rights statutes. Consider two of them: the Enforcement Act of May 31, 1870, and the Ku Klux Act of March 28, 1871.[19]

Section 1 of the Enforcement Act announced that "all citizens of the United States" were "entitled and allowed to vote . . . without distinction of race . . . any constitution, law, custom, usage, or regulation of any State or Territory . . . to the contrary notwithstanding." With the partial exception of section 16, which might be considered the Chinese American Civil Rights Act of 1870, twenty-one more sections of the Enforcement Act put the federal government in the business of (1) protecting citizens' exercise of their Thirteenth, Fourteenth, and Fifteenth Amendment rights by defining the violation of their rights either by public officials or by private individuals (by "any person") as felonies and by providing for criminal sanctions against such violation, (2) attacking fraud in congressional elections (under authority of article 1, section 4) and by defining such fraud as subject to criminal sanctions, and (3) attacking violations of office-holding provisions of section 3 of the Fourteenth Amendment as misdemeanors punishable by imprisonment or fines or both. The act provided for private action against public officials' Fifteenth Amendment violations, establishing a schedule of fines and permitting the recovery of legal fees by counsel for plaintiffs from defendants. In addition to encouraging a private enforcement bar, the act explicitly directed United States district attorneys to bring violations described in the act into the federal courts, and it required United States marshals and United States court commissioners to arrest, imprison, and bail offenders against citizens' constitutional rights "at the expense of the United States" and to form posses or call for military aid in support of the service of process, noting further (in section 13) that "it shall be lawful for the President of the United States" to use federal or state military forces to "aid in the execution of judicial process."[20]

A critical aspect of the legislative debate concerned the federal government's authority to act on behalf of or against *private* citizens. Senator John Pool (R-N.C.) authored sections 5–7 of the act (modeling them after North Carolina's anti-Klan provisions); they dealt with individuals as well as public officials. In discussing them, Pool claimed that "the United States has the right . . . to go into the States to enforce the rights of the citizens against all who attempt to infringe upon those rights." He noted that "it is upon individuals that we must press our legislation. It matters not whether those individuals be officers or whether they are acting upon their own responsibility; whether they are acting singly or in organizations. If there is to be appropriate legislation at all, it must be that which applies to individuals."[21]

This issue of what the United States could and could not do vis-à-vis private citizens resurfaced a year later in the deliberations of the Forty-second Congress concerning the Ku Klux Act. This Congress's first session opened immediately after the close of the lame-duck third session of the Forty-first Congress, during which a joint investigating committee had taken testimony concerning activities of Klan-like organizations in North Carolina. The new Congress then launched a much broader investigation whose gravity and unprecedented scope reflected a consensus among Republicans regarding the appropriateness of national enforcement of rights.[22]

The Ku Klux Act (parts of which survive in the United States Code) provided for redress of rights violations by persons acting "under color of . . . law"; it defined each of two kinds of conspiracy, (1) schemes directed against public officials or citizens either acting in their official capacities or acting to enforce the "equal protection of the laws" and (2) schemes intended to obstruct voting and political advocacy, as a "high crime"; it authorized federal suits for recovery of damages by persons "deprived of . . . rights and privileges" against the conspirators whose actions caused the deprivation and injury; it authorized presidential military intervention when either state governments or the United States faced violent conspiracies that resulted in the deprivation of constitutional rights; it provided procedures for temporary suspension by the president of the writ of habeas corpus; and it denied the privilege of jury service in the United States courts to anyone complicit in the conspiracies forbidden by the act.[23]

Two interesting articulations (among others) of Reconstruction constitutionalism occurred in the House and in the Senate. Representative John Coburn (R-Ind.) stated: "Where there is domestic violence and aid is asked by the State, the nation must exercise its authority. Can it do so without invitation? Before the fourteenth amendment it could not unless that violence amounted to an overthrow of republican institutions."[24] Coburn then refined this point to argue that either state or federal *inaction* was effectively a denial of "the equal protection of the law": "A systematic failure to make arrests, to put on trial, to convict, or to punish offenders against the rights of a great class of citizens is a denial of equal protection." Consequently, it was "the plain duty of Congress to enforce by appropriate legislation the rights secured by . . . the fourteenth amendment."

As to the method of enforcement, "Shall we deal with individuals or with the State as a State?" Coburn then argued that direct federal action against individuals, if states did not take action against individuals (presumably under their police powers), actually did *less* damage to federalism because no supersession of civil government occurred by means of imposition of martial law and suspension of the writ of habeas corpus. He was, however, perfectly willing to adopt, if necessary, "the more thorough method of superseding State authority" once "the deprivation of rights and the condition of outlawry was so general as to prevail in all quarters." In other words, Congress had "both remedies" at its disposal—and indeed both were written into the act.[25]

In the Senate, the Fourteenth Amendment's principal architect, Lyman Trumbull (R-Ill.), doubted the Ku Klux Act's constitutionality, arguing something close to a "state action" view: "I do not believe . . . that the Congress of the United States has a right to pass a general criminal code for the States of the Union . . . that would be destructive at once of the State governments." Yet the Senate manager of the Ku Klux Act, George Edmunds (R-Vt.), explicitly disagreed with Trumbull. Before passage of the Reconstruction Amendments it was true, Edmunds said, that "national citizenship was the consequence of a State citizenship." This meant that "if any [black] citizen of another State chose to go [to South Carolina]" and thus run the risk that he might be enslaved "he must take his chances and the Constitution could not help him." He continued: "Now, sir, to put this question at rest . . . the thirteenth and fourteenth amendments came in," with the consequence that "*the language of the old Constitution is reversed absolutely.*" Finally, "Instead of declaring, as it did before, that the citizen of a State was entitled to the privileges of a citizen in another state, it declared that every person born within the territory of the United States was a citizen of the nation, and, by consequence, a citizen of any State in which he might from time to time reside." Edmunds therefore wanted direct national action against "any man who infracts" the Fourteenth Amendment.[26]

So, to summarize, many Republicans were sensitive to preserving federalism. But such conservative constitutionalism also had a broad equitable streak. Republicans saw that the civil and political rights acquired by America's new citizens now had both life *and* vulnerability. Members of

Congress processed large quantities of information about the fragility of blacks' rights. For the state of Louisiana alone, Republicans generated (between the Thirty-ninth and the Forty-fourth Congresses) twenty-two reports about violence in that state and fifteen congressional reports using executive branch information. They knew clearly that the question whether the law could effectively bring black southerners into electoral politics hung in the balance.[27]

Using the Power to Protect Voting Rights

The story continues, of course. What happened next was influenced by the lower federal judicial system and by the Grant presidency.

Although Reconstruction constitutionalism provided a theoretical foundation for an electoral-regulatory system, several institutional weaknesses plagued the only recently revived southern federal courts. Under the 1869 Judiciary Act, circuit and district judges were paired in the circuits, thus instituting tensions between circuit judges (including Supreme Court justices, who then rode circuit)—who were inclined to support Republican constitutional theory—and southern district judges (who were sometimes inclined to support conservative pro-southern constitutional theory.) The number of enforcement cases greatly exceeded the number of competent federal judges available to hear them (twenty-one judges in all, not counting Supreme Court justices on circuit). Also, courts and judges lacked stenographers, clerks, and libraries. Other factors were the hostility of local law enforcement officers and the fear for life and property often voiced by black witnesses as they contemplated their fate should the United States fail in court. Federal marshals in service of process often faced real bodily danger. Finally, the U.S. attorneys were badly overworked.[28]

On the other hand, the resources put into the effort were substantial. Even by twentieth-century American standards the Grant administration and Congress were highly activist. Grant certainly grasped and was guided by the tenets of Reconstruction constitutionalism.[29]

One vital resource for the Grant administration was the quality and élan of the government's first set of lawyers. The federal legal officers initially implementing the Enforcement and Ku Klux Acts were Attorney General Amos Akerman of Georgia and Solicitor General Benjamin Bristow of Kentucky, both of whom had been vigorous United States attorneys. Bristow, in particular, had acted forcefully in Kentucky to secure the constitutionality of the 1866 Civil Rights Act.[30]

Also, to support the Department of Justice and the federal courts the United States increased its judicial expenditures about 214 percent between the late 1860s and the early 1870s. The enforcement effort by no means drove the entire increase, but it certainly played a major role. The enforcement cases on the docket of the southern federal courts during the height of the enforcement effort in the early 1870s numbered 271 (1870), 879 (1871), 1,890 (1872), and 1,960 (1873).[31]

Convictions did not mean severe punishment, particularly in Mississippi, where the district judge developed a policy of exchanging light sentences for open court confessions (which, however, quickly ended the violence). Also, the Grant administration eventually pardoned most federal prisoners and suspended the remaining prosecutions. Nonetheless, by 1873 the massive nocturnal organized violence against black men, women, and children, white carpetbaggers, and the occasional northern lady school instructor had melted away—if only briefly.

In South Carolina and Mississippi the federal government was reasonably effective in court. In 1871 and 1872 the United States won convictions in, respectively, 48 percent and 90 percent of its South Carolina prosecutions, after which it essentially withdrew from further intervention in that state. In Mississippi it won convictions in 77 percent of the prosecutions it carried out between 1872 and 1874.[32]

Noticing these outcomes requires some modification of the common judgment that the Grant administration's judicial effort to secure black political rights from private violence was weak and cynical. This seems to ignore the governance element of the situation. The administration clearly did not intend either full justice for victims and criminals or full peace in every southern state. Instead, it apparently intended a cessation of regionwide violence. In this it succeeded, if briefly.[33]

The government's jurisprudential accomplishments were, of course, tentative. Judges and lawyers uncertainly made their way across new and rapidly changing constitutional territory. Sometimes they displayed confusion, at other times visionary creativity. In an 1871 South Carolina (Fourth Circuit) anti-Klan case, *United States v. Allen Crosby,* for instance, one sees United States lawyers, and to a certain extent the United States circuit judge, having real difficulty with concrete applications of the 1870 Enforcement Act and of the Fifteenth Amendment's meaning. During argument the United States conceded that the amendment did "not clothe any one absolutely with the right of suffrage." But the United States then immediately asserted that "practically, really, as a great public fact . . . the fifteenth amendment does secure and does guarantee to this class of our citizens the right to vote, and it was so regarded by Congress."[34]

As for the court, it upheld conspiracy counts but also quashed others pertaining to crimes committed in connection with conspiracy. In discussing the

Enforcement Act the court opined that Congress "may have thought that legislation most likely to secure the end in view," that is, to punish individuals. But beyond that supposition the Fourth Circuit evidently could not go and simply added, "If the act be within the scope of the amendment, and in the line of its purpose, Congress is the sole judge of its appropriateness."[35]

Much if not most ambivalence of this type reflected argument and judicial reasoning on the fly. The dockets of the southern courts were terribly congested, leading to haste. Also, the protean character of the Reconstruction Amendments and enforcement statutes baffled and surprised federal judges and government lawyers.[36]

Another window into the difficulties of using the new jurisprudence to protect black voting rights is provided by a colloquy between a federal judge and Associate Justice Joseph Bradley. In 1871 the federal district judge William B. Woods wrote to Bradley to ask whether an armed, violent assault on a Republican political meeting in Alabama, undertaken by private parties, violated the Fifteenth Amendment and federal elections laws. Bradley wrote back that a "mere firing into a political meeting" was certainly a "private municipal offence," beyond the capacity of the United States to correct or punish. But the question was different, he suggested, if there was a conspiracy to violate the Fifteenth Amendment. Such a conspiracy could be recognized by the "banding" or "confederating" together of armed assailants, and the violation could be recognized by the firing into a political meeting, an action that was "evidently an attempt to prevent persons from exercising the right of suffrage, to whom it was guarantied under the Fifteenth Amendment." Clearly, two smart men were trying to make their way through a new jurisprudence.[37]

Sometimes uncertainty gave way to vision, though. Consider the Fifth Circuit, on which Bradley traveled. In May and June 1870, Bradley undertook to resolve one of Louisiana's major legal disputes. In 1869 the Republican legislature, under the state's police power in public health, reorganized the butchering and slaughterhouse industry in New Orleans by entitling one company to dominate the trade for twenty-five years. Several of the state's courts entered the ensuing legal fray between the companies disadvantaged by the regulation and the firm to which the legislature had granted special privileges.[38]

Justice Bradley drew the case into the federal courts when he issued a writ to one of the disadvantaged companies, which eventually requested the Fifth Circuit to enjoin implementation of the state regulation pending a Supreme Court decision. The antimonopoly lawyers were led by former U.S. Supreme Court justice John Campbell, an Alabamian who resigned from the Court in

1861 to join the Confederacy. Campbell mounted a remarkably daring claim. In preventing most of the butchers in New Orleans from making a living as they saw fit and effectively subjecting them to the dictates of a legislatively instituted monopoly, Louisiana had created an involuntary servitude for these butchers that was illegal under the Civil Rights Act, unconstitutional under the Thirteenth Amendment, and unconstitutional under the Fourteenth Amendment.

Initially disagreeing, Bradley then changed his mind. In fact, and this is astonishing, he issued injunctive relief for "flagrant violation of the fundamental rights of labor" secured to "the citizen of the U.S." by the Fourteenth Amendment. Bradley's ruling suggested that there was *a right to work* directly secured by the United States. This was breathtakingly experimental.[39]

THE SUPREME COURT AND THE *SLAUGHTERHOUSE CASES*

But Bradley's expansive view still lacked Supreme Court sanction. How would his brethren on the Court treat it?[40] This book holds that the key factor governing jurisprudence-building after coalition formation was the stance taken by the Supreme Court when the results of coalition-making *first* received Court scrutiny. The entire arc of jurisprudence-building was influenced by this "critical moment."[41]

April 14, 1873, saw the first full test before the Supreme Court of the emerging jurisprudence described above. The vehicle came from Louisiana in the *Slaughterhouse Cases*. As Justice Samuel Miller noted in his majority opinion in a 5–4 ruling, the Court was "called upon for the first time to give construction" to the Thirteenth Amendment and to section 1 of the Fourteenth Amendment.[42]

On one level the controversy had nothing to do with voting rights but instead turned on whether Louisiana could regulate sanitary conditions in New Orleans slaughterhouses. Miller showed that Louisiana's statute was nothing exceptional. Did the Reconstruction Amendments change matters so much that those firms who disliked the regulation now had a constitutional case against Louisiana? Hardly, Miller thought. The Reconstruction Amendments were overwhelmingly about "the freedom of the slave race."

But Miller's decision wounded the new electoral statutes. Picking up on plain distinctions in the Fourteenth Amendment's first section, Miller animated two previously inarticulate elements of Reconstruction constitutionalism, the concepts of "dual citizenship" and "dual federalism." Miller showed that citizens of the states had had a rich array of rights before the Civil War. Correlatively, there had been very few national rights. Did

Congress now intend to transfer all the erstwhile state rights and their enforcement to the United States? If so, Congress must engage in constant legislation. And "such a construction . . . would constitute this court a perpetual censor upon all legislation of the States." Such horrible consequences were absurd on their face. To take a nationalist view of the amendments meant a great "departure from the structure and spirit of our institutions." The Court was "convinced that no such results were intended" by Congress or the ratifying states.

Miller evoked a stern sense of judicial guardianship. The Court must preserve, "with a steady and even hand, the balance between state and federal power." With such reasoning, then, he dropped a confining net over Reconstruction constitutionalism.[43]

Scholars still debate what Miller was up to. One thing seems certain: Miller wanted to proceed cautiously in construing the new amendments. But as noted in both Bradley's dissent and subsequent commentary, Miller thereby disregarded the implications of his narrow dual-citizenship approach for voting rights jurisprudence. Miller may in fact have stumbled into a trap set by John Campbell, counsel for those seeking to overthrow the monopoly. If he supported Campbell he risked stretching the Fourteenth Amendment, but by ruling for Louisiana he necessarily watered down Reconstruction constitutionalism.[44]

In short, the Court was now suddenly a genuine danger to voting rights and civil rights. Another Louisiana case, *United States v. Cruikshank*, soon amplified the repercussions of the *Slaughterhouse Cases*.

UNITED STATES V. CRUIKSHANK IN THE FIFTH CIRCUIT

A black militia company enters the story at this point; it was under the command of William Ward and Levi Allen, both black Union veterans. In March 1873, they sought to bring order to a Louisiana jurisdiction named after Grant's first vice president, Schuyler Colfax, which was the seat of a parish named after the president himself. They installed the new (more radical) Republican governor's appointed sheriff and parish judge, and they established informal martial law. In response, on Easter Sunday, April 13, 1873, a white militia consisting of about three hundred men, firing a cannon, successfully assaulted Colfax and then set about executing the entire black militia company. One black man feigned death, however. He survived to become a witness for the federal prosecution.[45]

Initially the United States indicted nearly one hundred perpetrators of the Colfax massacre but then settled on a strategy of prosecuting nine ringleaders. This did little good. Over the course of two trials from February to June 1874, a well-funded defense proved spectacularly successful. It argued the unconstitutionality of the Enforcement Acts, secured the acquittal of six defendants, prevented the conviction of the remaining three for conspiracy to murder, and restricted conviction only to the conspiracy to interfere with such rights as the right to vote. Most important, the defense team seemed to split the Fifth Circuit.

At trial Judge William Woods, the district judge, adopted a robust Reconstruction constitutionalist reading of the United States' case, in apparent defiance of the Supreme Court. But Justice Bradley, again riding circuit, supported the defense motion for arrest of judgment on the ground that the United States attorney had incorrectly drafted his indictment. This division meant certification to the Supreme Court.[46] What did Bradley think he was doing? It is hard to know—and examination of Bradley's personal papers only deepens one's puzzlement. There are intriguing hints in the papers which suggest that the president and the Senate elevated Bradley to the Supreme Court in the first place on the basis of a specific understanding that he would be the "point man" of the Supreme Court in the former Confederacy and would govern the Fifth Circuit. If so, then Bradley' action in splitting the Fifth Circuit and breaking from his colleague, Judge Woods, may have been meant as a gambit for rescuing Reconstruction constitutionalism from the *Slaughterhouse Cases*. Bradley had, after all, dissented furiously from the ruling in the *Slaughterhouse Cases*.

One possible interpretation is that Bradley had to get around the *Slaughterhouse Cases* and *also* satisfy his own strong desire to fashion what he considered some sort of workable national policy for (in his words) the "war of race" and its "outrages, atrocities" and "conspiracies." Bradley appears to have recognized that he could find a broad national power to protect the right to vote against racial discrimination under *the Fifteenth Amendment*. If sustained on appeal to the Supreme Court, his view also meant a partial Thirteenth- and Fourteenth-Amendment civil rights policy. Bradley was apparently deeply satisfied with his circuit opinion. He circulated printed copies to his brethren on the Court and, significantly, to members of Congress and the attorney general.[47]

THE "WHITE REVOLUTION" IN THE BLACK MAJORITY STATES

Yet Bradley's initiative was a terrible blunder, precisely because he was so closely watched by his regional opponents for clues to the Grant administration's southern policy. His circuit opinion touched off a disastrous reversal of the fragile southern peace that the administration had earlier secured. In a remarkable coincidence, a tornado blew the roof off his home the day after he mailed out copies of his opinion—a meteorological portent of things to come.[48]

Many Louisiana Conservatives considered Bradley's action in *Cruikshank* an unmistakable signal of a deliberate shift in national policy. First of all, he issued it *after* taking an extended trip to Washington and then returning to New Orleans; second, the circuit opinion suggested that some of the elections enforcement statutes were either unconstitutional or needed to be rewritten.[49]

Literally within days of Bradley's decision Louisiana Conservatives completed their statewide establishment of a private army under full regimental organization, the White League. The United States Attorney for Louisiana correctly thought that the price of Bradley's fateful ruling would be "five hundred lives" in the fall election campaign.[50] The process of Republican collapse in Louisiana continued into early 1877. It spread to Mississippi and led in 1875 to that state's "redemption" and indeed the establishment of a hegemonic racial conservatism that lasted for a century. South Carolina's redemption, modeled on Mississippi's, began in the latter part of 1876 and continued through the first months of 1877.

Certain vital elements were common to the "white revolution" in each of these black majority states. The Democratic-Conservative opposition to the governing Republican parties was initially organized by a moderate wing that explicitly argued for fighting it out with the Republicans on issues of waste and fraud as a way to keep peace and order. However, the "unificationist" or "accommodationist" groups in every single party were outflanked by "straight outs" who called for violence, intimidation, and frank assertion of white racial supremacy. The weakness of the moderates was both signaled and deepened by frenzied and murderous white riots—the Coushatta (Louisiana) Massacre and the Battle of Liberty Place in New Orleans (August 30 and September 14, 1874), Vicksburg's two riots of December 7, 1874 and September 2, 1875, the Clinton (Mississippi) riot of September 5, 1875, and the Hamburg and Ellenton (South Carolina) massacres of July 4 and September 16, 1876.

Anticipating federal intervention as election day neared in the fall of 1874 (Louisiana), the fall of 1875 (Mississippi), and the fall of 1876 (South Carolina), the dominant white supremacist factions of the Democratic parties revamped their movements. They organized separate political clubs for black voters and made explicit appeals to black voters in order to split or discourage the Republican base. This step achieved its greatest success in Charleston,

South Carolina, and led to the endorsement of former Confederate general Wade Hampton, running for governor, by the black nationalist leader Martin Delany (once the highest-ranking black Union Army officer).[51]

Also, in several localities office-sharing "fusion" arrangements between Democrats and Republicans were made. The straight-outs sponsored torch-light parades, joint campaign appearances with Republicans, barbecues, open nominating conventions, and (in Louisiana and Mississippi) the active involvement of the Grange. Most effective of all was the organization of white marching "rifle clubs," armed with live ammunition and appareled in special uniforms. The "white liners" of Mississippi and South Carolina combined the threat (and on a few occasions the actuality) of truly massive violence, the militancy and energy of semipopulist mass movements, and, late in the campaigns, the feigning of sincere interest in black participation.[52]

Louisiana's "white liners" were the most overtly insurrectionary of such groups in all three black majority states. In mid-September 1874, White League forces launched a successful military coup against the Republican governor of Louisiana and defeated the state militia (which had a biracial staff commanded by the former Confederate general James Longstreet of Gettysburg fame) on the streets of New Orleans, the famous Battle of Liberty Place. Only Grant's military intervention sustained the de jure government. In early 1875 a second coup attempt racked New Orleans. However, shortly afterward a congressional committee successfully brokered a treaty between the state's warring parties.[53]

In response to this growing southern whirlwind, the Department of Justice and the federal judiciary were tragically inactive. Bradley's widely publicized circuit ruling paralyzed federal legal officers into awaiting Supreme Court clarification of national enforcement powers.[54]

The Grant administration was also irresolute. It had earlier bungled the defense of southern regimes, a pattern that began in the spring of 1870, when it washed its hands of Governor Rufus Bullock's regime in Georgia. Indeed, Grant truly disliked interventions. When it appeared necessary to protect law and order generally, Grant could follow the signal Congress gave him with the statutes it crafted implementing the Fifteenth Amendment—hence the moderately successful effort against the Klan throughout the South in 1871 and 1872. Also, open violence that plainly rose to the level of insurrection quickly triggered his decisive intervention, as in Louisiana. But Grant did little to settle the Brooks-Baxter War in Arkansas, which appeared to be a comic opera of a conflict between two Republican factions; in fact, it evolved into the redemption of Arkansas. During Mississippi's chilling redemption in the fall of 1875, Grant ignored Governor Adelbert Ames and made a separate peace with the state's Conservatives.[55]

UNITED STATES V. REESE AND UNITED STATES V. CRUIKSHANK IN THE SUPREME COURT

Against this backdrop *United States v. Reese,* a Fifteenth Amendment case from Kentucky, and *United States v. Cruikshank*, the Colfax massacre case, both were heard by the Supreme Court in 1875. Then, on March 27, 1876, the Court handed down its decision in *Reese*.

First, a majority of seven did accept some of Justice Bradley's attempt in his earlier circuit ruling in *Cruikshank* to save Reconstruction constitutionalism as it applied to the Fifteenth Amendment. To that extent, they deferred to the colleague who had the requisite expertise from his circuit experience. But they accepted his argument in a quite confusing way: they in effect told Congress to rewrite its enforcement legislation. By then, however, Democrats had regained control of the House! The Court gave no comfort to the Republican Party and to black voters.

Reese had come out of Kentucky in a division of opinion between the district judge, who considered the Enforcement Acts unconstitutional, and Circuit Judge Halmor Edmunds, who like other circuit judges was far more nationalist. The defendants were municipal elections officials who participated in a complex conspiracy to snare black voters of Lexington, Kentucky, in a Catch-22 fraud. In an 1873 city election they refused to accept blacks' ballots on the ground that the plaintiffs had not paid their municipal poll tax—but the city government (which established the tax) had earlier refused black voters' efforts to pay the tax. The defendants' actions clearly violated section 3 of the 1870 Enforcement Act, which had been written precisely for the purpose of blocking such schemes.[56]

Writing for the Court in *Reese*, the new chief justice, Morrison Waite, declared sections 3 and 4 of the Enforcement Act unconstitutional under the Fifteenth Amendment. In writing the statute Congress had misunderstood the true scope of the amendment. It did not establish the right to vote (a point already ventured in a women's suffrage case decided the previous year, *Minor v. Happersett*). The Fifteenth Amendment *did* create a new national right against racially discriminatory action that Congress could indeed actively and positively secure. But sections 3 and 4 of the Enforcement Act made for the wrong vehicle; they were written too broadly. The United States had therefore not indicted Reese under "appropriate legislation" per section 2 of the amendment. The Court therefore sustained the defense's demurrer that the United States lacked jurisdiction.[57]

The Court's 8–1 decision in *Cruikshank* was handed down the same day as was *Reese*. It was even worse news for the Republican Party, its southern constituencies, and Reconstruction constitutionalism. Writing for the Court, Waite scrutinized every single count in the indictment of the defendants drawn up by the United States, and he systematically shattered the implicit justification in Reconstruction constitutionalism of every count, except for those based on the Fifteenth Amendment. He wrapped the entire exercise in a grand statement of "dual citizenship" theory that elaborated what Justice Miller had said in the *Slaughterhouse Cases*. As for the Fifteenth Amendment counts, in principle they could have been good counts under the doctrine announced in *Reese*, but they were not properly written because they did not explicitly mention racial animus. "We may suspect that 'race' was the cause of the hostility"—Waite unctuously referred here to the Colfax massacre—"but it is not so averred."[58]

THE STATUS OF THE POWER TO PROTECT BLACK VOTING RIGHTS

At this point let us step back. Having followed these cases, the reader is surely asking the bottom-line question: What was the ultimate status of the jurisprudence-building effort? The answer, it so happens, is maddeningly ambiguous. But that also tells us all we need to know. By the end of Reconstruction, jurisprudence-building was far, far weaker than it could have been. That the first cycle of jurisprudence-building *ended* in ambiguity is the point. Reconstruction constitutionalism was, after all, unambiguous. Had its full clarity survived both the *Slaughterhouse Cases* and the Court's review of the enforcement statutes, the first reconstruction would have been less vulnerable to final reversal.

The coalition of 1867–1868 did not come away from the judicial process completely empty-handed. Though this is seldom noticed, Justice Bradley's clever if costly strategy to save it via *Cruikshank succeeded*—albeit to a slight extent only. In *Reese* Waite wrote:

> The Fifteenth Amendment . . . prevents the States, or the United States . . . from giving preference . . . to one citizen of the United States over another on account of race . . . Previous to this amendment, there was no constitutional guaranty against this discrimination; now there is. *It follows that the amendment has invested the citizens of the United States with a new constitutional right which is within the protecting power of Congress.* That right is exemption from discrimination in the exercise of the elective franchise on account of race. . . ."[59]

In principle, in this statement, buried in an otherwise devastating opinion, Waite expressly accepted national action as part of the "protecting power of Congress"—which was exactly what had been at stake during this period.[60]

Furthermore, technically speaking, the national elections statutes were *not* constitutionally invalidated by *Cruikshank* and *Reese*. Recall from the discussion in chapter 3 that Congress reenacted these statutes when it issued the Revised Statutes of 1874. When it did, it also provided that prosecutions under the earlier statutes could proceed. Thus the Court merely concluded final prosecutions under laws that really no longer existed. The shell of a nationalist jurisprudence of voting rights and of a regulatory system survived via the revised United States statutes.

Nonetheless, by 1876 the Supreme Court had obviously damaged Reconstruction constitutionalism. In the end the genuinely expansive implications of the Republican-led rights revolution frightened the Court. For one thing, Reconstruction constitutionalism betokened a fundamental change in federalism. As Miller had said in the *Slaughterhouse Cases*, the Court had a duty to preserve "with a steady and even hand, the balance between state and federal power." For another, the fear that the judiciary itself would be over-burdened—and perhaps become highly politicized in the process—played a role for Miller and the majority.

Bradley, in his dissent in the *Slaughterhouse Cases,* rejected this view, noting that "great fears are expressed" concerning whether the kind of nationalist jurisprudence that he (then) espoused would lead to "Congress interfering with the internal affairs of the States . . . abolishing the State governments in everything but name; or else, that it will lead the Federal courts to draw to their cognizance the supervision of State tribunals on every subject of judicial inquiry, on the plea of ascertaining whether the privileges and immunities of citizens have not been abridged." For him such fears were overblown: "[E]ven if the business of the National courts should be increased, Congress could easily supply the remedy by increasing their number and efficiency. . . . The argument from inconvenience ought not to have a very controlling influence in questions of this sort. The National will and National interest are of far greater importance." But Bradley's expansive view of the "National will and National interest" ultimately meant little. A majority of the Court declined to actively protect black electoral inclusion by following what Congress had done.[61]

This chapter has thus added to the previous chapter's discussion of party-building. It has shown that jurisprudence-building ended the same way that party-building ended—flawed and incomplete. A majority of the Court did not reject the new jurisprudence outright. But because the first set of decisions testing Reconstruction jurisprudence-building provided so little support for the basic ideas of this jurisprudence, there was much less political pressure for the coalition's opponents to comply with the new constitutional law that had been devised to protect the rights essential for the new coalition's survival. Consequently, the Court's stance became a serious political problem for the coalition of 1867–1868. Already much weaker than it was when it first formed, it now faced the task of finding effective ways to either bypass the Court or to bring it over to the coalition's side.

Circumvention of the Court occurred openly in 1876, which saw a truly massive federal presence for securing a free ballot. The national electoral-regulatory system was alive and well. Grant deployed infantry in Louisiana and South Carolina. The new attorney general, Alphonso Taft, by means of legal legerdemain, found a way to skirt the Court's recent rulings and provided for 166 deputy marshals in North Carolina, 338 in South Carolina, 745 in Florida, and 840 in Louisiana. His circular to U.S. marshals and U.S. attorneys read, in part, "The laws of the United States are *supreme*, and so consequently is the action of officials of the United States in enforcing them. There is . . . no officer of any state whom you may not by summons embody in your own posse." That was about as full-throated an expression of Reconstruction constitutionalism as one could find.[62]

But these were stopgap measures. To be sure, Taft's actions underscored the truth that the Supreme Court's holdings were (and are) not self-enforcing. But flouting the Court would not work over the long haul.

In key respects, then, we have the answer to Frederick Douglass's question for the 1876 Republican national convention: "What does it all amount to . . . ?" The answer is: quite a lot, indeed, more than most educated Americans probably realize. But the limited extent of both party- and jurisprudence-building left the first reconstruction vulnerable to rollback. The institutional vulnerabilities of the great coalition of 1867–1868 pointed, in fact, to African American disenfranchisement.[63]

Chapter Six

The Vortex of Racial Disenfranchisement

Previous chapters have shown that the coalition of 1867–1868 never became well institutionalized. Party-building was plagued by weaknesses that were inherent in making eleven brand-new state parties on a crash basis. Jurisprudence-building fared badly, too. Between 1873 and 1876, a majority on the Supreme Court deflated the expansive constitutional vision of the Reconstruction Amendments and the elections statutes that had quickly developed within Congress, the presidency, and the federal circuit courts.

Despite the consequent vulnerability of African American electoral inclusion, its collapse was far from becoming a complete certainty. During Benjamin Harrison's administration (1889–1893), Republicans devised a strong measure, the Federal Elections Bill of 1890, that would have protected federal elections from fraud. It built on new Supreme Court doctrine developed in the late 1870s and the 1880s. If the 1890 bill had been enacted and implemented, it would likely have committed Republicans to doing something about the process of disenfranchisement then just getting under way in Florida, Mississippi, and Tennessee. But this belated strategy of coalitional renewal failed in early 1891. The first flat-out southern filibuster in American history killed it. The 1890 elections bill was the first substantive legislation in the history of the U.S. Congress that was supported by the House, the president, and a Senate majority *and* was killed by a southern filibuster.[1]

Following this filibuster came Republican losses in the 1892 elections. Democrats gained unified control of national government during the second Cleveland administration in 1893. This was the first instance of unified Democratic control since the Buchanan administration before the Civil War. They used it to destroy the national government's capacities for enforcing the Fourteenth and Fifteenth Amendments. All of the vulnerabilities analyzed in previous chapters then came home to roost. This chapter treats what happened as a result.

In comparative perspective, black disenfranchisement is a unique outcome. No major social group in Western political history other than African Americans ever entered the electorate of an established democracy en masse and then was more or less democratically pushed out, without accompanying change in the basic forms of the political regime. With the disintegration of the first reconstruction's legacies, a second reconstruction of southern electoral politics became necessary for America to again become the kind of biracial democracy that the United States pioneered after the Civil War.[2]

Consider table 6.1, which communicates the brute fact that disenfranchisement pushed huge portions of the population in the southern states, and huge areas of these states, out beyond the boundaries and ordinary protections of liberal democratic politics. Furthermore, disenfranchisement affected nonsouthern jurisdictions. Two non-Confederate states, Oklahoma and Delaware, also acquired (or already had) institutional obstacles.

Table 6.1 Racial Demography of the South in 1900

State	Percentage of State Population Black	Percentage of Counties Majority Black
Alabama	45	33
Arkansas	28	20
Delaware	17	0
Florida	44	27
Georgia	47	49
Louisiana	47	52
Mississippi	58	51
North Carolina	33	18
South Carolina	58	75
Tennessee	24	3
Texas	20	5
Virginia	36	36

Source: Frederick D. Wright, "The History of Black Political Participation to 1965," in *Blacks in Southern Politics*, ed. Laurence W. Moreland, Robert P. Steed, and Tod A. Baker (New York: Praeger, 1987), pp. 9–30, tables 1.1 and 1.3, pp. 10, 15.

Eventually, in thirteen of forty-eight states, *27 percent of the Union,* African Americans were disenfranchised or strongly discouraged from voting by legal devices.[3]

I illuminate this stunning development by covering several topics. First, I discuss the making of disenfranchisement. Second, I trace northern Republican acceptance of disenfranchisement. Third, I discuss other groups that might have stood by African Americans and how they did (or could) not make common cause with their fellow citizens. Fourth, I trace the direct impact on African Americans. Finally, I draw in broad strokes the metamorphosis the polity underwent in response.

THE MAKING OF DISENFRANCHISEMENT

James Wigg, a black delegate from Beaufort to the 1895 South Carolina constitutional convention, which disenfranchised black Carolinians, warned his white colleagues that the Constitution forbade them from doing what they had gathered to do. "The two amendments to the Federal Constitution stand like the two angels at the gate of Paradise with flaming swords, barring the way. They warn you in tones of thunder that you must make no change in the suffrage."[4] Wigg's vivid admonition points to the first thing to know about disenfranchisement: the disenfranchisers thought that they would, in fact, get past the "flaming swords" of the Reconstruction Amendments. They hoped to generate formal-legal mechanisms that could *appear* constitutional.

That the Reconstruction Amendments could be legally circumvented was well known. During the drafting of the Fifteenth Amendment, several Republicans—southern Republicans in particular—warned their party colleagues that they ought to textually inhibit any future efforts at apparently color-blind property and educational restrictions on suffrage. They urged their colleagues to draft language that could prevent such tactics. But eventually Republicans agreed that the important thing was to write an amendment that could be ratified as quickly as possible, and the version of the Fifteenth Amendment that is now in the Constitution appeared to fill that bill.[5]

Consequently, the second thing to point out about legal disenfranchisement is that it took place in one of two basic ways. Tennessee, for instance, legislated a poll tax based on an enabling provision of its constitution. The 1890 Mississippi constitutional convention, the first of several such gatherings, modeled the other way: several other former Confederate states built on what was known as the "Mississippi Plan." Disenfranchisement in each state was thus either primarily a *statutory* or primarily a *constitutional* process.

Third, disenfranchisement proceeded by means of learning and imitation. States have been called the American polity's "laboratories of democracy." In this instance, the lab technicians put their energies toward figuring out how to make American democracy as white as possible. Leading lawyers and journalists traveled to other states to testify at or to observe another state's process. Though never recognized as such in the political science literature, disenfranchisement in fact resembled the kind of "policy diffusion" for which the states are often noted by political scientists.[6]

Fourth, however, disenfranchisement was not *fully* legal. It required considerable trickery and intimidation on the part of its backers. A little-known contrasting instance, the state of Maryland, sheds light on such subtle (and sometimes far from subtle) corruption of the democratic process. In the former Union slave state of Maryland, Democrats also attempted to disenfranchise blacks. After a period of Republican rule from 1896 to 1900, Democrats regained control of state government on a white supremacy platform (a response to the increase in black office-holding that took place in Baltimore and elsewhere while Republicans were in charge). Maryland Democrats then followed the southern disenfranchisement plan in every detail, first introducing a ballot law that would cut black voting in heavily black counties, then making three separate attempts (the Poe Amendment of 1905, the Straus Amendment of 1908–1909, and the Digges Amendment of 1910–1911) to amend the state constitution so as to disenfranchise black Marylanders.

Each of these efforts was defeated in a referendum, however. Maryland Democrats evidently differed from their southern counterparts in one crucial respect. They did not commit massive electoral fraud. Nor did they strategically foster race riots that would scare enough black voters away from the polls to carry the day, as was the case in North Carolina. In short, Maryland Democrats played, or were somehow forced to play, reasonably fairly.[7]

In the former Confederacy matters were different. The disenfranchisers displayed *some* obedience to democratic norms, but it was strategic and partial. They evidently recognized that any general acceptance of disenfranchisement required a show of democracy. Consider the way the Florida Democratic party accomplished its goal. It launched a coherent, extended program of institutional change by first calling for a constitutional convention in 1885. The Pensacola convention then authorized reapportionment. A new, reapportioned legislature, with a much weaker Republican opposition, then established personal registration. When implemented, it diminished black and Republican voting for the 1889 legislature. Capping off what was, in effect, an open conspiracy against blacks, the 1889 Florida legislature was free to adopt a poll tax and other restrictive measures.[8]

The following year, Mississippi's legislature provided for the election of a constitutional convention, which gathered after a very low turnout and did its work—but then simply declared the new constitution to be in force. In Louisiana the constitutional convention was elected—but on the basis of timed voting that allowed three minutes to mark a four-foot-long ballot. In addition, the enabling statute held that the result of the convention would become active once the convention adjourned. In Virginia, the disenfranchisers reneged on a promise to permit popular ratification.

In South Carolina and Alabama, disenfranchisers did go through a formally democratic sequence of (1) holding a referendum on whether there should be a new constitution, (2) electing a constitutional convention, and (3) ratifying the new constitution. Also, in Arkansas, Florida, Georgia, North Carolina, Tennessee, and Texas, the electorate approved constitutional amendments after the legislature submitted them for approval. But legislatures generally rigged the constitutional phase of the process by changing voter registration requirements, thus constructing electorates *likely* to approve the contemplated constitutional change. By means of such legerdemain, the rules of the electoral game gradually changed throughout the region. Just as it took new laws to bring black southerners into electoral politics, it took new rules and laws to finally push African American voters all the way out. This was how disenfranchisement developed into a vast, interlocked institutional program.

Table 6.2 offers a synoptic overview of the new regime's elements according to time, place, and type of formal-legal device used to achieve disenfranchisement. It shows, in particular, two quite well-known devices: the poll tax and the literacy test. (Two familiar devices, the grandfather clause and the white primary, are treated in chapter 8.) For most of the nineteenth century the poll tax had little relation to voting; in most places it was a minor per capita tax collected, often, to support public education. In its new guise, it required voters to pay money before they could vote. If a voter got behind, arrears going back one, two, three or more years, depending on the state, had to be paid up.

The reason why the poll tax appealed so much to white supremacists may not be entirely obvious at this late date. The amount of money involved does not seem large. But the poll tax was actually a lot of money. Consider the percentage of annual income of a southern black farm laborer taken by a $1.00 poll tax and compare it to a contemporary equivalent payment. One dollar was about one-half of 1 percent of a black farm laborer's annual income circa 1900, assuming he worked every day of the year. That translates into about $135.00 in 2001 dollars.[9]

Table 6.2 Emergence of the Southern Electoral-Regulatory System for Disenfranchising African Americans

Year	Poll Tax Enactment	Poll Tax Ratification or Year Put into Force	Literacy Test Enactment	Literacy Test Ratification	State Residence Requirement Enacted	County Residence Requirement Enacted	City/Town Residence Requirement Enacted	Precinct or Ward Residence Requirement Enacted
1885	Florida							
1889		Florida						
1890	Mississippi	Mississippi	Mississippi		Mississippi	Mississippi	Mississippi	Mississippi
1892	Arkansas			Mississippi				
1893		Arkansas*						
1895	S. Carolina	S. Carolina	S. Carolina	S. Carolina	S. Carolina	S. Carolina		S. Carolina
1898	Louisiana	Louisiana	Louisiana	Louisiana	Louisiana	Louisiana		
1900	N. Carolina							
1901	Alabama	Alabama	Alabama					
1902	Virginia	Alabama N. Carolina Texas Virginia	Virginia	North Carolina Virginia	North Carolina Virginia	Virginia	Virginia	North Carolina Virginia
1903				Alabama				
1907	Arkansas							
1908		Arkansas Georgia	Georgia	Georgia	Georgia			

Sources: J. Morgan Kousser, *The Shaping of Southern Politics: Suffrage Restriction and the Establishment of the One-Party South, 1880–1910* (New Haven: Yale University Press, 1974), table 9.1; Alexander Keyssar, *The Right to Vote: The Contested History of Democracy in the United States* (New York: Basic/Perseus, 2000), tables A.13–A.14; Jerrold G. Rusk, *A Statistical History of the American Electorate* (Washington D.C.: CQ, 2001), tables 2-8 to 2-11; tables 2-15 to 2-17.

*U.S. Circuit Court invalidates Arkansas poll tax in 1905, requiring reenactment (1907) and ratification (1908).

As for the literacy test, it often contained three separate tests, requiring voter registrants to demonstrate to the satisfaction of local registrars their capacity to read, to write, and to properly interpret a public document, usually a passage from the state constitution (or, ironically, the U.S. Constitution). It obviously required local administration—and thus opened the way for discretionary abuse, which was, in fact, the whole point.[10] In a similar vein were new residence requirements, also shown in table 6.2. These were covert literacy tests because they required competent record-keeping by voters in order to prove residence.

In this connection another, less commonly recognized piece of the system came into play: the Australian ballot, that is, the publicly printed, publicly provided ballot, marked by voters in secret within a polling booth. The spread of the Australian ballot created an administrative context that gave an enormous advantage to the disenfranchisers. This type of ballot is generally considered a major advance in democratic practice because it prevented fraud and removed social pressures, both crude and subtle, from voters. Yet for two reasons the Australian ballot was, in the former Confederacy, less of an advance in democratic practice than is commonly thought.[11]

First, a printed ballot was by itself a literacy test. About half of black adult males in the former Confederacy circa 1900 were illiterate. The Australian ballot was therefore expected to suppress black voting. Second, party officials performing the central function of the balloting process—physically handing out the ballots—were no longer directly linked to black voters. Previously, parties printed and provided the ballots, subject to certain regulations concerning size and paper weight. Under the party-strip balloting system, parties colored the ballots, stamped them in special ways, or even perfumed them. Any voter, literate or not, could easily vote for his choice. But with the Australian system, Republican and third-party workers could no longer show up with their own ballots on election day.[12] Small wonder, then, that in his 1896 report the Arkansas secretary of state noted with satisfaction that the Australian ballot's introduction in Arkansas had "minimized the pernicious and demoralizing effects of the Fifteenth Amendment to the United States Constitution."[13]

Table 6.2 communicates, in short, the profusion and interplay of formal-legal change. A corollary of that theme is the role of institutional complementarity. The operation of each part of the emerging regime was all the stronger because it worked in a larger context of other measures.

Now that key aspects of disenfranchisement's various forms have been covered, we can turn to a vital issue. Once the intermeshed rules were put in place, was it actually these rules that finally pushed blacks out? Or did the rules simply formalize black defeat?[14]

Consider table 6.3, which offers a bird's-eye view of the process, a snapshot devised by Kent Redding and David James. They generated ecological regression estimates for two presidential elections that can be reasonably assigned to the post-Reconstruction, pre-disenfranchisement period (1880 and 1892) and for two that can be assigned to the disenfranchisement period (1900 and 1912.) The 1900 estimate ranks as something of a mid-point. The estimate for 1912 captures the full effect of disenfranchisement, after the dust had settled.[15]

Notice that between 1892 and 1900 there were, quite strikingly, sizeable drops in black voting in four states—Alabama, North Carolina, Texas, and Virginia. Yet these states had not moved toward legal disenfranchisement. Extralegal factors such as fraud, violence, and intimidation probably were at work. In other words, the *diminution* of black voting strength could be and was accomplished extralegally, if Democrats were willing, as discussed in chapter 3. Yet diminution was not enough for the southern disenfranchisers. They wanted complete and lasting exclusion of African Americans from American life altogether. The development of a new electoral-legal regime was essential for that purpose.

Table 6.3 The Extent of Black Disenfranchisement

State	Redding-James Ecological Regression Estimates of Black Voter Turnout in Presidential Elections, 1880–1912 (percentage)			
	1880	1892	1900	1912
Alabama	55	55	21	2
Arkansas	57	36	**12**	3
Florida	84	**14**	7	2
Georgia	42	**33**	7	2
Louisiana	44	30	**4**	1
Mississippi	45	*1*	**4**	2
North Carolina	81	63	44	1
South Carolina	77	17	**4**	2
Tennessee	70	**31**	**14**	1
Texas	59	53	32	2
Virginia	59†	58	38	2

Source: Kent Redding and David R. James, "Estimating Levels and Modeling Determinants of Black and White Voter Turnout in the South: 1880 to 1912," *Historical Methods* 34.4 (2001): 141–158.

Notes: Cell entries in boldface denote *poll tax* in effect. Cell entries in bold italics denote *both a poll tax and a literacy test* in effect.

†This figure is not in boldface because the poll tax in effect in 1880 was repealed in 1881 and had been in effect only since 1879.

Note that table 6.3 internally indexes the relative effects of the two most consequential rules changes: literacy tests and poll taxes (on which more below). The cell entries that are in boldface display turnout with a poll tax alone. Cell entries that are in boldface italics display turnout with both a poll tax and a literacy test. Both types of cell entries suggest that the rules changes were, by themselves, very significant in stopping blacks from voting.

Other things besides new elections laws were certainly at work in sharply depressing voter turnout. Nonetheless, Kent Redding's recent multivariate test of several factors discovers huge effects for the elections rules, even as it finds statistical significance for other variables, including growing one-party dominance, an increase in white and black tenancy rates, the emergence of manufacturing wage labor, and indirect measures of racial intimidation. For instance, for the presidential elections of 1880, 1892, 1900, and 1912, Redding finds that an increase of about .2 to .5 percent in the percentage of county residents who are black will decrease county-level black voter turnout by 1 percent, suggesting the role of intimidation. These are large effects. Likewise, decreases in the extent of party competition of approximately the same magnitude will depress county-level black voter turnout by 1 percent in his model—again, large effects. In contrast, the adoption of the poll tax depresses black voter turnout by 4–18 percent for three of these four elections, and the adoption of the literacy test depresses county-level black voter turnout by approximately 17 percent in 1892, 15 percent in 1900, and 3 percent in 1912. These are mammoth effects.[16]

Table 6.3 is thus consistent with Redding's multivariate findings. One sees that early in the process of disenfranchisement the rule changes had enormous effects, as suggested by the remarkable cases of Florida and Mississippi. Likewise, midway through the overall process, rule changes had large effects, as the case of Louisiana suggests. Finally, states that had not moved toward formal disenfranchisement before 1900 still had quite significant black turnout. But that changed drastically after disenfranchising rules were set up in these states.

The reasons why these rules decreased turnout had to do with the enormous and paralyzing increase in the cost to an individual of voting. The new system required from voters genuine material sacrifice, psychological stamina in the face of official screening processes, and disciplined preparation for registration in the form of recordkeeping. A voter, white or black, also had to know when and where to pay a poll tax. Often payment was required many months in advance, which also increased a voter's recordkeeping tasks because voters were required to present poll-tax receipts on election day. In multiplying voters' tasks, the new system threatened black voters with the certainty of humiliation, or in some cases abuse and assault, in a public setting by minor public officials empowered to declare the registration faulty.

Although the conceptualization was paternalistic, a federal judge grasped the point of the emerging system in his 1894 decision striking down South Carolina's especially difficult personal registration system: "Our most intelligent voters would dread this ordeal. . . . With what crushing force, then, must it strike the weaker race." In 1929 a Brookings Institution political scientist described the way the new "ordeal" worked in Mississippi. "In Mississippi a Negro attorney, graduate of Harvard, determined to register and vote, and applied to the precinct registrar, a blacksmith. The registrar asked him to give an interpretation of the due process clause, which he did with a considerable amount of learning and ability. When the Negro attorney had completed his 'interpretation,' the registrar ruled that it was not 'reasonable' and refused to register him." The registrar in fact was faithful to the intention expressed at the 1890 Mississippi constitutional convention by the delegate who proclaimed that "if every Negro in Mississippi was a graduate of Harvard . . . he would not be as well fitted to . . . suffrage as the Anglo-Saxon farm laborer."[17]

The new rules worked, in other words. That was an *intended* outcome. The disenfranchisers realized that violence and intimidation were ultimately inefficient. Such tactics did not make for a long-term solution. They would always have a tendency to inflame northern opinion. Furthermore, violence and intimidation *without* a demobilizing structure of election rules could never really crush black resistance.[18] For the disenfranchisers, a far better solution was the new electoral-legal system that they created. With a formal-legal system, maximum exclusion was possible. That is why they bothered to devise it.

Furthermore, if the new regime was condoned by other actors in the political system as legitimate, it became structurally protected by American federalism. Once disenfranchisement was excused, only another revolution from above—one that again recast American federalism—could uproot the institutional bases of disenfranchisement. Only another large-scale coalition of black and white voters would create the momentum for that.

One last point about the South's new panoply of rules is in order. Looking at tables 6.2 and 6.3, one can discern a key feature of the process that is obvious once it is pointed out: that it was indeed a *process*. The tables show how much time it took to erect disenfranchisement as a system. Its backers could not and did not do all of what they wanted right away. It took effort and political organization for them to exploit democratic processes for the purpose of building new institutional foundations for white supremacy. This matters for the simple reason that there was plenty of time to stop disenfranchisement if anyone cared to. But one vital force capable of stopping it, the northern wing of the Republican Party, chose not to. The following section deals with what it did and did not do, and why.

SIGNALS FROM A CHANGED NORTHERN WING

The northern branch of the Republican Party was confronted with two issues when it regained dominance over national politics by the late 1890s. It had to figure out what to do about the rise of state-level disenfranchisement. There was also the matter of whether to respond to Democrats' cancellation of federal elections law, which took place during Democrats' brief moment of unified control of national government during the first half of the second Cleveland administration.

During the Fifty-third Congress, 1893–1895, Democrats repealed the sections of the Enforcement Act of May 31, 1870 (the first statute to enforce the Fifteenth Amendment) that proscribed poll taxes and literacy tests and that criminalized election fraud and interference by state and local election officials with the voting rights of those voting in national elections. A House report recommending such annulment demanded that "every trace of reconstruction measures be wiped from the books." Democrats also rescinded the statutes establishing federal supervisory control of national elections.[19]

In the face of the crisis in the former Confederacy and the statutory sweep at the national level, what did northern Republicans do when they regained control during the McKinley administration? Nothing. The great coalition of 1867–1868 finally flew apart. One side simply defected. More precisely, the northern wing split into two factions. One was willing to live with the changes, the other wished to mount some sort of protest and response. But, as soon will become clear, the latter faction was quite weak.

This schism can be traced to 1872, with the rise of the liberal Republicans, who sharply criticized Reconstruction. There had always been friction within the northern wing about the costs of sustaining the coalition of 1867–1868. Now the division erupted again. The difference this time was a powerful shift in the strength of the two factions. The turning point in northern Republicans' attitudes was particularly obvious in 1898, when Democrats in North Carolina mounted a fierce, race-baiting challenge to a Populist-Republican fusion that then governed North Carolina. On election day, the South's lone Republican governor, Daniel Russell, faced grave danger. Russell was nearly lynched by a Democratic mob that stopped his train; he escaped death only because he managed to find a good hiding place on the train. In

Raleigh another mob menaced his family as it cowered in the governor's mansion.

A few days later Democrats staged a savage armed revolt against the Republican city government of Wilmington, North Carolina, shattering a prosperous black community in the process. The governor ordered in the militia, but state units simply joined the Democratic paramilitary forces. Following these events the Democratic-controlled legislature set about planning the disenfranchisement of black voters. From North Carolina came a plea for federal help by African American leaders, among them U.S. Representative George White of the state's second congressional district. In the U.S. Senate, North Carolina's two fusionists, Marion Butler and Jeter Pritchard, also spoke up.[20] But the McKinley administration did—and said—nothing. Instead it signaled to the South's white Democrats that it would not intervene. Shortly after the Wilmington coup, the president visited Atlanta for an ostentatious show of "sectional reconciliation."

Much disenfranchisement occurred, perhaps not coincidentally, during and after the McKinley administration. North Carolina is a case in point. Also, between 1898 and 1900 Louisiana constitutionally disenfranchised blacks. Alabama came next, in 1901, followed by Virginia. Texas established a poll tax in 1902. Georgia established a literacy test, a property test, and an understanding test in 1908.

Signs of coalitional break-up continued during the Roosevelt administration. Accounts of Theodore Roosevelt's presidency (1901–1909) emphasize his unwillingness to do anything about disenfranchisement. Indeed, Roosevelt privately regarded Reconstruction as "folly."[21]

Some congressional Republicans did challenge Roosevelt's stance. After introduction of several bills calling for congressional investigation into the prospect of Fourteenth Amendment enforcement, which would have penalized southern Democrats for their new disenfranchisement rules, the 1904 Republican platform proposed such a move. In December 1904, Senator Thomas Platt of New York introduced a bill implementing the platform plank.[22] But Roosevelt opposed the platform plank on the ground that it would weaken his presidency and divide the party. A detail that speaks volumes comes from Senator Henry Cabot Lodge, who introduced an elections bill in 1890 as a member of the House. He wrote Roosevelt to convey his agreement: "The proposition is an absolutely righteous one, but your objection and mine still holds that it is demanding something in all probability we shall not have the nerve to do." The president responded: "I am sorry they put in the suffrage plank, just as I should deprecate a plank endorsing your so-called 'force bill,' which I believed in thoroughly as a matter of abstract right, but which there is no use in backing when we are perfectly certain to be unable to carry it through." The bill died in committee.[23]

It was Roosevelt's successor who made the Republican Party's new policy regarding black voting rights explicit, however. In his inaugural address, March 4, 1909, President William Howard Taft said that he looked "forward with hope to increasing the already good feeling between the South and the other sections of the country." Pronouncing as a failure the effort by "Northerners who sympathized with the negro . . . to give him the suffrage," the president noted that the Fifteenth Amendment was nonetheless still in the Constitution and that states needed to meet "the test of compliance with that amendment." He added, "This is a great protection to the Negro." But immediately before saying this, Taft also praised "the tendency of southern legislation" to be in compliance with the amendment. Here the disenfranchisers' conscious strategy of writing textually color-blind rules paid off. He said, "it is clear to all that the domination of an ignorant, irresponsible element can be prevented by *constitutional laws* which shall exclude from voting both negroes and whites not having education or other qualifications thought to be necessary for a proper electorate." The president thus explicitly accepted the claim that the southern poll tax and literacy test were valid conditions of good government. In doing that, he made his peace with black disenfranchisement.[24]

Constitutionally speaking, there was, to be sure, a small—very small—victory for African Americans shortly after Taft's inauguration. For some time political pressure for direct election of U.S. senators had been building. In 1910, William Borah, Republican of Idaho, led the introduction in the Senate of an amendment whose wording provided both for the direct election of senators *and* for exclusive state regulation of the process. State regulation was the price of southern Democratic support, and Borah accepted it, denouncing colleagues who opposed the idea as hypocrites on the subject of black suffrage. But a few leading Senate Republicans—Chauncey Depew, Henry Cabot Lodge, and George Sutherland—insisted on retaining federal control of Senate elections. They would sacrifice neither the Fifteenth Amendment nor article 1, section 4. (In the process they could also obstruct the direct election movement.) Depew offered his own version of an amendment for direct election of senators. Reviving much of the design of the Federal Elections Bill of 1890, it required that voter qualifications be uniform everywhere in the United States and that Congress be granted authority to federally register voters and supervise congressional elections.[25]

Eventually, compromise language emerged in the Senate that mooted the division between federal-control and state-regulation senators. This was the cryptic article 1, section 2 language today emblazoned on the Seventeenth Amendment, which stipulates that federal voting qualifications equal those for the larger house in each state legislature. For a year, however, the House would not go along, insisting on the "southern" version or nothing. Finally it relented in mid-May 1912 and accepted the ambiguous version now in the Constitution.[26]

In short, a part of the GOP symbolically defeated a bold southern attempt to embed protection for black disenfranchisement in the Constitution itself. This was the good news. The bad news was that the GOP also participated in pulling out the remaining Reconstruction devices for actually enforcing the Fourteenth and Fifteenth Amendments.

During the administrations of Presidents Roosevelt and Taft (1905–1909; 1909–1913), there were *additional* repeals of Reconstruction-era elections statutes—principally the Ku Klux Act of April 20, 1871, but also the elements of the first Enforcement Act that Democrats left unrepealed during the Fifty-third Congress. By 1911, only a minor provision or two and two criminal conspiracy sections originally in the Ku Klux Act were left. The northern wing of the Republican Party thus played a major role in finishing what the Democrats began during the second Cleveland administration.[27]

Why did the northern wing evolve into a dominant faction willing to accept disenfranchisement, more or less unchecked by an impotent minority of conscience Republicans? One vital factor was an exchange of coalition partners. The black-white North-South coalition of 1867–1868 was supplanted by a new *white-white* North-West coalition. In a sense, the northern wing was compensated for the loss of its investment in southern party-building. The enormous and rapid growth of the Republican Party in the late 1890s outside the South substituted for lost black voters at the margin.

The strength of the Republican Party outside the South after 1896 became quite pronounced. In 1904, in their presidential platform, Republicans announced that their party had entered a "period of complete supremacy." They were correct. Republicans eventually enjoyed unified government for fourteen straight years, across seven Congresses, from the Fifty-fifth through the Sixty-first. This became the longest such stretch of unified government up to that point in U.S. history, longer than the previous record (six Congresses), which had been set during the Jackson–Van Buren era (1829–1841), and later to be matched only during the Roosevelt era (1933–1947). Across these seven Congresses Republicans enjoyed an average of twenty-six U.S. representatives more than the number needed for control of the House, and in the Senate their average "surplus" was about eleven senators more than needed to control the chamber.[28]

At the national level, Republicans were firmly in the saddle. Had they wanted to react to events in the South, they could have, just as they had in the Fifty-first Congress. Another elections bill, or simply the enforcement of the federal voting rights laws that still survived from the Democratic repealer of 1894–1895, or even a high-profile congressional investigation—any or all of these measures would have politically reinforced the opponents of suffrage restriction on the ground. But for northern Republicans they were politically unnecessary.

Recall that before the unified government of the McKinley administration, Republicans had achieved unified government only twice, from 1881 to 1883 and from 1889 to 1891. In both of these cases, Republican investment in southern politics had paid critical dividends. Indeed, it was essential for unified government in the first case: no involvement with the Virginia Readjusters, no control of the Senate, which had proved crucial to the passage of the trade legislation benefiting the Republican party in the North.

Between 1896 and 1908, however, the average Republican percentage of the electoral vote (not the popular vote) was 65.7 percent, and from the Fifty-fifth Congress to the Sixtieth, the party averaged 56.9 percent of House seats and 60.7 percent of Senate seats. The southern contribution to Republican House and Senate strength during this time was significant only from 1897 to 1899, during the Republican-Populist fusion in North Carolina. Thus all of the party's considerable strength lay outside the South.[29]

The main reasons for these nonsouthern sources of Republican strength were nonsouthern electoral shifts that began in the massive swing toward Republicans in the 1894 off-year national elections. The change in the partisan balance in the electorate was concentrated in a pro-Republican direction outside the former Confederacy and the Border States. Paul Kleppner has closely analyzed several aspects of the electoral metamorphosis. One telling aspect that he developed, the Republican Party's greater success in gaining unified control of nonsouthern state governments, is visible in table 6.4. It suggests the strong buildup of pro-Republican electoral change. Particularly striking is the jump in the "Unified Republican" category between 1892 and 1894. Part B of the table is helpful for understanding another important change visible in part A: the 25 percent drop in split control in favor of unified Republican control.

Kleppner also calculated "competitiveness categories" for nonsouthern counties for presidential elections from 1896 to 1908. These are visible in table 6.5. For the first three of the four elections one sees a Republican Party growing stronger in the North at the expense of the Democratic Party. Even in

Table 6.4 Growing Republican Control of State Governments

A. Control in Nonsouthern States (percentage)

Year	Unified Democratic Control	Unified Republican Control	Split Control
1892	30.3	24.2	45.4
1894	6.0	57.4	36.3
1896	6.0	60.6	27.2

B. The Trend Toward Unified Control, 1894–1896

Became Democratic		Became Split		Became Republican			No Change		
R → D	Split → D	D → Split	R → Split	D → R	Split →R	D → D	R → R	Split → Split
0	0	3.0	9.1	9.1	30.3	6.1	33.3	9.1

Source: Paul Kleppner, *Continuity and Change in Electoral Politics, 1893–1928* (Westport: Greenwood, 1987), pp. 32–33.

1908 the Republican Party is comfortably dominating the Democratic Party outside the South.

The precise extent to which it mattered that the Republican Party grew stronger outside the South is communicated by table 6.6, which shows the proportion of individuals from a given region elected to the House or the Senate for the period or the percentage of votes in the Electoral College for the region for the period. What the information presented for the former Confederacy suggests is very clear: so long as Republicans dominated Democrats outside the South, they did not need black southerners' votes to stand a good chance of gaining unified control of national government.

Table 6.5 The Republican Party's Dominance Outside the South

Nonsouthern Counties Falling into Range	1896	1900	1904	1908
20.0%+ Democratic	15.7	7.5	3.4	5.8
10–19.9% D	8.9	7.1	3.2	6.4
5–9.9% D	6.4	5.8	2.9	5.5
0–4.9% D	7.2	6.4	4.1	8.2
0–4.9% Republican	8.2	8.0	3.4	8.5
5–9.9% R	7.4	9.5	5.7	10.1
10–19.9% R	15.1	16.8	11.5	20.7
20.0%+ R	31.1	39.7	65.8	34.9

Source: Paul Kleppner, *Continuity and Change in Electoral Politics, 1893–1928* (New York: Greenwood, 1987), p. 41.

Table 6.6 Shifts in Regional Bases of National Politics

Region	Presidential Electoral Vote			House			Senate		
	1876 to 1892–94	1896 to 1908–10	% Change	1876 to 1892–94	1896 to 1908–10	% Change	1876 to 1892–94	1896 to 1908–10	% Change
Former Confederacy	26	25	–4	19	13	–31	28	24	–14
Northeast	29	26	–10	31	29	–6	23	20	–13
Midwest	21	19	–9	26	27	+3	13	12	–7
Border	11	10	–9	11	12	+9	13	12	–7
West	13	19	+46	13	19	+46	25	33	+32

Source: Charles Stewart III, "Lessons from the Post–Civil War Era," in Gary W. Cox and Samuel Kernell, *The Politics of Divided Government* (Boulder: Westview, 1991), pp. 208–212.

A particularly striking shift shown in table 6.6, furthermore, is the increased importance of western states. Relative to the other regions, the West was the "winner" in the shifts that occurred. Although Democrats gained temporary strength in the West in 1896, they lost ground thereafter. Thus Republicans' long-standing hopes for this region were eventually realized. The same kind of political insecurity that had pushed the Republicans during and after the Civil War to bring West Virginia, Nebraska, Nevada, and Colorado into the Union *also* motivated a western policy in the 1880s. As a senator, Benjamin Harrison led the party in continuing a western statehood policy. At the outset of his presidency, six new states, the largest number ever to be admitted in any presidency and several pro-Republican, joined the Union: North and South Dakota, Montana, Washington, Idaho, and Wyoming.[30]

By developing a western policy, the Republicans partly compensated themselves for their troubles in the former Confederacy. As far as I know, no member of the national Republican Party *intended* the Western policy as insurance against a potential collapse of Republican or fusionist strength in the former Confederacy. But in the end the western policy had that effect. Of the fifty-six members of the House elected from these states from 1898 to 1908, fifty-one, or 91 percent, ran and won as Republicans. Of the thirty-six men who went to the U.S. Senate from these states during this period, twenty-eight, or 78 percent, were Republicans.[31]

In short, owing to electoral growth in both old and new states, Republicans no longer needed black southerners' votes. Yet in 1867 they had needed black voters to block Andrew Johnson's party-building scheme. Black voters had helped cement the Republicans' nation-building vision and consolidated the Civil War's revolutionary potential for American political development. Also, in the 1870s and to a lesser extent the 1880s, Republicans had protected black voting rights in order to protect the party. In 1890–91, Republicans had contemplated the launch, via the Federal Elections Bill, of a new system of federal electoral regulation based in the federal courts. They had done so to correct for fraudulent losses in southern House races by Republicans and third-party candidates, with hopes for allowing House Republicans to organize slim majorities for chamber control. But, despite having served as critical players in the Republican Party's maturation into a stable, national organization, African Americans in the South became expendable.

Senator William Chandler (R-N.H.), for many years the Republican Party's chief southern strategist, grasped and denounced this rather bitter irony. In a speech delivered in Fairfield, Vermont, on August 19, 1903, to celebrate the completion of a monument to President Chester Arthur at his birthplace, Chandler asked what his old boss would do "if he lived in this beginning of a new century when the condition of the colored race . . . is being radically and wickedly changed." Chandler sketched the subversion of each of the Reconstruction Amendments in considerable detail, noting disenfranchisement, lynching, and the "virtual enslavement of colored laborers." He then got to the heart of the betrayal—the fact that though the Republican Party's strength for decades had depended on black southerners they now were thrown overboard:

> [T]he wrongs to which I am calling attention are real and terrifying, and they will not down because it is disagreeable for the politicians of both parties to face the uncomfortable situation. Because the negro is black the Republican party has existed and practically controlled the government for forty-seven years with great power, prominence, and profit to the greatest Americans of the last half century. It will not serve for the Republican party now to find fault because the negro is black, and to abandon him to subjugation, peonage, and barbarous slaughter without trial because his oppressors are southern whites.

But, of course, it did serve.[32]

THE WITHDRAWAL OF ALLIES

A public reversal as enormous as disenfranchisement profoundly and radically isolated African Americans. Once the Republican Party abandoned them in about 1898, they faced a context in which both national parties effectively agreed to allow southern Democrats a free hand in structuring American race relations. Who else besides the northern Republicans might have stood by African Americans? The answer is: several actors could have, but they would not or could not step into the breach.

First among these other actors was the Supreme Court. Here the record is startling. The new tacit bipartisan consensus seems to have cued it to adapt the Constitution to full white supremacy. Considering in 1895 a petition in equity from a black South Carolinian, the Court held that it could not block South Carolina's establishment of a disenfranchising constitution in *Mills v. Green*.[33] Then, in 1898, the Court washed its hands of the petition of Henry Williams, sentenced to death by an all-white Mississippi jury. Williams held that Mississippi denied him the equal protection of the law on racial grounds because it restricted the jury pool to white voters. The Court, however, sent Williams to his maker. It accepted Mississippi's argument that its electoral provisions were facially neutral and complied with the Reconstruction Amendments in *Williams v. Mississippi*.[34]

In 1903, the Court treated disenfranchisement far more frankly and openly—but still refused to act. Justice Oliver Wendell Holmes, writing for the Court in a case from Alabama, *Giles v. Harris,* cogently summarized the racially discriminatory mechanisms of Alabama's disenfranchising constitution of 1901. He held, however, that the Court could not order any relief: "The bill imports that the great mass of the white population intends to keep blacks from voting. To meet such an intent something more than ordering the plaintiff's name to be inscribed upon the lists . . . will be needed. If the conspiracy and the intent exist, a name on a piece of paper will not defeat them." Holmes and the Court accepted Giles's characterization of disenfranchisement in Alabama as a public white "conspiracy" against blacks. But courts, the reasoning went, were just no good for stopping such conspiracies.[35]

Ten days later, the Court handed down its decision in *James v. Bowman,* a case brought by the United States in connection with the bribing of black voters in Kentucky to keep them from voting in a congressional election.[36] The Court dismissed the case for want of jurisdiction under the remaining federal elections statutes, incidentally ignoring the decisions of the 1880s, for example, *Ex parte Yarborough*.

In 1904, in *Giles v. Teasley,* the Court again rebuffed Jackson Giles, a federal postal employee in Montgomery, Alabama, and leader of a small group known as the Colored Men's Suffrage Association of Alabama. Unbeknownst to him, his representation was secretly financed by Booker T. Washington, the great (though deliberately enigmatic) political entrepreneur. Giles engineered a test of the Alabama constitution by the Alabama Supreme Court. His lawyer stated, "The record clearly shows that nothing but a Federal question was therein presented to the highest court of Alabama . . . and that the judgment rendered by the Supreme Court of Alabama could not have been rendered without deciding the Federal question."[37] But with only Justice John Marshall Harlan in dissent, the Court flatly disagreed. No federal question was at stake because the Alabama Supreme Court had correctly framed the issue, ruling that if the Alabama Constitution and implementing statutes were invalid, then Giles still had his federal rights and therefore had not suffered an injury. If, on the other hand, the Alabama Constitution was valid, then Giles likewise had no business before a federal court.

Finally, in *Jones v. Montague,* handed down two months after *Giles,* the Court dismissed a challenge to Virginia's disenfranchising constitution. Jones's lawyer, an old Readjuster Republican, pointed out the obvious: that the injury of disenfranchisement was continuing and that the petition was broad in its scope. The Court instead followed *Mills v. Green*. Judicial equity, it held, could correct political wrongs only prospectively, not retrospectively.[38]

New legal challenges to disenfranchisement did come after Oklahoma entered the Union in 1907. In 1910, the state's legislature revised the 1907 constitution to insert both a good understanding clause (meant to block black voting) and a grandfather clause (meant to exempt white voters from the good understanding provision). The 1910 amendment held that "[n]o person shall be registered . . . or be allowed to vote . . . unless he be able to read and write any section of the Constitution of the state of Oklahoma; but no person who was, on January 1, 1866, or any time prior thereto, entitled to vote under any form of government . . . and no lineal descendant of such person, shall be denied the right to register and vote because of his inability to so read and write sections of such Constitution."[39]

Oklahoma's exemption device recapitulated an earlier strategy to divide the Populists. Disenfranchisers wanted to obstruct the electoral participation of poor whites as well as end black voting. During the heyday of Populism white farmers had shown themselves as all too likely to organize along class, not racial, lines. To get the requisite white votes for poll taxes and literacy tests, the disenfranchisers promised these exemptions. These laws accorded special treatment to whites. Military service during the Civil War or descent from someone who had served would warrant registry without a literacy test. The disenfranchisers hedged their bets, though, by setting forth only brief periods for white voters to use the exemptions.

The U.S. Supreme Court blocked the implementation of Oklahoma's provision in *Guinn and Beal v. United States* in 1915. It invalidated "old soldier" and "grandfather" exemptions from literacy tests. In addition to Oklahoma, several other states—Alabama, Georgia, Louisiana, North Carolina, and Virginia—were also affected by *Guinn*. The Court thus partly deracialized elections rules.[40]

Still, *Guinn* carried an absurd implication, namely, that the only electoral rules in the South that violated the Constitution were these devices. Oklahoma quickly revealed *Guinn's* triviality by passing a law automatically registering everyone qualified to vote in 1914, when the grandfather clause was in effect. New registrants were required to register in a special twelve-day period or forfeit the franchise. Oklahoma thus disenfranchised black Oklahomans by setting an impossible condition for their acquisition of registered status.[41]

The Supreme Court's unwillingness to protect African Americans' voting rights was a measure of how extremely politically isolated African Americans were. The Readjuster lawyer who litigated *Jones v. Montague* captured this point when he wrote that "Congress doesn't want to do anything, the Supreme Court doesn't want to do anything, and so it goes. The Supreme Court passes the question along to Congress, and Congress politely passes it along to the Supreme Court. It is a game of 'After you, my dear Alphonse,' and it is amusing to everybody, except the Negro."[42]

Yet another indication of political isolation was the course of women's suffrage politics. The National American Woman Suffrage Association (NAWSA), the main women's suffrage organization by the end of the nineteenth century, severed its cause from any defense of black voting rights. It perpetuated a split between the causes of black and women's suffrage that dated to the initial moment of coalition formation in the late 1860s. In bringing in black men, Republicans had built a "winning coalition" that did not require women to save the party. As the abolitionist Wendell Phillips had put it: "I say, One question at a time. This hour belongs to the negro." To be sure, one side of the women's suffrage movement worked to maintain good relations with such figures as Frederick Douglass, an early, steadfast advocate of women's suffrage. Another wing, though, understood the failure of female suffrage as a betrayal.[43]

But many female leaders went further than refusing to lift a finger to protest black disenfranchisement. They *exploited* it. Hoping to leverage the process, they regularly appeared in the 1890s at the southern conventions and legislative sessions that redesigned voting laws. They asked, in effect, whether it was not high time to also seriously consider female enfranchisement as long as the franchise was being reformed so markedly. Marjorie Spruill writes that "an organized southern suffrage movement with strong national support came into existence at the time that it did because many leading suffragists—southern and northern—believed the South's so-called negro problem might be the key to female enfranchisement."[44]

And, once the Nineteenth Amendment was ratified and adopted in 1920, NAWSA's successors, the League of Women Voters and the National Women's Party, did nothing to aid "colored women's leagues." These sprouted up in southern cities to direct a black female voter registration drive for the 1920 elections. Despite appeals for help, white officials of the League of Women Voters and National Women's Party stayed quiet as southern elections officials obstructed black female voter registration. No white female activist appears to have said a word when a black schoolteacher led about one thousand black women in 1926 to register to vote at the Jefferson County courthouse in Birmingham, Alabama, only to find herself arrested for vagrancy.[45]

Yet another source of African American political isolation was the demobilization of poor white southerners. Disenfranchisement was not only about

pushing African Americans out; it was also in considerable part about managing political conflict among whites. Hence the device that was simultaneously
racially discriminatory and inclusive of whites, namely, the well-known
grandfather clause, a heritage requirement for voting that whites alone could
meet.

White southerners were hardly united along racialist lines in the 1890s.
In several of the states the disenfranchisers did not in fact trust the electorate to formally ratify what they had done. The architects of constitutional
revision in Louisiana, Mississippi, and Virginia refused to submit their new
constitutions for final voter approval. The Democrats who pushed for
disenfranchisement had to jury-rig enough white racial unity to get the
statutes, constitutions, and amendments on the books. In the 1890s, biracial
Republican-Populist electoral coalitions threatened the ascendancy of regular
white Democrats. Large fractions of the white yeoman farmer electorate in
most of the southern states suspected that the proposals for a new formal-
legal context of elections would actually keep them out, too, and were part of
a larger battle between the "classes" and the "masses," to use Populist termi-
nology. If they were careless, they might be suckered into approving their
own political demobilization.

Hence the grandfather clause, a device first dreamed up in South Carolina
by the Ben Tillman wing of the Democratic Party for splitting the white opposition to black disenfranchisement in South Carolina. Offering it was symbolic politics. Big change was afoot, after all. To win, disenfranchisers needed
to find a way to reassure just enough whites that whites generally would be
exempt from the exclusionary purposes of the new legal order. The extrusion
of blacks from electoral politics would be coupled with a guarantee of inclusion for the poor and unlettered whites whose participation would otherwise
also be blocked by poll taxes and literacy tests. Such provisions in the letter of
the law as a "good understanding" or "good character" clause also hinted that
local registrars would be sure to take care of white registrants.

Yet the white Populists were right to be suspicious. After disenfranchisement, hundreds of thousands of ordinary, illiterate and semiliterate whites
found the new electoral-regulatory environment of printed ballots, literacy
tests, and poll taxes enormously intimidating. In effect, the Populists had
their base chopped away from underneath their feet. An organization and a
movement that had argued against white supremacy, holding that it was
nothing but a smokescreen blocking consideration of more fundamental
questions of social justice, soon died out.[46]

To summarize, three forces or institutions besides the northern wing of
the Republican Party could have stood by black southerners. But both the

Supreme Court and the women's suffrage movement instead added to the political quarantine of black Americans. The Populists, for their part, were targets of disenfranchisement who in the end did not dodge the fate that the disenfranchisers intended for them.

Costs to African Americans

Isolated, with no one in white America willing or able to help, black southerners soon were made to pay very dearly for their disenfranchisement. It coincided with, and also fueled, an increase in lynching. A formalization of segregation ensued. Finally, educational opportunities were taken from black southerners.

Lynching

Space precludes a full discussion of the way disenfranchisement affected the rise of lynching, but some sense of the connections between these phenomena can be offered. Ida Wells-Barnett, the great antilynching crusader, once characterized the cost of votelessness: "With no sacredness of the ballot there can be no sacredness of human life itself. . . . The mob says, 'This people has no vote with which to punish us . . . therefore we indulge our brutal instincts.'"[47] Public figures thus generally blamed the victims. President Theodore Roosevelt issued a letter in 1903, for instance, condemning lynching—but he also sternly advised blacks to stop tolerating black criminality and to keep their own house in order.[48]

The national rate of lynching dropped as the disenfranchisement process rolled to a finish. But as late as 1922 a lynching occurred, on average, *every week*. Lynchings indeed became legitimate popular entertainment for whites, with railroads running excursions to a "lynching bee," hotels advertising rooms with a good view, photographers printing postcards for spectators, children being let out of school, and body parts actually offered for sale. The North had its boardwalks; the South had its lynchings. Prominent national, state, and local white politicians from the South proudly noted their direct involvement.[49]

Segregation

Segregation, too, was abetted by disenfranchisement and the political friendlessness of African Americans. It came in many forms. Two of its most damaging were labor and residential segregation. They of course emerged in the

South before disenfranchisement. But they both became further entrenched between 1889 and 1908.

During downturns in the business cycle, labor segregation meant informal restriction of both the private labor market and the governmental safety net, such as it was, to whites. Blacks were therefore disproportionately jobless, indeed highly vulnerable to convict leasing and forced labor. Custom, law, and powerlessness combined to disconnect black men and women from the chance to have a skill-enhancing career.[50] During booms, certain job categories in the private sector were informally restricted by white-led trade unions and local "opinion" to whites only. These were better paid and more likely to impart skills. Labor segregation also allocated public employment, for example, police and public works, to whites. At the federal level, there was formal segregation in U.S. government workplaces and restriction of the better-paid civil service jobs to whites.

Residential segregation meant all-black and all-white neighborhoods. Black neighborhoods received markedly inferior provision of public services of all kinds (sanitation, crime control, infrastructure, electrification, and so on). Residential segregation began as an informal practice. After disenfranchisement, it became codified in municipal law, in and outside the former Confederacy. Though the Supreme Court outlawed official municipal legal segregation early in the twentieth century, residential segregation persisted everywhere in the United States because of a combination of informal market practice and racial covenanting in private sales.[51]

The weakness of political representation of black interests within Congress and within the Electoral College fostered a segregationist climate throughout the entire United States. The rest of the nation differed, however, from formerly Confederate jurisdictions in one vital respect: below the Mason-Dixon line, labor and residential segregation were part of a *general* regulation of all interracial contact.[52] White-dominated states and localities devised such constant reminders of white supremacy as separate drinking fountains, public parks, warehouses for school texts, waiting rooms, railroad cars, and seating on streetcars and other forms of municipal transportation. State and local governments, and companies licensed by them for public conveyance, insulted African Americans by keeping "colored" public facilities extremely shabby. White clerks and ticket takers were notorious for their abusive demeanor toward blacks.[53]

Public Education

Finally, disenfranchisement established severe educational injustice. Here a stillborn reform initiative has a poignant relevance. From 1870 to 1890 the

Republican Party promoted and several times approved in Congress but ultimately failed to enact a program of federal aid to southern common schools.
In 1890 Congress did revise the Civil War–era land-grant system to provide
support for black land-grant college education. But aid to primary and secondary education would have been even more helpful.[54]

Within this void in federal aid, the region's whites robbed black southerners of a better future. After disenfranchisement, county school boards in
black majority areas took the state funds allocated per capita and used them
largely for the white children. States and counties restricted state expenditures on education for blacks to elementary education and held off on high
school education. States paid black teachers much less than white teachers.
Counties operated black schools for fewer days than white schools. States
and counties provided markedly inferior plant and facilities.[55]

White plantation lords were delighted by all of this. As a Louisiana newspaper stated in 1889, "God never intended the negro to be educated." After
disenfranchisement, planter representatives in state legislatures became leading players in lobbying for separate and highly unequal education.[56]

In summary, disenfranchisement was like the locomotive of a train.
Attached to it were the rise of lynching into nothing less than popular entertainment for whites, the rise of de jure segregation, and a sharp diminution in
educational opportunities.

NATIONAL EFFECTS OF LACK OF REPRESENTATION

Having gained a sense of the way disenfranchisement deepened the separation of African Americans from the body politic, we should also assess the
national effects. The almost total absence of political representation in
Congress and in the executive branch paved the way for profound statutory
and institutional changes.

A vital feature of the situation created by disenfranchisement was the
nonenforcement of the second section of the Fourteenth Amendment.
Section 2 reduces congressional representation for states that deny the suffrage on racial grounds. Had it been enforced, disenfranchisement would
have cost its backers politically. But they never paid the price specified in the
Constitution. That itself was a major if silent constitutional change, a tacit,
extraconstitutional amendment of the Fourteenth Amendment.

This nonenforcement did two important things to American politics.
First, because Democrats had an Electoral College bonus that they would not
otherwise have had, Woodrow Wilson was able to best Charles Evans Hughes
in the 1912 presidential election. Because Wilson was a Democrat and occu-

pied the White House when Democrats also controlled Congress for the first time since the early 1890s, his election altered race relations. Wilson authorized a truly thorough program of segregating the federal civil service. Federal territory—the District of Columbia—came to resemble a southern state capital such as Montgomery or Jackson.[57]

The same nonenforcement that made Wilson's election possible also gave the Democratic South about twenty-five extra seats in Congress for each decade between 1903 and 1953. Their added presence, in turn, altered about 15 percent of roll call outcomes in the House during this period.[58]

In addition, the elimination of two-party competition in southern House districts and states meant that southern members of the House and Senate could expect long careers (unless they were unseated in Democratic white primaries). Not surprisingly, they supported organizing congressional committee appointments according to seniority. As Senator "Pitchfork" Ben Tillman wrote president-elect Woodrow Wilson in January 1913, "My long service here . . . entitles me to select from the committees of which I am a member a chairmanship."[59] A strict seniority norm, that is, a right to a chairmanship (when one's party controlled the chamber) based on the longest continuous service on a given committee, took hold by about 1920. Southerners thus became disproportionately represented within the Democratic-run leadership structures of the House and Senate.

There was therefore little or no representation of black interests in Congress. Instead, white supremacy was dominant. That skew influenced the design of government housing credit, income assistance, and other forms of social subsidy. Strong, activist regulatory government began during the Wilson administration and continued during and after the New Deal. But because African Americans lacked power within Congress, and because no blacks with decisionmaking influence were in the cabinet, many statutes—and many administrative rules in agencies monitored by Congress, such as the adoption of redlining by federal housing credit agencies—tended to neglect the interests of most African Americans.

For instance, when Congress and the president devised the old-age income insurance component of the Social Security program in 1935, they did not include agricultural workers or domestics, who made up much of the black participation in the labor force. Unemployment was then disproportionately concentrated among blacks, distancing another large fraction of African American adults from program enrollment. The point is not that statutory design was consciously racist. Rather, statutory design reflected who was represented—and who was not.[60]

All in all, the vortex of disenfranchisement did much to entrench white supremacy in the United States. Lacking robust political representation, black Americans became vulnerable not merely to Jim Crow, a de jure phenomenon, but also to a strengthening of de facto color lines in the nation as a whole. Color lines grew brighter in public settings (for example, the District of Columbia, the federal civil service, the dining rooms of Congress), in national institutions (for example, the armed forces), and in national policies (for example, agricultural credit and federal work relief in the 1930s). Such public segregation in turn legitimated efforts by northern party machines with white ethnic clienteles to establish color lines in public employment, schooling, and housing. The stage was set, in other words, for the ghettos that greeted black migrants from the South. By the 1930s and 1940s color lines were so much a feature of national life that Gunnar Myrdal aptly characterized their existence as "an American dilemma."[61]

CONCLUSION

This chapter has traced the more or less total breakup of the coalition of 1867–1868. It underscored the exceptional nature of America's development as a political democracy—no other democracy in the world has ever enfranchised a large group and then disenfranchised it. It also showed that the second reconstruction has indeed been a *second* reconstruction of the South's electoral politics—and of America as a whole. Assembling the grand coalition of 1867–1868 generated new institutions; the effort to smash it also generated new institutions.

We saw how northern Republicans finally abandoned black southerners. The electoral changes of the mid-1890s north of the Mason-Dixon line gave the GOP a vastly expanded, largely white voter base. The black part of the party's coalition was now left to its own devices, and new white voters replaced black southerners at the margin. In addition, we saw how disenfranchisement generated deep political isolation for African Americans, placing them in a dangerous political and social borderland that was racked by hideous private violence. Finally, we saw that law and institutions generated and reinforced deep material and educational disadvantage.

A second reconstruction of southern electoral politics became necessary in order for America to again become a biracial democracy. When did that second reconstruction start? How did it develop? Why did it evolve in the ways that it did? The next several chapters address these questions.

Chapter Seven

Heralding the Second Reconstruction: The Coalition of 1948

Coalition-making and coalition protection drove the second reconstruction and its dynamics as they had driven the first. Party politicians faced political dangers; they met them by bringing in new voters. But rather than a national party *collectively* agreeing to bring in new voters, the most important member of a divided national party, the president, responded to his electoral insecurity and brought one wing of his party along. Three Democratic presidents—Harry Truman, John F. Kennedy, and Lyndon Baines Johnson—conspicuously embraced the rights concerns of African Americans. Each needed alliances with black voting blocs. Truman and Johnson, former vice presidents unexpectedly thrust into office, needed help for a second term. Kennedy's initial motive was simply to buy himself black cooperation with pressing foreign policy needs. All three, in the end, became racially progressive presidents. All thereby confronted the southern wing of their own party.[1]

This chapter traces how, in the late 1940s, the Democratic Party's New Deal faction built a small-scale successor to the coalition of 1867–1868. Franklin D. Roosevelt's death in 1945 suddenly thrust Vice President Harry Truman into the Oval Office. Anticipating a loss in the 1948 presidential election, much as congressional Republicans feared a terrible reversal led by Andrew Johnson in 1868, he sought to stay in the national political game by emphatically reaching out to African American voters. President Harry Truman became the first openly civil rights–oriented Democratic president.

Responding to this new opportunity in American politics, blacks in the North voted for Truman. In the South, in the kingdom of voter disenfranchisement, a regional Democratic replacement for the coalition of 1867–1868 began to emerge. In 1944, the Supreme Court (in a decision described below) had announced that the putatively private primary elections of southern Democratic parties were in fact public processes and could not be racially discriminatory. Black southerners began to participate in voter registration drives and sought to vote in Democratic party primaries. Truman's northern mobilization accelerated this process. His stance openly acknowledged the importance of black voters for the Democratic Party.

But this was only the beginning. Southern Democrats inevitably resisted the emerging alliance between New Deal Democrats and black voters and leaders. "Dixiecrats," to employ a journalist's pithy neologism, stormed out of the Democratic Party in mid-1948 to set up their own States' Rights Party. Their bolting from the party underscored both the extent to which the Democratic base now differed and the Dixiecrats' concerns about that change. *Full* black electoral reinclusion would require a long interfactional battle within the Democratic Party.

Still, the Dixiecrats were in trouble. Not only had the presidency shifted against them, but a major institutional support of Dixiecratic power, the white primary, died between 1944 and 1952. In a white primary, according to a rule issued by a local or state Democratic party, electoral participation in Democratic party primaries was restricted to white voters. But, as already noted, the Supreme Court turned against this institution. Black southerners therefore gained a jurisprudential foothold for beginning to rebuild the black southern electorate. Furthermore, unlike the first reconstruction, an entire national political party did not stand in the way—only half a party, squeezed by insurgency from below and reform from above.

Black southerners stood to inherit mass party organizations that were among the oldest in the world. With their implementation of new Supreme Court doctrine, black southerners who were grouped within the southern state conferences and local chapters of the National Association for the Advancement of Colored People (NAACP) and other associations built what I call a "party-in-waiting," one that heralded the great changes that occurred when the second reconstruction reached its apogee. In states and locales throughout the South, the kernels of a new biracial Democratic party-in-waiting had an associational existence, parallel and connected to the regular Democratic Party. Their principals laid claim to rightful membership in a party from which they were excluded. Like a shadow cabinet, they were ready to come in and take over.[2]

In short, processes that played out sequentially and rapidly during the first reconstruction played out in tandem and slowly during much of the second. After Congress enacted military reconstruction of the South, coalition-making gave way to forceful party- and jurisprudence-building. Coalition came first, *then* came efforts to institutionally protect voting rights. In contrast, and particularly in the decades before passage of the Voting Rights Act of 1965, similar processes took place interactively and more gradually, but often as violently as during the first reconstruction.

This chapter shows how the basic conditions for such change came into being. As we shall see, black migration to the North between 1910 and 1950 created a structural possibility. If and when an insecure presidential candidate came onto the historical stage, black voters would be physically located in places where they could vote freely.

The coalition of 1948 had a "latent" period, in other words, prior to its manifest phase. During the New Deal, a warmer relationship between African Americans and the Democratic Party emerged because Roosevelt refused to stigmatize, insult, or ignore African Americans. Although he was not a figure who depended for his own political success on black votes, Roosevelt (with his spouse Eleanor) nonetheless became a patron of black hopes, welcoming a large number of black leaders and professionals into a wide array of new bureaucratic positions. Also, the New Deal provided considerable material relief to African Americans. Roosevelt effectively laid a foundation for an open coalition.

This chapter sketches black migration from the former Confederacy, the emergence of a significant black electorate in northern states, and this electorate's adoption of the Democratic Party despite the highly racialized limits of the New Deal. It segues to the role of the white primary in protecting Dixiecrat power within the Democratic Party, introducing the twin topics of interfactional conflict within the party and the long erosion of the Dixiecrats' institutional power. The chapter then turns to the coalition of 1948 itself and traces Truman's electoral insecurity as well as his exceptional outreach. From there it moves to the southern effects of that outreach.

The impact of Truman's actions in the South was in a sense deeply curious. Truman's efforts, after all, targeted *northern,* not southern, black voters. But his executive orders, his support for a presidential civil rights commission (the precursor of today's U.S. Commission on Civil Rights), his public statements, and his arduous, close-up campaign style, which included a deeply symbolic visit to Harlem, encouraged NAACP mobilization in the South.

As the NAACP implemented the Supreme Court's invalidation of the white primary, its strategy was favored by Truman's coalition-making.

A cross-regional, biracial coalition *within the Democratic Party* came into view—for the first time in American political development.

OUT-MIGRATION FROM THE EX-CONFEDERACY

In what is known as the great migration, from 1900 to 1910, net out-migration of black southerners totaled 175,000. From 1910 to 1920, net out-migration jumped to 450,000. From 1920 to 1930 the figure was 750,000. About half that many blacks went North from 1930 to 1940. The total for the period was nearly two million. Increased levels of demand in nonsouthern labor markets during and after World War I clearly fueled it. World War I suddenly shut off unskilled white immigrant labor; restrictions on immigration in the 1920s kept the spigot shut.[3]

Despite its later political significance, there was certainly no intent to switch parties behind these waves of out-migration. Economists and sociologists have convincingly emphasized that the migration was largely a job search, a case of factor mobility in action. Nonetheless, the exodus inevitably signified political hope as well. Out-migration was a reprise of the age-old flight to basic civil freedom. Black migration invigorated the citizen right of mobility. It bordered on civil disobedience. Crowds jumped onto trains, giving the slip to the police. Families fled at night, evading plantation overseers.

A black editor and lawyer, W. T. Andrews, once bluntly told an audience at the 1917 South Carolina Race Relations Conference, held at the height of the great migration, that "the chief causes of the Negro unrest" were "the destruction of his political privileges . . . no protection of life, liberty, and property under law; Jim Crow cars; residential and labor segregation; no educational facilities worthy of the name." His point was clear: America's political counterrevolution made life for black southerners oppressive—and it was small wonder that they went north.[4]

Out-migration eventually had significant electoral consequences. It brought a huge fraction of black southerners back into electoral politics—in a new location. African Americans were still only a quite small percentage of the nonsouthern electorate, taken as a whole. But within certain local jurisdictions they increasingly formed electoral majorities. A quick "case sketch" will highlight what was possible as a result of the migrants' partial reincorporation into electoral politics.[5]

Between 1900 and 1930, the percentage of African American voters in the Chicago electorate, concentrated in the "Black Belt" on the city's South Side, more or less tripled, rising from 2.9 percent to 8.7 percent. In a pioneering study of black urban politics, Chicago-style, Harold Gosnell, a University of

Chicago political scientist, found a participatory political subculture, one in which both "Colored women from the South" and "their men folks" shared "an intense interest in politics." Black voters were players in a biracial Republican party machine.[6]

In 1928, the Black Belt elected a black congressman, former alderman Oscar DePriest, himself a migrant to Chicago. Self-made, the son of ex-slaves, wealthy and politically skillful, he represented Illinois' First Congressional District, a black-majority district. DePriest symbolically desegregated Congress, serving three consecutive terms of office. He was the first African American elected to Congress since George White of North Carolina had retired in 1901. He was a "race man," speaking to North and South, mailing thousands of copies of the Declaration of Independence and the Constitution to black citizens and standing up for racial fairness within the House.[7]

Migration created new possibilities in national party politics, in short. Furthermore, because African Americans settled in "big" states with big cities, they became likely to affect *presidential* electoral politics. The Electoral College now advantaged black voters.[8]

MIGRATION INTO THE DEMOCRATIC PARTY

Enter the New Deal. Roosevelt never made an open effort to address disenfranchisement. Indeed, he committed himself to postponing any attempt at such a program. As he said one afternoon to a New Deal official who suddenly asked him, in the intimacy of a train compartment, about black voting rights, "Politics is the art of the possible. At the present time the passage of a law abolishing the poll tax is impossible." Interviewed by the historian Nancy Weiss in 1977, James Roosevelt, the president's eldest son and for several years his secretary in the White House, "could not remember 'a single discussion' among family members or friends 'with respect to . . . voting rights in the South.' "[9]

Also, large parts of the New Deal were internally redlined. The Social Security program happened to exempt job categories that were disproportionately filled by African Americans. The Wagner Act did not cover agricultural workers. The implementation of the Agricultural Adjustment Act allowed white landlords to throw black tenants off the land, thus achieving the production control that netted them federal checks. The Home Owners Loan Corporation, established in 1933, and its successor agency, the Federal Housing Administration, borrowed the discriminatory policies of local real estate boards and of the National Association of Real Estate Boards in the allocation of federal housing credit.[10]

Even when New Deal programs benefited blacks, their administration often perpetuated racial stigma and isolation. The Public Works Administration, for instance, reshaped Atlanta's racial geography by razing the homes of about five thousand black citizens. "Slum clearance" was advertised in PWA literature as a benefit to the ladies of white Atlanta society, who could proceed downtown to their shops on Peachtree Street without encountering "blight." Blacks received public housing in Atlanta. But the housing sites were carefully situated to assure the prospect of residential segregation.[11]

When all is said and done, though, there was a significant political migration of African Americans into the Democratic Party, and for good reasons. In 1936 most blacks who were eligible to vote followed the advice that the black editor of the *Pittsburgh Courier,* Robert Vann, first offered in Cleveland on September 11, 1932, in a speech that made him famous: "Instead of encouraging Negro support, the Republican party, for the past twelve years, has discouraged Negro support . . . I see millions of Negroes turning the picture of Lincoln to the wall. This year I see Negroes voting a Democratic ticket."[12] By 1936 most of the "turning" had taken place. Probably the great majority of African Americans supported FDR and the New Deal by then. A striking indicator of the change was Oscar DePriest's loss of his congressional seat from Chicago in 1934 to Arthur Mitchell, a black Republican who switched his party affiliation to become America's first black Democratic member of the House of Representatives.

Table 7.1 shows voting in predominantly black areas of several northern cities. In these cities there were also sharp increases in black voter turnout from 1932 to 1940—an average of 37 percent for Chicago, Cleveland, Detroit, and New York. Data for black voting outside these areas are not available, so it is not possible to know whether and to what extent these data are representative. But massive qualitative evidence of black support for FDR and the New Deal suggests that these data are, in fact, representative.[13]

Very little is known, of course, about the partisanship of black southerners. Nonetheless, Karen Ferguson's recent study of Atlanta's large community of African American professionals—college professors, social workers, economists, and city planners—and their response to the New Deal plainly suggests strong affective attachment to the New Deal. Hortense Powdermaker's classic ethnography of Indianola, Mississippi, published in 1939, similarly pictured black southerners as closet New Deal Democrats: "The author's impression is that, if they had had the chance, most Negroes during the period of this survey would have voted the Democratic ticket because of their faith in the New Deal." When Ralph Bunche interviewed black southern farm

Table 7.1 Voting for and against FDR in Black Districts of Selected Northern Cities

City	1932		1936			1940		
	Republican (%)	Democratic (%)	Republican (%)	Democratic (%)	Increase for FDR (in percentage terms, not percentage points)	Republican (%)	Democratic (%)	Increase for FDR (in percentage terms, not percentage points)
Chicago	75.1	21.0	50.5	48.8	132	47.3	52.2	7
Cincinnati	71.2	28.8	34.9	65.1	126	33.1	66.9	2.8
Cleveland	82.0	17.3	38.2	60.5	250	35.3	64.7	7
Detroit	67.0	31.0	31.8	66.2	114	24.3	74.8	13
New York	46.0	50.8	17.1	81.3	60	18.6	81.0	No change
Philadelphia	70.5	26.7	29.7	68.7	157	31.2	68.4	No change
Pittsburgh	56.2	41.3	23.5	74.7	81	17.6	82.0	10

Source: Nancy J. Weiss, *Farewell to the Party of Lincoln: Black Politics in the Age of FDR* (Princeton: Princeton University Press, 1983), tables IX.2, XII.2. Weiss defined "black district" as based on census tracts in which the population of the tract became 90% African American by 1940.

laborers as part of Gunnar Myrdal's research team, he found them strongly pro-Roosevelt. As one said, "Negroes should vote for Mister Roosevelt if they can. . . . They've talked more politics since Mister Roosevelt been in than ever before."[14]

In terms of access to decision makers, symbolism, electoral mobilization, and group benefits, the New Deal was racially inclusive. In 1936 and 1940 the Democratic Party's campaign apparatus appealed to black northern voters, establishing its own black voter mobilization bureau, sponsoring radio addresses, making a movie to be shown outside the South, mailing out literature, and working with churches and civic groups to contact black voters. The president, when he dedicated a new chemistry building at Howard University the week before the 1936 election, offered the first presidential radio address ever specifically directed at black voters. Finally, the New Deal provided material benefits on a scale literally unmatched by the federal government since the operation of the Freedmen's Bureau. For instance, 20 percent of the Works Progress Administration workforce was African American. Seven million dollars' worth of new schools were built by the Public Works Administration in the South. Such large benefits symbolized a new if partial inclusion. They were inadequate to meet blacks' needs. But in absolute and historical terms they were enormous outlays on behalf of black Americans.[15]

By the late 1930s, then, African Americans attached themselves to the Democratic Party's forward-looking social democratic faction. New Deal Democrats acquired both an electorally active northern black constituency and, down South, an "electorate-in-waiting." The elements of a new coalition were coming together. At this juncture, yet another piece fell into place: a Supreme Court decision, *Smith v. Allwright*, invalidating the white primary.

THE WHITE PRIMARY

The white primary was a vital institutional foundation of southern white supremacy by the late 1930s, having first emerged in the late 1870s as a way to generate white voter solidarity among Democrats before the general election. The idea was to prevent defections to new white independent candidacies that began to emerge (such as those of the Readjusters and the Populists). It then served to regularize factional conflict within the Democratic parties. The white primary's significance as a barrier to southern *blacks'* participation thus emerged after the South's transformation into a one-party system.[16] South Carolina formally established its statewide primary system in 1896. Arkansas followed in 1897, Georgia in 1898, Florida and Tennessee in 1901,

Alabama and Mississippi in 1902, Texas in 1904, Virginia in 1904, Louisiana in 1906, and North Carolina in 1915.[17]

The white primary then unexpectedly faced a little-known crisis as the primary caught on more generally. Diffusion brought the new institution within the purview of federal regulation. Did the United States have a basis for regulating the direct primary in federal elections to the House and Senate under article 1, section 4? This question lurked in the background as the direct primary became a significant feature of American politics. If the United States had such regulatory authority, then the Fourteenth and Fifteenth Amendments could be made to apply to the federal primary. In turn, if federal primaries for national elections to the House (and, after ratification of the Seventeenth Amendment, the Senate) could not be reserved for whites, then there was a gaping hole in the wall of legal disenfranchisement.[18]

In 1921, however, the white primary was inadvertently protected by the Supreme Court. When it ruled in *Newberry v. United States,* a case that tested a federal corrupt election practices statute, that "there is no Federal interest in a primary," southern Democrats saw instantly how this decision reinforced formal disenfranchisement of blacks. In Texas, indeed, the legislature felt free to settle a factional dispute within the Texas Democratic Party by passing the White Primary Law, which stated that "[i]n no event shall a Negro be eligible to participate in a Democratic primary election."[19]

The white primary's value to conservative southern Democrats subsequently grew for two reasons. Although the Supreme Court ruled in *Breedlove v. Suttles* that Georgia's poll tax, then sixty years old, was constitutional, the poll tax and the literacy test no longer guaranteed the electoral and policy results preferred by white conservatives.[20] As the real value of the nominal tax decreased, and as literacy increased, these devices could no longer reliably restrict the electorate to a white oligarchy, particularly in towns and cities. Three states in fact abolished the poll tax—Florida (1936), Louisiana (1934), and North Carolina (1920).

But as long as the white Democratic primary remained constitutional, conservative southern Democrats had the whip hand in the South and therefore remained a force to be reckoned with in the national Democratic Party. The Democratic primary *was* the general election in Dixie. In the period from 1940 to 1943, the total vote registered in five Deep South states in the general gubernatorial elections was a mere 24 percent, on average, of the total vote registered in the Democratic gubernatorial primary or runoff immediately preceding the general election. In four Peripheral South states (Arkansas, Florida, Texas, and Virginia), the total general election vote on average was 63 percent of the preceding Democratic primary vote.[21]

The white primary, in the one-party context, also advantaged Dixiecrats because it was the only way for any racial liberal within the party to gain office. There was no other party to jump to. In order to have careers, then, all Democratic politicians in the South inevitably agreed on keeping black voters away from the election that mattered most in the South's one-party system—the white primary.[22]

Smith v. Allwright

Enter the Supreme Court.[23] As we have seen, the Court's stance toward the white primary was a condition of conservative power. If it ever killed the white primary, the institutionally privileged position of white supremacist politicians would erode.

It did, in fact, attack the white primary. The *Smith v. Allwright* decision stunned the South.[24] On April 3, 1944, the Supreme Court responded favorably to a voting rights suit brought from Texas by the NAACP, holding that the Texas Democratic Party's racial restriction on voting in its primaries was "in violation of the Fifteenth Amendment." This decision was all the more disquieting because conservative white southerners considered themselves safe. The Court had announced only nine years earlier, in *Grovey v. Townsend*, that the white primary was constitutional.[25] But by 1944 three different groups of actors coalesced against the white primary: the NAACP's new and sophisticated legal team, Justice Department lawyers holding a new commission to battle for civil rights, and justices of the Supreme Court determined to deepen the Court's civil liberties and civil rights orientation.

Why and How the Supreme Court Turned against the White Primary

In the years between World War I and the New Deal the Court gradually adopted more libertarian attitudes, particularly with regard to the First Amendment, in reviewing cases from states and localities. From there it was but a short step, conceptually, to the Court's beginning to "incorporate" other parts of the Bill of Rights via the Fourteenth Amendment—that is, gradually creating a textually based national rights jurisprudence that would apply not only to the federal government but also to state and local governments. It was also just a short step toward a focus on the robustness and fairness of political processes. Taking that step, in turn, would necessarily reframe the meaning of restrictions on the right to vote.

As is well known, the articulation of these various evolving themes culminated in a famous footnote in an otherwise mundane case involving the 1923

Fluid Milk Act. In footnote 4 to the decision in *United States v. Carolene Products,* Justice Harlan Fiske Stone speculated that state and local legislation that seemed "within a specific prohibition of the Constitution, such as those of the first ten amendments," would receive closer scrutiny from the Court than ordinary "rational basis" commercial regulation (such as the Fluid Milk Act). Significantly, he added that "[i]t is unnecessary to consider now whether legislation which restricts those political processes which can ordinarily be expected to bring about repeal of undesirable legislation, is to be subjected to more exacting scrutiny under the general prohibitions of the Fourteenth Amendment than are most other types of legislation." His first example of types of political process–restricting legislation that might eventually "be subjected to more exacting scrutiny" was legislation concerning the "right to vote." Here he cited two earlier Texas white primary cases, *Nixon v. Herndon* and *Nixon v. Condon.*[26]

In short, the changed intellectual climate of the Supreme Court foretold an attack on the white primary. However, the danger was at first imperceptible. The Court, after all, had unanimously supported the white primary in *Grovey v. Townsend* three years earlier. In doing so it had retreated from precisely the holdings that Stone cited favorably in *Carolene Products.*

In *Nixon v. Herndon* the Court found that Texas's 1923 White Primary Law was an "obvious infringement" of the Fourteenth Amendment's equal protection clause. The Texas legislature then instructed the executive committee of the Texas Democratic Party to set its own rules, but the resulting rule still violated the Fourteenth Amendment (in *Nixon v. Condon*) because the state had instructed the party to issue rules, and the party acted as the state's agent.

But at its convention in May 1932, without formal instruction from the legislature about any of its rules, the Texas Democratic Party unilaterally forbade black participation in its primaries. The state attorney general issued an opinion that the rule was valid. Responding to a test of the rule, the Texas Supreme Court agreed with the attorney general. Responding to a legal challenge carried out by a black Houston businessman, Richard Grovey, the entire Supreme Court supported Justice Owen Roberts's acceptance (in his *per curiam* opinion) of the Texas Supreme Court's claim that the white primary was now essentially a private matter, beyond public regulation.[27]

Government Lawyers

The new ideas percolating on the Court needed some form of expression. Enter the Justice Department. The New Deal realignment created a different, more activist approach to government lawyering. Many new public policies faced tests in the federal courts and before the Supreme Court. Government lawyers consequently became highly attuned to these bodies. In such a legal environment the 1938 *Carolene Products* footnote could not help but have an impact on government lawyers—and it did. It was U.S. Attorney General Frank Murphy who finally took notice of the announced preference for strengthening rights and due process and acted unilaterally within his own agency, a major and well-documented case of "rights entrepreneurship."[28]

In the winter of 1939, shortly after assuming office, Murphy established a Civil Liberties Unit (CLU) within the Justice Department's Criminal Division (changed in 1941 to the Civil Rights Section [CRS]). Its purpose, as he explained it, was "to make an exhaustive study of the Federal civil liberties statutes enacted following the Thirteenth, Fourteenth and Fifteenth Amendments" and "to determine the effect of those statutes under modern conditions in local communities."[29]

The CLU and CRS lawyers focused quickly on what was then section 51 of the U.S. Code, also section 19 of the Criminal Code (today section 241 of the U.S.C.). This statute punishing conspiracies to violate "the free exercise or enjoyment of any right or privilege secured to [any citizen] by the Constitution or laws of the United States" was originally section 6 of the Enforcement Act of May 31, 1870, and later section 5508 of the Revised Statutes of 1874, which figured in *Ex parte Yarbrough* (1884). The CLU and CRS lawyers concluded that this Reconstruction remnant could in fact be used again to protect black voting—but only if the Supreme Court could be persuaded to reverse its holding in *Newberry v. United States* (1921) that "there is no Federal interest in a primary."

In *United States v. Classic,* federal lawyers persuaded the Court to do just that.[30] Pursuant to section 51 of the U.S.C. and article 1, section 4, of the Constitution, authorizing Congress to regulate federal elections, the United States prosecuted a Democratic election official who conspired to stuff ballot boxes in the September 10, 1940, Second Congressional District primary of the Louisiana Democratic Party. This was exactly what the United States had done in *Yarbrough*—with the difference that it now intervened in a federal *primary* rather than a federal general election.

The Supreme Court took the issue just as the United States presented it: the question was whether the United States correctly extended federal criminal regulation to party primaries. In a 4–3 opinion written by Justice Harlan Fiske Stone, author of the 1938 *Carolene Products* footnote, the Court gave the United States what it wanted. Indeed, the decision was explicitly offered as a lineal descendant of *Yarbrough*. Under article 1 of the Constitution and surviving Reconstruction law, the federal government could now use criminal law to protect voters' rights in both general *and* primary elections.[31]

The NAACP's Litigation Strategy

Here, however, we come to the third line of attack on the white primary. The Justice Department thought that *Classic* spelled the end of the white primary. But in fact the case only coaxed the white primary closer toward the judicial guillotine.[32] The Supreme Court would have to stretch yet again in dealing with the white primary. Government lawyers took the self-important view that, thanks to their *Classic* litigation, "At last the Negro could vote!" But black voters in Texas who afterward sought to vote in Democratic primaries had no luck. Queried by the NAACP, the Justice Department refused to litigate the white primary directly or even participate as amicus for fear of southern reaction to its participation.[33]

Finally killing off the white primary fell, therefore, to the NAACP. Yet two issues stood in its way. The first was *Grovey* itself. By holding that a primary was an "integral part" of the electoral process, *Classic* obviously implied that *Grovey* was overruled. Nonetheless, the United States had explicitly distinguished *Grovey* when it argued *Classic*. Also (before the Supreme Court granted certiorari in *Smith*), both a federal district court and a circuit court of appeals had relied on *Grovey* in ruling *against* the NAACP in the new Texas white primary case of *Smith v. Allwright*.

Second, *Classic* involved a criminal conspiracy statute. But the Supreme Court obviously would be loath to announce that the hundreds of officials administering white primaries were criminal conspirators. Therefore, some civil basis for a decision would be necessary. But, in contrast to the criminal precedents (for example, *Yarbrough* or, for that matter, *Guinn v. United States*), no positive civil precedent existed for Fourteenth or Fifteenth Amendment or for article 1 enforcement.

The new white primary case, involving ballot denial in a Democratic primary to nominate House and Senate candidates, was handled by Thurgood Marshall, later the first African American associate justice of the Supreme Court. By now, Marshall was an important figure in American legal circles. He and several associates were the enactors of a vision of civil rights litigation first articulated by the great black lawyer and dean of the Howard University School of Law, Charles Hamilton Houston. In argument before the Court, Marshall strongly emphasized the *Classic* doctrine that the Texas white primary was an "integral part" of the election process. He also demonstrated several dozen ways in which the Texas primary process was embedded in Texas law, making it state action under both the Fourteenth and Fifteenth Amendments. Moreover, he found two bases in civil law for the plaintiff's case, both from the Reconstruction, and argued that his client suffered a Fifteenth (not Fourteenth) Amendment violation.

Writing for the Court in an 8–1 decision, Justice Stanley Reed accepted the argument: "Here we are applying, contrary to the recent decision in *Grovey v. Townsend*, the well-established principle of the Fifteenth Amendment, forbidding the abridgement by a State of a citizen's right to vote. *Grovey v. Townsend* is overruled."[34]

THE COURTS OVERRULE DIXIECRATIC RESISTANCE

Not surprisingly, southern Democratic parties immediately devised several formal-legal types of resistance to *Smith*. The first, the South Carolina "private primary" plan, repealed *all* state laws regulating parties and elections, about 140 statutes. The second, the Arkansas plan, separated state and federal primaries. The third, tried in Alabama with a formal amendment to the 1901 Constitution, required registrants to read and understand the U.S. Constitution. The fourth (in Texas) involved a pre-primary slating election restricted to whites.[35]

In addition, in several states Democratic leaders and party officials fiercely denounced the threat they faced. The Alabama state party chairman mailed an open letter warning that *Smith* "opened the way to a flood of negro registration and negro domination." After a federal court struck down Georgia's white primary in 1946, gubernatorial candidate Herman Talmadge, later a U.S. senator, stated, "The most important issue of all now faces the people of Georgia and the Southland—the Democratic white primary. If elected governor . . . I shall see that the people of this state have a Democratic white primary unfettered and unhampered by radical, communistic and alien influences."[36]

But a federal judge in Charleston, South Carolina, struck down that state's private primary plan; his decision was affirmed by the Supreme Court on appeal. A three-judge federal court struck down the Alabama plan for violating the Fifteenth Amendment. Also, the NAACP persuaded the Fifth Circuit Court of Appeals that following a 1939 Supreme Court decision in an Oklahoma case, *Lane v. Wilson*, it must overrule a New Orleans district court ruling that the United States lacked jurisdiction prior to the exhaustion of state remedies in response to *Smith*. In 1953, the Supreme Court struck down the pre-primary plan devised in Texas.[37]

In short, many of the local federal courts held firm in the face of intense pressure to break from *Smith*. So did the Fifth Circuit. Finally, the Supreme

Court did not waver. This was a remarkable record of judicial solidarity. Such unity became a key factor in motivating NAACP leaders to use the opportunity provided by the case. Increasingly, they referred to *Smith* and the follow-on supporting decisions as the most important steps taken by the federal government since emancipation. This was predictable hyperbole to some extent. But it also reflected a real sense of optimism.[38]

THE INSURANCE POLICY

To recapitulate, one condition of the coalition of 1948's emergence was the New Deal's "latent coalition." Second, with the attack on the white primary came legal mobilization that helped the NAACP grow. There is another vital piece of the history to sketch—the irony of Harry Truman's selection as FDR's running mate in 1944. By 1944, the succession of Franklin D. Roosevelt, the longest-serving president in American history, was a palpable issue within the Democratic Party. At the Chicago nominating convention, southern Democrats acted to protect their interests. They supported Truman, grandson of a slaveholder, for vice president. They saw him as white supremacy's insurance policy. Southerners expected Roosevelt to die in office during his fourth term. His choice of running mate was not a small matter. His third-term vice president, Henry Wallace, represented everything about the New Deal that most southern Democrats disliked—he was pro-labor and pro–civil rights.[39]

For conservative southern Democrats, several events during Roosevelt's third term besides *Smith* signaled the importance of containing New Deal liberalism. In 1941, in response to a black "march on Washington" protest movement organized by A. Philip Randolph, president of the Brotherhood of Sleeping Car Porters, the president agreed to establish a Fair Employment Practices Committee within the Office of Production Management. Its purpose was bringing an end to the flagrant racial discrimination in the hiring practices of industries contracting with the federal government.[40]

In 1942, the House passed a bill to ban the poll tax (though it eventually met death by filibuster in the Senate). In 1943, the Soldiers' Voting Act of 1942, a separate measure that abolished the poll tax payment for servicemen but that otherwise had little effect, was brought up for amendment and strengthening at the president's request. The plan for revision, if enacted, meant creation of a War Ballot Commission, which would supervise separate federal balloting by servicemen at armed forces facilities. Senator James O. Eastland of Mississippi hysterically insisted that this new measure "would send carpetbaggers into the South to control elections." He and his colleagues successfully watered it down by requiring states to pass enabling legislation for its implementation.[41]

Senator Harry Truman's selection as the 1944 running mate thus encouraged southern Democrats. When Roosevelt died on April 12, 1945, they quickly commended his successor. They took satisfaction in his appointment of a South Carolinian to be secretary of state, the first major cabinet appointment from the South in decades. A Texas Democrat became attorney general.

CANDIDATE INSECURITY

But the advent of divided national government for the first time since the Hoover administration suddenly altered the conservative white South's strategic situation. Divided government in 1866 and 1867, it will be recalled, helped trigger the formation of a historic new coalition. It had the same effect nearly a century later. In November 1946, the Republican Party recaptured control of Congress. Reeling from the historic defeat, the first really major breach in Democratic Party strength since FDR's election in 1933, top Democratic strategists concluded that without an innovative campaign strategy Truman would not be elected president in 1948.[42]

Truman soon displayed a new self. He had to. Probably he had it in him. But the analytically interesting element here is the sudden emergence of behavior consistent with deep candidate insecurity. In December 1946, just after the off-year elections produced divided government, Truman emphatically responded to a wave of violent white-on-black murders and assaults that seemed targeted against returning black servicemen in the South. He established the President's Committee on Civil Rights. In issuing Executive Order 9808, which established the committee, the president called attention to the problem of "inadequate civil rights statutes. The protection of our democratic institutions and the enjoyment by the people of their rights under the Constitution require that these weak and inadequate statutes should be expanded and improved."[43] Truman's State of the Union address in 1947 continued his new focus on the issue of civil rights. Two days later, he also proposed a permanent Fair Employment Practices Committee.

Then Truman made a point of reaching out to the NAACP in an address delivered in front of the Lincoln Memorial in June, 1947. He sought to score points with an association that was now far more electorally consequential than it had ever been. From 1941 to 1945, the number of new chartered units in the NAACP jumped by about 250 percent. The organization now boasted more than one thousand units nationwide.[44] Truman's advisers recommended only a brief parting reference to civil rights in his speech, "not to exceed one minute." But he rejected this advice. The entire speech was about civil rights. Truman began by congratulating the NAACP on its "effective work for the improvement of our democratic processes." America, he said, was at a "turning point in the long history of our country's efforts to guarantee freedom and equality to all our citizens. . . . When I say all Americans I mean all Americans." The federal government would now have to become active in protecting civil rights. "We cannot wait another decade or another generation. . . . Our National Government must show the way."[45]

Although white-controlled media were mostly silent about the speech, black publications that served subscribers all over the country covered it fully. Newspapers such as the *New York Age*, the *Norfolk Journal & Guide*, and the *Pittsburgh Courier* reprinted it. The *Chicago Defender* applauded its "bold, unequivocal language." The *Philadelphia Afro-American* called it "the strongest address on civil rights ever made by any president." In short, the word got out.[46]

On October 29, 1947, the President's Committee on Civil Rights issued its report, *To Secure These Rights,* whose title evoked the Declaration of Independence. Clearly and succinctly it described the extent of racial hierarchy in labor and housing markets, the provision of medical care, the armed forces, the District of Columbia, criminal justice, public transportation and accommodations, and public education. It recommended the abolition of all of these aspects of racial hierarchy everywhere in the country. It called for upgrading the Civil Rights Section of the Criminal Division of the Department of Justice to a Civil Rights Division. It called for the abolition of poll taxes, federal protection of voting in federal elections, and enforcement of the Fifteenth Amendment.

In November 1947, special counsel to the president Clark Clifford forwarded a now very famous memo to his boss, presenting him with a campaign strategy. Actually written by James Rowe, it advised a strong civil rights stance in order to attract black voters to Truman's imminent presidential candidacy. "Unless there are new and real efforts . . . the Negro bloc . . . will go Republican," the Rowe-Clifford memo warned. Therefore Truman should "go as far as he feels he possibly could in recommending measures to protect the rights of minority groups." Furthermore, the president should not worry about southern Democrats. They were "safely Democratic" and could be "safely ignored."[47]

At the presidential nominating convention of 1948, Minneapolis mayor Hubert Humphrey gave a fiery speech meant to bind Truman to his new commitments. Truman preferred a toned-down civil rights plank, but party liberals wanted the platform to restate the ideas in *To Secure These Rights*.

Humphrey's carefully planned speech electrified the convention, leading it to vote for the stronger plank and prompting a walkout of southern delegates.[48]

The Democratic Party literally cracked from its reorientation. Meeting in Birmingham, Alabama, in mid-July 1948, just days after the party nominated Truman, the party's conservative southern wing gathered to plot strategy. It wanted to punish Truman and his advisors.[49] Led by South Carolina governor Strom Thurmond and Mississippi governor Fielding Wright, the Birmingham convention set a goal of winning the South's 127 votes in the Electoral College. The bolters anticipated doing this either by assuring (by means of state conventions or legal action) that Democratic electors were legally unpledged to Truman or by electing separate electors under a different label than the Democratic label. Given the anticipated strength of the Republican presidential contender, Thomas Dewey, they had high hopes for creating a phalanx of unpledged or third-party electors. Such an outcome might prevent either major-party candidate from gaining the necessary 266 votes to win the Electoral College. In the House of Representatives the former Confederacy would then vote as a bloc of eleven (or 23 percent) of the forty-eight votes deciding the election. The South could cut a grand bargain to protect itself.[50]

The Dixiecrat strategy was made all the more threatening by the Progressive Party challenge. This third party emerged from a network of political clubs favoring accommodation of a Soviet sphere of influence in Europe (the Progressive Citizens of America), and it enjoyed support from still-vital Communist-led trade unions. The ticket was headed by venerable New Dealers who knew a lot about how to conduct a national campaign: former vice president Henry Wallace and Senator Glenn Simpson, Democrat of Idaho.[51]

Under the circumstances it was possible that Truman would seek an accommodation with the Dixiecrats. Because his left wing might defect, he might see no choice but to move right toward Birmingham. The alternative to these twin threats, of course, was to reach out, mobilizing and turning out new voters—black voters who were manifestly pro-Democratic in key northern states essential for winning the Electoral College. By so doing Truman could trump the threats of defection on the left and the right and win reelection. But would he do that?

He did. On July 26, he issued two historic executive orders. With Executive Order 9981, Truman announced that it is "the policy of the President that there shall be equality of treatment and opportunity for all persons in the armed services without regard to race, color, religion, or national origin." To implement the policy "as rapidly as possible" the order established the President's Committee on Equality of Treatment and Opportunity in the

Armed Services. A second order established the Fair Employment Board in the Civil Service Commission.[52]

On August 17, 1948, a second Rowe-Clifford memo told the president that "Negro votes in the crucial states will more than cancel out any votes" that Truman might lose in the southern states where the States' Rights Party was strong. Not surprisingly, on the eve of the election Truman campaigned to cheering throngs in Harlem. New York was, of course, one of the "crucial states" identified in the memo.[53]

To summarize, despite trying to "bind the future" by selecting Roosevelt's successor, southern Democrats could not block Truman from adopting much stronger civil rights stances than his predecessor's. Historians have shown that his actions were sincere. But they were also politically prudent, even necessary. The return of divided government in 1946 and the likelihood of a strong challenger in 1948 generated candidate insecurity.

This kind of situation was ripe for coalition formation. For the first time in the twentieth century, *black voters were necessary* for the continued success of a national party—in this case, the Democratic Party's hold on the American presidency. Truman and his campaign advisors recognized the "balance-of-power position" of "Negro voters in northern and western industrial cities." From 1940 to 1950, black migrants were responsible for more than 50 percent of the increase in the number of northern urban black voters. In New York, Chicago, and Detroit, migrants accounted for 83 percent of the increase. If black voters were mobilized and turned out at high rates, their participation could spell the difference between victory and defeat in important Electoral College states.[54]

THE NAACP'S DEVELOPMENT OF A PARTY-IN-WAITING

Meanwhile, on the ground in the South, Truman's outreach interacted with startling political change. Truman's efforts were, of course, directed toward northern, not southern, black voters. But his sudden expansion of the Democratic Party's once latent biracial coalition encouraged further NAACP mobilization in the South, as the NAACP undertook a vast effort to implement the Supreme Court's invalidation of the white primary. This new dynamic in southern politics—the intersection of coalitional outreach at the national level and movement politics at the regional level—inaugurated the building of a cross-regional, biracial coalition within the Democratic Party. As a result of intense state and local efforts to implement a new jurisprudence, both a "party-in-waiting" and an "electorate-in-waiting" emerged. Jurisprudence and party-building thus worked in tandem.

A brief bit of background is in order. The evolution of black group politics is a little-known aspect of American pluralism. When the Republican Party abandoned African Americans to disenfranchisement, it also suddenly devalued the black political networks that it had built up. Disenfranchisement turned a large, multistate infrastructure of black male political activists, party officials, federal officeholders, and patronage brokers into an obsolete hulk. Black Republican politics persisted, to be sure. The historic black-Republican alliance still had vital uses for African Americans. In the early 1920s, for instance, despite the Republican failure to finally pass federal antilynching legislation, rates of lynching did drop considerably in the aftermath of a major Republican push to make it a federal crime.[55]

But black group politics had to be built in order to establish channels of representation for African American interests. This was a daunting task. A key part of the process was the politics of the "Tuskegee machine," headquartered at that estimable utopia of group self-determination founded by Booker T. Washington in 1881 in Alabama. Tuskegee lay at the center of a large but nearly invisible network of black business and professional notables guided by Washington in secret, prudential ways that are even today hardly known. As educational sociologists have recently shown, Washington's greatest accomplishment was a far-reaching strategy of private-public partnership that launched a revitalization of public education for black southerners.[56]

By the time of Washington's death in 1915, however, northern black intellectuals had discredited him for his overt accommodationism. His rise to fame had, after all, featured the 1895 Atlanta address in which Washington disavowed a role for African Americans in politics in return for assistance with vocational education. In establishing the NAACP, Washington's critics formed their own alternative to the Tuskegee machine. But the NAACP could not develop a southern wing despite some success just after World War I. It also was forced into fierce battles with Marcus Garvey's Universal Negro Improvement Association (in the 1920s), which did have a substantial southern wing, and the Communist Party, which had a tiny but determined and courageous southern cadre in the 1930s.[57]

By the mid-1940s, however, the black group system looked entirely different. The NAACP exploded in size. It became the dominant African American association in the country. The cold war and anti-Left political repression soon asphyxiated any influence that black Communist intellectuals and labor organizers might have wielded. As the NAACP rose to hegemony within the black group system, its leadership became predominantly black. This had everything to do with its growth in the South. From 1936 to 1940, the number of *new* separate NAACP units (local branches, youth councils, and college chapters) doubled, with about 80 percent of the growth occurring in the South. From 1941 to 1945, the number of new chartered units jumped by about 250 percent, with about three-quarters of the new units being chartered in the South, and between 1946 and 1950 the number of new units slightly exceeded the previous five-year increase, with, again, most of the growth occurring in the South. The NAACP boasted somewhere between eleven hundred and sixteen hundred units nationwide by this time, and at least half of its membership and infrastructure was now in the South.[58]

Its new southern wing became loosely coupled to a larger "NAACP-centered" network of separate but allied associations. They were sometimes successors to movement nuclei established in the 1930s such as the "citizenship schools" organized in various southern cities and at black colleges in the early and mid-1930s by the black college fraternity Alpha Phi Alpha and its talented leader, the historian Rayford Logan. They also included such traditional organizations as the Prince Hall Masons. They built on the advertising and subscription networks of black newspapers or the clientele of such institutions as black-owned insurance companies and even beauticians' parlors. Returning black veterans also helped energize the NAACP-centered network.[59] Finally, voter league organizations were spun out of the NAACP (in order to protect it). They typically charged moderate white candidates fees for elections services and eleventh-hour endorsements in agreements usually reached in secret back-door arrangements.[60]

Such exchange was possible, particularly in cities, because many southern Democrats now lacked any visceral commitment to white supremacy. In each southern state there were New Deal and more conservative wings of the Democratic Party. The New Deal approach was represented by men such as Lyndon Baines Johnson of Texas (later president, 1963–1969), James Folsom of Alabama (governor, 1946–1950), Lister Hill of Alabama (U.S. senator, 1938–1969), John Sparkman of Alabama (U.S. senator, 1946–1979), and Claude Pepper of Florida (U.S. senator, 1936–1951, U.S. representative, 1962–1989). White supremacy for its own sake meant little or nothing to them. They wanted to focus instead (as the southern Populists earlier had done) on class tensions and general social welfare.

SEIZING THE DAY

Between 1944 and 1946 the NAACP's national leadership forcefully exploited the new possibilities. It called on "every branch to conduct a registration and voting drive." What this meant in practice varied from state to state and from locale to locale. The Houston chapter's plans, as described by the historian

Merline Pitre, had several elements, however, that were probably typical. "First was encouraging poll tax payment. Second was collective endorsement of certain candidates." Third was voter education: "many organizations conducted clinics on how to mark ballots and how to use voting machines." Leaders worked through churches, "local organizations, the black press, and members of the NAACP." They were relentless. "Whether [the Houston chapter executive secretary] was speaking before Franklin Beauty School graduates, a civic club, or people on the street, her message was the same: 'Pay your poll tax and get out to vote.' "[61]

The activity of the units composing the "party-in-waiting" left a record of remarkable photographs that can today be viewed in secondary sources. A Richmond, Virginia, newspaper reported on a common scene when it noted the action at downtown municipal offices in early May 1947: "A Negro man wearing a NAACP badge on his coat lapel was supervising the poll tax payments and registrations of many Negroes yesterday. . . . Meanwhile a truck equipped with loud speakers continued to make the rounds of . . . Negro residential areas urging them to pay their poll taxes and to register."[62] The results of this regional registration drive were quite significant, for black voter registration had nowhere to go, after all, but up.[63] The results are displayed in table 7.2.

There were also inklings of a new biracial public sphere. The Atlanta Police Department hired black officers. An African American man was elected to the Richmond City Council in 1948, and in 1947 a black minister was elected alderman in Winston-Salem, North Carolina.[64] In short, a "party-in-waiting" came into being. New cadres of voters and activists served notice that they belonged to a party from which they were excluded. They were ready to come in and remake the party. Conservative regulars faced a new, unnerving prospect: they now had to patrol the boundaries of organizations that they long took for granted.[65]

CONCLUSION

This chapter has explored the way in which a cross-regional, biracial coalition *within the Democratic Party* came into view for the first time. After black southerners relocated in large numbers in northern cities, African Americans as a group were politically repositioned. Black migration before the New Deal "primed" the party system for reincorporation.

Soon after Franklin D. Roosevelt's death in 1945 thrust Harry Truman into the Oval Office, something similar to the coalitional trigger of 1867–1868 occurred: the emergence of divided government. With its arrival,

Table 7.2 Estimates of the Number of Successful African American Voter Registrants in the Former Confederacy, 1940–1956

State	1940	1947	% Increase, 1940–47	1952	% Increase, 1947–52	1956	% Increase, 1952–56
Alabama	2,000	6,000	200	25,596	326	53,366	108
Arkansas	21,888	37,155	69	61,413	65	75,431	23
Florida	18,000	49,000	172	120,919	147	137,535	14
Georgia	20,000	125,000	525	144,835	16	163,389	13
Louisiana	2,000	10,000	400	120,000	1,100	152,378	27
Mississippi	2,000	5,000	150	20,000	300	20,000	0
North Carolina	35,000	75,000	114	100,000	33	135,000	35
South Carolina	3,000	50,000	1,566	80,000	60	99,890	25
Tennessee	20,000	80,000	300	85,000	6	90,000	6
Texas	30,000	100,000	233	181,916	82	214,000	18
Virginia	15,000	48,000	228	69,326	44	82,603	19

Source: Adapted from Steven F. Lawson, *Black Ballots: Voting Rights in the South, 1944–1969* (New York: Columbia University Press, 1976), p. 134.

Truman feared defeat in the 1948 presidential election. He energetically reached out to African American voters. Such proactive coalition formation is predicted by the theoretical claim that, if elites believe that "their long-term capacity to reproduce their elite status" is at stake and that they "will be unable to compete . . . in the future," then they will strengthen their base by expanding it.[66]

Truman's coalition-making began shortly after the Supreme Court decisions concerning the white primary. It coincided with the NAACP's development of southern chapters and state conferences and its push to privately implement the Court's decisions. The effort to make the new jurisprudence actually apply on the ground strengthened a new galaxy of African American associations. Jurisprudence-building of this type nurtured an electorate-in-waiting and a party-in-waiting.

Still, the second reconstruction had only just begun. The great majority of voting-age black adults, 75 to 80 percent, were *not* registered to vote as of 1956, a decade after the NAACP launched its regional voter registration drive. Furthermore, actual black participation in the southern Democratic Party primaries was much lower than black registration. White Democratic officials resisted black voting much more than black registration. From their perspective, the southern Democratic parties were still all-white parties.[67] Further, where voting did occur, it often rose to levels too low to prevent white establishment figures from deflecting or manipulating its impact, generating patron-client politics: "A Georgia sharecropper, commenting on open-handed whites in his locality, said, 'They do all they can. Furnish you whiskey and cars before elections and bullets after the election.'" In addition, much of the legal structure of disenfranchisement was still in place. Finally, and tragically, outside the big cities there were murderous echoes of Reconstruction violence—shootings of activists, bombings, and instances of police brutality.[68]

The second reconstruction, in other words, proceeded in phases. The structure of party politics made this method of implementing African American electoral reincorporation likely. This differed from the rapid ballooning of the Republican electoral coalition in the period between the spring of 1867 and the ratification of the Fifteenth Amendment in April 1870, when the exceptional unity of a northern regional party guided electoral-coalitional expansion in another region. But that sort of coalition-making was not in the cards during the second reconstruction. The factional strife of the Democratic Party instead regulated coalitional enlargement. Reinclusion of blacks would be a protracted process. The Democratic Party was the eye of the needle through which it had to pass.

Chapter Eight

The Coalition of 1961–1965

The processes that made the coalition of 1948 were important parts of black southerners' long electoral struggle. But there was also much more to do. By the early 1950s southern Democrats figured out how to neutralize the impact of *Smith v. Allwright*. The two wings of the Democratic Party also ceased their open hostilities. Another coalition was required, an alliance that would resemble—but greatly improve on—the one engineered by Truman and the NAACP.[1]

As with the previous cases described in this book, a new episode of coalition-making began in 1961 with insiders reacting to a threat or combination of political dangers and problems. They realized that bringing outsiders in would help to resolve a major difficulty. The dominant condition at this juncture was a threat to a policy goal. During the Kennedy administration, a danger to the realization of U.S. foreign policy goals at the height of the cold war emerged from fierce racial conflict in southern locales. Concerned about the international ramifications of growing black protest and local official violence in the South, the Kennedy administration negotiated an agreement in 1961 with the civil rights movements. It offered to fund voter registration efforts by these organizations—what might be called the voting rights pact of 1961.

But the 1961 pact was unstable. Far from calming racial tensions, the focus on voter registration had quite the opposite effect.

Renewed voter registration efforts in Deep South states triggered fierce back-lash from state and local officials and judges. Such repression also encouraged private violence against blacks and violent white supremacist conspiracies.

Yet the pact not only held, but it was reestablished on stronger terms in a successor pact that undergirded the Voting Rights Act of 1965. Kennedy's successor, Lyndon Baines Johnson, also had incentives for coalition-making, though his were electoral, unlike the policy imperative to which Kennedy responded. Much like Truman before him, Johnson was determined to secure his leadership of the Democratic Party and his reelection. Candidate insecurity motivated him. He therefore promoted civil rights fiercely in the months leading up to his party's 1964 nominating convention.

Johnson's stance gave black leaders a subtle advantage: the ability to renegotiate the 1961 pact. They did that in early 1965, in Selma, Alabama, where Martin Luther King Jr. and his associates unfolded a carefully envisioned protest. Their local struggle escalated steadily, reaching a climax on March 7 with a peaceful civil rights march from Selma to Montgomery that encountered a brutal assault by Alabama state troopers. Much of the nation witnessed the drama on television.

The Selma march set the national agenda as few local struggles ever have. Shortly afterward Johnson addressed a joint session of Congress. He called for swift passage of a voting rights statute. In doing so, he emphasized that "[t]he real hero of this struggle is the American Negro. His actions and protests, his courage to risk safety and even to risk his life, have awakened the conscience of this Nation. . . . He has called upon us to make good the promise of America." In that moment, Johnson pictured a kind of great compact of the whole, a union between black and white Americans that redeemed "the promise of America."[2]

The long interfactional battle within the Democratic Party now reached a new phase. Chapter 7 outlined the opening skirmishes; this chapter focuses on a decisive set of encounters, starting with a discussion of the way black political will framed the entire era. It emphasizes tactical innovation within the civil rights movements, historicist consciousness, the grounding of political inventiveness in a protest philosophy of nonviolent direct action, and the transformation of African American associational politics from an NAACP-centered system into a rivalrous system with its different organizations competing to find the best way to dethrone white supremacy.

The chapter then considers how the new context for coalition-making emerged during Kennedy's presidency, at a time when many in his administration were unhappy about the unbending nature of black political will. The administration's response: encouragement of seemingly safe direct action—voter registration. Two meliorative statutes with relatively untested voting rights provisions were at hand: the 1957 and 1960 Civil Rights Acts. (Their political origins are briefly treated in chapter 10.) Kennedy's sponsorship of the Voter Education Project (VEP) and of the Lawyers Committee on Civil Rights (LCCR) launched the various civil rights organizations on an arduous effort to implement these two Eisenhower-era statutes. But the endeavor flew apart. The statutes that the VEP and its grantee organizations sought to implement assumed that state and local officials would comply in good faith with federal law. Southern violence and obstructionism—as one set of Democratic officeholders fought a pitched battle against the other—made the Civil Rights Acts nearly impossible to implement in the Deep South. The party-in-waiting of 1948 met with brutal repression.

Enormous tensions between the civil rights movements and the Kennedy administration consequently emerged. The party-in-waiting expected protection but did not receive it. One way out of the stand-off was for the civil rights organizations to force consideration of an entirely new statute. That was the purpose of the Selma campaign. In mounting it, the principals generated a crisis that was impossible for the president and Congress to ignore. From that emergency came the voting rights pact of 1965. It was an emergency rooted in the development of nonviolent direct action.

Black Political Will

Lunch-counter sit-ins, jail-ins, freedom rides, the children's crusades—these now-famous protest tactics of the civil rights era sprang from black political will. A 1963 survey found that among ordinary African Americans (people who could be classified as "nonleaders"), 51 percent said they were willing to march in a demonstration, 49 percent said they were willing to take part in a sit-in, 47 percent said they were willing to go to jail, and 46 percent said they were willing to picket a store. Other less famous types of protest included "swim-ins" at segregated public pools and the peaceful "read-in" intended to immobilize a recalcitrant city council.[3]

From a longer historical perspective, it is worth nothing the parallel between the heyday of civil rights insurgency between 1953 (the Baton Rouge bus boycott) and 1965 (the march on Selma) and the movement cycle of 1866–1867, as well as other incidents in between these two historical poles. Recall from chapter 2 the labor strikes, actions to desegregate streetcars in southern cities, and outdoor demonstrations of marching companies. Recall, too, the lightning-fast spread of the Union Leagues, so similar to the rapid proliferation of civil rights organizations in the 1940s and in the late 1950s and early 1960s. The nineteenth-century phenomena all prefigured the modern civil rights era.

Consciousness was an important political resource, just as postemancipation hope, confidence, and group consciousness had shaped coalition-making politics in the late 1860s. Consciousness acquired vocal and visible presence in the "mass meeting"—a semipublic action pioneered in Montgomery during the bus boycott of 1955. A white-owned rural Mississippi newspaper unwittingly paid homage to the power of this innovation when it noted that "these people accumulate into crowds and then by their speeches are exhorted into frenzy and then seek to march in a body to register." Consciousness also came from movement organizers patiently engaging in "the spade work," as the NAACP organizer and SNCC founder Ella Baker once put it. One example of spade work is the citizenship school, invented by Septima Clark, a South Carolina teacher, and sponsored by Myles Horton's Highlander Folk School in Tennessee. The Highlander trained scores of civil rights movement leaders in its workshops (and also diffused the anthem "We Shall Overcome"). It supported Clark's schools, which grew out of her experience as a teacher in the Sea Islands of South Carolina. In citizenship schools semiliterate adults learned and taught others how to write using voter-registration forms, discussed citizenship and public affairs, mastered the art of reading newspapers, and acquired essential skills such as handling money order forms. Eventually ten thousand people passed through a system of two hundred schools, becoming local leaders in the process.[4]

Such self-awareness was reinforced by quite profound spiritual experience. Many people in the civil rights movement, it appears, had religious epiphanies. The historian Charles Payne writes, "When explaining their own decision to join the movement, my respondents constructed answers primarily in terms of either religious belief or preexisting social networks of kinship and friendship. . . . Emma Lou Allen was drawn into the movement by her son, a junior-college student. Though she was often afraid, she was sure the Lord would see her through. . . . Susie Morgan was drawn in partly by the activity of her daughters. She prayed and prayed over the decision to join, and finally she could see that it was what the Lord wanted her to do. Ethel Gray was drawn into the movement by an old friend. After she had joined, people would drive by and shoot into her home . . . but 'we stood up. *Me and God stood up.*' "[5]

Coupled to the consciousness and often the religious understanding with which civil rights organizations were suffused was a moral and political philosophy: nonviolent direct action. Nonviolence is partly self-explanatory, but the direct action element is more subtle. Bayard Rustin, executive secretary of the New York–based War Resisters League and earlier a youth organizer in A. Philip Randolph's March on Washington movement, was a key exponent. Rustin, in fact, converted King to complete nonviolence, persuading him to stop keeping weapons in his home for self-defense.

Rustin had thought long and hard about how best to fuse together mass militance and Gandhian tactics. He held that "nonviolence . . . makes humble folk noble and turns fear into courage." The idea was to adopt a principle of collective behavior that could create a mass base in which every individual could do something brave, direct, and purposive among like-minded people. It meant constantly and deeply challenging the personal, individual-level aspects of white supremacy. Nonviolence called for unexpected, startling, and highly courageous behavior.[6]

Again, religion—specifically the institutional foundation of religious experience among black southerners—played an important role by creating a context for the diffusion of nonviolent direct action. Using OLS regression on data drawn from a little-known but extensive Harris-*Newsweek* 1966 survey of 1,037 black respondents, Fredrick C. Harris found that Baptist and Methodist churchgoing (a trait that captured 76 percent of the sample) very strongly inhibited African Americans' attraction to such ideas as favoring a separate black state or a belief in the political necessity of black violence.[7]

Thus, tactical innovation and a religious, historicist awareness, reinforced by a coherent philosophy of nonviolent direct action, characterized participants in the civil and voting rights struggles. These elements are already known, of course. What may be fresh to readers, however, are the parallels and contrasts. What happened between 1953 and 1965 was an extended cycle similar to the concentrated cycle of 1866–1867. The first cycle featured the truly vast Union League movement rising and falling over a brief period; the second featured many burgeoning and loosely cooperating movement organizations functioning for a long period.

The Role of the NAACP and Its Significance

Among these organizations, one deserves special notice. The most recent scholarship on the civil rights era considers the NAACP far more central in the second reconstruction than previously thought. Aldon Morris was the first scholar to emphasize the organization's importance. A new crop of British historians of the period have amply validated his insight.[8] I add to this view an accent on the causal role of the NAACP's legal repression (described below). Tracing the NAACP's central role underscores the links between the coalition-making of the 1940s and the better-known dynamics of the late 1950s and early 1960s.

The claim is not that the NAACP was stodgy and risk-averse and therefore that its weakening happily assured "real" struggle and association-building. On the contrary, in the 1940s and into the 1950s it played a major role in seeding the ground. Key NAACP leaders—Harry Moore of Florida and Medgar Evers of Mississippi—paid with their lives for their determination. The NAACP organized (indeed partly caused) the enormous shift upward in voter registration from 1946 to 1956.[9] Rather, the organization's loss of its hegemony over black associational life in the South because of repression had a significant if unintended consequence. It meant that in many locales new participants in the struggle could develop fresh associational frameworks for themselves without facing strong community pressure to work through the NAACP's local structures.[10]

That new aspect of the system—and this is crucial for understanding the context of the 1961 pact—promoted rivalrous tactical experimentation. The proliferation of movement associations and actions encouraged interorganizational competition regarding tactics, and it stimulated a competitive search for venues for nonviolent protest and defiance. As we shall see, such competition made protest seemingly untamable. The Kennedy administration needed to "do something" to calm a rising tide. Turn, therefore, to a quick background sketch of the crisis of the NAACP.

The Crisis of the NAACP

Why did this organization, at the moment of its greatest strength, suddenly weaken? The answer: it was forcefully attacked by the Southern Democratic parties. They criminalized it by means of antisubversive legislation. It was the NAACP's success in attacking segregated public schools that prompted the backlash. If it could do so much to implement *Smith*, then it followed that any effort to implement the famous Supreme Court decision *Brown v. Board of Education* would also be successful. The white Democratic establishment feared an aggressive implementation of *Brown* by the NAACP Legal Defense and Educational Fund, Inc.[11]

John Scott, an NAACP leader in Louisiana, writes in his autobiography, "After the Citizens' Council had organized in many towns across Louisiana, they, along with the joint legislative committee on segregation, put into action the first phase of their plan, which was to destroy the NAACP. . . . [A] 1924 law originally passed to break up the Ku Klux Klan was now used to break up the NAACP. . . . Twelve state NAACP officers were charged with breaking the 1924 law. By the end of March [1956], the state attorney, who was also an executive in the Citizens' Council, had seized the NAACP's state bank account, and the judge who heard the case had put an injunction against the NAACP, banning all meetings in the state until we all produced our membership lists. The newspapers that supported segregation were filled with victory stories. They called the NAACP ban a turning point 'in maintaining the social and economic status of the Negro.' "[12]

Table 8.1 outlines the repressive assault on the NAACP for its role in the *Brown* school desegregation case. Louisiana Democrats used anti-Klan legislation to shut it down. An Arkansas statute labeled the NAACP a "captive of the international communist conspiracy." Although the organization rebounded, the tactics deployed against it cumulatively took a serious toll. From 1956 to 1958, the number of branches in the South dropped by about 17 percent, and membership by about 38 percent.[13]

This erosion (which continued until a series of Supreme Court decisions reversed the official attack) suddenly left a significant vacuum. The South had made a mistake. It had inadvertently rearranged black associationalism.[14] Into the leadership crisis stepped the movement that is synonymous with Martin Luther King Jr., namely, the Southern Christian Leadership Conference (SCLC), an organization that emerged alongside the NAACP in many states. That the SCLC's founding leaders were current or former local NAACP officials helped the SCLC to quickly enter the associational system of black southerners.[15] Soon, furthermore, it was joined by two other organizations— the Student Nonviolent Coordinating Committee (SNCC) and the Congress of Racial Equality (CORE).

On February 1, 1960, four freshmen at North Carolina Agricultural and Technical College in Greensboro sat down at the whites-only lunch counter in the town's Woolworth's store. The following day, thirty students appeared and sat in, closing their protest with a prayer. On the third day, three white students from a different local college joined a large group of black students. Hundreds of black students, and a crowd of angry whites, showed up on the fourth day. The following week, twelve such black or biracial student sit-ins at whites-only facilities erupted throughout the South; the third week there were eight sit-ins, the fourth week nine, the fifth week fourteen, and the sixth week seven. To defy segregation, students simply showed up. Arrest became a badge of honor, not something to be feared.[16] As the student-led riptide surged, the SCLC quickly organized an Easter weekend conference in Raleigh, North Carolina. From this was formed the SNCC.[17]

Table 8.1 The Southern Official Assault on the NAACP, 1956–1957

Types of Official Action Taken	AL	AR	FL	GA	LA	MS	NC	SC	TN	TX	VA
Suit by state attorney general to prevent some or all NAACP operation	✓									✓	
Suit by attorney general to require NAACP to release membership and/or other records	✓									✓	
Judicial injunction against some or all NAACP operations or jailing of an NAACP official	✓				✓					✓	
Judicial fine levied against NAACP in connection with legal action	✓			✓	✓						
Legislative prohibition of NAACP activity within the state, or counties with large black populations, or both	✓			✓							
Establishment of an investigative body, e.g., a "state sovereignty commission"		✓	✓			✓					
Requirement of registration with some state authority and/or requirement for payment of fees for process or recordkeeping		✓	✓	✓			✓	✓	✓		✓
Grant to governor of powers to control emergencies created by civil rights activity			✓								
Legislative investigation of the NAACP or of associations described in general terms but clearly recognizable as the NAACP			✓		✓			✓		✓	
Raids of NAACP offices by state agencies, state police, or local police to seize membership lists and other records				✓			✓				
Cordoning off by police or other official intimidation of an NAACP meeting	✓										
Anti-barratry legislation (or similar authority) outlawing and/or criminalizing litigation by NAACP staff or representation of state residents by the NAACP			✓		✓	✓	✓	✓	✓		✓
Prohibition against state employees belonging to the NAACP				✓	✓	✓		✓			

Sources: American Jewish Congress, 'Assault upon Freedom of Association: A Study of the Southern Attack on the National Association for the Advancement of Colored People* (New York: American Jewish Congress, n.d. [1957]); Aldon D. Morris, *The Origins of the Civil Rights Movement: Black Communities Organizing for Change* (New York: Free Press, 1984), pp. 30–39; Adam Fairclough, *Race and Democracy: The Civil Rights Struggle in Louisiana, 1915–1972* (Athens: University of Georgia Press, 1995), chap. 8; Andrew Buni, *The Negro in Virginia Politics, 1902–1965* (Charlottesville: University Press of Virginia, 1967), p. 186.

On a parallel track, a venerable northern (but to this point invisible) Gandhian organization, the Congress of Racial Equality, grew along with the sit-ins. Like the NAACP in the 1940s (or, for that matter, the Union League movement of 1867), CORE was diffused southward from a northern base. It already had a student operation in several places in the South and had helped start the Greensboro movement. By February 1961, with SNCC help, CORE also added a vital new tactic, the "jail-in," which involved embracing prison and refusing bail in order to dramatize the official coercion that reinforced discrimination in public accommodations. That too helped attract adherents and expand nonviolent direct action.

Thus by 1961 the NAACP's associational hegemony in the South was in abeyance. The southern black associational system became instead a diverse constellation of highly competitive organizations seeking to outdo each other in creative nonviolent direct action. The South became like a blinking map, filled with recurring protests, first here, then there.

The Emergence of a Coalition-Making Context

Between nonviolence and organizational rivalry, an essential new context for coalition-making emerged. White supremacist reaction and violence, analysts have found, regularly surged after peaceful protest. The more black nonviolent protest there was, the more white violence followed.

There were, Joseph Luders has ingeniously shown, distinct state-by-state variations. The personal decisions of the governors—whether to tolerate or to smother white violence—were decisive factors. Governor Fritz Hollings of South Carolina effectively shut down white violence, but his colleagues in Alabama, Louisiana, and Mississippi tolerated white counterprotest and mayhem.[18]

Whatever the jurisdictional variation, the overall level of white-on-black violence was astonishing—a degree of civil disorder during the rebellious sixties that eclipses the oft-remarked violence of the northern student Left. More than eighty people lost their lives during the civil rights era, bombed, beaten, or shot to death. Southern white supremacists were willing and able to sharply escalate confrontation. They influenced or controlled several state and many local governments. They had public resources and institutions at their disposal. Finally, they were angry at the national government.[19]

The contempt for federal law that many white southerners appeared to share was galvanized by several factors: (1) the Southern Manifesto, a statement of defiance produced by 101 southern Democrats in Congress, (2) gubernatorial election campaigns, which brought ardent segregationists out of the southern Democratic parties' woodwork, and (3) the rapid spread of a respectable middle- and upper-class white resistance movement, the Citizens Councils. The Councils, founded in Mississippi by prominent lawyers, dedicated themselves to organizing "massive resistance." Within five years, in fact, southern legislatures produced more than two hundred anti-desegregation statutes and resolutions of "interposition," that is, declarations of noncompliance with *Brown*.[20]

Doug McAdam has quantitatively sketched the interracial conflict by using the *New York Times Index*. After reading through twenty-six thousand entries, he generated estimates of "white supremacist events" and "movement-generated events." Though his estimates have to be treated cautiously, they succinctly communicate the sharp increase in turbulence just around the time that Kennedy became president (see table 8.2).[21]

There were other classes of events that McAdam did not or could not code. He probably failed to record most economic reprisals for protest such as cut-offs of Aid to Families with Dependent Children, job loss, and credit withdrawal. Violent official abuse inside southern jails and police stations, away from any *Times* or wire service reporter, could not have made it into the *Index*. Finally, a wide range of hostile white actions surely never surfaced in the *Times*: verbal slurs, offensive gestures, bomb scares, appearances of signs, flyers, or graffiti, suspicious incidents (swerving vehicles, vandalism), the local publication of the names of those who had sought to register to vote, or low-level police harassment. After all, racial oppression was woven into daily life as well as into law. It had grim local enforcers—such as the white manager and employees of a Nashville lunch counter who retaliated against a sit-in by abruptly closing for the day, switching on the establishment's fumigator, and locking the exit, thus nearly killing the black students.[22]

Table 8.2 Racial Conflict in the Former Confederacy, 1955–1965

	1955–1960	1961–1965	% Change
Violent white-supremacist events	176	248	+41
Nonviolent white-supremacist events	540	427	−21
Nonviolent movement-initiated events	438	1,040	+137
Total N	1,154	1,715	+49

Source: Adapted from Doug McAdam, *Political Process and the Development of Black Insurgency, 1930–1970* (Chicago: University of Chicago Press, 1982), pp. 152, 173 for data, pp. 172–173 for description, and appendix 1 for coding, esp. pp. 242, 249.

Note: "Violent white-supremacist events" likely refers to beatings, murder, harassment, or intimidation by officials or individuals affiliated with segregationist organizations; "nonviolent white-supremacist events" likely refers to speeches, formation of an organization, rallies, or official actions; "nonviolent movement-initiated events" likely refers to boycotts, sit-ins, jail-ins, marches, speeches, rallies, court action, petition campaign, and voter registration action.

In short, by 1961 southern racial conflict was at a much higher and *constant* level than at any point in the twentieth century—and with no prospect of ending by itself. Simultaneously, outside the United States, the cold war suddenly assumed a new form. The Soviet Union acquired new leadership following Stalin's death. The Cuban Revolution generated a revolutionary socialist state off the coast of Florida. The Congo split into camps affiliated with the two great powers. In Angola, the Portuguese government launched a brutal counterinsurgency.[23]

Fatefully, the presidency changed from Republican to Democratic hands in the most closely contested election until that point in the century. The untested incoming president, John F. Kennedy, was likely to want domestic peace and an image of national unity as he pursued American foreign policy. Coalition-making would be a way to achieve those ends. To allow domestic racial conflict would be to risk the realization of major foreign policy goals.

THE VOTER REGISTRATION PACT OF 1961

The immediate trigger for coalition-making as the conflict intensified was the CORE-sponsored Freedom Ride of the spring of 1961. That was the direct action crusade that threw the Kennedy administration into disarray. It did so in large part because civil disorder during interstate travel tested—and put into sharp conflict—state and *federal* law enforcement authority. To solve the emergency resulting from the Freedom Ride, the administration proposed to help the civil rights movements with voter registration campaigns—and they accepted.

The Freedom Ride was meant to fuse two tactics: the "jail-in" and the "protest journey" (first pioneered in the little-known 1947 Freedom Ride by CORE.) The new Freedom Riders would test state and local compliance with a just-released Supreme Court decision that banned local official segregation within terminals that served interstate travelers. If arrested, they would conduct a jail-in. Southern lack of compliance with national constitutional law would be highlighted by the flooding of local jails with protesters who refused to participate in a sequence of bail, summary judgment for violation of unconstitutional local ordinances, and acceptance of scheduled fines. Instead they would insist on jail until such time as full process on the merits was complete. The Riders would, they thought, force southern officials and the nation to grasp just how absurd and repressive segregation really was.

On May 4, 1961, the second Freedom Ride departed from Washington. In time, 416 black and white Freedom Riders, recruited by CORE and the SNCC, faced—and survived because of their training in nonviolent self-protection—extraordinary mob violence, police and judicial excess and misbehavior, and severe abuse in the state and local jails of the Deep South. One bus was bombed in Alabama with a Molotov cocktail; a local hospital then refused to treat black Freedom Riders suffering from smoke inhalation. An elderly white Detroit doctor suffered permanent brain damage from his severe beating in the Birmingham bus terminal.[24]

On May 21 and 22, the Kennedy administration deployed in Montgomery six hundred federal officers recruited from the Border Patrol, the Bureau of Prisons, the Bureau of Alcohol, Tobacco, and Firearms, and U.S. Marshals' offices in several states. Sworn in as deputy marshals for the Middle District of Alabama, they were under the command of Deputy Attorney General (and later U.S. Supreme Court justice) Byron White. They prevented a violent mob attack on a black church where Martin Luther King Jr. was speaking. The governor of Alabama then placed Montgomery under martial law.[25]

By now the president was alarmed, and he pleaded with his civil rights advisors to find a way to stop the Freedom Riders, who had announced that they would travel from Montgomery to Jackson, Mississippi. The president believed that the controversy "was 'embarrassing him and the country on the eve of the meeting in Vienna with Khrushchev.'" After the Jackson city police arrested the Freedom Riders as they stepped off their bus, Robert Kennedy, the attorney general, publicly asked for a "cooling-off period." Observing that "the President was about to leave for a summit conference with the leader of the Soviet Union, he asked that people refrain from any activity that might bring discredit on the United States, for it could harm the President's mission."[26]

The Democratic Party was again ripe for coalitional expansion. In the case of Harry Truman, the dominant condition for such enlargement of the Democratic Party's base was candidate insecurity. In the case of Kennedy, the dominant condition was the need to resolve a threat to the highly valued foreign policy goal of successfully managing the bipolar tension between the United States and the Soviet Union.

Recall that a threat to the realization of highly valued policy goals was a key part of the danger that Andrew Johnson posed to the Republicans. A similar instance occurred in 1881, when Republicans helped the Readjusters remobilize black Virginians in order to achieve just enough unified national control to pass tariff legislation. In this instance, the Democratic Party needed help from African Americans in order to achieve a major goal: manage U.S.-Soviet relations competently.

Seeking to land a harness on the direct action movements, the administration soon proposed a mass voter registration drive. Carl Brauer, the historian of the Kennedy administration's relation to the second reconstruction, writes: "Soon after the May crisis subsided, several key government officials, including Robert Kennedy, Burke Marshall, and Harris Wofford, encouraged civil rights leaders to launch a large-scale voter registration project. They would have been reluctant to admit it, but the channeling of civil rights activism into voter registration work offered a much lower risk of the kind of violence that had accompanied the Freedom Rides—violence that had almost necessitated federal military intervention."[27]

Harris Wofford's "insider" memoir parallels Brauer's account. He writes: "At the June 1961 meeting of the Subcabinet Group on Civil Rights, Jack Conway, Deputy Administrator of the Housing and Home Finance Agency, remarked that the idea of nonviolent direct action against segregation had caught fire. . . . The Assistant Postmaster General, Richard Murphy, said the movement would grow and counsels of caution or efforts to 'cool off' the situation were futile. It was agreed that if federal agencies . . . used their full power to protect and promote equal rights, the necessity for popular pressure could be removed or at least reduced. Burke Marshall said that he and the Attorney General were encouraging vigorous voting registration efforts and thought 'it would be valuable if some of the present energy were channeled into this vital work.' "[28]

In a decision that effectively set America on a course toward the Voting Rights Act of 1965, the SCLC, the SNCC, and CORE accepted the Kennedy administration's proposal. Their acceptance was fostered, no doubt, by their already robust organizational investments in voter registration, along with other types of protest. The first voter registration drive of the civil rights era began February 12, 1958, when the newly formed SCLC kicked off a "Crusade for Citizenship" in twenty-two southern cities. Not to be outdone, the NAACP also committed itself to a huge voter registration campaign. From 1957 to 1960 the parallel drives consciously sought to strengthen the 1957 Civil Rights Act.[29]

The end result was a formal agreement to register black voters and thus to further implement the 1957 and 1960 Civil Rights Acts. The Voter Education Project emerged from several conferences in the late spring of 1961 that brought together philanthropists, civil rights leaders, and Justice Department officials. Coordinated by the Southern Regional Council of Atlanta, the VEP disbursed nearly about $870,000 in 1962 dollars (or about $6,117,500 in 2003 dollars) to the four major civil rights organizations. A nonprofit agency that officially collected reports on local obstacles to voting from volunteers provided by the leading civil rights organizations, VEP clearly meant to stimulate voter registration and perhaps to affect the 1964 elections.[30]

Just as the NAACP had earlier implemented *Smith v. Allwright,* the new organizations would implement federal law. In 1944, however, the Roosevelt administration had offered the NAACP no help, and the Truman Administration had continued that hands-off approach. In 1961, in contrast, executive branch officials promised and gave the NAACP's successors substantial resources, private and public.

Indeed, by 1964, fifty-six federal lawyers gave fifty thousand hours, or twenty-four years' worth of forty-hour work weeks, of *unpaid overtime* to voting rights enforcement via litigation. Between 1957 and 1964 the annual budget for Justice Department voting rights enforcement increased 440 percent and the number of personnel 186 percent. In 1964 federal civil rights personnel observed twenty-five hundred rights demonstrations and sent sixty thousand communications, up from thirteen thousand in 1960.[31]

On the ground, the registration across the South of voting-age African Americans jumped 48 percent from 1962 to 1964, from approximately 29 percent of voting-age black southerners to approximately 43 percent. Strictly speaking, the causal role of the VEP in the *regional* increase is still uncertain and has not been econometrically modeled. Nonetheless, in their study of CORE, Meier and Rudwick sketched the geography of CORE operations for the VEP. Besides Mississippi's Fourth Congressional District, they included nineteen counties in South Carolina, rural areas in northern Florida, Tallahassee, and Miami, and several northern Louisiana parishes as well as Louisiana's Sixth Congressional District. Meier and Rudwick estimated that "monthly registration in CORE's area" in South Carolina "rose from 400 in May 1963 to a high of 1900 in January 1964." Other locales where the VEP evidently increased registration were Jacksonville, Savannah, Raleigh, Petersburg and Portsmouth, Virginia, Richmond, Charlotte, Birmingham, Nashville, and Rome, Georgia. The VEP was, in short, probably a major cause of the regional increase in black voter registration, given its door-to-door canvassing, citizenship schools, and gathering of citizens to register.[32]

Despite such success, the 1961 voting rights pact did *not* achieve the Kennedy administration's ulterior goal in coalition-making: lowering the political temperature. Intended to manage interracial conflict, it actually set in motion exceptionally centrifugal forces. The pact eventually needed renegotiation. In that need, there was a possibility for a stronger version of the Riker-Gamson coalition that this book has explored. Nothing guaranteed a better voting rights pact. But having committed itself to direct voter registration, the northern wing of the Democratic Party would soon encounter a test of its resolve.

The Instability of the Kennedy Administration's Voting Rights Pact

It does no disservice to administration officials, to the movement members that were parties to the pact, or to the dedicated officers of the Voter Education Project to characterize institutional sources of the 1961 pact's deep instability. Doing so is essential for understanding the new set of possibilities that emerged by 1965. Turn first to the provisions of the 1957 and 1960 Civil Rights Acts.

The 1957 act was largely about voting rights, and it created institutions for promoting them that have proven durable and important: the United States Commission on Civil Rights and a separate Civil Rights Division in the Justice Department based on the Criminal Division's old Civil Rights Unit. As for the 1960 statute, it strengthened government litigation and fact-finding capacities. It also criminalized new forms of white-on-black violence.

Several threads connect the statutes. First, they lowered the stakes in federal litigation against local elections officials. They did this by requiring federal action to be a *civil* rather than a criminal action. The federal government would not punish; instead, it would prod. This was a very important shift; it was also inevitable. The South had hundreds of state and local elections officials. The switch in about 1890 from party-strip balloting to the Australian ballot and disenfranchisement created an army of such officials. To place them all under the threat of criminal proceedings would have been an impossible task in 1957, or really at any time after the rise of the Australian ballot.[33]

Second, all of the statutes sought to strengthen black voting rights by means of federal acquisition of information from state and local officers and citizens about actual voting rights practices in the South. This would happen via the Civil Rights Commission and the Justice Department. Such information was necessary for successful government litigation in the federal courts and for revising policy.[34]

Third, both statutes made civil litigation against state and local elections officers in the federal district courts, and the threat of such litigation, *the* basic federal mechanism for generating increases in levels of African American voter registration. Litigation proceeded according to the 1957 law on the basis of individual sworn complaints concerning discriminatory or intimidating treatment by private individuals or public officials, the circumstances of which were investigated by the FBI. With respect to the 1960 law, government attorneys and their assistants traveled through the South collecting data to support a federal claim of a "pattern or practice" of racial discrimination in elections administration.

Here, however, we come to the two basic limits of the 1957 and 1960 acts. First, because litigation was inherently complex and time-consuming, the framers of the statutes counted on a great deal of voluntary compliance from state and local elections officials for their efficacy. Second, the civil rights statutes presumed a compliant federal judiciary, eager to work with federal lawyers to change race relations.

In the Deep South, neither assumption worked. Burke Marshall, the assistant attorney general for civil rights, freely conceded this in public lectures given at Columbia University in March and April 1964. At the first lecture he displayed the results of thirty-five federal cases in the South from the Eisenhower administration to the Kennedy administration. Ninety-one percent of these cases sought to increase black voter registration in the Deep South. Despite the Kennedy administration's assertive enforcement, the results were "not encouraging"—as table 8.3 shows. Although jurisdictions that saw interventions during the Eisenhower administration showed relatively large increases in black voter registration by 1963, such change could not be attributed to federal intervention. Many other factors played a role in the intervening five years. The impact of federal lawyering was clearest in cases that were filed in 1963. The jurisdictions involved witnessed an increase of seven-tenths of a percentage point. What explained so meager a record?[35]

Southern elections administration officials in several states did not, first of all, comply with federal law or federal investigations. They instead

Table 8.3 Impact of Federal Voting Rights Litigation in the Deep South, 1958–1963

Number of Cases Filed against Local Jurisdictions (30 counties, 2 cities), by year*	Filings per State	(Average) Voting-Age Adults Registered within Local Jurisdiction(s) at Time of Filing (%)	(Average) Black Voting-Age Adults Registered by December 1, 1963 (%)
1958 (1)	GA (1)	1	4.6
1959 (2)	AL (1); LA (1)	8.8	33
1960 (1)	LA (2)	.64	14
1961 (14)	AL (3); LA (5); MS (6)	2.2	6.1
1962 (5)	AL (2); LA (1); MS (2)	6.7	8.5
1963 (9)	AL (3); LA (4); MS (2)	5.6	6.3

Source: My calculations are based on Burke Marshall, *Federalism and Civil Rights* (New York: Columbia University Press, 1964), pp. 25–27.
*Three of 35 cases are not listed. One was filed outside the Deep South (Fayette County, TN); two of the Deep South cases aimed to desegregate voting practices (e.g., separate lines on election day) rather than force registration.

withheld valuable information and destroyed records. To up the ante, Louisiana and Mississippi legislators proved their willingness to stay one step ahead by adding *new* registration requirements. This tactic cleverly turned the pattern or practice requirement of the 1960 law against the federal government, for the concept inherently required a record of years' worth of official behavior, after all, before there could be enough facts to show a pattern or practice.

The premise of a compliant federal judiciary often turned out to be illusory as well. Marshall pointed out that "the bench reflects the customs and attitudes of the community." In appointing district judges the president relied on the recommendations of the U.S. senators in the states where vacancies on the bench occurred. "This is one of the facts of the federal system," Marshall noted. "It is inevitable that most district judges want to do as little as possible to disturb the patterns of life and politics in their state and community." Thus it was a district judge in Georgia who in April 1959 stopped Justice Department efforts to compel officials in Terrell County to register black citizens by declaring the 1957 Civil Rights Act unconstitutional.[36]

Recalcitrant federal judges could and did use the opportunities for delay built into the deliberate, slow-moving nature of judicial proceedings to frustrate Justice Department efforts. They could also rule against the United States. More than one hundred Justice Department actions failed in this way.[37]

These limitations of the 1957 and 1960 Civil Rights Acts were rooted in a further characteristic that they shared: minimal renegotiation of federalism. Although they created new central governmental tasks and capacities and a new federal judicial role, they also went easy on federalism as it existed then. As Marshall said, "The national effort is to realize the constitutional rights of Negroes in states where they are now denied, but to do so with the smallest possible federal intrusion."[38]

Marshall expressed sympathy with civil rights workers' great frustration concerning the limits they faced. But extensive mobilization of federal law enforcement (or military personnel) to protect civil rights workers was simply too costly, he thought, for the larger constitutional scheme. He also rejected an idea first proposed in 1959 by the Civil Rights Commission, namely, direct federal registration. Indeed, he glumly associated that idea with Reconstruction. His view captured misgivings that others shared. "The sole alternative [to government litigation] with any precedent is the use of federal registration officials, as in the early Reconstruction period—a system which worked then only because of immediately available military force, and which ceased to work at all when that force was removed."[39]

The upshot of all this was a grim situation. Far from lowering the political temperature, the voting rights pact set in motion an appalling ordeal. The VEP encountered fierce official resistance and private violence in what were known as the "hardcore" areas of the drive: southwest Georgia, western and northern Louisiana, "Black Belt" Alabama, and all of Mississippi. Rampant, deliberate abuse of local elections administration awaited them. Very little prevented local elections registrars or boards from operating as they saw fit. They would close offices arbitrarily on scheduled days of operation, fail to open, process applicants as slowly as possible so that people would have to stand in line in the hot sun, or process registrations but subsequently reject them as invalid. Registrars were known to physically attack applicants, who would then be arrested and jailed for disturbance of the peace.[40]

Civil rights workers were hung on the horns of what Marshall called "the inescapable dilemma of the federal system." Yet the Kennedy administration was loath to intervene, believing that doing so would cause a white backlash that would sharply split the Congress from the presidency. The administration sought, in effect, to reconstruct the Democratic Party on the cheap. Or perhaps Kennedy, not being a white southerner, simply did not see what Johnson would later see: a great opportunity.[41]

The Kennedy administration and civil rights field workers grew angry with each other. Voter Education Project workers expected federal protection, certain that the administration had promised it to them in the spring of 1961 when the VEP was being set up. Some SNCC workers occupied Justice Department offices in Washington in protest, while others sued the federal government, asking the court to order the attorney general and the FBI to protect civil rights workers from Mississippi law enforcement officers. But from its perspective the Justice Department constantly faced unrealistic demands that were rooted in, to use Burke Marshall's sarcastic retort, "an immense ignorance, apparently untouched by the curricula of the best universities, of the consequences of the federal system."[42]

The result was the exposure of black citizens and civil rights workers to private violence. Direct action organizers and the often-terrified targets of their operations faced beatings, shootings, and bombings. Citizens in certain places actually turned and jogged the other way rather than be caught on the main street of a Deep South village holding a VEP flyer. Daily life was thick with menace as local law enforcement turned a blind eye. As one CORE organizer in Louisiana wrote to her parents, "We've got to travel many miles, spend much time just talking, before we convince one Negro to go to the registrar's office. In a typical week I contact 150 people, train 60, send 18 to the registrar's office, and have 9 of them get registered."[43]

The local police, judiciary, and prosecutors did a lot of white supremacy's dirty work. They assiduously surveilled, harassed, arrested, and jailed movement participants as often as they could, typically on minor or trumped-up infractions of little-known but sweeping and vaguely written ordinances. They would sometimes put them in cells with prisoners known to be violent. The idea was to tie up time, money, and manpower long enough to break or inhibit SNCC, SCLC, CORE, or local operations, to cause them physical and psychic injury, or to scare them badly.[44]

The official abuse was frequently Kafkaesque. On May 8, 1963, a black registration activist's home in Mississippi was bombed; the next day he was arrested and charged with arson. On August 9, 1963, four student workers were arrested in Georgia and charged with insurrection, a capital offense under Georgia law. The local prosecutor held them without bail until January 1964, when a federal court invalidated the statute. A September 19, 1963, letter to the mayor and district attorney of Clinton, Louisiana, from twelve local African American citizens politely requesting a biracial civil rights and community relations committee led to their arrest on December 3 on the charge of seeking to intimidate public officials. Each was required to post a $4,000 bail bond.[45]

Finally, a mass violent white underground emerged. This was most notable in Mississippi, where the local police and state authorities were unable and unwilling to control it. On the contrary, they colluded in it.[46] By the winter of 1964, the respectable Citizens Council, which had been founded in Mississippi, no longer controlled white supremacy's defense. The White Knights of the Ku Klux Klan took its place. Mississippi literally burned. On one night alone in May 1964, Klan crosses burned in sixty-four of the state's eighty-two counties. Murders and bombings of black leaders occurred. A state highway patrolman stopped four SNCC workers traveling to Atlanta and badly beat them.[47]

By then, local civil rights leaders agreed to accept and work with white student volunteers organized by white liberals on northern campuses. This effort would be known as Freedom Summer 1964, an extraordinary biracial movement. Veterans of the SNCC and CORE and new volunteers helped with establishing local freedom schools. At these community centers local people learned to read, talk freely about their rights, and build local solidarity. The idea was to keep the momentum for protest, sustain nonviolence, and socialize the conflict in Mississippi by generating national attention.[48]

Yet the violence and harassment hardly slackened. An "incident summary" for only one rural area reads, in part, as follows:

June 21: Homes of two NAACP members bombed. . . . Seven dynamite sticks
found on lawn of Mrs. Corine Andrews.

July 8: SNCC Freedom House bombed.

July 17: Mount Zion Hill Baptist Church . . . burned to the ground.

July 22: Mount Vernon Missionary Baptist Church . . . burned to the ground.

July 24: Mr. Brock, owner of local Negro cafe, beaten and then arrested.
Policeman threatened to kill him.

July 26: Two bombs thrown at home of Charles Bryant . . . a shot was fired into
the house.

July 27: Staff member Mendy Samstein arrested . . . while driving local Negro
children for voter registration canvassing.

August 4: Two Negro boys, students at Freedom School, who had been
receiving harrasing [sic] phone calls were arrested for using profanity over
the phone, tried without counsel, and sentenced one year each to jail
under Mississippi's phone harrassment law.[49]

Not surprisingly, Freedom Summer leaders expected that *something*
would finally seize national attention. Their premonitions became real
on June 21, 1964, when three volunteers, Andrew Goodman, Michael
Schwerner, and James Chaney, disappeared in Neshoba County. The governors of Mississippi and Alabama claimed that their disappearance was a hoax.
But the missing men were soon found dead from bullet wounds in an earthen
dam. Eventually, the United States proved that a local sheriff's deputy belonging to a klan abducted them so that klansmen could execute them.[50]

Frank R. Parker, a voting rights lawyer who spent most of his legal career
in Jackson, Mississippi, once wrote that the "ultimate test of whether the
promises of the fourteenth and fifteenth amendments can ever be made a
reality has always been Mississippi. . . . Mississippi has had the highest percentage of black people of any state . . . and has been the scene of the most
intransigent resistance to the constitutional rights of black people."[51] As the
civil rights movements encountered the "ultimate test"—for further klan-
style violence seemed likely—what prospects were there for full electoral
reinclusion? Indeed, how could the coalition-making process survive the
deep distrust between civil rights organizations and the Democratic Party?

The answers are to be found in the famous Selma campaign. In the story
of the battle there, and of its national effects, that follows, no original facts are
presented. Rather, the point of the vignette is to lay bare, again, actual
dynamics of coalition formation and, in particular, to stress the behavior
specified by that theoretical concept. In the original Riker-Gamson formulation, elites are the primary actors. But this book has stressed the importance

of *both* coalition partners behaving purposefully. The tale thus underscores the tactical cunning of the civil rights organizations and of Lyndon Johnson. Civil rights leaders appear to have known that they were racing the clock. Evidently Johnson knew, too. His race relations advisor, Louis Martin, reported that "[h]e used to say, 'We don't have much time.' He knew the country's mood was not going to remain that way." At some point, northern white backlash would kick in. When the moment for a stronger voting rights pact came, it had to be seized right then.[52]

THE TURNING POINT IN SELMA

Toward the end of 1964, local civil rights activists in Selma, Alabama, asked Martin Luther King Jr. for help with their long-standing voter registration campaign. King announced in Selma on January 2, 1965, that movement leaders meant "to arouse the federal government." Selma would show why America needed a strong national voting rights statute. In Dallas County, where Selma was located, only 2 percent of all voting-age African Americans were registered despite several years of effort.[53]

Events in Selma threw a lurid light on how far state and local officials in the Deep South really would go to block black registration. National newspapers recorded wild assaults by the local sheriff on blacks applying to vote. On February 18, in the nearby town of Marion, the Alabama state police attacked reporters from NBC News and the *New York Times* and launched a frenzied attack on black citizens. Troopers trapped several protest marchers in a local cafe and beat them. An unarmed twenty-six-year old pulpwood cutter and church deacon, Jimmie Lee Jackson, punched one of several troopers beating his mother as she lay pinned to the floor. In response, an officer shot him. Other troopers beat Jackson as he staggered outside.

Jimmie Lee Jackson's subsequent death in a hospital on February 26 spurred a march to Montgomery in his honor. It set out on March 7. Fifty mounted Alabama state troopers and the local sheriff and his "possemen" halted the march. They teargassed, clubbed, horsewhipped, and trampled the marchers in front of television reporters from the major networks. The video footage of the scene, a full fifteen minutes of which were broadcast that evening to forty-eight million viewers on ABC, could not have been more damning. The audiotape added to its power. Viewers heard racist yells from the police and the dull thuds, again and again, of police clubs hitting people. The day became known as "Bloody Sunday."[54]

The newly elected Johnson suddenly swung into action. On March 15, he delivered an extraordinary televised address to a joint session of Congress urging rapid, forceful legislation: "[T]here must be no delay, or no hesitation or no compromise with our purpose. . . . I ask you to join me in working long hours, nights, and weekends." During a dramatic moment the president invoked the civil rights anthem, saying, "We shall overcome!" It was a resonant choice, for the song really was sung at tense moments in southern churches and meetings for many years. It is said that, watching in Selma, Martin Luther King Jr. wept.[55]

Johnson's tribute was sincere. Although he had rather carefully planned for voting rights reform from the moment of his landslide election in 1964, he also preferred keeping the precise timing open. At the White House in mid-December 1964, King, on his return from receiving the Nobel Peace Prize, pressed Johnson for new federal voting rights legislation. But he replied, "Martin, you're right about that. I'm going to do it eventually, but I can't get a voting rights bill through in this session of Congress." The president perhaps did not want to risk Great Society legislation in 1965 by also requesting a voting rights bill. But the time came in 1965.[56]

By August 6, a bill that, among other provisions, bypassed state and local resistance and established direct federal voter registration was ready. Johnson traveled to the Capitol to sign it in the "President's Room," just off the Senate chamber, in a ceremony carried live on national television. King sat near the president as he signed the bill. The president called it "one of the most monumental laws in the entire history of American freedom."[57]

In retrospect there is, of course, an air of inevitability about the Voting Rights Act. It is hard to imagine that something so important to American national life could not have happened in the end. Quite possibly, though, the compelling nonviolent protest in Selma that did so much to empower Johnson to procure the act came at the last possible moment. Race riots in August 1965 and public alarm about such organizations as the Black Panthers crystallized a long-building northern white backlash. Governor George Wallace of Alabama nearly rode it into the White House in 1968. The Johnson administration was in disarray by then. The Voting Rights Act would have been less likely after the spring and summer of 1965.

The civil rights organizations were therefore crucial. Here in the story one sees the full importance of African American political will in coalition formation, in particular the awareness of history's rhythms that could be found among the people of the civil rights organizations. As activists sought to implement the pact with the Kennedy administration, movement leaders found that local officials' resistance to nonviolent direct action was stronger and more brutal than they anticipated. They drew a key—and fateful—distinction in their thinking. Some law enforcement officials, they noticed, were unprofessional, bloodthirsty, and manic; others, however, were quite controlled and efficient. The latter style was what they encountered in Albany, Georgia, in the fall of 1961. The cool professionalism of law enforcement in shutting down protest actually led the national media to denounce Martin Luther King as a failure and the administration to publicly praise the local police for their calm demeanor.[58]

In the spring of 1963 civil rights leaders came to the realization that, tactically and strategically, the deranged police response provided a critical political lever that the professional response did not. Midway through the Birmingham campaign of early 1963, a key SCLC official, Wyatt Tee Walker, appears to have argued to his colleagues that national media attention increased with police violence and that federal official attention grew in the wake of heightened media scrutiny. Soon, in fact, movement leaders interpreted the Kennedy administration's proposal of the 1963 Civil Rights Act as a direct response to the terribly troubled and riotous Birmingham campaign. If Birmingham got a federal response, then the implication for the future was clear: a big voting rights statute would surely emerge from another setting in which official frenzy was likely.[59]

They needed such a law. The 1964 Civil Rights Act was not it. Its first title provided for expedited adjudication of voting rights cases and for several federal standards (for example, written literacy tests only and presumption of literacy if the applicant had completed the sixth grade) that local registrars were required to observe. But that is all that the 1964 act did for voting rights. Hence Selma, where a voting rights campaign of several years' duration was stalled. There a local judge enjoined *any* meeting of more than three people convened to discuss or to promote voting or civil rights. The Dallas County Sheriff vigorously enforced the injunction. Often visibly frantic with rage, he liked using electric cattle prods on bystanders and prisoners alike. Alabama, like Mississippi, also had an active and murderous klan underground. The state's governor, George Wallace, was proving himself to be a talented, reckless defender of white supremacy. Rounding out this semiauthoritarian tableau was the director of the state police, Colonel Al Lingo, brutal, eager for battle, and probably klan-connected.[60]

In the end, the scope and barbarity of official violence in Alabama stunned America's public officials and the attentive public. The belief that Congress and the Johnson administration ought to do something decisive and vital about black voting rights as quickly as possible became overwhelming and pervasive.[61]

That political pressure, it bears repeating, was a *construct*. It was an outcome intended by the civil rights organizations who gathered in Selma. Time was running out on the coalition that Kennedy and his colleagues had created. The process of making it work generated shocking savagery, as the deaths in Mississippi showed. Who knew what the future held if somehow Congress and the president were not really and truly prodded into making a strong voting rights statute? That was the question hanging over the leaders of the organizations on the ground—and Democratic leaders in Washington.

The civil rights organizations understood, of course, that they had an unparalleled opportunity in Kennedy's succession. His vice president, Lyndon Baines Johnson, showed that as president he would be nothing like the wily Senate majority leader who brokered the 1957 Civil Rights Act or the man who balanced the ticket in 1960 so that Kennedy could carry the South. On November 27, 1963, only five days after Kennedy's assassination in Dallas, Johnson addressed a joint session of Congress, urging the "earliest possible passage of the [1963] civil rights bill" as a monument to Kennedy, who had first proposed it. Around this time, he also brought his old friend and former mentor, the arch-segregationist senator Richard Russell of Georgia, to the White House to explain what would happen. "Dick, you've got to get out of my way. I'm going to run over you. I don't intend to cavil or compromise." Russell replied, "You may do that. But, by God, it's going to cost you the South, and cost you the election."[62]

Johnson never backed down. Why? Here we see the role of candidate insecurity. It did not generate coalitional expansion specifically with respect to voting rights. But it did create an essential context for the 1965 expansion.

In a 1989 interview with the political scientist Mark Stern, Lawrence O'Brien, who advised both Kennedy and Johnson, noted that "Johnson believed the Kennedy people were going to try to deny him the nomination in '64. At Atlantic City . . . a coup might be pulled to stop him from being nominated." Johnson told his confidante, Doris Kearns, "I knew that if I didn't get out in front on this issue [the liberals] would get me. I had to produce a civil rights bill that was even stronger than the one they'd have gotten if Kennedy had lived. Without this, I'd be dead before I could even begin." And he delivered: the 1964 Civil Rights Act was a towering piece of legislation.[63]

But Johnson also knew that he wanted some sort of voting rights statute. He planned to reform the Kennedy administration's voting rights pact. In late December 1964, after his smashing landslide election, the attorney general, Nicholas Katzenbach, sent Johnson a sketch of his statutory options. Johnson was exactly the right person in the Oval Office to make the most of the opportunity that the civil rights organizations handed him in the first half of 1965. As the Selma crisis unfolded, he exhorted his team at the Justice Department to find a formula for decisive change that, in the words of a department staffer, "would by-pass the litigation, in effect, and put the presumption in favor of the voter."[64]

He enjoyed, furthermore, one of the rare moments in American party history of unified party government based on supermajority control of the Senate and the House. One had to go back to the seeming high point of the New Deal, the Seventy-fifth Congress, to find a numerically greater margin of control. Even so, Roosevelt's working liberal majority was smaller than Johnson's in 1965 because the Seventy-fifth Congress included so many southern Democrats in positions of seniority and leadership.

Southern Democrats went into the Eighty-ninth Congress with a significantly weaker blocking position. Thanks to the 1964 national elections, the number of nonsouthern Democrats in the party's two congressional wings *grew*. Southern Democrats as a percentage of House Democrats dropped from 38 percent to 32 percent. Also, NOMINATE scores devised by Poole and Rosenthal suggest that House newcomers were more racially liberal than previous House members. Thirty-six southern Democrats voted on final passage for the VRA.[65]

Somewhat similarly, southern Democrats as a percentage of Senate Democrats dropped slightly, from 31 percent to 29 percent. But three of the southern senators were actually liberals who supported the VRA. Further, Richard Russell of Georgia, the master of Senate procedure who usually led the obstructionist bloc, was seriously ill at this time. The size of the working obstructionist bloc was now 23 percent, not 31 percent. The leadership permitted a brief southern filibuster—as a courtesy!—and then handily suppressed it with a 70–30 cloture vote. America now had a Voting Rights Act.[66]

Conclusion

This chapter has explored the vital coalitional breakthroughs concentrated in a four-year period from 1961 to 1965. Much like the previous cases described in this book, coalition-making began with insiders reacting to a threat or combination of political dangers and problems by working to bring in others. During the Kennedy administration, foreign policy goals seemed to be in danger from growing unrest in the South, so it offered to fund and to protect voter registration efforts by civil rights organizations. But the pact of 1961 led to an increase in conflict instead. Therefore, even before Kennedy's tragic assassination, the tactical advantage in cementing the new biracial coalition shifted to the civil rights organizations, simply because it fell to them—and them alone—to maintain nonviolent self-discipline.

They succeeded in both restraining growing pressures for militant self-defense politics *and* simultaneously pushing for a major change in federal voting rights law. This pressure galvanized the Johnson administration. Given his own startling emergence as the most ardent white civil rights figure in national politics since Charles Sumner, Johnson cooperated with the civil rights organizations on *his* end, completing the coalitional process that Kennedy had begun four years earlier. Despite the deep distrust between civil rights organizations and the Democratic Party that violence in Mississippi and elsewhere created, the coalition came together.

But what would happen next? It is fitting to let King have the last word. In mid-January 1965, Johnson called King on his birthday, now a national holiday. The two quickly focused on current events in general and black voter registration in particular. King said to Johnson, "It's very interesting, Mr. President, to notice that the only states you didn't carry in the South . . . have less than 40 percent of the Negroes registered to vote. . . . It's so important to get Negroes registered to vote in large numbers in the South. It would be this coalition of the Negro vote and the moderate white vote that will really make the new South."[67] Chapter 9 considers how this vision came into being.

How the Second Reconstruction Stabilized

By the year 2001, the states of Mississippi and Alabama combined had more African American elected officials, 1,628, than the entire United States had had in 1970. Black office-holding was indeed widespread in the South. Black voting, too, was routine. Southern governments' fiscal allocations for such things as hospitals, libraries, roads, and jobs, responded to the renewal of black suffrage and office-holding.[1]

Glaring problems have emerged, to be sure. A tendency to regard the Voting Rights Act (VRA) suspiciously broke forth in the 1990s among a conservative 5–4 majority of the Supreme Court. The rate of felony disenfranchisement among black adult males rose considerably. Racial bias in elections administration has resurfaced as a serious issue since the presidential election of 2000, temporarily halting, for instance, California's gubernatorial recall election in the fall of 2003.[2]

Many whites evidence plain misgivings about black office-holding. Party politicians indeed openly refer to such qualms. When the Texas congressional redistricting struggle of 2003 ended in the way that U.S. House Majority Leader Tom DeLay wanted it to, two white Democrats with long service in the House complained about the packing of Texas districts with high concentrations of minority voters who were likely to elect African American or Latino politicians to Congress. "A Republican tactic against the Democrats," one of them said, "is to eliminate all white officials of consequence, so white voters will not identify with the Democratic party."[3]

Still, as the twenty-first century began the second reconstruction was a thriving concern. It had produced a well-developed, biracial public sphere that was now a fairly normal part of U.S. political life. Yet the second reconstruction's relative success was not obvious for some time. From 1966 to 1967, four civil rights murders occurred in Mississippi. Among the victims was Vernon Dahmer, an NAACP leader whose home was firebombed the day he issued a statement on the radio announcing that he would personally pay poll taxes. Voter registration workers in Mississippi in 1971 "were shot at, arrested on false traffic charges, and had their auto tires slashed." From 1966 to 1974, the Justice Department deployed 7,359 elections observers in Alabama, Georgia, Louisiana, Mississippi, and South Carolina, 77 percent of those in Alabama and Mississippi. Drew Days III, the assistant attorney general for civil rights during the Carter administration, has written that "[b]etween early 1977 and the end of 1980, the attorney general . . . authorized the assignment of over three thousand federal observers to monitor elections . . . upon a judgment that physical interference, intimidation, or pressure was likely to be directed at minority voters if the federal observers were not there."[4]

Just as insidious was a rush by racially conservative white legislators to exploit the VRA's silence regarding black office-holding. The act clearly proscribed racialized impediments to casting a ballot. But some sorts of legal structures were not patently in violation of the act. Seeking to prevent black office-holding, southern states and localities quickly switched their rules in ways that exploited the antipathy of white voters to black candidates for public office. Southern governments shifted to at-large voting for local assemblies, required run-off voting between the two top vote-getters, sought to annex areas with largely white populations, changed the responsibilities or terms of elective offices (or simply made them appointive), redrew district lines, and sought to have legislative districts with artificially large white majorities by means of multimember districting, which, in turn, could keep an entire legislature lily-white, so long as the rules encouraged them to do so. The generic name for these racially conservative strategies came to be "vote dilution"—that is, dilution of black voters' influence over government.[5]

Given the initial resistance, just how the second reconstruction became a success after 1965 requires concise description. In doing that, this chapter will lead us toward chapter 10's account of *why* the second reconstruction stabilized but the first did not. This chapter also illustrates, as did chapters 4 and

5, one of this book's basic points: that what happened *after* coalition formation revealed the coalition's prospects for entrenchment.

Below I trace both jurisprudence-building and party-building. I discuss
the Voting Rights Act's architecture, initial Supreme Court tests, and the act's
renewals. I pay particular attention to how legal change promoted the desegregation of the South's Democratic parties in essential ways. At the conclusion, I also quickly outline the broader VRA that has emerged out of the
original act. The second reconstruction not only has survived but has been
able to do more work than the first reconstruction. The VRA today addresses
many forms of minority voting discrimination. I begin by tracing the
oft-noted clever design of the original Voting Rights Act.

THE VOTING RIGHTS ACT IN ITS ORIGINAL FORM

To grasp the VRA's ingenuity, it helps to first quickly review the legal, administrative, and political situation before 1965. The pre-VRA environment structurally shrank the black (and white) electorate by means of literacy tests, poll
taxes, stringent residency requirements, requirements that registration occur
months before actual elections, and inconvenient hours and arrangements for
registration. For those who nonetheless banged at the doors, there was targeted retaliation: rejection at the discretion of local electoral administrators,
arrest, intimidation, job loss, and sometimes violent death.

This legal and political context was, furthermore, relatively immune to
the pre-1965 national voting rights statutes—the 1957, 1960, and 1964 Civil
Rights Acts. They "sought to strengthen litigation remedies" and "were the
vehicle for the Justice Department's litigation program." But, as chapter 8
showed, that program, despite rapid increases in manpower and other
resources, had little effect.[6]

The design of the Voting Rights Act efficiently got around the earlier difficulties. As a leading voting rights lawyer noted, the "1965 statute simply outlawed the major devices that had been employed to prevent blacks from
voting . . . and set up a system to monitor changes in existing voting regulations." Three elements interacted: the coverage formula, which took in the
Deep South states, the requirement that any proposed electoral rules changes
survive review by the Justice Department, and the suspension of tests and
devices.[7]

First, the VRA formally suspended the continued operation of the older
legal and administrative structure. Section 4 of title I of the act applied the
statute to any state or county that maintained a voting test or device on
November 1, 1964, and where the census showed voter registration or

turnout for the 1964 presidential election below 50 percent of the voting-age population. These tests or devices were now stopped for five years. The act covered all of Alabama, Alaska, Georgia, Louisiana, Mississippi, South Carolina, and Virginia, twenty-six North Carolina counties, three Arizona counties, one Hawaii county, and one Idaho county. The act also prevented the state of New York from enforcing its English-language competence test against voting-age Puerto Ricans residing in New York. Section 6 of the act authorized appointment of federal examiners in jurisdictions covered by section 4.

Second, section 5, creating a device called "preclearance," required the submission of any planned changes in voting rules in the covered jurisdictions to either the attorney general or a three-judge district court of the District of Columbia for prior approval. This was a potent instrument. As one associate justice of the Supreme Court said in conference when the Court first reviewed the VRA, "Section 5 shocks me, because a state must go for approval to the Attorney General."[8]

Third, the act built on the Twenty-fourth Amendment to the Constitution. This amendment resulted from an anti–poll tax campaign that first emerged in the 1930s as New Deal liberals sought to build a southern base, and it was finally ratified in 1964. But it covered only poll taxes for federal elections. The poll tax was still used in state and local elections in Alabama, Arkansas, Mississippi, Texas, and Virginia. Mississippi's administration of the tax was particularly onerous. The county sheriff collected it; payment was legally restricted to the Christmas season. New registrants had to pay not only the current year's levy but also that for the previous year and the following year. That amount, eight dollars, captured about 20 percent of monthly family income in some rural areas. The VRA thus directed the attorney general to finish off what the Twenty-fourth Amendment left standing by suing states and localities that still used the poll tax.[9] Also, in title II, the VRA struck down durational residency requirements and required all states to establish registration periods of no more than thirty days before an election. In addition, title II encouraged states to ease registration even further if they wished.

THE FIRST SUPREME COURT TESTS

But would the statute's clever construction acquire jurisprudential life? Here we come to a decisive element in both reconstructions: the initial Supreme Court tests of implementing statutes. The Voting Rights Act very quickly faced such tests. The State of South Carolina petitioned the Supreme Court, under the Court's original jurisdiction, to hear the state's claim against the

Johnson administration. Along with Louisiana, it asked the Court to immediately enjoin administration of the VRA. The act exceeded Congress's powers under the Fifteenth Amendment; it infringed on states' rights; it impermissibly treated states unequally; and it was a bill of attainder because it punished individual states and counties by legislative means.

In early 1966 the Court forcefully validated the act in an 8–1 decision (*South Carolina v. Katzenbach*). Chief Justice Earl Warren's opinion for the Court stressed the "great care" that Congress exercised in its deliberations. "Two points emerge vividly from the voluminous legislative history": first, that Congress believed that it faced "an invidious and pervasive evil" of "unremitting and ingenious defiance of the Constitution" among southern states, largely because previous federal remedies had been unsuccessful, and, second, that "sterner and more elaborate measures to satisfy the clear commands of the Fifteenth Amendment" were well in order. Congress was free under section 2 of the Fifteenth Amendment to do what it wished and was not "circumscribed by . . . artificial rules." Indeed, Warren praised Congress for the "inventive manner" with which it crafted the Voting Rights Act.[10]

In other words, a majority of the Supreme Court strongly supported the VRA—a stance quite different from that taken by a majority of the Court when it crippled the first reconstruction between 1873 and 1876. The majority announced, in essence, "Let the voting rights revolution roll." In several more decisions in the late 1960s it continued its firm support for the VRA.

THE 1970 AND 1975 RENEWALS OF THE VOTING RIGHTS ACT

Another vital aspect of jurisprudence-building was serial renewal by Congress of the VRA's powerful temporary provisions. Although the VRA enjoyed bipartisan support in 1965, similar bipartisan support was not a certainty when the act came up for renewal in 1970. But in the end, the 1970 renewal was actually a stronger statute than the original.

The 1970 renewal retained preclearance, first of all. It also required *all* states to limit the residency requirement for registration to no more than thirty days before a presidential election. It abolished literacy tests and "good character" tests everywhere in the country, thus changing the rules of fourteen nonsouthern states. Finally, the extension lowered the national voting age to eighteen. Richard Nixon, who initially seemed bent on subverting the renewal, signed the act with considerable good grace on June 22, 1970.[11]

In the wink of an eye, however, the VRA faced a renewal deadline of August 1975. Gerald Ford—despite a bit of last-minute wavering—strongly backed the VRA's renewal. The only major point of contention, in fact, was whether the act should be renewed for ten years, as many in Congress proposed, or five years, as the Ford administration proposed. In the end, the second renewal was for seven years, until 1982. The new statute reinstated such temporary enforcement provisions as preclearance, federal provision of federal examiners, and, if a jurisdiction requested them (an echo of the Federal Elections Act of 1872), provision of federal elections observers. The 1975 statute also made permanent the 1970 national ban on literacy tests. It authorized voting rights suits by the attorney general and the assignment of federal examiners on the basis of the Fourteenth as well as the Fifteenth Amendment. Also, it extended the horizon for "bailout from coverage" from ten to seventeen years for states and jurisdictions that in 1965 were brought under coverage because they met the original "coverage trigger" formula of (1) low voter turnout and (2) use of a voter registration test or device.

In addition, the 1975 statute targeted barriers to Hispanic and Native American voting. One of the first African American officeholders in Congress since the Reconstruction, and the first from Texas, Representative Barbara Jordan, pushed for this change. By facilitating the growth of an Anglo-African-Hispanic American electoral base, her plan developed the party- and coalition-building logic of the 1965 act. The 1975 statute extended the same basic "coverage trigger" formula and preclearance process to states and jurisdictions that, in the 1972 presidential election, had lower than 50 percent voter turnout, contained voting-age citizens composing a "language minority" of 5 percent of the voting-age population, and, finally, did not provide bilingual ballots or language assistance. In short, the VRA had a major impact on Latino electoral incorporation.[12]

PARTY-BUILDING

Stabilization and entrenchment of the second reconstruction demanded more than the jurisprudence-building engendered by the periodic reauthorizations of the Voting Rights Act. It also meant fundamentally changing state and local parties that had been dedicated to white supremacy since their rise in the 1820s. Three essential processes were involved: reconstruction of the South's parties-in-the-electorate, reconstruction of the region's Democratic parties-as-organizations, and an arduous struggle to desegregate the South's parties-in-government.

Party-in-the-Electorate

Constructing a biracial Democratic party-in-the-electorate required, first of all, black voter registration. In an echo of the "registration summer" of 1867, a federal workforce did much of the work. In the South as a whole, not only the states covered by the VRA, about 930,000 black citizens registered to vote in the two years following passage of the act. Of these, federal examiners directly enrolled about 16 percent.[13]

But the direct federal approach ended with the Johnson administration. Federal examiners listed 158,384 newly registered African Americans from 1965 to 1969 but only 1,974 from 1970 to 1974. Ninety-six percent of all those enrolled by federal examiners were enrolled within the first two years, three-quarters in the first year.[14]

Further electoral expansion would take place without a direct federal role. Johnson himself foresaw that prospect. Before he signed the Voting Rights Act on August 6 at the Capitol, he summoned SNCC leader (now Congressman) John Lewis to the White House. Lewis remembers that "near the end of the meeting the President leaned forward and said, 'Now John, you've got to go back and get all those folks registered. You've got to go back and get those boys by the *balls*. . . . You've got to get 'em by the balls and you've got to *squeeze,* squeeze 'em till they *hurt.*'" Lewis went back to "get all those folks registered" in 1970, when he succeeded Vernon Jordan as executive director of the second Voter Education Project of the Southern Regional Council (VEP II). Lewis writes, "The job was a perfect fit, a direct extension of the work I'd done during all those years with SNCC."[15]

Before Lewis arrived, VEP II had already been quite active under Jordan's direction. It funded about one hundred voter registration drives in 1966 and 1967 conducted by the SCLC and local voter leagues, established citizenship schools, and held conferences for black officeholders and aspirants to public office. This level of activity continued under Lewis, who headed a staff of thirty-eight, "spearheading get-out-the-vote drives, presenting seminars for young black people interested in politics, and offering technical and financial assistance to black community groups interested in political education." One vital tactic was having black politicians tour the South's "little villages and hamlets, places where people had never *seen* a black elected official, and give them a chance to meet a Julian Bond; or a state senator like Doug Wilder from Virginia. . . . On a given day we might make ten or twelve stops in one county" or "cover ten counties in one day."[16]

Similar mobilizations also occurred after VEP II shut down in the mid-1970s. The initial run by a black politician for national office was, for one

thing, a major impetus for registration. Thus, in 1982, there was voter regis-
tration in North Carolina's Second Congressional District to support Mickey
Michaux, a former U.S. district attorney during the Carter administration.
Churches and tenant organizations pitched in. So did the black labor–backed
civil and voting rights organization formed in 1965, the A. Philip Randolph
Institute (which is still in operation).[17]

After 1965, in other words, black southerners continued the *group implementation* of federal voting rights law that has been so important in the entire
history since 1867. During the first reconstruction the Union Leagues—and
later the black militias—implemented federal elections statutes and gave life
to the Fifteenth Amendment. The second reconstruction began, really, when
the NAACP implemented *Smith v. Allwright*. The NAACP, the SCLC, CORE,
the SNCC, and the VEP then implemented the 1957 and 1960 Civil Rights
Acts. Yet a third wave of group implementation of a federal statute, the Voting
Rights Act, took place after 1965. The jumps in black voter registration can
be seen at a glance in table 9.1.

But there is another vital fact about black voters besides sharply increased
registration. They embraced a historically new partisan identity. Between
1937 and 1965, all African Americans became strongly pro-Democratic in
terms of partisan identity, as we saw in chapter 7 and at the end of chapter 8.
And when black southerners entered the electorate after 1965 they entered as
Democratic identifiers. This was an essential purpose of the coalition of
1961–1965.[18]

Desegregating Party Organizations

Organizationally speaking, the Democratic parties in the South nonetheless stood in the way of black political aspiration. In 1962, for example, the
state central committee of the Alabama Democratic Party openly changed its
rules to prevent black participation on the committee. The Democratic
Executive Committee of Barbour County, Alabama, switched representation
on the committee to at-large voting in 1966.[19]

No sooner was the VRA passed than black leaders turned to desegregating
the Democratic Party. The leader of the Mississippi NAACP, Charles Evers
(brother of the assassinated leader Medgar Evers), put the problem well: "We
are trying to change this Democratic racism structure. . . . I feel always [that]
to change anything is to become a part of it and destroy it from within. That is
why I ran as a Democrat, to let them know that we are challenging them, that
we will meet them head-on . . . to let them know they didn't have the
Democratic party to themselves anymore."[20] Evers could just as well have

Table 9.1 African American Voter Registration in the Former Confederacy since World War II (%)

State	1947	1956	1964	1968	1976	1986	1988	1990	1992	1994	1998
Alabama	1.2	11.0	23.0	56.7	58.4	68.9	68.4	74.9	71.8	69.2	74.3
Arkansas	17.3	36.0	49.3	67.5	94.0	57.9	68.0	62.6	62.4	65.8	51.8
Florida	15.4	32.0	63.8	62.1	61.1	58.2	57.7	53.3	54.7	53.1	50.4
Georgia	18.8	27.0	44.0	56.1	74.8	52.8	56.8	57.0	53.9	64.6	64.1
Louisiana	2.6	31.0	42.0	59.3	63.0	60.6	77.1	72.0	82.3	71.9	69.5
Mississippi	0.9	5.0	6.7	59.4	60.7	70.8	74.2	71.4	78.5	67.4	71.3
N. Carolina	15.2	24.0	46.8	55.3	54.8	58.4	58.2	60.1	64.0	65.5	57.4
S. Carolina	13.0	27.0	38.7	50.8	56.5	52.5	56.7	61.9	62.0	64.3	68.0
Tennessee	25.8	29.0	69.4	72.8	66.4	65.3	74.0	68.5	77.4	65.7	64.8
Texas	18.5	37.0	57.7	83.1	65.0	68.0	64.2	60.0	63.5	63.2	62.1
Virginia	13.2	19.0	45.7	58.4	54.7	56.2	63.8	58.1	64.5	64.0	53.6

Sources: James E. Alt, "The Impact of the Voting Rights Act on Black and White Voter Registration in the South," in ed. Chandler Davidson and Bernard Grofman, *Quiet Revolution in the South: The Impact of the Voting Rights Act, 1965–1990*, (Princeton: Princeton University Press, 1994), pp. 351–377, table 21.1; U.S. Department of Commerce, Economics and Statistics Administration, Bureau of the Census, Current Population Reports, Population Characteristics, Series P-20, nos. 440, 453, 466, "Voting and Registration in the Election of November 1988," "Voting and Registration in the Election of November 1990," "Voting and Registration in the Election of November 1992"; figures for 1994 and 1998 from www.census.gov.

been talking about all of the southern Democratic parties. Their proceedings were often secret. Party officials were openly hostile to black voters on election day. In 1968, there were about seventeen hundred state committee positions in ten former Confederate states, of which .6 percent were held by African Americans.[21]

Evers's strategy of boring from within was only part of the pressure being used in the region to break down the Democratic Party's internal segregation. Another approach was the formation of parallel parties in Mississippi, Alabama, and South Carolina. Hanes Walton Jr. writes that a "black satellite or parallel political party . . . revolves in the orbit of a major political party on the national level and runs parallel with the state party . . . which it seeks to displace." A little-known precursor of this approach was the South Carolina Progressive Democratic Party of 1944–1946, which challenged the credentials of the conservative delegation at the 1944 Democratic National Convention, ran a statewide candidate for U.S. Senate, and pressed the Senate to investigate South Carolina's electoral practices. Similarly, the Mississippi Freedom Democratic Party, which grew out of a mock 1963 election called "the Freedom Vote," mounted a dramatic, nationally televised credentials challenge by its delegates at the 1964 Atlantic City nominating convention of the Democratic Party. It also instigated a protracted elections contest meant to block the seating of five regular House Democrats from Mississippi at the congressional session that convened in January 1965.[22]

In 1968, the Alabama Democratic Conference divided over whether to function as a faction in the Alabama Democratic Party, dominated by George Wallace, or go it alone. One group—influenced by both the Mississippi Freedom Democratic Party and the SNCC-sponsored Black Panther Party of Lowndes County (formally known as the Lowndes County Freedom Organization)—formed the National Democratic Party of Alabama, whose constitution listed as its first principle the goal of support for "the platform and programs of the Democratic Party of the United States," hence the need "to provide a vehicle in Alabama for their expression and implementation." It vigorously sought to displace regular Democrats and to become *the* Democratic party in Alabama.[23]

In South Carolina, the United Citizens Party was formed in 1969 at the annual meeting of the South Carolina Voter Education Project. By 1971 it had engineered considerable organizational growth—and the election of three state legislators and several local officeholders.[24]

Meanwhile, at the level of the national Democratic Party, pressure grew for integration of the entire party and all of its national, state, and local units. In response to the Mississippi Freedom Democratic Party's 1964 credentials challenge, the 1964 nominating convention ruled that the 1968 delegations must not be tainted by racial discrimination. In July 1967, the Special Equal Rights Committee sent a letter to the chairs of all state Democratic parties list-ing "basic" requirements for all the parties to meet: open, well-advertised public meetings, abolition of racist party loyalty tests, support for nondis-criminatory voter registration, and proper publicizing of the procedures and qualifications for the filling of national, state, and local party offices. The Democratic National Committee then adopted these criteria as prerequisites for seating delegations at the 1968 national convention.[25]

A second party commission, led by Governor Harold Hughes of Iowa, entered the reform process. A key member was Julian Bond; on its staff was former SNCC leader John Lewis. Its report stressed that "[f]ull political par-ticipation . . . requires an entree to intra-party proceedings as well as general elections—a fact recognized since the white primary cases of the 1940s," and it warned, presciently, against "tokenism" at the 1968 convention.[26]

The 1968 Chicago convention honored the nondiscrimination goal in its handling of the credentials challenge to the "regulars" from Mississippi. Officials of the Mississippi Freedom Democratic Party, the NAACP, and the Mississippi AFL-CIO coalesced to form the Loyal Democrats of Mississippi, which then successfully blocked the "regulars" from being seated. Also, the challenge to the segregationist Georgia delegation, led by Governor Lester Maddox, ended in an integrationist outcome—but not because the party enforced its own rules. The Credentials Committee recommended seat-ing both Georgia delegations and splitting their votes, though both dele-gations opposed the solution. The convention backed the committee in a voice vote. It also rejected the committee minority report in favor of ejecting the Maddox-led delegation in favor of the group led by Julian Bond. Maddox then stormed out with his delegates, ceding the field to his challengers.

The National Democratic Party of Alabama had less luck, however, than did the Loyal Democrats of Mississippi and liberal Georgia Democrats. Its rivals were the Alabama "regulars" (a delegation with two black members and controlled by George Wallace) and a rump group, the all-white but anti-Wallace Alabama Independent Democratic Party. The Credentials Committee seated the "regulars," in part to aid the nomination prospects of Hubert Humphrey. The irony was that Humphrey personally symbolized the emer-gence of robust racial liberalism within the Democratic Party owing to his famous 1948 convention speech (see chapter 8).[27]

The North Carolina, Tennessee, and Texas delegations also faced formal con-tests. Whether Louisiana's delegation was chosen in a racially discriminatory fashion was yet another case considered by the Credentials Committee. But "regulars" from all of these states were seated at the convention.[28]

These outcomes underscore the extent to which the special circumstances of the 1968 presidential election—a mounting white racial backlash and the rise of George Wallace's presidential candidacy—affected the Democratic Party's internal integration. The precedent set in Chicago was dangerous. In the end, though, the Democratic Party thoroughly reformed itself via two national commissions. One, the McGovern-Fraser Commission, revamped party representation. Seating at the 1972 convention depended on full compliance with new rules. The first of these, Guideline A-1, required (1) that the "basic elements of the Special Equal Rights Committee"—disseminated in July 1967—"be added to all the state party rules" and (2) "affirmative steps to overcome past discrimination, including minority presence in the state delegation in reasonable relationship to group presence in the state as a whole."[29]

The governors of Georgia, South Carolina, and Tennessee protested the change, as did party leaders in Louisiana. But their weakness became apparent when, led by Maddox, they sought to defeat the McGovern-Fraser Commission within the federal judiciary by casting delegate allocation as a Fourteenth Amendment issue. They lost all the way up to the Supreme Court.[30]

The 1972 national convention saw fully integrated state delegations. The average percentage of black delegates among the nine "unreformed" delegations of 1968 was 7.7 percent; that average in 1972 jumped to 22.4 percent.[31]

By 1984, according to the Comparative State Party Activist Survey, which included Arkansas, Louisiana, Mississippi, North Carolina, South Carolina, and Texas, 28 percent of delegates at southern Democratic party state conventions (about eight hundred) were African American. Of these, 96 percent reported always having been Democrats.[32]

In summary, the second reconstruction's stabilization partly—and critically—depended on integrating the South's Democratic Party organizations *as organizations*. As a result of the pressure from temporary biracial protest parties in Alabama, Mississippi, and South Carolina and from national committees set up by the Democratic Party, the Democratic parties-as-organizations were integrated.

But such internal organizational reform was insufficient. Parties are, after all, influenced by their officeholders and professional politicians. Barriers to black office-holding therefore had to come down. Just how did this critical change occur? It was one thing to change rules for representation at the national convention; it was another for large numbers of black candidates to win elective office.

THE PROBLEM OF SEGREGATED PARTIES-IN-GOVERNMENT

Party-building during the second reconstruction thus had a vital third face: *desegregation of the Democratic parties-in-government.* In 1965, there were about thirty-six thousand local, state, and national elected officials in the entire former Confederacy. But only about seventy-two—a tiny fraction of 1 percent of the total—were black, and of these there were only two serving in state legislatures.[33]

Table 9.2 schematizes the strategic situation prevailing that year. The region's "inventory" of offices was monopolized by the Democratic Party's southern wing. Southern Democrats intended to protect that monopoly. Reading the handwriting on the walls in 1965 (often, in fact, shortly before), many southern state legislatures and local bodies quietly but quickly threw a variety of procedural barriers around state and local government.[34] Immediately before Congress enacted the VRA in 1965, for instance, two Georgia counties with single-member districts for electing their county commissions switched to at-large voting; four counties did so in 1967, two in 1968, two more in 1970.

In an echo of the first reconstruction's expulsion of black legislators, the Georgia General Assembly refused in 1965 to seat Julian Bond (elected from District 136) until ordered to do so by a federal court and after Bond won two more elections.[35]

Many Georgia counties selected their boards of education by vote of a local grand jury, a holdover from Jim Crow. But as jury commissioners faced

Table 9.2 Freezing the Second Reconstruction's Full Potential after 1965

Level of Black Office-Holding	Level of Black Voter Registration	
	High	Low
High	Outcome that the 1965 Voting Rights Act did not immediately generate (preventable via vote dilution strategies)	[No Historical Case]
Low	Situation in the South (1965–1969) before the emergence of the anti–vote dilution program authorized by the Supreme Court and Congress	Situation in the South before passage of the 1965 Voting Rights Act

lawsuits for discrimination, several counties suddenly adopted at-large elections for their boards of education.

In 1968, the Georgia General Assembly enacted majority vote requirements for cities in the state. Cities with plurality vote charters were exempt, but twenty-three of them nonetheless repealed their charters.

Even after Congress and the Nixon administration renewed the VRA in 1970, eighteen Georgia counties joined the resistance to the VRA by switching to at-large voting for the county commission and the board of education. The cities of Augusta, Alapaha, Ashburn, Athens, Bainbridge, Butler, Cairo, Camilla, Cochran, Crawfordsville, East Dublin, Hartwell, Hinesville, Hogansville, Homerville, Jesup, Jonesboro, Lakeland, Louisville, Lumber City, Madison, Monroe, Nashville, Newnan, Palmetto, Sandersville, Thomson, Wadley, Waynesboro, and Wrens all sought to adopt majority vote requirements after the 1970 extension, in several cases after African Americans were elected to the city councils on plurality votes. In 1972 the city of Butler, Georgia, changed the plurality vote system used for its mayoralty. When sued in 1986 by local black plaintiffs for noncompliance with the VRA, Butler refused to conduct any local elections at all until ordered to do so by a federal court in 1995.[36]

What became clear, in other words, in Georgia and elsewhere, was that the large body of white southern officeholders already in place, and many of their white constituents, showed little intention of opening the doors to office. In 1962, while president pro tem of the Georgia Senate, Carl Sanders, later governor, pushed successfully for at-large legislative elections. One of his colleagues defended the policy by saying, "I am not going to vote for anything that would . . . put a member of a minority race in the Senate." The politicians who set up vote dilution counted on the persistence of racial affect of one sort or another, ranging from bigotry to unease, among some fraction of whites. Athalie Range, a prominent black businesswoman in Miami, Florida, found in her first bid for a seat on the city commission that "a loud-speaker went through the community stating, 'Unless you vote on Tuesday you will have a Negro on the City Commission.'"[37]

Long-established dilutive electoral rules bolstered the post-1965 strategy of preventing black office-holding. The role of institutional legacies can be seen, for instance, in Virginia school board elections. During the first reconstruction, local election of Virginia school boards clearly favored black voters in black majority areas. Virginia Conservatives substituted central appointment of school boards when they gained control. After Readjusters promoted black voter influence on school boards, Conservatives, when they returned to power as Democrats, established a complex system of local selection of school boards via special school trustee electoral boards. Furthermore, during the 1901–1902 formal disenfranchisement of African Americans in Virginia, drafters of the new state constitution discussed how to strengthen this system against any possibility of future black voter influence and settled on central appointment of the local school trustee selection boards. This system was perpetuated *into the 1980s* by white majority state legislative sessions that have left a record of racially discriminatory intent.[38]

At the national level, conservative white House and Senate Democrats had no trouble hanging onto their offices if they wanted to. They had name recognition and the resources of incumbency. White voters who had been Democrats all their lives were disinclined to punish them for the sins of northern racial liberals. The pool of talented African American politicians able to challenge them in Democratic primaries was minuscule and growing all too slowly owing to the racial lock-out of state and local offices. Only death and retirement would create opportunities for black politicians—but then they would have to figure out how to build a stable biracial coalition that would give them a majority, no easy matter given whites' initial deep distrust of black officeholders.[39]

This problem of desegregating the former Confederacy's Democratic parties-in-government was severe. The turn toward vote dilution, which began before passage of the Voting Rights Act and continued long after, rested on powerful historical and institutional legacies. The South's thirty-six thousand elective political offices were ensconced within a racial Maginot Line. Without a solution, party-building would be incomplete. It might well evolve into an unhealthy relationship between black voters and paternalistic white politicians doling out crumbs of public largesse to their clientele.

THE IMPACT OF ANTI–VOTE DILUTION JURISPRUDENCE

The solution lay in a remarkable confluence of party-building *and* jurisprudence-building. In 1969, the basic foundation for anti–vote dilution jurisprudence was more or less invented by the Supreme Court in a decision interpreting section 5 of the VRA (see below). Between 1969 and 1982 black Democratic office-holding grew somewhat at the state and local levels. Then, in 1982, Congress amended the VRA so that it would explicitly include the principles of jurisprudence limiting vote dilution. After 1982 black office-holding in the South grew even more; it came to include national office-holding in the U.S. House of Representatives. By 1993, the Democratic party-in-the-House became the most biracial it had ever been.

The result was enormous *intra*partisan change. That outcome was not intended, of course, by the Justice Department, the voting rights bar, or the courts. Their goal was securing the right to office. As a vital by-product, though, Democratic parties-in-government became biracial.

The first major step in making the jurisprudence that would help revamp the southern Democratic parties came in a quartet of cases (three from Mississippi, one from Virginia). These two states argued that the VRA targeted only the acts of balloting and voter registration and not the kinds of rules changes that occurred in Mississippi and Virginia after passage of the VRA. These included an amendment of Mississippi statutes permitting county boards of supervisors to change election procedures to at-large voting rather than district voting, a statute eliminating the election for county superintendent of education in eleven Mississippi counties and making these offices appointive, a change in general election regulations for independent candidates in Mississippi (note that Mississippi then had a largely black third party, the Mississippi Freedom Democratic Party), and a change in Virginia's procedures for helping illiterate voters cast a write-in ballot.

But Chief Justice Earl Warren wrote in *Allen v. State Board of Elections* that "[w]e must reject a narrow construction that appellees would give to § 5. The Voting Rights Act was aimed at the subtle, as well as the obvious, state regulations which have the effect of denying citizens their right to vote because of their race. . . . Congress intended that state enactments such as those involved in the instant cases be subject to the § 5 approval requirements." Only Justice Black dissented entirely from the holding (on the ground that section 5 was unconstitutional.)[40]

With *Allen,* an administrative basis for inhibiting vote dilution came into being. The problem of getting rid of existing rules was not, to be sure, solved by *Allen.* Nor did the case have any significance for states and local jurisdictions where racially motivated vote dilution existed that were not regulated by the coverage formula in section 4 of the act. But preventing future vote dilution in covered jurisdictions was now possible.

After the Court's strengthening of section 5, the Justice Department sent a barrage of letters to covered states and localities advising them that the section 5 preclearance system was now up and running. The frequency of compliance with the section 5 administrative process rose sharply in covered jurisdictions. Full compliance did not emerge, to be sure. Before the VRA's 1975 renewal, the Justice Department researched compliance and found 316 unsubmitted state session laws. The General Accounting Office found in 1983 that of the 262 objections issued by the department between January 1975 and June 1981, eleven—about 4 percent—were simply ignored by the submitting jurisdictions. Nonetheless, from 1966 to 1970 there were only 255 submissions from southern states, yet from 1971 through 1975 there were 5,337, an increase of nearly 2,000 percent in the scope of the preclearance process. In addition, between 1973 and 1980 the Supreme Court supported Justice Department regulations implementing section 5, gave a broad reading to what it meant by "covered jurisdiction," and protected relevant decisions of the attorney general from legal challenge.[41]

The next phase in the development of anti–vote dilution jurisprudence involved discovery of ways to roll back existing dilutive structures in covered jurisdictions and to block or reverse vote dilution in noncovered areas. Initially, there was a major stumbling block. The problem, briefly, was that evidence of *purpose* was generally necessary in a Fourteenth Amendment case against the pre-1965 forms of vote dilution. That was a very high standard. For instance, in a pair of major vote dilution cases from Alabama conducted in accordance with a purpose standard, counsel for the plaintiffs devoted six thousand hours of their time and seven thousand hours of the expert witnesses' time.[42]

This sort of problem disappeared when the Supreme Court eased proof-of-intent requirements. In a unanimous decision in *White v. Regester* (1973), the Court held that an accumulation of indirect evidence concerning a reapportionment plan for the Texas House of Representatives sufficed to show discriminatory intent.[43] This became known as the Court's "totality of circumstances" test. A large accumulation of circumstantial evidence sufficed to infer intent.

Within months of *White,* in *Zimmer v. McKeithen,* the Fifth Circuit Court of Appeals codified *White* and further eased its probative requirements.[44] It did so in order to aid plaintiffs seeking to stop at-large elections for the police jury (county commission) and board of election of a Louisiana parish. The decision in *Zimmer* (later affirmed *per curiam* by the Court) catalogued four "primary" and four "enhancing" factors. Their presence, when demonstrated, showed that an electoral change or practice was either motivated by racial intent *or* had the effect of vote dilution, regardless of intent.

For the next several years, a lively voting rights bar that had sprung into existence after 1965 led a wide frontal assault on vote dilution. Two members of the voting rights bar based in Mobile, Alabama, have written that "the so-called *Zimmer* factors pre-empted the field and were used—practically to the exclusion of all other evidentiary criteria—to govern the outcome of scores of reported and unreported at-large dilution cases."[45] In short, in 1969 the Supreme Court construed section 5 of the VRA in the same kind of broad terms that characterized all its voting rights decisions in the late 1960s. This inhibited *future* vote dilution. Then, in *White*, a Court majority made proof of discriminatory purpose much easier. This greatly facilitated private litigation against *previous* vote dilution, that is, against pre-*Allen* dilutive structures.

There was still more essential jurisprudence-building, however. The fight against vote dilution seemed to face a crisis in 1980, when the Supreme Court suddenly and inexplicably backed off from the experiment in the lowering of proof-of-intent requirements. But Congress corrected the Court, which got the message in subsequent vote dilution cases. The 1980 crisis originated in 1975, when African American plaintiffs sued the city of Mobile for operating a three-person city commission elected at large. Mobile was about 33 percent black, but no black had served on the city commission since its adoption in 1911, which was in fact an intended outcome. Using the *White-Zimmer* analytical framework, the federal district court held for the plaintiffs, and the Fifth Circuit affirmed.[46]

But in a plurality opinion in *City of Mobile v. Bolden,* the Supreme Court suddenly held that the Fifteenth Amendment applied only to registration and voting! The kind of crabbed formalism that has periodically intruded into voting rights jurisprudence made a devastating appearance. Associate Justice Potter Stewart claimed, in the opinion for the Court, that "[t]he 15th Amendment does not entail the right to have Negro candidates elected." A valid vote dilution claim was certainly possible under the Fourteenth Amendment. But that required proof of intent. The Court thus seemed to abruptly demolish the *White-Zimmer* framework. It remanded the city commission case and a companion case concerning at-large elections to the Mobile County school board for retrial at the district level.[47]

Fortuitously, the jurisprudence was rescued by the scheduled expiration on August 6, 1982, of the VRA's temporary provisions. This provided the occasion for Congress to address the Court's actions.

Justice Stewart inadvertently left a loophole for Congress in the *Mobile* opinion. His gloss on the Fourteenth and Fifteenth Amendments posed a deep problem, given that it was a reading of the Constitution itself, not of a statute implementing the Constitution. But Stewart *also* glossed a previously obscure section of the VRA, reading section 2 as merely a restatement of the Fifteenth Amendment. There was the opening. Congress met his attack on the new anti–vote dilution jurisprudence by radically amending and rewriting section 2. Statutory revision, after all, was its prerogative, not the Court's.

Section 2, in its original form, stated that "[n]o voting qualifications or prerequisite to voting, or standard, practice, or procedure shall be imposed by any State or political subdivision to deny or abridge the right of any citizen of the United States to vote on account of race or color." Congress extensively

rewrote the section to contain both a results test and the "totality of circumstances" test established in *White* and *Zimmer*. The new section 2 forbade any
device "which results in a denial or abridgement" of the right to vote and further stated that a voting rights violation "is established if, based on the totality
of circumstances, it is shown that the political processes leading to nomination or election . . . are not equally open to participation by a class of citizens
protected by subsection (a) in that its members have less opportunity than
other members of the electorate to participate in the political process *and to
elect representatives of their choice*."[48]

In October 1981 the House of Representatives passed a version of this
language by a vote of 389 to 24. A further elaboration (the current section 2),
crafted by Edward Kennedy and Robert Dole, passed the Senate in June 1982
by a vote of 85 to 8. President Ronald Reagan signed a new Voting Rights Act
eleven days later, on June 29.[49] Congress thus explicitly banned vote dilution
and rectified what the Supreme Court had done. Congress could hardly have
been more emphatic. It renewed the Voting Rights Act for twenty-five years,
more than three times the previous renewal period.[50]

The Court heeded the signal. Only days after Reagan signed the bill, the
Court invalidated at-large elections in Burke County, Georgia, as unconstitutional under the Fourteenth Amendment in *Rogers v. Lodge*. The facts were
nearly identical to those in *Mobile*. The Court thus recommitted itself to the
jurisprudence that it had seemed to abandon two years earlier.[51]

Further, in 1986, Justice William Brennan led the Court (5–4) to adopt
a simplified "totality of circumstances" formula in *Thornburg v. Gingles*.[52] It
highlighted only three factors. Meeting these three prongs was and is not
sufficient in the courts, but it takes one a long way toward success. The
holding in *Gingles*, like the decisions in *White* and *Zimmer* before it, reener-
gized the campaign against vote dilution. Three election law experts later
wrote that "much Section 2 litigation became routinized . . . and involved
municipal and county governments which were both financially and func-
tionally ill-equipped to defend the lawsuits: they lacked access to the
expertise developed by the small but specialized plaintiffs'-side voting
rights bar."[53]

In summary, anti–vote dilution jurisprudence faced an unexpected challenge in 1980. But because the scheduled renewal of the Voting Rights Act
coincided with the ruling in *Mobile*, there was a legislative opportunity to
restore the jurisprudence. Majorities in both houses of Congress did just that,
adopting the new jurisprudence and placing its principles in the statute itself.
Afterward, in *Thornburg v. Gingles*, the Supreme Court went far toward implementing the act's new amendment.

One last set of interlocked successes require introduction and characterization. They have to do with the partisan effects of jurisprudential change.

INTRAPARTISAN IMPACT OF FAIR DISTRICTING

The building of jurisprudence from *Allen* to *Gingles,* in the courts and in Congress, created strong remedies. Under section 5 of the VRA, the Justice Department would refuse preclearance to proposed election rules that perpetuated vote dilution. Also, the private voting rights bar would present jurisdictions that maintained vote dilution with section 2 or *Gingles* litigation. Such litigation could not be ignored. Losers in a voting rights suit owed plaintiffs' fees: section 14 (e) of the 1975 Voting Rights Act provided that "[i]n any action or proceeding to enforce the voting guarantees of the fourteenth or fifteenth amendment, the court, in its discretion, may allow the prevailing party, other than the United States, a reasonable attorney's fee as part of the costs." The financial incentives for southern governments to settle anti–vote dilution lawsuits were therefore substantial.[54]

Fairer ways to district—already under way in the 1970s—thus became more common in the 1980s and early 1990s. Consider the impact at each level of government—local, state, and national.

At the local level, fair districting meant getting rid of such devices as at-large elections. In their place came ward and precinct elections. These, in turn, became springboards for local black officeholders. The resulting changes, for both a restricted set of local officeholders and for *all* local elected officials, are displayed in table 9.3. Several things stand out in the table. First, rates of increase were hardly uniform across states. Second, increase was gradual. Third, the arrival of local black office-holding was delayed. These features suggest that at the local level vote dilution was both real and effective until a serious campaign was mounted against it.

At the state level, fair districting meant getting rid of multimember legislative districts. Because of the one-person, one-vote apportionment revolution of the mid-1960s, such districts were inevitably large. In the South, such large districts generally diluted black votes because whites would outnumber blacks. And, because white voters very seldom voted for black candidates, multimember districts inevitably sent multiple white candidates to the legislature. The result was overwhelmingly white legislatures. Yet the former Confederate states contained large black electorates. The most egregious case was Mississippi, where continuous legislative obstruction and resistance from reactionary federal judges were particularly pronounced, keeping the legislature almost completely white in America's most biracial state. The obvious

Table 9.3 Change in Local Office-Holding by Blacks in Southern States Completely Covered by the VRA

	Total LEOs [1]	Total BLEOs [1]	BLEOs as % [1]	All LEOs [2]	All BLEOs [2]	All BLEOs as % [2]	Blacks as % of voting-age pop.
AL (1974)	2,634	110	4.2	N.A.	N.A.		23
AL (1984)	2,795	241	8.6	3,125	292	9	23
AL (1993)	2,936	605	20.6	3,237	672	20	22.7
GA (1974)	4,077	120	2.9	N.A.	N.A.		22.9
GA (1984)	4,209	250	5.9	4,950	276	5.6	24
GA [1993]	4,428	459	10.3	5,760	498	8.6	24.6
LA [1974]	2,577	141	5.5	N.A.	N.A.		26.6
LA [1984]	2,651	374	14	2,779	425	15.3	27
LA [1993]	3,235	511	15.8	3,362	600	17.8	27.9
MS [1974]	2,252	190	8.4	N.A.	N.A.		31.4
MS [1984]	2,462	296	12	3,226	410	12.7	31
MS [1993]	2,477	546	22	3,241	708	21.8	31.6
SC [1974]	1,961	113	5.8	N.A.	N.A.		26.4
SC [1984]	1,817	229	12.6	2,252	242	10.7	27
SC [1993]	2,213	407	14.5	2,602	423	16.2	26.9
TX [1974]	11,467	117	1	N.A.	N.A.		11.3
TX [1984]	12,587	183	1.5	18,749	215	1.1	11
TX [1993]	12,474	438	3.5	18,636	447	2.4	11.2
VA [1974]	2,002	61	3	N.A.	N.A.		16.6
VA [1984]	1,994	86	4.3	2,451	100	4	18
VA [1993]	1,999	125	6.2	2,456	141	5.7	17.6

Sources: National Roster of Black Elected Officials, vol. 5 (Washington, D.C.: Joint Center for Political and Economic Studies, July 1975); *Black Elected Officials: A National Roster 1984* (New York: UNIPUB/R.R. Bowker, 1984, for the Joint Center for Political and Economic Studies); *Black Elected Officials: A National Roster 1993* (Washington, D.C., Joint Center for Political and Economic Studies Press, 1993, by arrangement with University Press of America); Richard M. Valelly, "Net Gains: The Voting Rights Act and Southern Local Government." In *Dilemmas of Scale in America's Federal Democracy*, ed. Martha Derthick (Woodrow Wilson Center Press and Cambridge University Press, 1999), pp. 298–321, esp. pp. 309–310 and n. 17. Figures on the left-hand side (denoted as [1]) are for a restricted set of local officeholders (county commissioners, members of municipal governing bodies, sheriffs, and school board members). Figures on the right-hand side (denoted as [2]) are for all local elected officials including coroners, municipal "sergeants," probate judges, and commissioners of special boards. The black voting-age population as a percentage of the total voting-age population is displayed as a benchmark.

solution was single-member districting, often with an eye toward creating districts with black populations in excess of 50 percent.[55]

Table 9.4 offers a time line to show the increase in the number of black legislators associated with the change from multimember districting to fairer districting. By 1993, as table 9.5 shows, African American membership in most state legislative chambers was substantially greater than 10 percent of the total membership.[56]

The final aspect of fairer districting involved congressional representation. By 1990, a total of only seven black southerners had served in the U.S. House of Representatives, representing districts in Georgia, Mississippi, Tennessee, and Texas. Further, only five black southerners were elected in 1990 to serve in the 101st Congress. Yet a historic opportunity beckoned to the emerging cadres of black state legislators. They could now affect the congressional districting process. As they did, they found the Justice Department eager to help reshape southern House districts in ways that would afford African American office-seekers a chance of election to the House, a goal several had had for many years.[57]

The result of southern legislatures' seeking to comply with section 2 of the VRA in the 1990 reapportionment could hardly have been more dramatic. *Thirteen* African American representatives were elected from the former Confederacy to the 103rd Congress, an increase of 160 percent over the previous Congress, bringing the total number of black members of the House to an all-time high of thirty-eight. Indeed, there had not been that many black

Table 9.4 Timing and Effects of Shifts from Multimember to Single-Member Districting

	Senate	House
1965	0	0
1970	Tennessee (0 → 2)	0
1975	Alabama (0 → 2)	Alabama (0 → 13)
	Arkansas (0 → 1)	Georgia (12 → 19)
	Louisiana (0 → 1)	Louisiana (1 → 8)
	Virginia (1 → 1)	South Carolina (0 → 13)
		Tennessee (6 → 9)
		Texas (2 → 9)
1980	Mississippi (0 → 2)	Mississippi (1 → 15)
1985	Florida (0 → 2)	Florida (4 → 10)
	North Carolina (1 → 3)	North Carolina (4 → 13)
	South Carolina (0 → 4)	Virginia (4 → 5)

Source: Bernard Grofman and Lisa Handley, "The Impact of the Voting Rights Act on Black Representation in Southern State Legislatures," *Legislative Studies Quarterly* 16 (February 1991): 111–128, table 6.

Table 9.5 Black Elected Officials as a Percentage of Legislative Chamber Size in the Former Confederacy, 1993

	Alabama	Arkansas	Florida	Georgia	Louisiana	Mississippi	North Carolina	South Carolina	Tennessee	Texas	Virginia
Upper house	11.4	8.6	12.5	16.1	20.5	19.2	14	15.2	9.1	6.5	12.5
Lower house	17.1	10	11.7	17.2	21.9	26.2	15	14.5	12.1	9.3	7

Source: Black Elected Officials: A National Roster 1993, 21st ed. (Washington, D.C.: Joint Center for Political Economic Studies Press, 1994), p. xxviii.

southerners representing the South in the House *at one time* since seven arrived to take their seats in the 43rd Congress.[58]

In short, the development of anti–vote dilution jurisprudence from *Allen* (1969) to *Gingles* (1986) and beyond had a major impact on black office-holding, the rates of which at all three levels of southern government clearly moved beyond tokenism. By the 1990s, the desegregation of American representative government had finally come. A significant concomitant of this victory was the simultaneous recasting of the southern Democratic parties-in-government and of the Democratic Party's southern wing in the U.S. House of Representatives. For the first time in American political history, these became substantially biracial parties.

Earl Warren did not, of course, intend such outcomes when he wrote the opinion in *Allen*. Nor did William Brennan when he wrote the opinion in *Gingles*. But the cumulative *partisan* effect of the campaign against vote dilution was far-reaching. The desegregation of Democratic parties-in-government has been so marked that it has independently affected public policy outputs. Kerry Haynie has shown that increased numbers of African Americans in state legislatures—as distinct from what he calls "political incorporation," that is, increases in the legislative influence of black legislators due to seniority, rise to leadership positions, and the like—by themselves change states' expenditures on health, education, and welfare. Political incorporation reflects the role of professionalism. But simple change in number of black representatives suffices to alter public spending in the states.[59]

To summarize, the rise of new legal ideas and remedies for addressing obstacles to black office-holding was a major element of the second reconstruction. Its development vitally affected southern city councils and state legislatures. As they became biracial, the process of rebuilding southern Democratic parties-in-government, so necessary for the second reconstruction to become a success, also became much easier.

Table 9.6   The Extended Voting Rights Act in 2004

Section 5 Preclearance	Section 4(f)(4) Language Assistance	Section 203 Balloting Assistance, by Number of Geographic Subdivisions and Languages
Alabama	Alaska (statewide)	Alaska (26): Eskimo, Aleut, American Indian and Native, Filipino, Athabascan
Alaska	Arizona (statewide)	Arizona (22): Apache, Navajo, Pueblo, Tohono O'Odham, Yaqui, Yuman, Spanish
Arizona	Texas (statewide)	
California (4)	California (3)	
Florida (5)	Florida (5)	
Georgia	Michigan (2)	California* (17): Non-US Indigenous, Chinese, Filipino, Japanese, Korean, Vietnamese, Yuman
Louisiana	North Carolina (1)	
Michigan (2)†	New York (2)	
Mississippi	South Dakota (2)	Colorado (10): Navajo, Ute, Spanish
New Hampshire (17)†		Connecticut (7): Spanish
New York (3)		Florida (10): Seminole, Spanish
North Carolina (40)		Hawaii (2): Chinese, Filipino, Japanese
South Carolina		Idaho (5): American Indian
South Dakota (2)		Illinois (2): Chinese, Spanish
Virginia‡		Kansas (6): Spanish
Texas		Louisiana (1): American Indian
		Maryland (1): Spanish
		Massachusetts (6): Spanish
		Michigan (1): Spanish
		Mississippi (9): Choctaw
		Montana (2): Cheyenne
		Nebraska (2): Sioux, Spanish
		Nevada (6): Paiute, Shoshone, Other tribe; Spanish
		New Jersey (7): Spanish
		New Mexico* (11): Navajo, Pueblo
		New York (7): Chinese, Korean, Spanish
		North Dakota (2): Sioux
		Oklahoma (2): Spanish
		Oregon (1): Spanish
		Pennsylvania (1): Spanish
		Rhode Island (2): Spanish
		South Dakota (18): Cheyenne, Sioux
		Texas* (3): Pueblo, other tribe, Vietnamese
		Utah (2): Navajo, Ute
		Washington (4): Chinese, Spanish

Sources: For section 5 coverage: http://www.usdoj.gov:80/crt/voting/ sec_5/covered.htm; for section 4(f)(4) and section 203 coverage: Bryan Cave LLP Public Elections Compliance News Alert, "Director of the Census Bureau Makes Determination of Jurisdictions Subject to the Minority Language Assistance Provisions of the Voting Rights Act," September 2002, at www.bryancave.com/pubs; Daniel Levitas, ACLU Voting Rights Project, "Reauthorizing the Voting Rights Act of 1965: Assessing the Geographic and Political Terrain" (ACLU Civil Liberties Union Foundation, Southern Regional Office: n.d. [2004?]); 67 Fed. Reg. 48,871 (July 26, 2002).

Note: In the section 5 column, numbers in parentheses refer to number of counties under coverage. Where there is a dagger (†), the number in parentheses refers to towns or townships, not counties. If no number is noted parenthetically, then the entire state is under coverage. The double dagger (‡) refers to three political subdivisions in Virginia that have bailed out from section 5 coverage via section 4 procedures: Fairfax City, Frederick County, and Shenandoah County. In the section 4(f)(4) and section 203 columns, numbers in parentheses refer to local jurisdictions under coverage, e.g., counties and towns. Both sections mandate language assistance, e.g., bilingual ballots. Section 4(f)(4) jurisdictions comply not only with section 203 but also with section 5 preclearance. When section 203 applies to an entire state (denoted by an asterisk,*), it applies only to state elections officials.

Conclusion

The second reconstruction eventually overwhelmed antiblack discrimination in both voting *and* office-holding. In the process, the southern Democratic party was internally reconstructed. But there is more—and this extra dimension is rather telling. In several stages Congress also deployed the second reconstruction's core statute, the Voting Rights Act, against *other* forms of minority voting discrimination besides antiblack discrimination. What might be called an "extended VRA" has therefore emerged out of the original VRA. Indeed, in only fourteen states are state and local government today wholly unregulated by some aspect of this extended VRA.

Fully discussing the broader VRA is beyond this book's scope. But, by way of conclusion, a very quick sketch is essential; it accentuates the second reconstruction's brighter history. Table 9.6 encapsulates both the original and the extended VRA. As it shows, about 64 percent of the former Confederacy is under the preclearance requirement. Think of this as the historic core of the VRA. But preclearance now also applies—under section 4(f)(4) of the statute (added in 1975)—to several nonsouthern states where nonblack minorities (Hispanic and Native Americans) historically faced electoral discrimination. Preclearance further applies to many local jurisdictions in other nonsouthern states with histories of voting discrimination. In addition, in 1975, 1982, and 1992 Congress added a balloting assistance system to the Voting Rights Act (Title II, section 203) that required bilingual election materials for four "language minorities": Native American, Asian American, Alaskan Native, and "Spanish heritage." The state and local application of this additional protection is in effect until August 6, 2007.

During the first reconstruction, protecting African American voting and office-holding was challenge enough for the coalition of 1867–68. But the VRA has become the foundation of a comprehensive program of correcting the discrimination that historically has hurt the voting rights of other minorities. That the second reconstruction thus exceeded the first in this regard nicely highlights its happier fate.

The second reconstruction's stabilization might seem inevitable in retrospect. But it was not. The fading of racially conservative resistance and backlash, the steady increase in black voter registration, the overthrow of vote dilution, the desegregation of representative government, the trends toward fairer expenditures by state and local governments, the emergence of an extended VRA—all were propelled by processes of party-building and jurisprudence-building. *Why,* however, did these twin processes evolve favorably? Chapter 10 addresses this question.

Chapter Ten

Institutions and Enfranchisement

W hy did party- and jurisprudence-building come more easily for the coalition partners of the second reconstruction than they did for their first-reconstruction predecessors? The answer developed in this chapter is that there were better institutional supports for these two processes than during the first reconstruction.

I do not mean to say that the prospects for success of the first and second reconstructions were otherwise identical but for such institutional foundations. Rather, my claim is that institutional differences between the two reconstructions differentially magnified probabilities for coalitional success. During both reconstructions, the same political framework of parties and courts empowered the biracial coalitions—but to very different degrees. In the first case, coalitional hopes eventually proved fruitless because the coalition did not have a good enough rendition of the "parties and courts" setup. In the second case the coalition had a better party system structure and a better initial jurisprudential test. In that sense, the twentieth-century coalition was just lucky in a way that the earlier one was not.

In making this claim, I offer a distinctive view of what institutions do in politics. One viewpoint stresses the way institutions force political actors to adopt perspectives on their strategic and political situations that differ from those they would hold in the absence of these institutions. The Madisonian separation of powers does this, in theory at least, by channeling self-interested political behavior into a system of complex interactions, out of which arises an ensemble of broad representational perspectives on policy questions.[1]

Another classic conjecture is that institutions enable coordination. They permit mutually beneficial arrangements between rational actors who otherwise would have difficulty achieving their goals—often, paradoxically, because of the actors' very rationality. The political party has been portrayed as such an institution. It critically introduces a time horizon into actors' calculations about how to realize their goals. A party permits better political bargains for its members across time, as it were. They are superior to the deals that would be negotiated by these same actors if they tried instead for one intricate and uncertain logroll after another.[2]

Yet a third hypothesis is that institutions are really not joint "solutions" for helping all similarly situated rational actors so much as subtle allocators of advantage and disadvantage whose effects escape detection in the short run but not in the long run. For instance, the internal committee structure and parliamentary rules of the U.S. House will periodically change in ways that solve problems for a majority coalition at the time of solution. But the losers will eventually realize that they lost and will seek later to renegotiate the partial equilibrium.[3]

The analysis in this book sees institutions in a way somewhat different from these. It builds on a core idea in each of the other views, namely, that institutions mesh with political action. I see institutions as a kind of technology that allows actors in a difficult and challenging situation to gain leverage—a fulcrum, as it were—on a demanding enterprise that they have set for themselves.[4]

Political reform, the activity central to the two reconstructions, depended on the disciplined performance of arduous tasks by a very wide range of actors. The "parties and courts" configuration fortunately gave these actors tremendous traction. Without it they never could have hoped to achieve the soaring social and political transformations that they intended.

As a superstructure by means of which an extraordinary reform of race relations was attempted, the parties and courts matrix had remarkable and complementary advantages. A broad-based party harnessed citizens' hopes and politicians' ambitions to each other and channeled these vital forces toward gaining control of government and government revenue. With such resources, reform coalitions could take on the job of bringing fairness to the question of who got what from government—educational, health, municipal, and police expenditures, access to government (or publicly supported) jobs and financial credits, and government occupations that enjoyed honor and status, for example, judicial, law enforcement, military, and diplomatic careers. The "courts" side of the framework was also essential. White backlash and efforts to sustain white supremacist practices spilled into the law as well as politics. This side gave a reform coalition authoritative support in negotiating such reaction.[5]

But at two comparable times the same basic matrix had subtle and decisive differences in its actual makeup—as underscored in table 10.1. During the first reconstruction, the reform coalition not only had to work on reform itself but also had to attend to strengthening the institutional framework that did so much to enable the reform project. It had two sets of tasks: reform *and* matrix-making on the fly. If the first reconstruction had pivoted around the lower level of task difficulty that characterized the second—in which the Supreme Court was cooperative and party-building really meant party *re*building, taking over the existing Democratic parties of the south—then the coalition of 1867–1868 might have experienced more success than it did. The appalling persistence of white supremacy late into the twentieth century, almost two centuries after the issuing of the Declaration of Independence and the ratification of the Constitution, might never have been.

Correlatively, if it had been necessary during the second reconstruction to do something as difficult as build eleven brand-new political parties all at once in the former Confederate states and to simultaneously contend with an uncertain Supreme Court, then the coalition of 1961–1965 might well have run into more trouble than it actually did after 1965. As a country we might never have gained real political leverage on the task of bringing African Americans fully into competitive electoral politics. We would today be awaiting the promise of a "third reconstruction."

Table 10.1 Political Processes after Coalition-Making

Coalition's Relation to Supreme Court	Coalition's Party-Building Options	
	Building a New Party	Reforming an Existing Party
Cooperative		"Parties and courts" matrix highly empowering for coalition
Uncertain or intermittently conflictual	"Parties and courts" matrix empowering for coalition but long-run prospects indeterminate	

Note: For the empty cells the expected outcome is intermediate between the two historical outcomes; i.e., the "parties and courts" matrix is expected to be fairly (but only fairly) empowering for the reform coalition.

None of this is to say that alternative institutional foundations were in the cards at either time. They were not, and that is the point. The impact of the parties and courts matrix on these two great moments in American political evolution reveals how such institutions have fundamentally regulated both race relations and the development of full political democracy in this country.

This chapter systematically compares party-building during the two reconstructions. After treating contrasts in party-building and their consequences, it turns to historical contrasts in jurisprudence-building and their results. The final section returns to considering how this book's historical analysis reframes the evolution of American politics.

PARTY SYSTEM STRUCTURE AND INSTITUTIONALIZING THE BIRACIAL COALITION

As suggested by the contrasting accounts of chapters 4 and 9, party-building differed critically during the two reconstructions. Why? The answer is that the thresholds for success were very dissimilar.

In the first reconstruction, the southern party system's institutional baseline was unpromising for the coalition of 1867–1868. For nearly a decade before the first reconstruction the South lacked strongly competitive two-party politics. The collapse of the Whig Party splintered southern politics. One-partyism then emerged during the Civil War. Only late in the life of the Confederacy was there factional opposition to the Davis administration. The Confederacy's Civil War experience with a "politics above parties" subtly framed any competitive organized opposition to the southern elite as an illegitimate politics.[6]

In this forbidding context the coalition poured enormous energy into building eleven state-level parties as rapidly as possible. Although essential for giving enfranchisement substance and meaning, this was very difficult business. The development of competitive, mass political parties before the Civil War took several decades. Now something similar needed to be set up almost overnight in the former Confederacy.

During the second reconstruction, in contrast, the coalition-making between the Democratic party's New Deal faction and black southerners only required them to take over long-standing, long-accepted party organizations. As early as 1961, such a strategy was in fact explicit. Harris Wofford, John F. Kennedy's civil rights advisor, urged the president during the period between election and inauguration to focus on black voter registration in order to strengthen white southern moderates' electoral chances: "[B]ehind their back, with their open or tacit approval, the Executive will be increasing the

Negro vote which can help re-elect them." He noted that the southern conservatives "who oppose any form of Federal action on civil rights are against most of the social legislation of the new administration anyway." The idea was to take their historic party away from them and give it to new people.[7]

Had the structural context for party-building been more favorable during the first reconstruction, the coalition of 1867–1868 would have become better institutionalized. When they are well-developed, political parties allow voters to clearly grant authority for using governmental resources in socially useful ways. Parties do this because they channel the ambition of talented political entrepreneurs into mobilizing the loyalty and participation of ordinary citizens on a regular basis. But such attractive properties of party politics did not fully emerge during the first reconstruction, given the structural context. They have, however, characterized southern party politics to a greater extent during the second reconstruction.[8]

PARTY SYSTEM STRUCTURE AND RACIAL REACTION

The regularization of southern party politics during the second reconstruction also depended on what the party system's structure implied for *other* party actors not in the incorporating coalition. As a result, they critically influenced the new biracial coalition's development.

During the first reconstruction all Democratic politicians, north and south, disliked black electoral incorporation. They did so because African American voting created a far more competitive and uncertain electoral and political situation, both regionally and nationally. What could Democrats do in response to the intense loyalty that African American voters showed for the Republican Party and yet stay within the rules of nonviolent political competition? If they let it proceed, they could say goodbye to any national influence for some time to come. Small wonder, then, that Republicans and Democrats were so far apart on the issues of black voting and office-holding.[9]

After the Compromise of 1877, southern Democratic politicians did face a more comfortable situation, given the drop in the Republican Party's southern strength. But third party efforts in the region soon revived the uncertainty that Democrats had earlier faced. Such independent parties as the Virginia Readjusters or, later, the North Carolina Populists advantaged the Republican Party and the coalition of 1867–1868, not Democrats. Third parties genuinely needed to attract black votes as well as white votes in order to have any success. Thus these independent organizations openly accepted black electoral incorporation. Their influence substituted, at the margin, for the loss in Republican strength during the Redemption.[10]

Southern third parties also helped reinstitutionalize black electoral incorporation in a second way. They bolstered the Republican Party nationally, in
the House and the Senate. They generally voted with Republicans and helped
them organize these two chambers. This is why Chester Arthur and his
southern strategist, William Chandler, then secretary of the navy, were eager
to build such parties.[11]

The national party system's structure during the first reconstruction thus
had two large consequences. First, its makeup meant that southern
Democrats could never peaceably accept black electoral incorporation via the
Republican Party—unless southerners developed an ethical commitment to
an acceptance of political uncertainty and possible national minority status
for an indeterminate length of time. Yet the South's historically violent political culture inhibited such leadership. Second, and for the same reason,
southern Democrats could not accept black electoral inclusion via populist
third parties.

The gains and losses allocated by the party system's structure, once
African Americans were electorally incorporated, generated fierce backlash.
Those who considered themselves the losers fostered turbulent racial reaction. In order to rally whites, Democratic politicians perpetuated and refurbished white supremacist symbols and discourse and tinged them with gore
during the Redemption. A new generation of fiery politicians such as Ben
Tillman did the same again, as they set about suppressing the budding biracial coalitions of the 1880s and 1890s.

In contrast, the second time around, the party system's structure *contained*
racial reaction. The rebuilding of the South's Democratic parties into biracial
organizations was aided by the unlikelihood of a durable, militant white
jacquerie.

Consider George Wallace, the governor of Alabama. He came close to giving white chauvinism a strong organizational foundation in 1964, when he
ran in Democratic presidential primaries; in 1968, when he launched his own
party; and in 1972, when he again ran in Democratic presidential primaries.
But Wallace's strategy of crisis-mongering on the basis of white mobilization
was ultimately impossible. He could hardly take the Democratic Party from
the inside. But an "outside" strategy—forming the American Independent
Party—required party-building on an even larger scale than Republican
party-building had during the first reconstruction. The burden, however,
now fell on *racial reactionaries*, not racial liberals.

Not surprisingly, in 1968 the American Independent Party did not have a
common label in the fifty states. Nor did it hold a national convention.
Instead, it was simply the extension of an Alabama clique led by Wallace, who

dominated the drafting of a platform and the choice of a running mate. Wallace's Alabama advisors ran his campaign and raised most of the money in Alabama. The other AIP national candidacies (eighteen altogether, fourteen in California) were a sideshow.[12] Yet the AIP's essential personalism was not an idiosyncrasy. It was necessary. Wallace really had to centralize all aspects of the AIP's decisionmaking. Otherwise he had no hope of controlling his message and preventing its hijacking by far-Right cranks.[13]

We will never know how the 1972 Democratic Party's nomination process might have turned out if Wallace had fought to the end. The attempt on Wallace's life in 1972 crippled him and forced his withdrawal from national politics. It also rapidly deflated his movement precisely because it was so personalistic.

Of course, if there had been a successful history of third-party formation for white supremacists or a deeper, more lasting split within the Democratic Party, then the 1961–1965 coalition would have faced more political trouble than it did. The second reconstruction might have encountered a bit of the fierce southern belligerence that characterized the first. Businessmen would have contributed to thriving backlash candidates; newspapers would have taken stands in favor of the third party; radio shows would have incited white voters during campaigns; underground violent movements might have maintained their strength. All of this would have made rebuilding the Democratic Party as a stable biracial coalition—one that could develop voter loyalty and attract the talents and energies of politicians and other sorts of leaders—far harder.

The improbability of continuing, organized white resistance, Wallace-style, was thus vitally important. It created a far more politically regular environment for the rebuilding process within the southern Democratic parties. In this way, the party system's structure aided the second reconstruction by blocking an independent white battle cry. Instead, as many researchers have shown, such combativeness eventually coursed into the Republican Party and transformed it. Today, only one in ten black southerners supports the GOP. But Republican party-building in the South in the second reconstruction also tamed and utterly changed the character of the region's white reaction. In a supreme historical irony, southern white racial backlash helped rebuild the party of African American emancipation and electoral incorporation—this time with a largely white, not largely black, regional base.[14]

In the end, therefore, *both* major parties reaped advantages from the revolutionary incorporation of black southern voters. That, too, stabilized the second reconstruction, in contrast to the zero-sumness for the major parties of African American incorporation during the first.

Precisely because the Democratic Party historically dominated the South, the Republican Party had an opening to grow in the region once the character of the southern Democratic parties changed. It could now offer an alternative to white southerners. One question was implicit in the moment: Did offering a partisan alternative to white southerners require open GOP opposition to the Voting Rights Act? No; the VRA was in a sense the GOP's golden goose. Without it, the party might not grow as quickly.

Hostility to the VRA would have been costly for the Republicans. Taking up a stance of open opposition to black southerners' full electoral reinclusion, and thus pushing for a rollback of the VRA, would only have caused a replication of the Democratic Party's schism between racial liberals and racial immoderates. Republican racial liberals played key roles, after all, in the passage of the Civil Rights Acts of 1957 and 1960.

Better for the GOP to signal a more subtle, even complex sort of racial conservatism. Interestingly, at this juncture in the history of the Republican Party, it fell to Richard Nixon to forge a strategy that simultaneously harmonized the party and allowed it to grow in the South by tapping into white racial reaction. Nixon was impressed by the Wallace movement's strength in and outside the South. But he also earlier played a key role in passage of the 1957 Civil Rights Act, the first national voting rights measure passed by Congress since Reconstruction. He ended up balancing conflicting impulses to exploit racial reaction, on one hand, and to assist the second reconstruction, on the other.[15]

In the 1968 presidential campaign Nixon developed a strategy of arguing to southern white voters that a vote for Wallace was a wasted vote. Nixon was aided by serious mistakes in the Wallace campaign such as the choice of an impolitic running mate, former Air Force general Curtis LeMay. Taking advantage of the sudden decline in Wallace's credibility, Nixon said in a radio ad, "[D]on't play their game. Don't divide your vote. . . . I pledge to you we will restore law and order in this country." Nixon's polling operation for the South showed a collapse in support for Wallace.[16]

Nixon learned that racially resentful whites, and whites startled by the rapid social and cultural changes swirling around them, would go to the Republicans if the latter could fuse voters' resentment and alarm to coherent views about policy and public philosophy. In the process Republicans could partly hide and transfigure the racial rancor at work among many whites. Barry Goldwater, his predecessor, had shown how. Although Goldwater lost badly outside the former Confederacy, in the Deep South he did extremely well. It was widely known that he opposed the 1964 Civil Rights Act. Goldwater sincerely espoused a philosophical conservatism of a limited federal role for correcting social wrongs. During his campaign he sometimes gave it subtle (and sometimes not-so-subtle) racial trappings.

All of this had, ironically, favorable implications for the Voting Rights Act. They surfaced when the act first came up for renewal in 1970. Initially, Nixon seemed bent on subverting the VRA. But in early 1970 a bipartisan Senate coalition led largely by Hugh Scott (R-Pa.), the minority leader, hammered out a workable alternative. Interestingly, the White House did nothing to fight Scott. A bipartisan House coalition then accepted the Senate version on June 17, 1970. The final result was a stronger statute than the original VRA (on which more below). With a show of graceful good cheer, the president signed the act on June 22, 1970.[17]

Nixon's apparent initial intent to subvert the VRA should not obscure the moment's importance. A new and complex southern strategy, one of tilting toward white racial resentments while decisively supporting black voting rights, now guided the GOP. What Nixon did, successors also did in one form or another. Gerald Ford discovered reasons at the last minute for opposing the renewal of the VRA's temporary provisions in 1975, and just as suddenly gave way. Ronald Reagan generally supported the act's renewal but then made a show of signing the renewal in a quite perfunctory way.[18]

Meanwhile, even as the Voting Rights Act was renewed by three successive Republican presidents, the GOP grew on the ground, particularly during Reagan's presidency. First, a combination of demographic exit by older whites, migration to the South of white voters inclined to vote Republican, and entry by new voters, that is, younger whites joining the electorate every two years, gradually created two additional new parties-in-the-southern-electorate. These were a largely white Republican Party and a largely white "nonparty" of avowed Independents. Both swelled the Republican Party's strength at election time. By the 1990s, only about 28 percent of Deep South whites thought of themselves as Democrats, and only 34 percent of Peripheral South whites were Democrats. Proportionately, the greatest number of white southerners, about 39 percent, considered themselves Independents. Younger whites increasingly (but not exclusively) elected partisan identities—Republican or Independent—that differed from those of their parents and grandparents.[19]

As the GOP built a southern white base, the governing prospects of southern Democrats obviously grew dimmer. This increase in Republican strength limited the number of southern Democrats, black and white, that could have careers in the state capitals and in the U.S. House and Senate.[20]

The bottom line for the coalition of 1961–1965, though, is that a century's worth of wide inter- and intraparty conflict over the electoral inclusion of African American voters finally came to a halt after passage of the VRA. The willingness of Republicans to live with (and sometimes embrace) the act critically assisted the rebuilding of the southern Democratic Party as a biracial party. The coincidence of the party system's historically received structure circa 1965 (on one hand) and of the Democratic Party's internal reconstruction (on the other) permitted *both* political parties to experience joint gains from black electoral inclusion. This has been a key difference from the first reconstruction.

THE WARTS ON PARTY CONVERGENCE

For the record, though, there are two large warts on this convergence between the two major parties. First, Republican mobilization of southern whites has sometimes involved playing a race card. This tactic began early. For instance, seeking to exploit white backlash after the Wallace phenomenon, the South Carolina GOP mailed "lurid leaflets 'exposing' the integrationist ties of our Democratic opponents . . . in plain white envelopes to all the white voters in the precincts George Wallace had carried."[21]

If the quite unapologetic use of the race card stratagem by the late 1980s is any indication, southern GOP strategists evidently honed its use over many years. Vice President George H. W. Bush's 1988 campaign for the presidency, guided by a South Carolina GOP operative, Lee Atwater, made an issue of Willie Horton, a black convict who went on a crime spree while on furlough from a prison in Massachusetts, the state governed by Bush's Democratic opponent, Michael Dukakis. Political scientists who researched the episode concluded that the Bush campaign deliberately activated white racial resentment in southern and nonsouthern states.[22]

In 1990, trailing Harvey Gantt, the former Democratic mayor of Charlotte, incumbent North Carolina senator Jesse Helms dropped a bomb in the closing days of the campaign. It was particularly incendiary because Gantt was a rising African American politician. Helms ran a famous reverse discrimination television ad. The camera focused on white hands crumpling a job rejection letter. The voice-over intoned, "You needed that job and you were the best qualified. But they had to give it to a minority because of a racial quota. Is that really fair? Harvey Gantt says it is. Gantt supports Ted Kennedy's racial quota law that makes the color of your skin more important than your qualifications."[23]

The second wart on the major party consensus in favor of the VRA is the occasional GOP abuse of the act. After passage of section 2—which, to recall, seeks to promote minority office-holding—GOP leaders sought to exploit its implications for congressional districting. Political scientists have debated whether the tactics actually worked for the GOP and what kind of impact they actually had, net of a strong general growth in Republican strength in the former Confederacy. But the facts of attempts to bend section 2 to partisan purpose are not in dispute.

John Griffin Dunne, the assistant attorney general for civil rights during the presidency of George H. W. Bush, intervened in congressional reapportionment in states partly or completely covered by the VRA. His promotion of section 2 compliance by states with respect to congressional districting promised not only to significantly change black office-holding but also to help Republicans. To comply with section 2, state legislatures concentrated black voters in certain districts. As some adjacent House districts became "whiter," Republican candidates seemed to pick up more seats in southern House contests.[24]

Some thought they saw a conscious Republican strategy of both weakening white Democratic office-seekers and sowing factional mischief within the Democratic Party along racial lines. Many Democrats believed that compliance with section 2 in the 1990 apportionment round cost them enough strength in southern districts to turn the House over to Republican control in 1994. What else, they thought, explained the vigor of the Bush administration in enforcing section 2 in the late 1980s? There was evidence, too, that the attack on vote dilution at the state level also cost Democrats numerical strength in southern legislatures.[25]

In short, racial appeals and strategies made their way into the competitive dynamics of the second reconstruction, just as they did during the first. But as we have seen, they did so in a far more favorable institutional context. If George Wallace could not disrupt the second reconstruction, these fainter echoes of racial politics were even less likely to do so.

JURISPRUDENCE-BUILDING

Having considered party-building during the two reconstructions, I turn next to jurisprudence-building. Let me begin with the more recent events and work backward.

Today, many Americans have the impression that a conservative 5–4 majority of the Supreme Court has reined in the Voting Rights Act. In fact, the Court has been split 4–4, giving the swing vote, Justice Sandra Day O'Connor, considerable leeway to reshape the Court's construction of the VRA in ways that usually (though not always) seem either ambiguous or disturbing. *Shaw v. Reno,* a 1993 congressional districting case from North Carolina's 1990 reapportionment round, signaled O'Connor's new influence. Like the 1980 decision in *Mobile v. Bolden*, the Court's 5–4 ruling in *Shaw* stunned observers of the second reconstruction. Some were outraged. Former federal judge Leon Higginbotham and two co-authors wrote in the *Fordham Law Review* that "the Court has created law that could make *Shaw v. Reno* equivalent for the civil rights jurisprudence of our generation to what *Plessy v. Ferguson* and *Dred Scott v. Sandford* were for previous generations."[26]

Such language had something to do with how breathtaking the holding in *Shaw* really was. The majority agreed with white plaintiffs' objection to a plan that increased the number of black House representatives for North Carolina. It accepted the plaintiffs' idea that *whites* could very well be *constitutionally* harmed by such political and regulatory processes. True, white citizens did not suffer vote dilution or vote denial, as African Americans previously had successfully claimed in voting rights cases. But whites could still legitimately have, under the Fourteenth Amendment, a claim to "equal protection" (that is, of the laws). They were potentially entitled—as a matter of *their* political rights—to so-called colorblind regulatory and political processes. In such color-blind processes, state legislators should mix both compliance with section 2 of the VRA and adherence to what the Court called "traditional districting principles." The Court therefore remanded to the lower federal courts the dispute about whether North Carolina properly drew its House districts in the 1990 reapportionment round.[27]

Placed in historical context the *Shaw* decision seemed "nutty," as Lyndon Johnson's attorney general, Nicholas Katzenbach said later. It appeared to constitutionally privilege the difficulty and resentment that whites have historically had in accepting African American office-holding. In fact, it came alarmingly close to tricking up the ancient epithet "Negro rule" into a valid "wrongful districting" cause of action before the Supreme Court.[28]

By the time the Court handed down *Shaw*, only three justices remained who had been on the Court during the previous renewals of the Voting Rights Act and had supported their implications. These were Justices Blackmun, Stevens, and White, appointed by, respectively, Nixon, Ford, and Kennedy. One of George H. W. Bush's appointments, David Souter, joined the voting rights jurisprudence of these three. But Bush's other appointment, Clarence Thomas, did not. Rehnquist, of course, came onto the Court during Nixon's presidency. Reagan nominated him for chief justice in 1986 and filled his associate justice seat with Antonin Scalia. In 1988, Reagan appointed Anthony Kennedy. These four—Rehnquist, Scalia, Kennedy, and Thomas—joined a key dissenter in *Gingles*, Sandra Day O'Connor. She had been Reagan's first nomination to the Court. Together they created *Shaw*.[29]

In additional cases known as the "*Shaw* progeny," the majority elaborated its colorblind philosophy. The most notable was a districting case from Georgia, *Miller v. Johnson*.[30] There the voting rights majority hardened the equal protection issue into a command that racial sorting in districting decisions and debate not be a "predominant" factor in reapportionment.

Besides *Shaw* and its progeny, which targeted section 2 of the Voting Rights Act, the Court's conservative majority also chipped away at section 5's preclearance device. An odd doctrinal position emerged in *Reno v. Bossier Parish School Board,* handed down on January 24, 2000. (It is also known as *Bossier II*, since it was the second opinion in a lengthy conflict.) In an opinion written by Justice Scalia, a majority of the Court held that clear evidence of constitutionally forbidden racially discriminatory intent by white officials— that is, smoking-gun evidence of purpose that, in turn, could be shown to have affected how the same officials devised new elections rules—did *not* bar preclearance of a redistricting plan by the Justice Department *if* the submitted plan did not "retrogress." By that the Court meant that so long as the plan did not cut back on, say, the number of black officeholders in a jurisdiction, whites were free to reveal a discriminatory purpose in the way they designed the plan. The Justice Department would still be required to approve it: "In light of the language of Sec. 5 and our prior holding in *Beer,* we hold that Sec. 5 does not prohibit preclearance of a redistricting plan enacted with a discriminatory but nonretrogressive purpose."[31]

Whether these changes have actually harmed black enfranchisement is not obvious, however. Furthermore, the Supreme Court's critical stances toward the Voting Rights Act have been relatively recent. For a quarter of a century the Court's relationship to the act was instead openly cooperative. The role of the Court is indeed a large part of explaining why the second reconstruction's jurisprudence-building evolved relatively well.

Before considering particulars, a brief review of what I have posited concerning the Court's role is in order. During both reconstructions, the key factor in the evolution of voting rights jurisprudence was the first stance taken by a majority of the Supreme Court, that is, when the constitutional and statutory products of coalition-making first received Court scrutiny. At such moments informed observers were both highly uncertain and highly self-conscious. Coalition-making was, after all, contentious; it altered power relations.

Which side of the post-coalition struggle would the Court's majority join? It had to choose. Protecting black voting and office-holding either appeared valid and commanding or it did not. Minimum political requirements—that constitutional amendments be taken seriously and that new statutes be respected by the courts—were either met or not met. For these reasons, the initial signal from the Court had one of two further effects during the two reconstructions. At the least, the favorable stance (the second reconstruction) generated pressure for compliance with the new policies. But the initially *un*favorable stance (the first reconstruction) produced something different than pressure for compliance. It created new and difficult follow-on tasks. It placed pressure on the incorporating coalition to (1) undertake some new litigation strategy or (2) change the Court's composition.

In other words, an unfavorable ruling did not mean the end of reform. It instead meant much more work. As we will see for the case of the first reconstruction, the Supreme Court's initially hostile rulings did *not* foreclose an ultimately favorable position on the national protection of black voting rights. This is rarely remarked. By the late 1880s, an alternative (though also more limited) constitutional basis for the protection of black voting rights became available within the original Constitution, not in the Reconstruction Amendments. The result was to encourage the Republican Party's final attempt to save some of the political gains of Reconstruction, namely, the Federal Elections Bill of 1890.

But by then a great deal of time had been lost. The coalition of 1867–1868 was much weaker. The jurisprudential opportunity cost, as it were, of the Supreme Court's initially unfavorable position was therefore high. Time and effort that could have gone into strengthening, revising, and advancing the legal basis for electorally including African Americans had to go toward solving the problem of the Court's hostility.

The extent of the jurisprudential opportunity cost becomes particularly clear in considering the second reconstruction, in which the coalition of 1961–1965 paid none. We will see below that the Supreme Court's very favorable stance this time explicitly encouraged further congressional elaboration and strengthening of the VRA. In addition to reducing political uncertainty about the status of the act and thereby generating pressure for compliance, the Court's approval of the act strongly energized the bipartisan consensus described above. It invited a virtuous circle of cooperative jurisprudence-building via the new bipartisan consensus forged by Nixon, Ford, and Reagan.

COOPERATIVE JURISPRUDENCE-BUILDING

The initial signal from the Court (as chapter 9 showed) was highly auspicious. The Court strongly emphasized the information-gathering and deliberative strengths of Congress as an institution.[32] In the opinion for the Court's

1966 review of the Voting Rights Act, *South Carolina v. Katzenbach,* the chief justice wrote that "Congress may use *any* rational means to effectuate the constitutional prohibition of racial discrimination in voting." Congress was not "circumscribed by . . . artificial rules" under section 2 of the Fifteenth Amendment; its remedy was "inventive," "legitimate," "permissible," "acceptable," based on "reliable evidence of actual voting discrimination," and "rational in both practice and theory." In *Katzenbach v. Morgan,* another 1966 decision construing the VRA, the Court went even further, stressing that just about *anything* Congress did to enforce the Fourteenth and Fifteenth Amendments, so long as the legislation was reasonably related to the enforcement of these amendments, would make sense. The only limit on Congress was any enforcement legislation that did not meet this standard. That is, Congress had "no power to restrict, abrogate, or dilute" the guarantees of equal protection and due process that the Court had found in the Fourteenth Amendment. But that was the sole limitation.[33]

In short, in its early reviews of the VRA the Court signaled that it would not, for its part, cast any shadow over how Congress proceeded with the act—as long as Congress acted forcefully and amelioratively. This was a vitally important sign. Because its enforcement features were not permanent legislation, the act was especially vulnerable. If a Supreme Court majority had initially adopted an unfavorable stance toward it, then a new legislative coalition overriding the Court would have been required at the time of the VRA's first renewal. That would not have been impossible. But it would not have been guaranteed.

The Court once again adopted an approving stance in 1969, shortly before the statutory renewal, when it reviewed the VRA's major temporary provision, section 5, establishing preclearance. In the first test of section 5, *Allen v. State Board of Elections,* the opinion said that the Court meant to "reject a narrow construction" of section 5. Instead, it was guided by Congress: "in passing the Voting Rights Act, Congress intended that state enactments such as those involved in the instant cases be subject to the § 5 approval requirements."[34]

In light of the Court's repeated emphasis on Congress's deliberative competence, it is no surprise that—once the Nixon administration chose bipartisan consensus—the VRA's temporary provisions were carried forward and a strengthening of the act occurred. (The details are in chapter 9.) This had two vital consequences. First, renewal of the act became an occasion for solidifying bipartisan consensus. Second, extension featured not only continuation of the temporary provisions; it also saw positive strengthening of the entire act.

Come the 1975 renewal, it too was bipartisan. It carried forward, as before, the temporary provisions, reinstating preclearance, federal provision of federal examiners, and, if a jurisdiction requested them, provision of federal elections observers. Congress made permanent the 1970 national ban on literacy tests and targeted barriers to Hispanic and Native American voting and office-holding.[35]

In short, the Supreme Court's initially favorable stance in 1966 did more than reduce the uncertainty of the Voting Rights Act's political status and thus invite statutory compliance. It also interacted with the bipartisan consensus analyzed above and prompted statutory innovation. The 1970 and 1975 renewals saw not only a continuation of the VRA's temporary provisions; they also saw a considerable strengthening of the act and a wide extension of its geographic and group coverage.

BLACK OFFICE-HOLDING

As I have emphasized, the Warren Court's initial view of Congress's competence as a factor in the Court's own stance, coupled with convergence of the parties, encouraged jurisprudential leadership by Congress at the scheduled renewals. Such legislative learning later had an unexpected synergy—one that was vital for the development of black office-holding: *Congress checked the Court itself.* It did this when the Court unexpectedly stepped back from its partnership by refusing to explicitly endorse a positive right to office.

When Congress asserted itself in this manner, it paved the way for a truly momentous change in voting rights jurisprudence: open statutory promotion of minority office-holding. Recall that in 1980, in a plurality opinion in *City of Mobile v. Bolden,* the Supreme Court suddenly held that the Fifteenth Amendment applied only to registration and voting, stating that "[t]he Fifteenth Amendment does not entail the right to have Negro candidates elected." A valid vote dilution claim was certainly possible under the Fourteenth Amendment. But that required proof of intent.[36]

Congress quickly reacted, given the scheduled expiration on August 6, 1982, of the VRA's temporary provisions. Congress rewrote section 2 of the act to counter Justice Potter Stewart's constitutional interpretation that there was no right to office guaranteed in the Fifteenth Amendment. Proof of racial intent was no longer necessary, and minorities could properly expect "representatives of their choice." Section 2 did not create a *right* to office, of course, but it did create a legal environment that would invite higher rates of office-holding by minority politicians. To underscore that it meant business, the coalition behind the amendment renewed the Voting Rights Act for twenty-five years. In a quarter century, minority office-holding would have plenty of time to root itself.

The Supreme Court then aided the implementation of section 2 for the next decade. It invalidated at-large elections in Burke County, Georgia, as unconstitutional under the Fourteenth Amendment (*Rogers v. Lodge*), a case with facts similar to those in *Mobile*. It was particularly cooperative in *Thornburg v. Gingles*. This decision defined impermissible vote dilution as occurring when three circumstances coincided: minority voting as a group, evidence of persistent racial-bloc voting among whites, and enough geographic concentration of minority voters to permit a remedy in the form of a majority-minority district. A simpler framework for forcing compliance with section 2 thus emerged.[37]

THE NEW VOTING RIGHTS BAR

Soon, also, the role of private lawyers became obvious. After *Gingles*, more than 90 percent of legal challenges to municipal at-large elections succeeded, most brought by minority plaintiffs supported by a specialized plaintiffs'-side voting rights bar.[38]

Where did this plaintiffs'-side voting rights bar come from? By the late 1960s, there were three pools of legal talent available for such a bar: voting rights lawyers affiliated with the NAACP (and later its Legal Defense Fund), a network of African American civil rights lawyers that had emerged in southern cities by the 1940s, and finally a volunteer voting rights bar encouraged by the Kennedy administration when it convened 246 African American and white lawyers drawn from the top levels of the American legal profession. This led to the emergence of the Lawyers' Committee for Civil Rights Under Law and to its opening of an office in Jackson, Mississippi. About 130 lawyers also donated summer vacation time during Freedom Summer under the auspices of a separate organization, the Lawyers' Constitutional Defense Committee. Many of the lawyers who "went South" stayed. They were legal carpetbaggers, as it were, who sharply expanded the work that had long been done by what the social movement literature calls "early risers," that is, the NAACP lawyers and the local black civil rights lawyers.[39]

In 1975, Congress created a profit motive by instituting fee awards. Section 14(e) of the 1975 Voting Rights Act provided that "[i]n any action or proceeding to enforce the voting guarantees of the fourteenth or fifteenth amendment, the court, in its discretion, may allow the prevailing party, other than the United States, a *reasonable attorney's fee* as part of the costs." It reinforced this step in 1976 by passing the Civil Rights Attorney's Fees Awards Act.[40]

Given the nature of the Voting Rights Act—i.e., that it was a civil statute—such steps promoted a vital support structure of "rights-advocacy" lawyers and organizations. During the first reconstruction, the support structure for black voting rights comprised only government lawyers and federal judges. This was the case because the federal election laws were criminal statutes, and by their nature they inhibited the formation of an additional, private support structure, despite the first Enforcement Act's encouragement of private action. During the second reconstruction, in contrast, such a support structure comprised not only the lawyers in the Civil Rights Division of the Justice Department but also a private voting rights bar. These lawyers became what Gregory Caldeira has called "repeat players."[41] Repeat players came back into court again and again. They had many chances to move the law in a certain direction. Government lawyers became responsible for only a very small percentage of voting rights cases—one estimate is 5 percent. As Caldeira put it, "Enforcement of voting rights is . . . very much an activity of the private sector."[42]

This was due to legislative design. When Congress fostered a private voting rights bar in its 1975 renewal of the Voting Rights Act, it also created a synergy with other parts of the act. Sections 4 and 5 (the temporary provisions renewed in 1970, 1975, and 1982) limit the Court's customary discretion over its docket. For instance, per section 4a(3)(5), "[a]n action pursuant to this subsection shall be heard and determined by a court of three judges . . . *and any appeal shall lie to the Supreme Court*" (emphasis added). Between subsidizing a voting rights bar and requiring appeal to the Supreme Court, Congress underwrote the expansion of liberal voting rights doctrine.

The role of this bar in shaping voting rights law can be seen particularly clearly in *Thornburg v. Gingles*. In this case Justice Brennan led the Court, over the dissent of Justices O'Connor, Burger, Powell, and Rehnquist, to adopt a highly simplified formula (described above) for making "vote dilution" claims against states and localities. But it is a little-known fact that Brennan borrowed part of his formula from a 1982 law review article penned by well-known members of the voting rights bar. The alliance between voting rights lawyers and the Court's liberal majority was apparently close.[43]

To summarize, during the second reconstruction the evolution of voting rights jurisprudence was decisively influenced by the early favorable stance of the Supreme Court. Key members of Congress in time learned to liberalize the Voting Rights Act. Indeed, when a changed Court announced in 1980 that there was no right to office in the Fifteenth Amendment, Congress quickly corrected the situation. In doing that, it amended the act to promote minority office-holding. A new legal infrastructure of voting rights attorneys then moved the statute's implementation along.

All of this contrasts sharply with the impact in the 1870s of Supreme Court hostility to voting rights legislation. The political talents and skills of the coalition of 1868–1867 would surely have gone toward building on favorable Court rulings—if such rulings had been forthcoming. Let us return, therefore, to the antagonism that emerged between the Court and the coalition of 1867–1868 during the first reconstruction.

SUPREME COURT HOSTILITY DURING THE FIRST RECONSTRUCTION

In reconsidering the Supreme Court's stance during this period, it is first essential to reiterate how close the Court actually came to adopting a friendly view of the Fourteenth and Fifteenth Amendments and of the federal elections statutes. The Court's opposition probably resulted from sheer contingency—the crisis of Chief Justice Salmon Chase's health.[44] Chase earlier had led the development of Reconstruction constitutionalism. For example, his circuit decision in *In re Turner* gave a muscular, innovative reading to the 1866 Civil Rights Act. Chase's position that there were national rights that the United States could positively protect was the essence of Reconstruction constitutionalism. Had Chase lived, similar ideas would have guided his leadership of the Court when tests of the elections statutes came before it. But Chase's health declined rapidly after March 1873, and he died in early May 1873. These events coincided with the first tests of the federal elections statutes.[45]

Imagine if Chief Justice Earl Warren suddenly had fallen ill in 1966. If Warren had died, would Johnson have been able to replace him with someone similar? Whom would Nixon have appointed if Johnson had not made the appointment? What would have happened with the first tests of the Voting Rights Act under these alternative scenarios? Such questions illuminate the kind of crisis that was caused by Chase's illness and death. Rather than having a clean, strong ruling in favor of Reconstruction constitutional theory, the coalition of 1867–1868 was forced to instead work around unfriendly decisions.

A key circumvention occurred after the *Slaughterhouse Cases* of 1873. Republican leaders seem to have anticipated that in any forthcoming elections cases the Court would extend the restrictive approach that Justice Samuel Miller enunciated in the *Slaughterhouse Cases*. The Forty-third Congress authorized a revision of the federal statutes. The revision commissioners completely tore apart the federal elections statutes and placed the various pieces all around the United States Code. Congress then enacted the Revised Statutes with the proviso that the revision supersede all previous statutes. Now several dozen electoral regulatory pieces existed in the Code. An invalidation of one did nothing to all the others.[46]

A similar circumvention happened the day after (and perhaps as a part of) the Compromise of 1877. Congress appointed George Boutwell, an author of the Fifteenth Amendment, to prepare a new edition of the Revised Statutes. Boutwell's handling of his assignment was clever: he made no substantive change at all to the elections provisions despite *Cruikshank* and *Reese* (discussed in chapter 5).[47]

Much more work was, of course, needed. The new chief justice, Morrison Waite, disliked Reconstruction constitutionalism, as his opinion for the Court in *Cruikshank* showed. In 1883, the Court struck again, this time against a provision that originated in section 2 of the Ku Klux Act. It provided for federal voter protection against private violence in House elections. One R. G. Harris and several companions, all whites from Crockett County, Tennessee, beat several African Americans and killed one in election-related violence. But in *United States v. Harris* the Court held that the Fourteenth and Fifteenth Amendments reached state action, not private violence.[48]

A comprehensive effort to revitalize voting rights jurisprudence was desperately needed. It came, finally, in 1889. The Republican Party moved vigorously after the election of Benjamin Harrison to establish national control over elections in the South. This initiative coincided with its fairly strong control of both houses of Congress. Key Republican leaders took a long, hard look at some useful regulatory machinery that they had at hand. They had at their disposal an electoral regulatory framework that had been originally devised to allow some measure of national control over *northern* national elections. But there was no reason it could not be extended to southern elections. Indeed, as we shall see, they had Court approval to do just that.[49]

Many American political scientists have encountered the following passage in Woodrow Wilson's classic study of Gilded Age national politics, *Congressional Government:* "The federal supervisor who oversees the balloting for congressmen represents the very ugliest side of federal supremacy." In glancing over this sentence, modern scholars read a diatribe against an electoral-regulatory system that no longer exists.[50] Wilson's comments referred to an article 1, section 4 electoral-regulatory system that functioned, with greater or lesser force, throughout the entire country. Its purpose was the supervision of congressional elections. This system could be strengthened, and thus it could be used to address Republican weakness in House elections within the former Confederacy.

Article 1, section 4 of the Constitution reads, "The Times, Places and Manner of holding Elections for Senators and Representatives, shall be prescribed in each State by the Legislature thereof; but the Congress may at any time by Law make or alter such Regulations, except as to the Places of Chusing Senators." Consistent with this were three statutes available to Republicans: an immigration and naturalization act dating to 1870, a federal elections bill of 1871, and another federal elections bill that was folded into the 1872 appropriations act.

Further, government lawyers, the circuit courts, and the Supreme Court grew increasingly attracted to article 1, section 4 as a basis for national electoral regulation. Three decisions in particular, *Ex parte Siebold, Ex parte Clarke,* and *Ex parte Yarbrough,* announced the new jurisprudential stance.[51] In these rulings, a majority of the Court adopted a nationalist reading of article 1, section 4. The Court literally took the view that nothing prevented Congress from regulating federal elections in any way it chose. "It must execute its power, or it is no government." The Court had no patience for exceptions or hedges to this authority, else "our institutions . . . cannot stand."[52]

The vital difference in *Yarbrough,* relative to *Siebold* and *Clarke,* was petitioners' request that they be held immune from federal criminal process because they were private individuals. Yet the Court held that the United States could, in fact, act against private individuals under its article 1, section 4 power. This is precisely what the Court had had such doubts about in *Cruikshank* in 1876. *Yarbrough* thus laid a key foundation for federal correction of private electoral fraud and voter intimidation.

The decision for the Court was striking in several ways. First, it was unanimous, a very strong message. Second, it was written by Justice Samuel Miller. In the *Slaughterhouse Cases* Miller's opinion for the Court was considerably more cautious about the national protection of rights than in this case. Third, the Court appeared genuinely alarmed over the disorder and violence of House elections in the South. Finally, the Court was certain that the Constitution provided forceful remedies to the problem. They were located in article I, section 4—and in the Fifteenth Amendment. The United States had firm bases for national regulation of the electoral process.

With casual assurance Miller distinguished the case from the holding in *Reese* that the Fifteenth Amendment "gives no affirmative right to the colored man to vote." Miller blandly noted that "it is easy to see that under some circumstances it may operate as the immediate source of a right to vote." After giving an illustration involving Delaware (where the Fifteenth Amendment automatically invalidated the state's constitutional "whites only" restriction), Miller noted that "[i]n such cases this fifteenth article of amendment does, *proprio vigore* [with its own force], substantially confer on the negro the right to vote." Also, in order to protect the electoral processes that made it a national representative assembly, Congress could protect the right to vote of any citizen "whenever that is necessary." Indeed, Congress could directly criminalize any individual behavior that tainted the integrity of national elections. All representative governments had this power.[53]

In light of Miller's articulation of dual federalist jurisprudence in the *Slaughterhouse Cases*, *Yarbrough*—which, again, the entire Court supported—was a radical departure. In it, Miller forged a conceptual link between article 1, section 4 of the Constitution and the Fifteenth Amendment broad enough to permit strong national protection of the electoral process.

The Republican Party now had a jurisprudential basis for addressing persistent elections fraud in southern House elections. The targets of fraud and intimidation were usually African American voters. About one-third of the eighty-five southern House districts were majority black, for a total of twenty-eight House districts that "should have" been under constant Republican control, following the 1880 apportionment.[54]

Fraud cost the Republican Party dearly. From the Forty-fourth Congress (1875–1877) to the Fiftieth Congress (1887–1889), which was the last to convene before introduction of the Federal Elections Bill, the Democrats always organized the House except during the Forty-seventh Congress, or about 86 percent of the time. Of those congresses, three—or 41 percent—had a close party division. It was plausible for Republicans to think that a few more seats in the former Confederacy would have given them control of the House in these periods.

Equally consequential for the party was the decline in Republican strength outside the South: "Democrats experienced a resurgence of support nationally, picking up strength in the border states equal to the strength they had had in the former Confederacy, winning about half the elections in the Great Lakes states from Ohio to Wisconsin, and even gaining two-fifths of the seats in the Northeast (concentrated in New York and Pennsylvania)." In other words, Republicans *needed* to shore up their strength in the South.[55]

THE FEDERAL ELECTIONS BILL OF 1890

Action on the opportunity presented by *Yarbrough* was promised in the 1888 Republican presidential platform: "We . . . demand effective legislation to secure the integrity and purity of elections. . . . We charge that the present Administration and the Democratic majority in Congress [the House] owe their existence to the suppression of the ballot by a criminal nullification of the Constitution and laws of the United States."[56]

On the ground, in the former Confederacy there was considerable antici-
pation. As the Fifty-first Congress considered the Federal Elections Bill,
Senator George Hoar of Massachusetts, the bill's architect, received petitions
and letters of support from the Afro-American League's Executive Committee
and from ordinary citizens in Mississippi.[57]

A national elections bill appears to have been particularly closely anticipated in Mississippi. The state Republican Party's African American leadership, principally former Mississippi House speaker and U.S. representative John Roy Lynch and former U.S. senator Blanche Bruce, traveled
in Republican circles, splitting their time between Washington and
Mississippi. One of the party's white leaders, former Confederate general
James Chalmers, had already worked with New Hampshire senator William
E. Chandler in drafting legislation that foreshadowed the 1890 elections
bill.[58]

Several of the former Confederacy's Republican and independent parties
also called for fair elections when they met at their state conventions in 1888.
The Alabama Republican Party called for a "national law to regulate the elec-
tion of members of Congress and Presidential electors"; the Arkansas Union
Labor Party, representing the Agricultural Wheel, the National Farmers
Alliance, and the Knights of Labor, fused with the state Republican Party and
called for the "consolidation of the elections, State and national"; the North
Carolina Republican Party called for protective state legislation that would
assure "free and just exercise of the elective franchise"; the South Carolina
Republican Party asked "Congress to enact such legislation as shall secure a
fair election at least for members of Congress and presidential electors"; and
the Texas fusion at a gathering in Waco of the State Alliance, Knights of Labor,
Union Labor, Prohibition, and Republican Parties called for a "free ballot and
a fair count."[59]

Introduced in the House by Henry Cabot Lodge of Massachusetts and in
the Senate by George Frisbie Hoar, the 1890 Federal Elections Bill became a
major element of the Republican Party's 1889–1891 legislative push. Senator
John C. Spooner of Wisconsin, a close collaborator of Hoar, thought that the
policy of national control of national elections would bring the party back "to
its old-time vigor."[60]

In the end, the Federal Elections Bill was filibustered to death. At that
time in the Senate's evolution, there were no procedures for cloture. With
their obstructionism Democrats consumed a total of thirty-three legislative
days. As mentioned in chapter 6, the 1890 elections bill was the first substantive legislation in the history of the U.S. Congress that was supported by the

House, the president, and a Senate majority and that was killed by a Senate filibuster. Thus the last window for national voting rights jurisprudence closed for decades to come.[61]

There are many lessons in the story of the Federal Elections Bill. The one that is relevant here has to do with the opportunity cost of the *Slaughterhouse Cases, Cruikshank,* and *Reese.* These holdings meant that it was not until 1890—twenty years after ratification of the Fifteenth Amendment—that the original coalition of 1867–1868 finally fashioned what could have been a workable statutory basis for protecting black voting rights. By then, though, any failure in legislation was extremely costly. As chapter 3 showed, the coalition was much weaker. The Republican Party's push for a new bill may even have played a role in goading the southern Democratic parties into developing the formal-legal devices that brought about black disenfranchisement.

Comparison of the jurisprudence-building process early in the two reconstructions underscores the critical importance of the initial statutory test. Had Salmon Chase been able to do in the mid-1870s what Earl Warren did in 1966 in *South Carolina v. Katzenbach,* statutory development during the first reconstruction might have been more favorable. Instead, a long and uncertain set of tasks confronted the coalition of 1867–1868 as it sought to work around the Court's initial stance.

In addition, comparison of jurisprudence-building relatively *late* in the course of these two reconstructions is also instructive. Late in its history, the coalition of 1867–1868 did receive help from the Supreme Court, but by then the impact of such assistance was limited. Today, the coalition of 1961–1965 faces the opposite situation: a majority of the Supreme Court has distanced itself from black enfranchisement. But the impact of that change has so far been fairly slight. The contrasting outcomes—the Federal Elections Bill's failure and the modest impact of *Shaw* and other cases—remind us that jurisprudence-building skills and energies were best put to use the *earlier* they were put to use.

In summary, different institutional foundations for party- and jurisprudence-building separated the two reconstructions. During both, the parties and courts framework empowered the biracial coalitions. Yet in the first case the coalition worked within a version of the parties and courts matrix that proved much harder to use. In the second case the coalition had a far more favorable party system structure and more advantageous initial jurisprudential outcomes. The twentieth-century coalition was fortunate, then, in a way that the nineteenth-century coalition was not.

PROGRESS AND POLICY

Taking notice of the similarities and differences of the two reconstructions has many implications. Perhaps the most important is that as a nation we have only just begun to truly experience the kind of full political democracy that we might have had if the first reconstruction had not collapsed. The United States is among the last of the advanced democracies to still be at the business of fully including all of its citizens in its electoral politics. The United States is the only democracy in which a major social group entered the electorate en masse and then was extruded via legislation, referendum, and constitutional revision, forcing that group to start all over again.

Consequently, as a country we still have very important business to do: we have to overcome the social and economic legacies of disenfranchisement. It is often thought that the persistence of black disadvantage is rooted in the experience of African American enslavement. But disenfranchisement is also an important cause. It may even be more significant than the experience of enslavement.[62]

Once black southerners were disenfranchised by the early 1900s, the stage was set for a systematic entrenchment of white supremacist norms and public policies. These exercised considerable influence over national public policy. This is because southern states escaped the representational penalty for disenfranchisement established in the second section of the Fourteenth Amendment. The former Confederacy's Democratic politicians thus received a political bonus in the census enumeration, bringing more of them to the U.S. House than they might otherwise have had. One-partyism in the South also assured long political careers for southern Democrats in Congress. They gained special advantages in congressional leadership politics into the early 1960s.

Not coincidentally, color lines grew brighter in the District of Columbia, the federal civil service, the dining rooms of Congress, and the armed forces. Such highly symbolic national segregation tacitly legitimated northern de facto segregation in public employment, schooling, and housing. Examples of de facto racial exclusions also occurred in old age income security, collective bargaining, direct housing subsidies, mortgage credit, insurance regulation, banking regulation, medical care, and government jobs. Statutory design reflected who was represented—and who was not. This remarkable state of affairs lasted into the mid-1960s.[63]

Racial hierarchy, in short, got a very strong second wind. As a result, when the coalition of 1961–1965 emerged, the second reconstruction had its work cut out for it. Because the links between electoral politics and policy impact are not tight and immediate, the beginning of full electoral inclusion circa 1965 could not quickly dissolve disenfranchisement's legacies. The second reconstruction has been instead a gradual solvent of economic and educational inequality.[64]

One day the hateful inequalities that disenfranchisement did so much to create or to entrench—in housing, jobs, medical care, and education—may be gone. When that happens the second reconstruction will finally be over. But not until then will it be over. And this has clear implications, I believe, for voting rights policy. The temporary provisions of the Voting Rights Act will come up for congressional consideration no later than 2007. When they do, they must not be allowed to lapse—at least not without putting protections of equal strength in their place.

There is an attitude that may tempt members of Congress and much of the public when the Voting Rights Act's temporary sections require reconsideration. In an essay in *Collier's Weekly* in 1906, W. E. B. Du Bois put his finger on it. "We have a way in America," he wrote, "of wanting to be 'rid' of problems. It is not so much a desire to reach the best and largest solution as it is to clean the board and start a new game. For instance, most Americans are simply tired and impatient over our . . . social problem, the Negro. They do not want to solve it, they do not want to understand it, they want to simply be done with it and hear the last of it. Of all possible attitudes, this is the most dangerous." Du Bois recommended instead a policy of—to use his Victorian but apt language—"Freedom and Friendship."[65]

Abraham Lincoln also understood the special obligations of our national history. As is well known, Lincoln's Second Inaugural offered the most soaring, historicist sorts of ideas, even speculating that divine providence might prolong the Civil War for another two and a half centuries. But Lincoln ended on just the right note. His voice will serve Congress and the president well when they reconsider the Voting Rights Act: "With malice toward none, with charity for all, with firmness in the right as God gives us to see the right, let us strive on to finish the work we are in."[66]

Notes

Preface

1. C. Vann Woodward first used the term "Second Reconstruction" in his article "The Political Legacy of Reconstruction," *Journal of Negro Education* 26 (Summer 1957): 231–240, reprinted in C. Vann Woodward, *The Burden of Southern History* (Baton Rouge: Louisiana State University Press, 1960). Among studies pursuing his view that the two periods were comparable, see J. Morgan Kousser, "The Undermining of the First Reconstruction: Lessons for the Second," in *Minority Vote Dilution,* ed. Chandler Davidson (Washington, D.C.: Howard University Press, for the Joint Center for Political Studies, 1984), pp. 27–46; Kousser, "The Voting Rights Act and the Two Reconstructions," in *Controversies in Minority Voting: The Voting Rights Act in Perspective,* ed. Bernard Grofman and Chandler Davidson, pp. 135–76 (Washington, D.C.: Brookings Institution, 1992); Kousser, *Colorblind Injustice: Minority Voting Rights and the Undoing of the Second Reconstruction* (Chapel Hill: University of North Carolina Press, 1999), chap. 1; William S. McFeely, "Two Reconstructions, Two Nations," *Massachusetts Review,* Spring 1991, pp. 39–53; Richard M. Valelly, "Party, Coercion and Inclusion," *Politics and Society* 21 (March 1993): 37–67.

2. A classic statement of this view is Gunnar Myrdal, *An American Dilemma: The Negro Problem and Modern Democracy* (New York: Harper and Brothers, 1944).

Chapter One

1. This is a reference to C. Vann Woodward, *The Strange Career of Jim Crow,* 3d rev. ed. (New York: Oxford University Press, 1974).

2. *Repeal of Federal Election Laws,* 53d Cong., 1st sess., 1893, H. Rep. 18, p. 7, also quoted by Justice Douglass in his dissent to the opinion for the court in *United States v. Classic,* 313 U.S. 299, 335 (1941). My thanks to Jacki Magagnosc, government documents specialist at the Swarthmore College Libraries, who tracked down this report for me. See also Xi Wang, *The Trial of Democracy: Black Suffrage and Northern Republicans, 1860–1910* (Athens: University of Georgia Press, 1997), pp. 294–299. The calculations are mine.

3. Thomas T. Mackie and Richard Rose, *The International Almanac of Electoral History,* rev. 3d ed. (Washington, D.C.: Congressional Quarterly, Inc., 1991); Ian Gorrin, ed., *Elections since 1945: A Worldwide Reference Compendium* (Harlow, Essex: Longman Group UK, 1989); John R. Freeman and Duncan Snidal, "Diffusion, Development, and Democratization: Enfranchisement in Western Europe," *Canadian Journal of Political Science* 15 (June 1982): 299–329.

4. Roy P. Basler, ed., *The Collected Works of Abraham Lincoln* (New Brunswick: Rutgers University Press for the Abraham Lincoln Association [Springfield, Illinois], 1953), 8:399–405. For the context of Lincoln's statement, see Peyton McCrary, *Abraham Lincoln and Reconstruction: The Louisiana Experiment* (Princeton: Princeton University Press, 1978); Herman Belz, "Origins of Negro Suffrage During the Civil War," *Southern Studies* 17 (Summer 1978): 115–130.

5. Alexander Keyssar, *The Right to Vote: The Contested History of Democracy in the United States* (New York: Basic Books/Perseus Books Group, 2000), table A.4.

6. On Booth, see William Hanchett, *The Lincoln Murder Conspiracies* (Urbana: University of Illinois Press, 1983), p. 37; David Herbert Donald, *Lincoln* (New York: Simon and Schuster, 1995), pp. 585–588, 592–599.

7. United States Bureau of the Census, *Ninth Census,* vol. 1: *The Statistics of the Population of the United States* (Washington, D.C.: Government Printing Office, 1872), pp. 618–619. For 1866 count Massachusetts, Rhode Island, and Vermont; for 1867 count these states and the District of Columbia, Colorado, the Dakota Territory, Nebraska, and the former Confederacy, including Tennessee. See also Leonard P. Curry, *The Free Black in Urban America, 1800–1850: The Shadow of the Dream* (Chicago: University of Chicago Press, 1981), pp. 217–224; William Gillette, *The Right to Vote: Politics and the Passage of the Fifteenth Amendment* (Baltimore: Johns Hopkins University Press, 1965), p. 30n13; Alrutheus Taylor, *The Negro in Tennessee, 1865–1880* (Washington, D.C.: Associated Publishers, 1941), pp. 24, 45–46.

8. James Ciment, *Atlas of African-American History* (New York: Checkmark, 2001), p. 96.

9. Steven J. Rosenstone and John Mark Hansen, *Mobilization, Participation, and Democracy in America* (New York: Macmillan, 1993), p. 200n67.

10. See James E. Alt, "The Impact of the Voting Rights Act on Black and White Voter Registration in the South," in *Quiet Revolution in the South: The Impact of the Voting Rights Act, 1965–1990,* ed. Chandler Davidson and Bernard Grofman, pp. 351–377 (Princeton: Princeton University Press, 1994) (my calculations are based on table 12.1 at p. 374).

11. Sasha Abramsky, "The Other Election Scandal," *Rolling Stone,* 30 August 2001, pp. 47–50; Angela Behrens, Christopher Uggen, and Jeff Manza, "Ballot Manipulation and the 'Menace of Negro Domination': Racial Threat and Felon Disenfranchisement in the United States, 1850–2002," *American Journal of Sociology* 109 (November 2003): 559–605.

12. David Gonzalez and Dexter Filkins, "In Palm Beach County, Tumult Grew Hourly," *New York Times,* 13 November 2000, pp. A1, A18; Mireya Navarro and Somini Sengupta, "Arriving at Florida Voting Places, Some Blacks Found Frustration," *New York Times,* 30 November 2000, p. A1; John Mintz and Dan Keating, "Analysis Shows Higher Vote Loss in Black Areas," *Washington Post,* 3 December 2000, p. A1; Dana Canedy, "Rights Panel Begins Inquiry into Florida's Voting System," *New York Times,* 12 January 2001, p. A20; Marc Lacey, "Bush, in Outreach Bid, Meets Black Caucus," *New York Times,* 1 February 2001, p. A1; John Lantigua, "How the GOP Gamed the System in Florida," *Nation,* 30 April 2001, pp. 11–17.

13. *United States v. Charleston County,* Order of Patrick Michael Duffy (D.S.C., March 6, 2003), p. 35.

14. Judith N. Shklar, *American Citizenship: The Quest for Inclusion* (Cambridge: Harvard University Press, 1991), p. 3. See also Donald R. Kinder and Lynn M. Sanders, *Divided by Color: Racial Politics and Democratic Ideals* (Chicago: University of Chicago Press, 1996), pp. 196–197.

15. Laughlin McDonald, "The Voting Rights Act Is the Only Hope against a Century of All-White Rule," *Civil Liberties,* June 1981, 3–4, quoted in *Quiet Revolution in the South: The Impact of the Voting Rights Act, 1965–1990,* ed. Chandler Davidson and Bernard Grofman, 16 (Princeton: Princeton University Press, 1994). See also http://archive.aclu.org/issues/racial/racevote.html#edgefield.

16. Henry McNeal Turner, "On the Eligibility of Colored Members to Seats in the Georgia Legislature (1868)," in *Respect Black: The Writings and Speeches of Henry McNeal Turner,* ed. and comp. Edwin S. Redkey, pp. 14–28, at pp. 14–19 (New York: Arno Press and the New York Times, 1971).

17. Quoted in Edmund Drago, *Black Politicians in Reconstruction Georgia: A Splendid Failure* (Baton Rouge: Louisiana State University Press, 1982), p. 59.

18. Ibid., pp. 57–58.

19. Katherine Tate, "Black Opinion on the Legitimacy of Racial Redistricting and Minority-Majority Districts," *American Political Science Review* 97 (February 2003): 45–56; Tate, "The Political Representation of Blacks in Congress: Does Race Matter?" *Legislative Studies Quarterly* 26 (November 2001): 488–492; Peter H. Schuck, "What Went Wrong with the Voting Rights Act?" *Washington Monthly,* November 1987, pp. 51–55; Carol M. Swain, *Black Faces, Black Interests: The Representation of African-Americans in Congress* (Cambridge: Harvard University Press, 1993); Kerry L. Haynie, *African American Legislators in the American States* (New York: Columbia University Press, 2001), chap. 4.

20. *Can a Negro Hold Office in Georgia?* [*White v. State of Georgia ex rel. Clements*] (Atlanta, Ga.: Daily Intelligencer Book and Job Office, 1869), p. 79.

21. See Jeffrey Haydu, "Making Use of the Past: Time Periods as Cases to Compare and as Sequences of Problem Solving," *American Journal of Sociology* 104 (September 1998): 339–371; Arend Lijphart, "Comparative Politics and the Comparative Method," *American Political Science Review* 65 (September 1971): 682–693; James Mahoney and Dietrich Rueschemeyer, "Comparative Historical Analysis: Achievements and Agendas" and James Mahoney, "Strategies of Causal Assessment in Comparative Historical Analysis," in *Comparative Historical Analysis in the Social Sciences,* ed. James Mahoney and Dietrich Rueschemeyer, pp. 3–40, 337–372 (New York: Cambridge University Press, 2003).

22. A good introduction to the scope of the path dependence concept is "Forum: Timing and Sequence in Political Processes," *Studies in American Political Development* 14 (Spring 2000): 72–119.

23. Michael Perman, *Struggle for Mastery: Disfranchisement in the South, 1888–1908* (Chapel Hill: University of North Carolina Press, 2001), pp. 13, 322; Dunning is quoted on p. 12.

24. Elaine K. Swift, Brian D. Humes, Richard Valelly, Kenneth Finegold, and Evelyn C. Fink, "The Overrepresentation of the South in Congress: Measuring the Impact of the Three-Fifths Clause and the Fourteenth Amendment," at http://mccubbins.ucsd.edu/mcbrady.pdf.

25. See Garth E. Pauley, *The Modern Presidency and Civil Rights: Rhetoric on Race from Roosevelt to Nixon* (College Station: Texas A&M University Press, 2001), pp. 172–175, and citations therein.

26. Elements of the calculation are as follows: (1) there were about twenty-nine thousand elective offices in the former Confederacy (border states are not counted) and (2) sixty-six total election cycles between 1868 and 2000; (3) thus, $66 \times 29,000 = 1,914,000$.

27. Stephen Skowronek, *Building a New American State: The Expansion of National Administrative Capacities, 1877–1920* (New York: Cambridge University Press, 1982), chap. 2, esp. pp. 24–31; J. Morgan Kousser, *The Shaping of Southern Politics: Suffrage Restriction and the*

Establishment of the One-Party South, 1880–1910 (New Haven: Yale University Press, 1974); Kousser, *Colorblind Injustice: Minority Voting Rights and the Undoing of the Second Reconstruction* (Chapel Hill: University of North Carolina Press, 1999).

28. Compare Paul Burstein, "Interest Organizations, Political Parties, and the Study of Democratic Politics," in *Social Movements and American Political Institutions*, ed. Anne N. Costain and Andrew S. McFarland, pp. 39–56 (Lanham, Md.: Rowman and Littlefield, 1998).

29. For a discussion of this view, see Tali Mendelberg, *The Race Card: Campaign Strategy, Implicit Messages, and the Norm of Equality* (Princeton: Princeton University Press, 2001), especially p. 122.

30. See Woodward, *Strange Career,* p. 103, quoting and discussing Sumner. A classic and methodologically elegant discussion of the cultural roots of southern violence is Sheldon Hackney, "Southern Violence," in *Violence in America: Historical and Comparative Perspectives,* rev. ed., ed. Hugh Davis Graham and Ted Robert Gurr, pp. 393–410 (Beverly Hills: Sage, 1979), reprinted from *American Historical Review* 74 (February 1969): 906–925.

31. See Benjamin I. Page and Robert Y. Shapiro, *The Rational Public: Fifty Years of Trends in Americans' Policy Preferences* (Chicago: University of Chicago Press, 1992), pp. 68–81, 327–328; Gavin Wright, "The Civil Rights Revolution as Economic History," *Journal of Economic History* 59 (June 1999): 267–289, esp. pp. 270–271, discussing Timur Kuran, *Private Truths, Public Lies* (Cambridge: Harvard University Press, 1995); Dennis Chong, *Rational Lives: Norms and Values in Politics and Society* (Chicago: University of Chicago Press, 2000).

32. Frances Fox Piven and Richard A. Cloward, *Poor People's Movements—Why They Succeed, How They Fail* (1977; reprint, New York: Vintage, 1979), chap. 4.

33. V. O. Key Jr., *Southern Politics in State and Nation* (1949; reprint, Knoxville: University of Tennessee Press, 1984), p. 9. See C. Vann Woodward, "The Price of Freedom" and George M. Fredrickson, "After Emancipation: A Comparative Study of White Responses to the New Order of Race Relations in the American South, Jamaica and the Cape Colony of South Africa," in *What Was Freedom's Price?* ed. David G. Sansing, pp. 93–94, 71–92 (Jackson: University Press of Mississippi, 1978); Dietrich Rueschemeyer, Evelyne Huber Stephens, and John D. Stephens, *Capitalist Development and Democracy* (Chicago: University of Chicago Press, 1992), pp. 60–61; see Heather Cox Richardson, *The Death of Reconstruction: Race, Labor, and Politics in the Post–Civil War North, 1865–1901* (Cambridge: Harvard University Press, 2001); David Quigley, *Second Founding: New York City, Reconstruction, and the Making of American Democracy* (New York: Hill and Wang, 2004).

34. David R. James, "The Transformation of the Southern Racial State: Class and Race Determinants of Local-State Structure," *American Sociological Review* 53 (April 1988): 191–208; James, "Local State Structure and the Transformation of Southern Agriculture," in *Studies in the Transformation of U.S. Agriculture,* ed. Eugene Havens, pp. 150–178 (Boulder: Westview, 1986).

35. Manfred Berg, "Soldiers and Citizens: War and Voting Rights in American History," in *Reflections on American Exceptionalism,* ed. David K. Adams and Cornelis A. Van Minnen, pp. 188–225, European Papers in American History (Staffordshire, U.K.: Ryburn Publishing/Keele University Press, 1994); Mary Frances Berry, *Military Necessity and Civil Rights Policy: Black Citizenship and the Constitution, 1861–1868* (Port Washington, N.Y.: Kennikat, 1977); Mary Dudziak, *Cold War Civil Rights: Equality as Cold War Policy, 1946–1968* (Princeton: Princeton University Press, 2000); Keyssar, *The Right to Vote*; Philip A. Klinkner and Rogers M. Smith, *The Unsteady March: The Rise and Decline of Racial Equality in America* (Chicago: University of Chicago Press, 1999).

36. Richard M. Valelly, "Party, Coercion, and Inclusion: The Two Reconstructions of the South's Electoral Politics," *Politics and Society* 21 (March 1993): 37–67. Anthony Marx's formulation is hardly identical to mine, because he emphasizes more than I do national elites' desire to diminish intrawhite conflict at the expense of blacks during the first reconstruction. The similarity in our arguments lies in the way Marx traces the growth of a conciliation policy as national leaders found themselves unable to cope with white violence in the South. During the second reconstruction, in contrast, placating southern whites was less salient because central governmental control over the South had grown. See Anthony W. Marx, *Making Race and Nation: A Comparison of the United States, South Africa, and Brazil* (New York: Cambridge University Press, 1998), pp. 13, 17, 120–157.

37. William H. Riker, *The Theory of Political Coalitions* (New Haven: Yale University Press, 1962), pp. 32–33; William A. Gamson, "A Theory of Coalition Formation," *American Sociological Review* 26 (June 1961): 373–382.

38. David Waldner, *State-Building and Late Development* (Ithaca: Cornell University Press, 1999), p. 29.

39. John H. Scott with Cleo Scott Brown, *Witness to the Truth: My Struggle for Human Rights in Louisiana* (Columbia: University of South Carolina Press, 2003), pp. 140, 187.

40. J. Mills Thornton III, *Dividing Lines: Municipal Politics and the Struggle for Civil Rights in Montgomery, Birmingham, and Selma* (Tuscaloosa: University of Alabama Press, 2002), pp. 4, 7.

41. Michael C. Dawson, *Black Visions: The Roots of Contemporary African-American Political Ideologies* (Chicago: University of Chicago Press, 2001), pp. 27–29. See also ibid., pp. 325–327; Taeku Lee, *Mobilizing Public Opinion: Black Insurgency and Racial Attitudes in the Civil Rights Era* (Chicago: University of Chicago Press, 2002), p. 31; Katherine Tate, *From Protest to Politics: The New Black Voters in American Elections* (New York: Russell Sage Foundation; Cambridge: Harvard University Press, 1993), p. 25.

42. See Jennifer L. Hochschild, "You Win Some, You Lose Some: Explaining the Pattern of Success and Failure in the Second Reconstruction," in *Taking Stock: American Government in the Twentieth Century,* ed. R. Shep Melnick and Morton Keller, pp. 219–246 (New York: Cambridge University Press for the Woodrow Wilson Center, 1999).

43. See J. Morgan Kousser, "The Voting Rights Act and the Two Reconstructions," in *Controversies in Minority Voting: The Voting Rights Act in Perspective,* ed. Bernard Grofman and Chandler Davidson (Washington, D.C.: Brookings Institution, 1992), pp. 135–176.

44. See Kousser, *Colorblind Injustice,* pp. 49–68.

45. Quoted in Xi Wang, *Trial of Democracy,* p. 87. The full quotation emphasizes that there is a "double danger" from the Court and the opportunity given to the Democratic Party to castigate Republicans for constitutional recklessness.

46. Frank J. Mizell Jr. to the Hon. George Wallace, Governor of Alabama, 25 October 1965, 7 pp. (emphasis in original). Copy provided to me by Peyton McCrary, Voting Section, Civil Rights Division, U.S. Department of Justice, from his personal collection of historical materials, cited with his permission. The original is at the Governors' Papers (Wallace), Alabama Department of Archives and History.

Chapter Two

1. On resistance in the North, see Leslie H. Fishel Jr., "Northern Prejudice and Negro Suffrage, 1865–1870," *Journal of Negro History* 39 (January 1954): 8–26; Forrest G. Wood, *Black Scare: The Racist Response to Emancipation and Reconstruction* (Berkeley: University of California Press, 1968), pp. 87–91.

2. See, among others, LaWanda Cox and John Cox, "Negro Suffrage and Republican Politics: The Problem of Motivation in Reconstruction Historiography," in *Freedom, Racism, and Reconstruction: Collected Writing of LaWanda Cox*, ed. Donald G. Nieman, pp. 125–145 (Athens: University of Georgia Press, 1997); Peyton McCrary, "The Party of Revolution: Republican Ideas about Politics and Social Change, 1862–1867," *Civil War History* 30 (December 1984): 330–350; C. Vann Woodward, "Seeds of Failure in Radical Race Policy," in *New Frontiers of the American Reconstruction*, ed. Harold M. Hyman, pp. 125–147 (Urbana: University of Illinois Press, 1966).

3. See chapter 1, note 7.

4. Richard H. Abbott, "Jason Clarke Swayze, Republican Editor in Reconstruction Georgia, 1867–1873," *Georgia Historical Quarterly* 79 (Summer 1995): 337–366, at p. 363.

5. See James M. McPherson, *Battle Cry of Freedom: The Civil War Era* (New York: Oxford University Press, 1988), pp. 699–703; Hans L. Trefousse, *Andrew Johnson: A Biography* (New York: Norton, 1989), pp. 196–197.

6. Except as noted below, this section is based on LaWanda Cox's "The Promise of Land for the Freedmen," *Mississippi Valley Historical Review* 45 (December 1958): 413–440, and Claude F. Oubre, *Forty Acres and a Mule: The Freedmen's Bureau and Black Land Ownership* (Baton Rouge: Louisiana State University Press, 1978).

7. McPherson, *Battle Cry,* pp. 808–811, 841–842. For an account of the Savannah meeting, see Josef James, "Sherman at Savannah," *Journal of Negro History* 39 (April 1954): 127–137.

8. For succinct discussion of the statute, see McPherson, *Battle Cry,* p. 842. See also W. E. B. Du Bois, "The Freedmen's Bureau," *Atlantic Monthly,* March 1901, pp. 354–365.

9. Except where noted otherwise, this section relies on Harold Melvin Hyman's monograph *Era of the Oath: Northern Loyalty Tests during the Civil War and Reconstruction* (Philadelphia: University of Pennsylvania Press for the American Historical Association, 1954), chaps. 3, 5–8, and appendix; the quotation is from the appendix. See also Hans L. Trefousse, comp., *Historical Dictionary of Reconstruction* (Westport: Greenwood, 1991), s.v. "Ironclad Oath."

10. See William C. Harris, *With Charity for All: Lincoln and the Restoration of the Union* (Lexington: University Press of Kentucky, 1997), esp. pp. 131–134, and Peyton McCrary, *Abraham Lincoln and Reconstruction: The Louisiana Experiment* (Princeton: Princeton University Press, 1978).

11. On Lincoln-Johnson policy continuities, see Harris, *With Charity for All,* pp. 258–275; on administrative problems see Hyman, *Era of the Oath,* chap. 5. More generally, see Albert Castel, *The Presidency of Andrew Johnson,* American Presidency Series (Lawrence: Regents Press of Kansas, 1979); Brooks D. Simpson, *The Reconstruction Presidents* (Lawrence: University Press of Kansas, 1998). On collapse, see McCrary, *Lincoln,* chap. 10.

12. James D. Richardson, comp., *Messages and Papers of the Presidents, 1789–1908* (New York: Bureau of National Literature and Art, 1908), 6:310–312; Harold M. Hyman, *To Try Men's Souls: Loyalty Tests in American History* (Berkeley: University of California Press, 1959), pp. 263–265.

13. Richardson, *Messages and Papers of the Presidents,* 6:312–331; Hyman, *Era of the Oath,* pp. 84–85.

14. See Hans L. Trefousse, "Andrew Johnson and the Freedmen's Bureau," in *The Freedmen's Bureau and Reconstruction: Reconsiderations,* ed. Paul A. Cimbala and Randall M. Miller, pp. 29–45 (New York: Fordham University Press, 1999).

15. Ibid; see also Willie Lee Rose, *Rehearsal for Reconstruction: The Port Royal Experiment* (1964; reprint, Athens: University of Georgia Press, 1999), pp. 351–355.

16. Edward McPherson, *The Political History of the United States of America during the Period of Reconstruction, April 15, 1865–July 15, 1870* (1871; reprint, New York: Da Capo, 1972), pp. 29–32.

17. Ibid., pp. 32–44. See also Roberta Sue Alexander, *North Carolina Faces the Freedmen: Race Relations during Presidential Reconstruction, 1865–67* (Durham: Duke University Press, 1985), chap. 3; Dan T. Carter, *When the War Was Over: The Failure of Self-Reconstruction in the South, 1865–1867* (Baton Rouge: Louisiana State University Press, 1984), esp. chaps. 4–6; Michael Perman, *Reunion without Compromise: The South and Reconstruction, 1865–1868* (New York: Cambridge University Press, 1973), esp. chaps. 3–4; James L. Roark, *Masters without Slaves: Southern Planters in the Civil War and Reconstruction* (New York: Norton, 1977), chaps. 3–4. On how the Black Codes conflicted with Republican political theory, see Harold M. Hyman, *The Reconstruction Justice of Salmon P. Chase: In Re Turner and Texas v. White* (Lawrence: University Press of Kansas, 1997), pp. 107–112.

18. Carter, *When the War Was Over,* pp. 228–230.

19. Hyman, *Reconstruction Justice,* chap. 8; Joseph B. James, *The Framing of the Fourteenth Amendment,* Illinois Studies in the Social Sciences, vol. 37 (Urbana: University of Illinois Press, 1956), pp. 37–38, 50; Eric L. McKitrick, *Andrew Johnson and Reconstruction* (Chicago: University of Chicago Press, 1960), pp. 277–282.

20. Quoted in James, *Framing of the Fourteenth Amendment,* p. 46, emphasis added.

21. Quoted in George P. Smith, "Republican Reconstruction and Section Two of the Fourteenth Amendment," *Western Political Quarterly* 23 (December 1970): 829–853. See also Maxwell Whiteman, ed., *Equal Suffrage: Address from the Colored Citizens of Norfolk, Va., to the People of the United States,* Afro-American History Series, Historic Publication no. 216 (Philadelphia: Historic Publications, n.d.) (a reproduction of an 1865 pamphlet), p. 5.

22. Because many (though by no means all) of the southerners could not take the 1862 "ironclad" loyalty oath, still in effect, Republican action to bar their seating seemed legally plausible. Richard Abbott, *The Republican Party and the South, 1855–1867* (Chapel Hill: University of North Carolina Press, 1986), pp. 52–53. The decision not to seat was signaled when Edward McPherson, a protegé of Thaddeus Stevens and clerk of the House of Representatives, announced before the Thirty-ninth Congress that he would "not put on the rolls of the new House nor call the names of persons claiming to be representatives from States that have been in rebellion." See McPherson, *Political History of the United States,* p. x.

23. See Benjamin B. Kendrick, *The Journal of the Joint Committee of Fifteen on Reconstruction, 39th Congress, 1865–1867,* Studies in History, Economics, and Public Law, vol. 62 (New York: Longmans, Green for Columbia University, 1914); Beverly Wilson Palmer and Holly Byers Ochoa, eds., *The Selected Papers of Thaddeus Stevens,* vol. 2, *April 1865–August 1868* (Pittsburgh: University of Pittsburgh Press, 1998); Hans L. Trefousse, *Thaddeus Stevens: Nineteenth Century Egalitarian* (Chapel Hill: University of North Carolina Press), chaps. 15–16.

24. See John H. Cox and LaWanda Cox, "Andrew Johnson and His Ghost Writers: An Analysis of the Freedmen's Bureau and the Civil Rights Veto Messages," *Mississippi Valley Historical Review* 48 (December 1961): 460–479; McPherson, *Political History of the United States,* pp. 74–80. McKitrick, *Andrew Johnson and Reconstruction,* is especially good at capturing the growing surprise and sense of betrayal among congressional Republicans; see chaps. 5–6, 9–10.

25. James, *Framing of the Fourteenth Amendment,* pp. 136–137.

26. See Joseph B. James, *The Ratification of the Fourteenth Amendment* (Macon, Ga.: Mercer University Press, 1984), chaps. 1–2. (Though informative, this source requires care in its use.) See also McKitrick, *Andrew Johnson and Reconstruction,* chaps. 12–13; Michael Les Benedict,

A Compromise of Principle: Congressional Republicans and Reconstruction, 1863–1869 (New York: Norton, 1974), chap. 9; Earl Maltz, *Civil Rights, the Constitution, and Congress, 1863–1869* (Lawrence: University Press of Kansas, 1990), pp. 118–122; Patrick W. Riddleberger, *1866: The Critical Year Revisited* (Carbondale: Southern Illinois University Press, 1979). A memoir of the campaign is James G. Blaine, *Twenty Years of Congress: From Lincoln to Garfield* (Norwich, Conn.: Henry Bill, 1893), vol. 2, chap. 10.

27. David Waldner, *State-Building and Late Development* (Ithaca: Cornell University Press, 1999), p. 29.

28. See McPherson, *Political History of the United States,* pp. 143–147, for Johnson's message. Not mentioning the Fourteenth Amendment at all, Johnson pictured the Thirty-ninth Congress (in his second annual message, December 4) as the remaining obstacle to a program of national unity that was otherwise complete and implied that its obstructionism risked "absolute despotism" and disregard for the "ancient landmarks" of "our fathers." See also McKitrick, *Andrew Johnson and Reconstruction,* p. 470, showing that Johnson initially wavered regarding whether to ignore the 1866 elections in his second annual message.

29. See Stanley I. Kutler, *Judicial Power and Reconstruction Politics* (Chicago: University of Chicago Press, 1968), pp. 33–34, 89–95; Martin E. Mantell, *Johnson, Grant, and the Politics of Reconstruction* (New York: Columbia University Press, 1973), p. 22; McKitrick, *Andrew Johnson and Reconstruction,* pp. 93–98, 101–103, 108–109, 465; Benjamin P. Thomas and Harold M. Hyman, *Stanton: The Life and Times of Lincoln's Secretary of War* (New York: Knopf, 1962), pp. 472–478, 513, 516–518.

30. See Benedict, *Compromise of Principle,* chap. 10; Larry G. Kincaid, "The Legislative Origins of the Military Reconstruction Act, 1865–1867," Ph.D. diss., Johns Hopkins University, 1968, chaps. 3–6. As a compromise between the two wings of the party, those who tended to see the Fourteenth Amendment as the last step in a process of change and those who saw it as merely the first, the Thirty-ninth Congress had adjourned its *first* session without any clear statement of the precise terms of readmission. Nonetheless, the "restorationist" wing of the Republican Party, for the most part the moderates, argued during the 1866 elections that the Fourteenth Amendment was a final settlement. The "reconstructionist" wing, for the most part the radicals, did not strongly challenge this construction of the amendment for the sake of party unity but clearly regarded the second session as the time to return to their program.

31. See Kincaid, "Legislative Origins," pp. 162–176; Perman, *Reunion without Compromise,* pp. 254–265; the former describes Johnson's suffrage compromise and Republican reactions, the latter the intentions of the compromise's proponents.

32. See Benedict, *Compromise of Principle,* chap. 10; Maltz, *Civil Rights,* pp. 122–131; John Lockhart McCarthy, "Reconstruction Legislation and Voting Alignments in the House of Representatives, 1863–1869," Ph.D. diss., Yale University, 1970, chap. 3; Walter L. Fleming, *Documentary History of Reconstruction: Political, Military, Social, Religious, Educational, and Industrial, 1865 to the Present Time* (1906; reprint, Gloucester, Mass.: Peter Smith, 1960), pp. 401–411. On the Local Prejudice Act, see Kutler, *Judicial Power and Reconstruction Politics,* p. 152 and notes.

33. Richard L. Hume, "The 'Black and Tan' Constitutional Conventions of 1867–1869 in Ten Former Confederate States: A Study of Their Membership," Ph.D. diss., University of Washington, 1969, pp. 1–2; James E. Sefton, *The United States Army and Reconstruction, 1865–1877* (Baton Rouge: Louisiana State University Press, 1967), chaps. 5–6.

34. On the role of violence in influencing public and elite opinion in the North, see Carter, *When the War Was Over,* pp. 248–253; McKitrick, *Andrew Johnson and Reconstruction,* pp. 330–331, 456–459; George C. Rable, *But There Was No Peace: The Role of Violence in the*

Politics of Reconstruction (Athens: University of Georgia Press, 1984), pp. 55–60. Some of the incoming information was "endogenous" to politicians' policy preferences, that is, structured to inform Congress a certain way, as suggested in Richard Lowe, "The Joint Committee on Reconstruction: Some Clarifications," *Southern Studies* 3 (Spring 1992): 55–65, but much of it was not. See also William S. McFeely, *Grant: A Biography* (New York: Norton, 1981), p. 260, discussing "thousands of carefully documented reports" of atrocities in the possession of General Howard of the Freedmen's Bureau. The quotation from the governor of Iowa is from Robert R. Dykstra, *Bright Radical Star: Black Freedom and White Supremacy on the Hawkeye Frontier* (Cambridge: Harvard University Press, 1993), p. 218.

35. See Edward L. Gambill, *Conservative Ordeal: Northern Democrats and Reconstruction, 1865–1868* (Ames: Iowa State University Press, 1981), chap. 2; Greeley is quoted in James P. Shenton, *Robert John Walker: A Politician from Jackson to Lincoln* (New York: Columbia University Press, 1961), p. 210 (Greeley then being in the pro-radical stage of his chameleon-like political career). See also Charles Sumner to John Bright, 13 March 1865, in *The Selected Letters of Charles Sumner,* ed. Beverly Wilson Palmer (Boston: Northeastern University Press, 1990), p. 273.

36. C. Vann Woodward, "The Political Legacy of Reconstruction," *Journal of Negro Education* 26 (Summer 1957): 235–236. The most thorough study is William A. Russ Jr., "Congressional Disfranchisement 1866–1898," Ph.D. diss., University of Chicago, 1933.

37. A technically sophisticated reappraisal of the Ninth Census can be found in J. David Hacker, "New estimates of census underenumeration in the United States, 1850–1880," Paper presented at the annual meeting of the Population Association of America, March 24, 2000. For an overview of the literature on nineteenth-century census underenumeration and a display of earlier estimates for the Ninth Census, see Richard H. Steckel, "The Quality of Census Data for Historical Inquiry: A Research Agenda," *Social Science History* 15 (Winter 1991): 579–599, and table 1, p. 588. See also Kenneth Winkle, "The U.S. Census as a Source in Political History," *Social Science History* 15 (Winter 1991): 565–578. On the quality of the Ninth Census in particular see Gerald Carson and Bernard A. Weisberger, "The Great Countdown," *American Heritage,* November 1989, pp. 3–23. The lowest estimate, around 6 percent, is provided in William Cohen, *At Freedom's Edge: Black Mobility and the Southern White Quest for Racial Control, 1861–1915* (Baton Rouge: Louisiana State University Press, 1991), p. 298, citing Roger L. Ransom and Richard Sutch, *One Kind of Freedom: The Economic Consequences of Emancipation* (New York: Cambridge University Press, 1977), pp. 54, 329.

38. See Peter Cozzens, *General John Pope: A Life for the Nation* (Urbana: University of Illinois Press, 2000), chap. 14; Harold M. Hyman, "Johnson, Stanton, and Grant: A Reconsideration of the Army's Role in the Events Leading to Impeachment," *American Historical Review* 66 (October 1960): 85–100; Lawrence N. Powell, "Correcting for Fraud: A Quantitative Reassessment of the Mississippi Ratification Election of 1868," *Journal of Southern History* 55 (November 1989): 633–658, at 656 (on Virginia); Clement Mario Silvestro, "None But Patriots: The Union Leagues in Civil War and Reconstruction," Ph.D. diss., University of Wisconsin, 1959.

39. By far the best single discussion in this connection is Steven Hahn, *A Nation under Our Feet: Black Political Struggles in the Rural South from Slavery to the Great Migration* (Cambridge: Harvard University Press, Belknap Press, 2003), chap. 4.

40. See, among others, Alexander, *North Carolina Faces the Freedmen;* Eric Foner, "The Meaning of Freedom in the Age of Emancipation," *Journal of American History* 81 (September 1994): 435–460; Tera W. Hunter, *To 'Joy My Freedom: Southern Black Women's Lives and Labors after the Civil War* (Cambridge: Harvard University Press, 1997), chap. 2; Peter Kolchin, *First*

Freedom: The Responses of Alabama's Blacks to Emancipation and Reconstruction, Contributions in American History, no. 20 (Westport: Greenwood, 1972); Leon F. Litwack, *Been in the Storm So Long: The Aftermath of Slavery* (New York: Knopf, 1979), esp. chap. 10; Donald G. Nieman, "African Americans and the Meaning of Freedom: Washington County, Texas as a Case Study, 1865–1886," *Chicago-Kent Law Review* (Symposium on the Law of Freedom, Part I) 70:2 (1994): 541–582.

41. See W. E. B. Du Bois, *Black Reconstruction in America, 1860–1880* (1935; reprint, New York: Atheneum, 1992); Ira Berlin, "Who Freed the Slaves? Emancipation and Its Meaning," in *Union and Emancipation: Essays on Politics and Race in the Civil War Era,* ed. David W. Blight and Brooks D. Simpson, pp. 105–122 (Kent, Ohio: Kent State University Press, 1997).

42. *Freedom: A Documentary History of Emancipation, 1861–1867,* ser. 2, The Black Military Experience, ed. Ira Berlin, Joseph P. Reidy, and Sheila Rowland (Cambridge: Cambridge University Press, 1982), including overview, "The Black Military Experience 1861–1867," pp. 1–34; Brooks D. Simpson, "Quandaries of Command: Ulysses S. Grant and Black Soldiers," in *Union and Emancipation: Essays on Politics and Race in the Civil War Era,* ed. David W. Blight and Brooks D. Simpson, pp. 123–150 (Kent, Ohio: Kent State University Press, 1997); Howard C. Westwood, *Black Troops, White Commanders, and Freedmen during the Civil War* (Carbondale: Southern Illinois University Press, 1992).

43. Ira Berlin, Barbara J. Fields, Steven E. Miller, Joseph P. Reidy, and Leslie S. Rowland, *Slaves No More: Three Essays on Emancipation and the Civil War* (New York: Cambridge University Press, 1992), pp. 187–233, table 1, p. 203.

44. Mary Frances Berry, *Military Necessity and Civil Rights Policy: Black Citizenship and the Constitution, 1861–1868* (Port Washington, N.Y.: Kennikat, 1977); Du Bois, *Black Reconstruction,* chap. 5. Regarding the military plantations, see Cohen, *At Freedom's Edge,* pp. 7–12.

45. The only thorough published treatment of black soldiers on occupation duty in the South is in Simpson, "Quandaries of Command." For black soldiers in Wilmington, North Carolina, see William McKee Evans, *Ballots and Fence Rails: Reconstruction on the Lower Cape Fear* (1967; reprint, Athens: University of Georgia Press, 1995), pp. 23–25, 79–81. Statistics are based on calculations using data from Sefton, *The United States Army and Reconstruction, 1865–1877,* Appendix B: Numbers and Locations of Troops.

46. "The Republican Party Must Be Maintained in Power: An Address Delivered in New Orleans, Louisiana, on 13 April 1872," in *The Frederick Douglass Papers,* ser. 1, Speeches, Debates, and Interviews, vol. 4, *1864–80,* ed. John W. Blassingame and John R. McKivigan, pp. 293–299, at pp. 297–298 (New Haven: Yale University Press, 1991); John Hope Franklin, "Reconstruction and the Negro," in *New Frontiers of the American Reconstruction,* ed. Harold M. Hyman, pp. 59–76, at p. 67 (Urbana: University of Illinois Press, 1966); Laura F. Edwards, *Gendered Strife and Confusion: The Political Culture of Reconstruction* (Urbana: University of Illinois Press, 1997), p. 193.

47. William H. Wiggins Jr., *O Freedom! Afro-American Emancipation Celebrations* (Knoxville: University of Tennessee Press, 1987); Norman R. Yetman, *Voices from Slavery* (New York: Holt, Rinehart and Winston, 1970); and Paul D. Escott, *Slavery Remembered: A Record of Twentieth-Century Slave Narratives* (Chapel Hill: University of North Carolina Press, 1979), introduction and chap. 5. For percentages, see p. 137. The estimate of total "usable" interviews is the sum of the figures at pp. 9 and 195. See also Yetman, *Voices from Slavery,* pp. 330–355, on the history of the WPA's Slave Narrative project and that of other ex-slave interview projects. The vast social significance of postemancipation migration is captured in Kolchin, *First Freedom,* chap. 1.

48. Edwards, *Gendered Strife,* pp. 31–54.

49. John W. Blassingame, "The Union Army as an Educational Institution for Negroes, 1862–1865," *Journal of Negro Education* 34 (Spring 1965): 152–159; Herbert Gutman, "Schools for Freedom: The Post-Emancipation Origins of Afro-American Education," in Herbert G. Gutman, *Power and Culture: Essays on the American Working Class,* ed. Ira Berlin, pp. 260–297 (New York: Pantheon, 1987); Jacqueline Jones, *Soldiers of Light and Love: Northern Teachers and Georgia Blacks, 1865–1873* (Chapel Hill: University of North Carolina Press, 1980); Litwack, *Been in the Storm So Long,* chap. 9; Robert C. Morris, *Reading, 'Riting, and Reconstruction: The Education of Freedmen in the South, 1861–1870* (Chicago: University of Chicago Press, 1976); Morris, "Educational Reconstruction," in *The Facts of Reconstruction: Essays in Honor of John Hope Franklin,* ed. Eric Anderson and Alfred A. Moss Jr., pp. 141–166 (Baton Rouge: Louisiana State University Press, 1991).

50. William E. Montgomery, *Under Their Own Vine and Fig Tree: The African-American Church in the South, 1865–1900* (Baton Rouge: Louisiana State University Press, 1993), pp. 97–127; Daniel W. Stowell, *Rebuilding Zion: The Religious Reconstruction of the South, 1863–1877* (New York: Oxford University Press, 1998), pp. 70–99; James D. Anderson, *The Education of Blacks in the South, 1860–1935* (Chapel Hill: University of North Carolina Press, 1988), pp. 12–15; Howard N. Rabinowitz, "Holland Thompson and Black Political Participation in Montgomery, Alabama," in *Southern Black Leaders of the Reconstruction Era,* ed. Howard N. Rabinowitz, pp. 249–280 (Urbana: University of Illinois Press, 1982), esp. pp. 249–253; Evans, *Ballots and Fence Rails,* p. 234.

51. Dorothy Sterling, ed., *The Trouble They Seen: Black People Tell the Story of Reconstruction* (Garden City: Doubleday, 1976), p. 4. See also Elsa Barkley Brown, "Negotiating and Transforming the Public Sphere: African American Political Life in the Transition from Slavery to Freedom," *Public Culture* 7 (Fall 1994): 107–146; Fleming, *Documentary History of Reconstruction,* vol. 1, plates 232–233; Whiteman, *Equal Suffrage,* pp. 9–15. For black newspapers in this period, see Henry Lewis Suggs, ed., *The Black Press in the South, 1865–1979,* Contributions in Afro-American and African Studies, no. 74 (Westport: Greenwood, 1983), pp. 3–21. See Michael W. Fitzgerald, *The Union League Movement in the Deep South: Politics and Agricultural Change during Reconstruction* (Baton Rouge: Louisiana State University Press, 1989), pp. 35–36, for a fascinating sketch of the Mobile *Nationalist.* See also James M. Russell and Jerry Thornbery, "William Finch of Atlanta: The Black Politician as Civic Leader," in *Southern Black Leaders of the Reconstruction Era,* ed. Howard N. Rabinowitz (Urbana: University of Illinois Press, 1982), pp. 309–334, esp. pp. 310–312, on the *Loyal Georgian* of Augusta, a publication of the Georgia Equal Rights Association.

52. Alexander, *North Carolina Faces the Freedmen,* pp. 16–31, 78–93; Evans, *Ballots and Fence Rails,* pp. 79–81 (on riots) and pp. 86–94 (on the Equal Rights League); John Cimprich, "The Beginning of the Black Suffrage Movement in Tennessee, 1864–65," *Journal of Negro History* 65 (1980): 185–195; Ruth Currie-McDaniel, *Carpetbagger of Conscience: A Biography of John Emory Bryant* (Athens: University of Georgia Press, 1987), pp. 57–61; Fitzgerald, *Union League Movement,* pp. 30–36; Philip S. Foner and George E. Walker, eds., *Proceedings of the Black National and State Conventions, 1865–1900* (Philadelphia: Temple University Press, 1986), 1: 80–108, 112–129, 177–182, 187–198, 229–236; William Cassidy Hine, "Frustration, Factionalism, and Failure: Black Political Leadership and the Republican Party in Reconstruction Charleston, 1865–1877," Ph.D. diss., Kent State University, 1979, pp. 33–43; Kolchin, *First Freedom,* chap. 7; Litwack, *Been in the Storm So Long,* chap. 10; C. Peter Ripley et al., eds., *The Black Abolitionist Papers,* vol. 5, *The United States, 1859–1865* (Chapel Hill: University of North Carolina Press, 1992), pp. 324–329, 334–349.

53. On the "Republic of St. Catherine," see Russell Duncan, *Freedom's Shore: Tunis Campbell and the Georgia Freedmen* (Athens: University of Georgia Press, 1986), chap. 1, and for the other experiments, Paul Cimbala, *Under the Guardianship of the Nation: The Freedmen's Bureau and the Reconstruction of Georgia, 1865–1870* (Athens: University of Georgia Press, 1997), chap. 7; Eric Foner, *Freedom's Lawmakers: A Directory of Black Officeholders during Reconstruction* (New York: Oxford University Press, 1993), pp. 115, 162.

54. Julie Saville, *The Work of Reconstruction: From Slave to Wage-Laborer in South Carolina, 1860–1870* (Cambridge: Cambridge University Press, 1994), chap. 5. On Florida, see Edward Magdol, "Local Black Leaders in the South, 1867–75: An Essay Toward the Reconstruction of Reconstruction History," *Societas* 4 (Spring 1974): 81–110, esp. 97–98. On Georgia, see Cimbala, *Under the Guardianship of the Nation*, pp. 168–169; Joseph P. Reidy, "Aaron A. Bradley: Voice of Black Labor in the Georgia Lowcountry," in *Southern Black Leaders of the Reconstruction Era*, ed. Howard N. Rabinowitz (Urbana: University of Illinois Press, 1982), pp. 281–308.

55. Compare J. Craig Jenkins, "Resource Mobilization Theory and the Study of Social Movements," in *American Society and Politics: Institutional, Historical, and Theoretical Perspectives*, ed. Theda Skocpol and John L. Campbell, pp. 289–306 (New York: McGraw-Hill, 1995), reprinted from *Annual Review of Sociology* 9 (1983): 527–553.

56. Fitzgerald, *Union League Movement*; Robert C. Schenck Papers, Rutherford P. Hayes Presidential Center Library, Microfilm Edition, Reel 6 (1866–1868), circulars of URCEC and a list of organizers and speakers in the 1867 portion).

57. This sketch is based on Abbott, *Republican Party and the South*, pp. 85–93; Fitzgerald, *Union League Movement*, chaps. 2–6; and Saville, *Work of Reconstruction*, chap. 5.

58. Abbott, *Republican Party and the South*, pp. 91–92; William C. Harris, *The Day of the Carpetbagger: Republican Reconstruction in Mississippi* (Baton Rouge: Louisiana State University Press, 1979), p. 97, quoting the Natchez *Weekly Democrat* of mid-April 1867.

59. On Turner's wartime service, see Edwin S. Redkey, ed., *A Grand Army of Black Men: Letters from African-American Soldiers in the Union Army, 1861–1865* (New York: Cambridge University Press, 1992), pp. 159–161; Schenck Papers, Microfilm Edition, Reel 6 (1866–1868), transcript of letter of July 23, 1867 from Turner to Thomas Tullock, secretary of URCEC. On Turner and the Georgia AME see John Dittmer, "The Education of Henry McNeal Turner," in *Black Leaders of the Nineteenth Century*, ed. Leon Litwack and August Meier, pp. 253–274, Blacks in the New World (Urbana: University of Illinois Press, 1988), esp. pp. 254–257.

60. Schenck Papers, Reel 6.

61. Fitzgerald, *Union League Movement*, chaps. 4–6, esp. pp. 248–253; Carl H. Moneyhon, *The Impact of the Civil War and Reconstruction on Arkansas: Persistence in the Midst of Ruin* (Baton Rouge: Louisiana State University Press, 1994), pp. 244–245; Saville, *Work of Reconstruction*, chap. 5; Jerrell H. Shofner, *Nor Is It Over Yet: Florida in the Era of Reconstruction, 1863–1877* (Gainesville: University Presses of Florida, 1974), pp. 166–170, 178.

62. Eric Foner, "Black Reconstruction Leaders at the Grass Roots," in *Black Leaders of the Nineteenth Century*, ed. Leon Litwack and August Meier, pp. 219–236, at p. 220, Blacks in the New World (Urbana: University of Illinois Press, 1988). See also Currie-McDaniel, *Carpetbagger of Conscience*, p. 65; Jeffrey R. Kerr-Ritchie, *Freedpeople in the Tobacco South: Virginia, 1860–1900* (Chapel Hill: University of North Carolina Press, 1999), pp. 73–75.

63. Saville, *Work of Reconstruction*, p. 160; see also chap. 5. Registration in Tennessee, which occurred before "registration summer" because Tennessee instituted black suffrage before Congress instituted it, was also collective and disciplined. See Thomas B. Alexander,

Political Reconstruction in Tennessee (Nashville: Vanderbilt University Press, 1950), pp. 155–156. For a case from Louisiana, see John C. Rodrigue, "Labor Militancy and Black Grassroots Political Mobilization in the Louisiana Sugar Region, 1865–1868," *Journal of Southern History* 67 (February 2001): 115–142.

64. Julie Saville, "Rites and Power: Reflections on Slavery, Freedom, and Political Ritual," *Slavery and Abolition* 20 (April 1999): 81–102, at p. 89; Elsa Barkley Brown, "To Catch the Vision of Freedom: Reconstructing Southern Black Women's Political History, 1865–1880," in *African-American Women and the Vote, 1837–1965,* ed. Ann D. Gordon, ed., with Bettye Collier-Thomas, John H. Bracey, Arlene Voski Avakian, and Joyce Avrech Berkman, pp. 66–99 (Amherst: University of Massachusetts Press, 1997). A fine overview of the registration process is Hahn, *A Nation under Our Feet,* pp. 189–198.

65. In this connection, see William A. Russ Jr., "Was There Danger of a Second Civil War During Reconstruction?" *Mississippi Valley Historical Review* 25 (June 1938): 39–58. See also Michael Les Benedict, *The Impeachment and Trial of Andrew Johnson* (New York: Norton, 1973), pp. 45–46, fn. 37.

66. On military discontent with presidential reconstruction, see Hyman, "Johnson, Stanton, and Grant," 85–100; Thomas and Hyman, *Stanton,* p. 518 and chaps. 21–25; Kutler, *Judicial Power and Reconstruction Politics,* p. 152 and n15. More generally see Mantell, *Johnson, Grant, and the Politics of Reconstruction.*

67. Abbott, *Republican Party and the South,* pp. 94–103; Cimbala, *Under the Guardianship of the Nation,* pp. 67–69; Robert C. Lieberman, "The Freedmen's Bureau and the Politics of Institutional Structure," *Social Science History* 18 (Fall 1994): 405–438, figure 4.

68. Quoted in Richard L. Hume, "The Freedmen's Bureau and the Freedmen's Vote in the Reconstruction of Southern Alabama: An Account by Agent Samuel S. Gardner," *Alabama Historical Quarterly* 38 (Fall 1975): 217–224, at pp. 222–223.

69. Harris, *Day of the Carpetbagger,* pp. 74–75.

70. Sefton, *United States Army and Reconstruction,* pp. 137, 183–184.

71. See John Pope to Robert C. Schenck, Chair, Executive Committee, Union Republican Congressional Executive Committee, May 20, 1867, Schenck Papers, Reel 6 (Schenck was a retired army general); Cozzens, *General John Pope,* chap. 14; Abbott, *Republican Party and the South,* pp. 98–99; Randolph B. Campbell, *A Southern Community in Crisis: Harrison County, Texas, 1850–1880* (Austin: Texas State Historical Association, 1983), pp. 275–276; Edmund L. Drago, "Georgia's First Black Voter Registrars during Reconstruction," *Georgia Historical Quarterly* 78 (Fall 1994): 760–793; Harris, *Day of the Carpetbagger,* pp. 67–77; Hume, " 'Black and Tan' Constitutional Conventions," pp. 8, 269, 387, 468; Kolchin, *First Freedom,* pp. 160–163; Richard Lowe, "Local Black Leaders during Reconstruction in Virginia," *Virginia Magazine of History and Biography* 103 (April 1995): 181–206, esp. 181–195; Charles William Ramsdell, *Reconstruction in Texas,* Studies in History, Economics, and Public Law, vol. 36, no. 1 (New York: Longmans, Green for Columbia University, 1910), pp. 149–165; Loren Schweninger, *James T. Rapier and Reconstruction* (Chicago: University of Chicago Press, 1978), pp. 44–46.

72. Richardson, *Messages and Papers of the Presidents,* Third Annual Message of President Andrew Johnson, 3 December 1867, 6:558–581, quotations at pp. 566, 569, emphasis added. Discussion of presidential inauguration of civil war for a higher cause is at p. 568.

73. Benedict, *Impeachment and Trial of Andrew Johnson,* p. 100.

74. For the Tenure of Office Act, see "An Act Regulating the Tenure of Certain Civil Offices," *The Statutes at Large, Treaties, and Proclamations of the United States of America,* ed.

George P. Sanger, vol. 14, December 1865 to March 1867, pp. 430–431 (Boston: Little, Brown, 1868).

75. Riker, *Theory of Political Coalitions*, pp. 32–33; Waldner, *State-Building and Late Development*, p. 29.

Chapter Three

1. Eric Foner, *Reconstruction: America's Unfinished Revolution, 1863–1877* (New York: Harper and Row, 1988), pp. 488–511, 524–534; Wilbert A. Ahern, "Laissez Faire vs. Equal Rights: Liberal Republicans and Limits to Reconstruction," *Phylon* 40 (March 1979): 52–65; Michael W. McConnell, "The Forgotten Constitutional Moment," *Constitutional Commentary* 11 (1994): 115–144, at p. 125; Eric Foner, *Freedom's Lawmakers: A Directory of Black Officeholders during Reconstruction* (New York: Oxford University Press, 1993), p. xiii.

2. "Looking the Republican Party Squarely in the Face: An Address Delivered in Cincinnati, Ohio on 14 June 1876," in *The Frederick Douglass Papers*, ser. 1, Speeches, Debates, and Interviews, vol. 4, *1864–80*, ed. John W. Blassingame and John R. McKivigan (New Haven: Yale University Press, 1991), pp. 440–442.

3. Eric Foner, *Reconstruction*, p. 577.

4. Ibid., p. 581. See also William Gillette, *Retreat from Reconstruction, 1869–1879* (Baton Rouge: Louisiana State University Press, 1979), pp. 323–331; Keith Ian Polakoff, *The Politics of Inertia: The Election of 1876 and the End of Reconstruction* (Baton Rouge: Louisiana State University Press, 1973), chaps. 6–7; Michael Les Benedict, "Southern Democrats in the Crisis of 1876–1877: A Reconsideration of *Reunion and Reaction*," *Journal of Southern History* 46 (November 1980): 489–524; Vincent P. de Santis, "Rutherford B. Hayes and the Removal of the Troops and the End of Reconstruction," in *Region, Race, and Reconstruction: Essays in Honor of C. Vann Woodward*, ed. J. Morgan Kousser and James M. McPherson, pp. 417–450 (New York: Oxford University Press, 1982); www.rbhayes.org.

5. See, e.g., Gilles Vandal, *Rethinking Southern Violence: Homicides in Post–Civil War Louisiana, 1866–1884* (Columbus: Ohio State University Press, 2000), pp. 86, 106, 195–196.

6. See Hanes Walton Jr., *Black Republicans: The Politics of the Black and Tans* (Metuchen, N.J.: Scarecrow, 1975).

7. See Lawrence D. Rice, *The Negro in Texas, 1874–1900* (Baton Rouge: Louisiana State University Press, 1971), pp. 116 (for Texas ballot regulation legislation in 1879), 28, 132 (for apportionment devices for reducing black office-holding). For South Carolina, see James Lowell Underwood, *The Constitution of South Carolina*, vol. 4, *The Struggle for Political Equality* (Columbia: University of South Carolina Press, 1994), pp. 38–39. For Wilmington, North Carolina, see Frenise A. Logan, *The Negro in North Carolina, 1876–1894* (Chapel Hill: University of North Carolina Press, 1964), pp. 61–63; on other measures, including changing county government to appointment rather than election, see pp. 49–60. On legislative attention to reduction of black voting and office-holding in cities, see Howard N. Rabinowitz, *Race Relations in the Urban South, 1865–1890* (New York: Oxford University Press, 1978), p. 323; Charles E. Wynes, *Race Relations in Virginia, 1870–1902* (Charlottesville: University of Virginia Press, 1961), p. 39. On Georgia, see J. Morgan Kousser, *The Shaping of Southern Politics: Suffrage Restriction and the Establishment of the One-Party South, 1880–1910* (New Haven: Yale University Press, 1974), pp. 62, 67–68. The tax was cumulative in that all annual payments owing were due before one could vote. On attacks on office-holding, see V. O. Key Jr., *Southern Politics in State and Nation* (1949; reprint, Knoxville: University of Tennessee Press, 1984), p. 541; Alwyn Barr, *Reconstruction to Reform: Texas Politics, 1876–1906* (Austin: University of Texas Press, 1971), p. 194.

8. Stephen Cresswell, *Multiparty Politics in Mississippi, 1877–1902* (Jackson: University Press of Mississippi, 1995), p. 42; Rabinowitz, *Race Relations in the Urban South*, pp. 321–322. See Barr, *Reconstruction to Reform*, pp. 194–201, chronicling the serial violent "redemption" of black majority counties in East Texas. See also Terence Finnegan, "Lynching and Political Power in Mississippi and South Carolina," in *Under Sentence of Death: Lynching in the South,* ed. W. Fitzhugh Brundage, pp. 189–218 (Chapel Hill: University of North Carolina Press, 1997).

9. William Warren Rogers and Robert David Ward, *August Reckoning: Jack Turner and Racism in Post–Civil War Alabama* (Baton Rouge: Louisiana State University Press, 1973), chaps. 4–7.

10. Ibid., pp. 69–78; Cresswell, *Multiparty Politics,* pp. 85–86, 213–214, 260n24, 271. On an important Senate investigation of Texas, see Rice, *Negro in Texas,* p. 119.

11. William Ivy Hair, *Bourbonism and Agrarian Protest—Louisiana Politics, 1877–1900* (Baton Rouge: Louisiana State University Press, 1969), p. 114. See Vandal, *Rethinking Southern Violence,* p. 196; Rabinowitz, *Race Relations in the Urban South,* pp. 319, 320–321; Joseph Patrick Harahan, "Politics, Political Parties, and Voter Participation in Tidewater Virginia during Reconstruction, 1865–1900," Ph.D. diss., Michigan State University, 1973, chap. 5.

12. Foner, *Freedom's Lawmakers,* s.v. "Robert Elliott," "John Hyman," "Alonzo Ransier," "James Rapier," and "Benjamin Turner."

13. After the federally conducted voter registration occurred in 1867–1868, voter registration was generally not done by the new state governments according to race, nor was their vote-counting done according to race. Thus no data for individual behavior exist—we have only what are known as "aggregate data," i.e., census data and partisan data at the level of a jurisdiction (ward, parish, county, or state). All that can be done, then, is to infer individual behavior by working with these two sets of aggregate data; this is known as "cross-level inference." Such inference is notoriously invalid, because it is statistically simple to prove that aggregates behave differently than the components that make them up. Ecological regression is an effort to resolve the problem reputably. It estimates how individuals behaved politically by algebraically combining and manipulating information about the population aggregates such as vote percentages for the political parties, on one hand, and census data about the numbers of black and white adult males in political jurisdictions, on the other. From such aggregate data, reasonably valid inferences can be made about black adult male electoral turnout and voting patterns when the results are compared carefully with qualitative data and corrected in commonsensical ways. For an introduction, see J. Morgan Kousser, "Ecological Regression and the Analysis of Past Politics," *Journal of Interdisciplinary History* 4 (Autumn 1973): 237–262. A computationally and mathematically advanced version is presented in Gary King, *A Solution to the Ecological Inference Problem: Reconstructing Individual Behavior from Aggregate Data* (Princeton: Princeton University Press, 1997). Old ER and new ER seem to produce similar estimates.

14. See United States Department of the Interior, Census Office, *Statistics of the Population of the United States at the Tenth Census* (Washington, D.C.: Government Printing Office, 1883), table IV.

15. William Cohen, *At Freedom's Edge: Black Mobility and the Southern White Quest for Racial Control, 1861–1915* (Baton Rouge: Louisiana State University Press, 1991), tables 10–12, pp. 214, 218, 240.

16. See Rogers and Ward, *August Reckoning,* chap. 7.

17. See Edmund L. Drago, *Hurrah for Hampton! Black Red Shirts in South Carolina during Reconstruction* (Fayetteville: University of Arkansas Press, 1998), pp. 40–43, on the role of black women in enforcing black male partisan identity. See also John William Graves, *Town and Country: Race Relations in an Urban-Rural Context, Arkansas, 1865–1905* (Fayetteville: University

of Arkansas Press, 1990), p. 173; Rabinowitz, *Race Relations in the Urban South*, chap. 12; Logan, *Negro in North Carolina*, pp. 22–23; Harahan, "Politics, Political Parties, and Voter Participation," p. 230. The quotation is from Sir George Campbell, *White and Black: The Outcome of a Visit to the United States* (New York: R. Worthington, 1879), p. 331.

18. Currents of political disaffection are described in Bess Beatty, *A Revolution Gone Backwards: The Black Response to National Politics, 1876–1896*, Contributions in Afro-American and African Studies (Westport: Greenwood, 1987), chs. 3–4; Janet Thomas Greenwood, *Bittersweet Legacy: The Black and White 'Better Classes' in Charlotte, 1850–1910* (Chapel Hill: University of North Carolina Press, 1994), pp. 160–162, 174–176; Carl V. Harris, *Political Power in Birmingham, 1871–1921* (Knoxville: University of Tennessee Press, 1977), chap. 4; Eugene J. Watts, "Black Political Progress in Atlanta: 1868–1895," *Journal of Negro History* 59 (July 1974): 268–286, on black voters playing off Democratic factionalism. See also Drago, *Hurrah for Hampton!* for Democratic voting and Kousser, *Shaping of Southern Politics*, p. 87, for black Democratic state legislators.

19. See Kousser, *Shaping of Southern Politics*, p. 131n34.

20. Joseph H. Cartwright, *The Triumph of Jim Crow: Tennessee Race Relations in the 1880s* (Knoxville: University of Tennessee Press, 1976), chap. 2. See also J. Morgan Kousser, "Post-Reconstruction Suffrage Restrictions in Tennessee: A New Look at the V. O. Key Thesis," *Political Science Quarterly* 88 (December 1973): 655–683, esp. pp. 660–661.

21. Justus D. Doenecke, *The Presidencies of James A. Garfield and Chester A. Arthur* (Lawrence: Regents Press of Kansas, 1981), p. 115.

22. The landmarks in Readjuster scholarship are Charles Chilton Pearson, *The Readjuster Movement in Virginia*, Yale Historical Publications (New Haven: Yale University Press, 1917), James Tice Moore, *Two Paths to the New South: The Virginia Debt Controversy, 1870–1883* (Lexington: University Press of Kentucky, 1974), and Jane Dailey, *Before Jim Crow: The Politics of Race in Postemancipation Virginia* (Chapel Hill: University of North Carolina Press, 2000). The best short introduction is Carl N. Degler, *The Other South—Southern Dissenters in the Nineteenth Century* (New York: Harper and Row, 1974), pp. 270–285.

23. See Dailey, *Before Jim Crow*, pp. 37–42, for Mahone the person and pp. 57–61 for patronage.

24. On the associational life of urban blacks in Virginia during the 1870s and 1880s, see Lawrence L. Hartzell, "The Exploration of Freedom in Black Petersburg, Virginia, 1865–1902," in *The Edge of the South: Life in Nineteenth-Century Virginia*, ed. Edward L. Ayers and John C. Willis, pp. 134–156 (Charlottesville: University Press of Virginia, 1991); Peter J. Rachleff, *Black Labor in the South: Richmond, Virginia, 1865–1890* (Philadelphia: Temple University Press, 1984), chap. 6.

25. Brooks Miles Barnes, "Triumph of the New South: Independent Movements in Post-Reconstruction Politics," Ph.D. diss., University of Virginia, 1991, pp. 157–58; Ronald Edward Shibley, "Election Laws and Electoral Practices in Virginia, 1867–1902: An Administrative and Political History," Ph.D. diss., University of Virginia, 1972, chap. 5 and pp. 90–94, especially, for details on mobilization before abolition of the poll tax.

26. The 47 percent estimate is from Wynes, *Race Relations in Virginia*, p. 21; the 30 percent estimate for 1881 to 1883 is from Degler, *Other South*, p. 280. Estimating the increase in gubernatorial elections is less straightforward than for the other two kinds of elections, because the 1877 election saw a Democrat run unopposed, so that the 1881 election resulted in an increase close to 100 percent. Comparing the 1873 voter total, when a Democrat and a Republican competed against each other, with the gubernatorial election of 1881 yields a much smaller increase of 5.3 percent. For House and gubernatorial elections, see *Congressional*

Quarterly's Guide to U.S. Elections, 2nd ed. (Washington, D.C.: Congressional Quarterly, Inc., 1985), pp. 532, 801, 805. On black office-holding, see James Hugo Johnston, "The Participation of Negroes in the Government of Virginia from 1877 to 1888," *Journal of Negro History* 14 (July 1929): 251–271, esp. p. 262; Rachleff, *Black Labor in the South,* pp. 102–105; Wynes, *Race Relations in Virgini,* pp. 22–27.

27. Dailey, *Before Jim Crow,* p. 68.

28. Moore, *Two Paths to the New South,* p. 92.

29. See Barnes, "Triumph of the New South," p. 151; Moore, *Two Paths to the New South,* pp. 87–88, 101–102; Pearson, *Readjuster Movement,* pp. 142–144.

30. Hartzell, "Exploration of Freedom," p. 140; Johnston, "Participation of Negroes," pp. 261–262; Moore, *Two Paths to the New South,* pp. 88–90, 102–104; Pearson, *Readjuster Movement,* pp. 144–145; Rachleff, *Black Labor in the South,* p. 103. For a fond and informative retrospective on the Readjusters, see the "Communications" section of the *Journal of Negro History* 11 (October 1926): 669–682, esp. the letters from George F. Bragg Jr., pp. 671–682.

31. Wynes, *Race Relations in Virginia,* pp. 29–34, 39–47; Harahan, "Voter Participation in Tidewater Virginia."

32. David Lublin, *The Paradox of Representation: Racial Gerrymandering and Minority Interests in Congress* (Princeton: Princeton University Press, 1997), pp. 19–21; J. Morgan Kousser, *Colorblind Injustice: Minority Voting Rights and the Undoing of the Second Reconstruction* (Chapel Hill: University of North Carolina Press, 1999), pp. 26–31. For particular districts, see George Brown Tindall, *South Carolina Negroes, 1877–1900* (Columbia: University of South Carolina Press, 1952), chap. 4 (for the seventh South Carolina district); Eric Anderson, *Race and Politics in North Carolina, 1872–1901: The Black Second* (Baton Rouge: Louisiana State University Press, 1981) (for the second North Carolina district); Wythe Holt, *Virginia's Constitutional Convention of 1901–1902* (New York: Garland, 1990), p. 86 (for the fourth Virginia District); and Cresswell, *Multiparty Politics,* pp. 40–41, 80–81 (for the second and sixth Mississippi districts).

33. See Donald G. Nieman, "African Americans and the Meaning of Freedom: Washington County, Texas as a Case Study, 1865–1886," *Chicago-Kent Law Review* (Symposium on the Law of Freedom, Part I) 70:2 (1994): 541–582; Finnegan, "Lynching and Political Power," p. 196, discussing Colleton County in the South Carolina Low Country; Edward L. Ayers, *The Promise of the New South: Life after Reconstruction* (New York: Oxford University Press, 1992), pp. 41–42 (Arkansas); James W. Leslie, "Ferd Havis: Jefferson County's Black Republican Leader," *Arkansas Historical Quarterly* 37 (Autumn 1978): 240–251; John C. Rodrigue, *Reconstruction in the Cane Fields: From Slavery to Free Labor in Louisiana's Sugar Parishes, 1862–1880* (Baton Rouge: Louisiana State University Press, 2001); and John Dittmer, *Black Georgia in the Progressive Era, 1900–1920* (Urbana: University of Illinois Press, 1977), pp. 98–99.

34. Cresswell, *Multiparty Politics,* pp. 92–93; Graves, *Town and Country,* chap. 6; Cartwright, *Triumph of Jim Crow,* chap. 5; Peter D. Klingman, *Neither Dies Nor Surrenders: A History of the Republican Party in Florida, 1867–1970* (Gainesville: University Presses of Florida, 1984), pp. 104–106; Thomas W. Hanchett, *Sorting Out the New South City: Race, Class, and Urban Development in Charlotte, 1875–1975* (Chapel Hill: University of North Carolina Press, 1998), pp. 78–81; Logan, *Negro in North Carolina,* p. 31; Canter Brown Jr., *Florida's Black Public Officials, 1867–1924* (Tuscaloosa: University of Alabama Press, 1998), pp. 143–184. To derive my counts for Florida I counted *number of terms* held by black officials during the 1876–1889 period relative to the 1867–1875 period.

35. For background on the convention and Hoar's role at it, see David M. Jordan, *Roscoe Conkling of New York: Voice in the Senate* (Ithaca: Cornell University Press, 1971), chap. 22;

Thomas C. Reeves, *Gentleman Boss: The Life of Chester Alan Arthur* (New York: Knopf, 1975), chap. 9; Richard E. Welch Jr., *George Frisbie Hoar and the Half-Breed Republicans* (Cambridge: Harvard University Press, 1971), pp. 94–98. On what was known as the Fifth Avenue Hotel Conference, see Stanley P. Hirshson, *Farewell to the Bloody Shirt: Northern Republicans and the Southern Negro, 1877–1893* (Bloomington: Indiana University Press, 1962), pp. 78–86; Reeves, *Gentleman Boss,* pp. 190–194.

36. James Garfield to George Frisbie Hoar, 10 July 1880, George Frisbie Hoar Papers, Special Collections, Massachusetts Historical Society. Note that these are the "special collections" of the Hoar Papers, personally arranged by Hoar, an important fact about the documents in them. I learned this thanks to the staff at the Massachusetts Historical Society.

37. Chester Arthur to George Frisbie Hoar, 15 July 1880, George Frisbie Hoar Papers, Special Collections, Massachusetts Historical Society, emphasis added.

38. Ibid. Arthur's precise phrasing is "the increased power derived from the enfranchisement of a race now denied its share in governing the country—wielded by those who lately sought the overthrow of the Government—is now the sole reliance to defeat" the Republican Party.

39. See David R. Mayhew, *Divided We Govern: Party Control, Lawmaking, and Investigations, 1946–1990* (New Haven: Yale University Press, 1991), p. 1, which refers to sixteen consecutive years of divided control between 1874 and 1896—but this estimate makes the common mistake of miscoding 1881–1883, a brief period of unified government for Republicans.

40. See John M. Taylor, *Garfield of Ohio: The Available Man* (New York: Norton, 1970), pp. 301–308.

41. For the particulars of the 1883 tariff, see Reeves, *Gentleman Boss,* chap. 20, and David Epstein and Sharyn O'Halloran, "The Partisan Paradox and the U.S. Tariff, 1877–1934," *International Organization* 50 (Spring 1996): 301–324, establishing the independent influence of party control on changes in tariff policy. Epstein and O'Halloran miscode, incidentally, for the Forty-seventh Congress, but this only strengthens their principal finding. See also Charles Stewart III, *Analyzing Congress* (New York: Norton, 2001), p. 347. On the politics of the conference, see Ada C. McCown, *The Congressional Conference Committee* (New York: Columbia University Press, 1927), chap. 6.

42. James M. McPherson, *Battle Cry of Freedom: The Civil War Era* (New York: Oxford University Press, 1988), pp. 758–760. At Petersburg, Mahone led a rout of black Union soldiers whose deployment was badly bungled by their white commanding officers. The quotation is from Reeves, *Gentleman Boss,* p. 310, emphasis added.

43. For general background on the Republican Party's economic policies, see Charles W. Calhoun, "Political Economy in the Gilded Age: The Republican Party's Industrial Policy," *Journal of Policy History* 8 (Summer 1996): 291–309, and Lewis L. Gould, "The Republican Search for a National Majority," in *The Gilded Age,* rev. and enlarged ed., ed. H. Wayne Morgan (New York: Syracuse University Press, 1963 and 1970), pp. 171–198. The best discussion is Richard Franklin Bensel, *The Political Economy of American Industrialization, 1877–1900* (New York: Cambridge University Press, 2000).

44. This section is based on Richard Valelly, "National Parties and Racial Disenfranchisement," in *Classifying by Race,* ed. Paul E. Peterson, pp. 188–216 (Princeton: Princeton University Press, 1995), esp. pp. 197–200.

45. See Robert Michael Goldman, " 'A Free Ballot and a Fair Count': The Department of Justice and the Enforcement of Voting Rights in the South, 1877–1893," Ph.D. diss., Michigan State University, 1976, chaps. 3–4.

46. Barr, *Reconstruction to Reform,* p. 196 (for Texas). For conversion, see Samuel H. Williamson, "What Is the Relative Value?" Economic History Series, April 23 2002, http://www.eh.net/hmit/compare/—I chose the median of five possible ways of estimating the relative value. Estimates ranged from $128,000 to $7,500,000; Cresswell, *Multiparty Politics,* pp. 77–80, detailing successful enforcement, and pp. 213–215, unsuccessful enforcement; Rogers and Ward, *August Reckoning,* p. 69, detailing how organization by black voters could allow them to make the most of the presence of U.S. officials, and pp. 69–78, on how organization could assist federal elections prosecutions.

47. The best recent discussion is Scott C. James and Brian L. Lawson, "The Political Economy of Voting Rights Enforcement in America's Gilded Age: Electoral College Competition, Partisan Commitment, and the Federal Election Law," *American Political Science Review* 93 (March 1999): 115–132.

48. See Harold M. Hyman and William M. Wiecek, *Equal Justice under Law: Constitutional Development, 1835–1875,* New American Nation Series (New York: Harper Torchbooks, 1982), pp. 467–468; Xi Wang, *The Trial of Democracy: Black Suffrage and Northern Republicans, 1860–1910* (Athens: University of Georgia Press, 1997), pp. 132–133, 207–208, 346–347, nn. 163–165.

49. *United States v. Harris,* 106 U.S. 629 (1883).

50. See Cass R. Sunstein, "Section 1983 and the Private Enforcement of Federal Law," *University of Chicago Law Review* 49 (Spring 1982): 394–439, esp. pp. 398–409, which provide a helpful discussion of the origins of the 1874 Revised Statutes.

51. Quoted in Wang, *Trial of Democracy,* p. 167.

52. *Ex parte Yarbrough,* 110 U.S. 651 (1884). This case resulted from the Arthur administration's encouragement, on one hand, of biracial fusion (in the state of Georgia) during the 1882 southern congressional election campaigns and, on the other, of voting rights enforcement intended to buttress such fusion. The case was initially prosecuted by a leading Georgia Independent, Emory Speer, a former congressman, a U.S. attorney in 1883–1884, and later a federal judge. For description of the facts of the case and the Justice Department's role, see Goldman, "Department of Justice," pp. 176–178, 196–200.

53. The supposedly unconstitutional sections of the Revised Statutes were sections 5508 (formerly section 6 of the first Federal Elections Act, May 31, 1870) and 5520 (a piece of section 2 of the third Federal Elections Act—the Ku Klux Act—April 20, 1871). See Wang, *Trial of Democracy,* pp. 294–299. The numbers there refer to the first and the second editions of the Revised Statutes; the first edition was published in 1875, the second in 1878.

54. *Civil Rights Cases,* 109 U.S. 3 (1883).

55. *Virginia v. Rives,* 100 U.S. 313 (1879).

56. Edward A. Purcell Jr., *Litigation and Inequality: Federal Diversity Jurisdiction in Industrial America, 1870–1958* (New York: Oxford University Press, 1992), pp. 142–147.

57. *Ex parte Yarbrough,* 110 U.S. 651, 664 (1884).

Chapter Four

1. For the estimate of two thousand, see Eric Foner, *Freedom's Lawmakers: A Directory of Black Officeholders during Reconstruction* (New York: Oxford University Press, 1993), p. ix; for an introduction, see Michael D. Cobb and Jeffery A. Jenkins, "Race and the Representation of Blacks' Interests during Reconstruction," *Political Research Quarterly* 54 (March 2001): 143–166. See also David R. Mayhew, *America's Congress: Actions in the Public Sphere, James*

Madison through Newt Gingrich (New Haven: Yale University Press, 2000), pp. 6, 19 and passim; Peter D. Klingman, "Race and Faction in the Public Career of Josiah T. Walls," in *Southern Black Leaders of the Reconstruction Era,* ed. Howard N. Rabinowitz, pp. 59–78 (Urbana: University of Illinois Press, 1982); John M. Matthews, "Jefferson Franklin Long: The Public Career of Georgia's First Black Congressman," *Phylon* 42 (Summer 1981): 145–156; George W. Reid, "Four in Black: North Carolina's Black Congressmen, 1874–1901," *Journal of Negro History* 44 (Summer 1979): 229–243; Alrutheus A. Taylor, "Negro Congressmen a Generation After," *Journal of Negro History* 7 (April 1922): 127–171; Melvin Urofsky, "Blanche K. Bruce: United States Senator, 1875–1881," *Journal of Mississippi History* 29 (May 1967): 118–141; Peggy Lamson, *The Glorious Failure: Black Congressman Robert Brown Elliott and the Reconstruction in South Carolina* (New York: Norton, 1973); Edward A. Miller Jr., *Gullah Statesman—Robert Smalls from Slavery to Congress, 1839–1915* (Columbia: University of South Carolina Press, 1995); Loren Schweninger, *James T. Rapier and Reconstruction,* Negro American Biographies and Autobiographies (Chicago: University of Chicago Press, 1978).

2. The vignettes are from Eric Foner, "Rights and the Constitution in Black Life during the Civil War and Reconstruction," *Journal of American History* 74 (December 1987): 863–883, at p. 878.

3. Constance McLaughlin Green, *The Secret City: A History of Race Relations in the Nation's Capital* (Princeton: Princeton University Press, 1967), chap. 6. See Donald R. McCoy and Richard T. Ruetten, *Quest and Response: Minority Rights and the Truman Administration* (Lawrence: University Press of Kansas, 1973), pp. 338–340, tracing restaurant desegregation in 1953.

4. Foner, *Freedom's Lawmakers,* s.v. "Robert Elliott," "John W. Menard," "Jefferson Long," "Joseph Rainey," and p. xxvii; Anne M. Butler, Wendy Wolff, and the U.S. Senate Historical Office, *United States Senate Election, Expulsion, and Censure Cases, 1793–1990* (Washington, D.C.: Government Printing Office, 1995), p. 154; Carter G. Woodson, *Negro Orators and Their Orations* (Washington, D.C.: Associated Publishers, 1925), sec. 7, pp. 262–410, esp. pp. 286–295, 309–328; Raymond W. Smock, "Black Members: Nineteenth Century," in *The Encyclopedia of the United States Congress,* ed. Donald C. Bacon, Roger H. Davidson, and Morton Keller, pp. 170–173, at p. 171 (New York: Simon and Schuster, 1995).

5. "Speech by the Hon. Henry M. Turner on the 'Benefits Accruing from the Ratification of the Fifteenth Amendment,' and Its Incorporation into the United States Constitution, Delivered at the Celebration in Macon, Georgia, April 19, 1870," in Philip S. Foner and George E. Walker, eds., *Proceedings of the Black National and State Conventions, 1865–1900* (Philadelphia: Temple University Press, 1986), 1:417–418, emphasis evidently in the original. Grant is quoted in W. E. B. Du Bois, *Black Reconstruction in America, 1860–1880* (1935; reprint, New York: Atheneum, 1992), p. 594.

6. Steven Hahn, *A Nation under Our Feet: Black Political Struggles in the Rural South from Slavery to the Great Migration* (Cambridge: Harvard University Press, Belknap Press, 2003), p. 248.

7. On *white backlash* see Joe Gray Taylor, "Louisiana: An Impossible Task," in *Reconstruction and Redemption in the South,* ed. Otto H. Olsen, pp. 202–236 (Baton Rouge: Louisiana State University Press, 1980); Carl H. Moneyhon, "The Failure of Southern Republicanism, 1867–1876," in *The Facts of Reconstruction: Essays in Honor of John Hope Franklin,* ed. Eric Anderson and Alfred A. Moss Jr., pp. 99–120 (Baton Rouge: Louisiana State University Press, 1991); Lou Falkner Williams, *The Great South Carolina Ku Klux Klan Trials,* Studies in the Legal History of the South (Athens: University of Georgia Press, 1996). On *"New Departure" Democrats,* see Eric Foner, *Reconstruction: America's Unfinished Revolution, 1863–1877*

(New York: Harper and Row, 1988), pp. 412–418, 505–506, 547–548. On *the failure of land reform* see Jay R. Mandle, *The Roots of Black Poverty: The Southern Plantation Economy after the Civil War* (Durham: Duke University Press, 1978); Dwight B. Billings Jr., *Planters and the Making of a 'New South': Class, Politics, and Development in North Carolina, 1865–1900* (Chapel Hill: University of North Carolina Press, 1979); Jonathan M. Weiner, *Social Origins of the New South: Alabama, 1860–1885* (Baton Rouge: Louisiana State University Press, 1978); Elsie M. Lewis, "The Political Mind of the Negro, 1865–1900," *Journal of Southern History* 21 (May 1955): 189–202, at 195; Robert Higgs, *Competition and Coercion: Blacks in the American Economy, 1865–1914,* Hoover Institution Publication P 163 (Cambridge: Cambridge University Press, 1977), pp. 77–80. On the *tension with female suffrage*, see Ellen Carol DuBois, *Feminism and Suffrage: The Emergence of an Independent Women's Movement in America, 1848–1869* (Ithaca: Cornell University Press, 1978); Rosalyn Terborg-Penn, *African American Women in the Struggle for the Vote, 1850–1920* (Bloomington: Indiana University Press, 1998), chaps. 1–3. On the *business cycle*, see Milton Friedman and Anna Jacobson Schwartz, *A Monetary History of the United States, 1867–1960,* Studies in Business Cycles (Princeton: Princeton University Press for the National Bureau of Economic Research, 1963), pp. 41–44. On *class conflict among black southerners*, see Michael W. Fitzgerald, "Republican Factionalism and Black Empowerment: The Spencer-Warner Controversy and Alabama Reconstruction, 1868–1880," *Journal of Southern History* 64 (August 1998): 474–494; Fitzgerald, *Urban Emancipation: Popular Politics in Reconstruction Mobile, 1860–1890* (Baton Rouge: Louisiana State University Press, 2002).

8. Lawrence N. Powell, "Correcting for Fraud: A Quantitative Reassessment of the Mississippi Ratification Election of 1868," *Journal of Southern History* 55 (November 1989): 633–658, esp. pp. 637–642 and table 1; Ronald F. King, "Hayes Truly Won: A Revisionist Analysis of the 1876 Electoral Vote in Louisiana, South Carolina and Florida," paper delivered at the 2000 Annual Meeting of the American Political Science Association, Washington, D.C., September, 2000; King, "Counting the Votes: South Carolina's Stolen Election of 1876," *Journal of Interdisciplinary History* 32 (Autumn 2001): 169–191, esp. table 1 and author calculation. Note that Charleston County figures are not available; therefore the actual turnout was higher than 78 percent.

9. See Edmund L. Drago, *Hurrah for Hampton! Black Red Shirts in South Carolina during Reconstruction* (Fayetteville: University of Arkansas Press, 1998); Gilles Vandal, *Rethinking Southern Violence: Homicides in Post–Civil War Louisiana, 1866–1884* (Columbus: Ohio State University Press, 2000), pp. 187–188.

10. See Alan Conway, *The Reconstruction of Georgia* (Minneapolis: University of Minnesota Press, 1966), pp. 172, 148–158, passim. See also "Address to the Colored People of South Carolina" and "Minority Report of the Ku Klux Klan Committee," in *Black Reconstructionists,* ed. Emma Lou Thornbrough, pp. 83–84, 95–99, Great Lives Observed (Englewood Cliffs, N.J.: Prentice-Hall, 1972); James S. Pike, *The Prostrate State: South Carolina under Negro Government* (New York: D. Appleton, 1874), once an oft-cited eyewitness report of the dangers of governmental "Africanization" (p. 4), and a more measured and factual work (built on a series for *Scribner's Monthly Magazine*), Edward King's *The Southern States of North America: A Record of Journeys* (London: Blackie and Son, 1875).

11. *Congressional Globe,* 41st Cong., 2d sess., pp. 1561–1563. See also Donald L. Singer, "For Whites Only: The Seating of Hiram Revels in the United States Senate," *Negro History Bulletin* 35 (March 1972): 60–63. On Republican conceptions of progress, see Harold M. Hyman, *A More Perfect Union: The Impact of the Civil War and Reconstruction on the Constitution* (New York: Knopf, 1973), and Hyman, *The Reconstruction Justice of Salmon P. Chase: In Re Turner and Texas v. White* (Lawrence: University Press of Kansas, 1997), pp. 111–112, treating

the relation between progress and God's will in Republican political thought. See also Victor B. Howard, *Religion and the Radical Republican Movement, 1860–1870* (Lexington: University Press of Kentucky, 1990.)

12. Daniel W. Stowell, *Rebuilding Zion: The Religious Reconstruction of the South, 1863–1877* (New York: Oxford University Press, 1998), pp. 149–155; "Speech by the Hon. Henry M. Turner," pp. 417–418.

13. Klingman, "Race and Faction," pp. 70–71; Foner, *Freedom's Lawmakers*, s.v. "James K. Green," pp. 90–91.

14. My calculations are based on the evidence given in Foner, *Freedom's Lawmakers*, pp. ix–xxv and s.v. "Oscar Dunn" and "Pinckney B. S. Pinchback."

15. Data on the Reconstruction sessions were coded by my research assistant, Jeremy Weinstein, using *Freedom's Lawmakers*. The data for women legislators come from Kristi Andersen, *After Suffrage: Women in Partisan and Electoral Politics before the New Deal* (Chicago: University of Chicago Press, 1996), table 5.1, p. 116.

16. Foner, *Freedom's Lawmakers*, p. xx. See also Katherine Tate, *Black Faces in the Mirror: African Americans and Their Representatives in the U.S. Congress* (Princeton: Princeton University Press, 2003), pp. 27–34. An interesting group portrait is A. E. Perkins, *A Résumé of Negro Congressmen's Office Holding* (New Orleans: n.p., 1944), located at the Massachusetts Historical Society.

17. See, among others, Richard Bensel, *Yankee Leviathan: The Origins of Central State Authority in America, 1859–1877* (New York: Cambridge University Press, 1990), pp. 380–395 and chap. 5.

18. For full treatments of these processes see Richard L. Hume, "The 'Black and Tan' Constitutional Conventions of 1867–1869 in Ten Former Confederate States: A Study of Their Membership," Ph.D. diss., University of Washington, 1969; Hume, "Carpetbaggers in the Reconstruction South: A Group Portrait of Outside Whites in the 'Black and Tan' Constitutional Conventions," *Journal of American History* 64 (September 1977): 313–330; Hume, "Negro Delegates to the State Constitutional Conventions of 1867–69," in *Southern Black Leaders of the Reconstruction Era*, ed. Howard N. Rabinowitz, pp. 129–154 (Urbana: University of Illinois Press, 1982). For a rare photograph of the Alabama Constitutional Convention delegates in 1867 see ibid., p. 131.

19. See John Hope Franklin, "Public Welfare in the South during the Reconstruction Era, 1865–80," *Social Service Review* 44 (December 1970): 379–392; Jack B. Scroggs, "Carpetbagger Constitutional Reform in the South Atlantic States, 1867–1868," *Journal of Southern History* 27 (November 1961): 475–493; Francis Newton Thorpe, comp. and ed., *The Federal and State Constitutions, Colonial Charters, and Other Organic Laws of the States, Territories, and Colonies Now or Heretofore Forming the United States of America* (Washington, D.C.: Government Printing Office, 1909).

20. David Tyack and Robert Lowe, "The Constitutional Moment: Reconstruction and Black Education in the South," *American Journal of Education* 94 (February 1986): 236–256, at pp. 245, 249.

21. Dale Baum, "Black Lawmakers and the Establishment of the Agricultural and Mechanical College of Texas," Remarks given at Texas A&M University, April 13, 1996, www.tamu.edu/gaines/bgsa.html; John W. Blassingame, *Black New Orleans, 1860–1880* (Chicago: University of Chicago Press, 1973), pp. 107–130; William C. Harris, *The Day of the Carpetbagger: Republican Reconstruction in Mississippi* (Baton Rouge: Louisiana State University Press, 1979), pp. 347–350; Joe Gray Taylor, *Louisiana Reconstructed, 1863–1877* (Baton Rouge: Louisiana State University Press, 1974), pp. 477–479; William Preston Vaughn,

Schools for All: The Blacks and Public Education in the South, 1865–1877 (Lexington: University Press of Kentucky, 1974), chaps. 3–5. On South Carolina, see W. Lewis Burke Jr., "The Radical Law School: The University of South Carolina School of Law and Its African American Graduates, 1873–1877," in James Lowell Underwood and W. Lewis Burke Jr., *At Freedom's Door: African American Founding Fathers and Lawyers in Reconstruction South Carolina* (Columbia: University of South Carolina Press, 2000), pp. 90–115.

22. Blassingame, *Black New Orleans,* pp. 173–196; Roger A. Fischer, *The Segregation Struggle in Louisiana, 1862–77* (Urbana: University of Illinois Press, 1974), chap. 4; John William Graves, *Town and Country: Race Relations in an Urban-Rural Context, Arkansas, 1865–1905* (Fayetteville: University of Arkansas Press, 1990), pp. 30–31; Harris, *Day of the Carpetbagger,* pp. 437–451; William C. Hine, "Dr. Benjamin A. Boseman, Jr.: Charleston's Black Physician-Politician," in *Southern Black Leaders of the Reconstruction Era,* ed. Howard N. Rabinowitz (Urbana: University of Illinois Press, 1982), pp. 335–362; Jerrell H. Shofner, *Nor Is It Over Yet: Florida in the Era of Reconstruction, 1863–1877* (Gainesville: University Presses of Florida, 1974), pp. 208, 291; Alrutheus Ambush Taylor, *The Negro in South Carolina during the Reconstruction* (Washington: Association for the Study of Negro Life and History, 1924), pp. 162–163; Taylor, *The Negro in Tennessee, 1865–1880* (1941; reprint, Spartanburg, S.C.: Reprint Company, 1974), p. 227.

23. See Cobb and Jenkins, "Race and the Representation of Blacks' Interests." For a succinct sketch of the act's origins, see William P. Vaughn, "Separate and Unequal: The Civil Rights Act of 1875 and Defeat of the School Integration Clause," in *The United States Congress in a Partisan Political Nation,* ed. Joel Silbey, 3:759–767 (Brooklyn: Carlson, 1991), reprinted from *Southwestern Social Science Quarterly* 48 (September 1967). See also Lamson, *Glorious Failure,* pp. 174–183; Schweninger, *James T. Rapier,* pp. 120–121, 125–130.

24. Bobby L. Lovett, *The African-American History of Nashville, Tennessee, 1780–1930: Elites and Dilemmas* (Fayetteville: University of Arkansas Press, 1999), pp. 77, 80; Foner, *Reconstruction,* p. 246.

25. Carol K. Rothrock Bleser, *The Promised Land: The History of the South Carolina Land Commission, 1869–1890* (Columbia, S.C.: University of South Carolina Press for the South Carolina Tricentennial Commission, 1969), appendix I; United States Bureau of the Census, *The Statistics of the Population of the United States* (Washington, D.C.: Government Printing Office, 1872), 1:5. What happened later is told in Elizabeth Rauh Bethel, *Promiseland: A Century of Life in a Negro Community* (Philadelphia: Temple University Press, 1981).

26. Harold D. Woodman, *New South—New Law: The Legal Foundations of Credit and Labor Relations in the Postbellum Agricultural South,* The Walter Lynwood Fleming Lectures in Southern History (Baton Rouge: Louisiana State University Press, 1995). See also Ronald L. F. Davis, "Labor Dependency among Freedmen, 1865–1880," in *From the Old South to the New,* ed. W. J. Fraser and W. B. Moore, pp. 155–166 (Westport: Greenwood, 1981).

27. Hyman, *Reconstruction Justice,* pp. 113–119.

28. As Thomas Holt points out in his study of South Carolina, "Reconstruction postponed, if not entirely forestalled, the development of an apartheid system of racial and economic relationships prefigured in the Black Codes." *Black over White: Negro Political Leadership in South Carolina during Reconstruction* (Urbana: University of Illinois Press, 1977), p. 152. See also Pete Daniel, "The Metamorphosis of Slavery, 1865–1900," *Journal of American History* 66 (June 1979): 89–99.

29. Graves, *Town and Country,* p. 35; Holt, *Black over White,* chap. 7; Shofner, *Nor Is It Over Yet,* p. 293; Woodman, *New South—New Law,* pp. 47, 78, 88. Note that freedmen overwhelmingly disliked wage labor and preferred to work the land individually as tenants or

sharecroppers. But many were drawn into wage labor in areas where rice and sugar were grown and because there was always a labor shortage at harvest time for all crops. Cohen, *At Freedom's Edge,* chap. 1 and pp. 131–134. On the 1876 "rice kingdom" strikes, see Eric Foner, *Nothing But Freedom: Emancipation and Its Legacy* (Baton Rouge: Louisiana State University Press, 1983), chap. 3.

30. Donald G. Nieman, "African Americans and the Meaning of Freedom: Washington County, Texas as a Case Study, 1865–1886," *Chicago-Kent Law Review* (Symposium on the Law of Freedom, Part I) 70:2 (1994): 541–582; William McKee Evans, *Ballots and Fence Rails: Reconstruction on the Lower Cape Fear* (1967; reprint, Athens: University of Georgia Press, 1995), pp. 137–138; Laura F. Edwards, *Gendered Strife and Confusion: The Political Culture of Reconstruction* (Urbana: University of Illinois Press, 1997), pp. 53–54; Christopher Waldrep, *Roots of Disorder: Race and Criminal Justice in the American South, 1817–80* (Urbana: University of Illinois Press, 1998), chap. 6; Eric Anderson, "James O'Hara of North Carolina: Black Leadership and Local Government" and James M. Russell and Jerry Thornbery, "William Finch of Atlanta: The Black Politician as Civic Leader," both in Howard N. Rabinowitz, *Southern Black Leaders of the Reconstruction Era* (Urbana: University of Illinois Press, 1982), pp. 101–128 and 309–334, respectively; Orville Vernon Burton, "The Rise and Fall of Afro-American Town Life: Town and Country in Reconstruction Edgefield, South Carolina," in *Toward a New South? Studies in Post–Civil War Southern Communities,* ed. Orville Vernon Burton and Robert C. McMath, Jr., Contributions in American History, no. 97 (Westport: Greenwood, 1982), pp. 152–192. There were, of course, places where local government and black office-holding were failures. For a modern study, free of bias, see Patricia L. Kenney, "LaVilla, Florida, 1866–1887: Reconstruction Dreams and the Formation of a Black Community," in *The African American Heritage of Florida,* ed. David R. Colburn and Jane L. Landers (Gainesville: University Press of Florida, 1995), pp. 185–206.

31. It seems to have originated with V. O. Key Jr. *Politics, Parties, and Pressure Groups,* 4th ed. (New York: Thomas Y. Crowell, 1958).

32. See Mark W. Summers, *Railroads, Reconstruction, and the Gospel of Prosperity—Aid under the Radical Republicans, 1865–1877* (Princeton: Princeton University Press, 1984). See also Horace Mann Bond, "Social and Economic Forces in Alabama Reconstruction," in *Reconstruction: An Anthology of Revisionist Writings,* ed. Kenneth M. Stampp and Leon F. Litwack (Baton Rouge: Louisiana State University Press, 1969), chap. 17, reprinted from Bond, "Social and Economic Forces in Alabama Reconstruction," *Journal of Negro History* 23 (1938). For further background on the growth agenda, see Richard Current, *Those Terrible Carpetbaggers: A Reinterpretation* (New York: Oxford University Press, 1988), pp. 157–160.

33. Terry L. Seip, *The South Returns to Congress: Men, Economic Measures, and Intersectional Relationships, 1868–1879* (Baton Rouge: Louisiana State University Press, 1983).

34. That the growth agenda had, indeed, clear potential for building white support might be inferred from the Ku Klux Klan's strong attacks on it as the entering wedge for "Negro rule." See Scott Reynolds Nelson, *Iron Confederacies: Southern Railways, Klan Violence, and Reconstruction* (Chapel Hill: University of North Carolina Press, 1999).

35. Summers, *Railroads, Reconstruction;* Maury Klein, "The Strategy of Southern Railroads," *American Historical Review* 73 (April 1968): 1052–1068.

36. On corruption, see Mark Wahlgren Summers, *The Era of Good Stealings* (New York: Oxford University Press, 1993), pp. x, 146–149, and chap. 11; Taylor, *Louisiana Reconstructed,* pp. 196–208.

37. Du Bois, *Black Reconstruction,* pp. 414–416, 428, 614–615; J. Mills Thornton III, "Fiscal Policy and the Failure of Radical Reconstruction in the Lower South," in *Region, Race,*

and Reconstruction: Essays in Honor of C. Vann Woodward, ed. J. Morgan Kousser and James M. McPherson, pp. 349–394 (New York: Oxford University Press, 1982).

38. William A. Muraskin, *Middle-Class Blacks in a White Society: Prince Hall Freemasonry in America* (Berkeley: University of California Press, 1975), pp. 37–39 and n108.

39. See Carl H. Moneyhon, *Republicanism in Reconstruction Texas* (Austin: University of Texas Press, 1980), pp. 134–135, 146–159, 172, 185–187, Moneyhon, "George T. Ruby and the Politics of Expediency in Texas," in *Southern Black Leaders of the Reconstruction Era,* ed. Howard N. Rabinowitz, pp. 363–392 (Urbana: University of Illinois Press, 1982), for discussion of both the League and other kinds of black associations. On trade unionism, see, e.g., Schweninger, *James T. Rapier,* chap. 7; Jerrell H. Shofner, "Militant Negro Laborers in Reconstruction Florida," *Journal of Southern History* 39 (August 1973): 397–408. See also Jonathan M. Bryant, "'We Have Chance of Justice Before the Courts': The Freedmen's Struggle for Power in Greene County, Georgia, 1865–1874," in *Georgia in Black and White: Explorations in the Race Relations of a Southern State, 1865–1950,* ed. John M. Inscoe, pp. 13–37 (Athens: University of Georgia Press, 1994); Bryant, *How Curious a Land: Conflict and Change in Greene County, Georgia, 1850–1885,* Fred W. Morrison Series in Southern Studies (Chapel Hill: University of North Carolina Press, 1996), p. 127; Current, *Those Terrible Carpetbaggers,* p. 323; Harris, *Day of the Carpetbagger,* pp. 640–664; William C. Hine, "Frustration, Factionalism, and Failure: Black Political Leadership and the Republican Party in Reconstruction Charleston, 1865–1877," Ph.D. diss., Kent State University, 1979, p. 432; Miller, *Gullah Statesman,* pp. 57, 63, 67, 122; Otis A. Singletary, *Negro Militia and Reconstruction* (Austin: University of Texas Press, 1957), chaps. 5–8.

40. Richard H. Abbott, *For Free Press and Equal Rights: Republican Newspapers in the Reconstruction South,* ed. John W. Quist (Athens: University of Georgia Press, 2004), chap. 5 and appendix. I thank John Quist for his kindness in making key portions of the page proofs available to me.

41. Reform politicians are well described in Du Bois, *Black Reconstruction,* pp. 414–416, 622–623.

42. See Robert H. Woody, *Republican Newspapers of South Carolina,* Southern Sketches, no. 10, 1st ser. (Charlottesville: Historical Publishing, 1936); Ted Tunnell, *Crucible of Reconstruction: War, Radicalism, and Race in Louisiana, 1862–1877* (Baton Rouge: Louisiana State University Press, 1984), pp. 148–149, 169–170.

43. On federal and state patronage disputes, see Current, *Those Terrible Carpetbaggers,* pp. 148–149, 169–171. On why patronage mattered so much to Republican officeholders and why they fought each other so fiercely, see Lawrence N. Powell, "The Politics of Livelihood: Carpetbaggers in the Deep South," in *Region, Race, and Reconstruction: Essays in Honor of C. Vann Woodward,* ed. J. Morgan Kousser and James M. McPherson, pp. 315–347 (New York: Oxford University Press, 1982), and a perceptive treatment by Evans in *Ballots and Fence Rails,* pp. 150–167. See also Fitzgerald, "Republican Factionalism and Black Empowerment." On the difference in payment between federal and nonfederal officials, see Canter Brown Jr., *Florida's Black Public Officials, 1867–1924* (Tuscaloosa: University of Alabama Press, 1998), pp. 34–35.

44. See Sarah Woolfolk Wiggins's able study, *The Scalawag in Alabama Politics, 1865–1881* (University: University of Alabama Press, 1977). See also Otto H. Olsen, "Reconsidering the Scalawags," *Civil War History* 12 (December 1996): 304–320. Compare Peter Kolchin, "Scalawags, Carpetbaggers, and Reconstruction: A Quantitative Look at Southern Congressional Politics, 1868–1872," *Journal of Southern History* 45 (February 1979): 63–76.

45. On *strong scalawags*, see Canter Brown Jr., *Ossian Bingley Hart: Florida's Loyalist Reconstruction Governor* (Baton Rouge: Louisiana State University Press, 1997), and a sturdy but less interesting biography, William Warren Rogers Jr., *Black Belt Scalawag: Charles Hays and the Southern Republicans in the Era of Reconstruction* (Athens: University of Georgia Press, 1993). On *Arkansas*, see Current, *Those Terrible Carpetbaggers*, pp. 132–142, 255–268, 299–305; Graves, *Town and Country*, chs. 2–3; Singletary, *Negro Militia and Reconstruction*, chap. 4; George H. Thompson, *Arkansas and Reconstruction: The Influence of Geography, Economics, and Personality*, National University Publications Series in American Studies (Port Washington, N.Y.: Kennikat, 1976); Gene W. Boyett, "The Black Experience in the First Decade of Reconstruction in Pope County, Arkansas," *Arkansas Historical Quarterly* 51 (Summer 1992): 119–134. For *Georgia*, see Conway, *Reconstruction of Georgia*; Ruth Currie-McDaniel, *Carpetbagger of Conscience: A Biography of John Emory Bryant* (Athens: University of Georgia Press, 1987), chap. 4; Edmund Drago, *A Splendid Failure: Black Politicians in Reconstruction Georgia* (Baton Rouge: Louisiana State University Press, 1982); Russell Duncan, "A Georgia Governor Battles Racism: Rufus Bullock and the Fight for Black Legislators," in *Georgia in Black and White: Explorations in the Race Relations of a Southern State, 1865–1950*, ed. John M. Inscoe, pp. 38–64 (Athens: University of Georgia Press, 1994); Duncan, *Entrepreneur for Equality: Governor Rufus Bullock, Commerce, and Race in Post–Civil War Georgia* (Athens: University of Georgia Press, 1994), pp. 39–87. For *Texas*, see Moneyhon, *Republicanism in Reconstruction Texas*.

46. See Michael Perman, *The Road to Redemption: Southern Politics, 1869–1879* (Chapel Hill: University of North Carolina Press, 1984), chap. 2; Peter D. Klingman and David T. Geithman, "Negro Dissidence and the Republican Party, 1864–1872," *Phylon* 40 (June 1979): 172–182; Loren Schweninger, "Black Citizenship and the Republican Party in Reconstruction Alabama," *Alabama Review* 29 (April 1976): 83–103.

47. The Louisiana story can be grasped by reading Current, *Those Terrible Carpetbaggers*, 122–131, 242–254, 276, 289–294; George Rable, *But There Was No Peace: The Role of Violence in the Politics of Reconstruction* (Athens: University of Georgia Press, 1984), chap. 8; Taylor, *Louisiana Reconstructed*, chaps. 5–6; and Hans Trefousse, ed., *Historical Dictionary of Reconstruction*, s.v. "William Pitt Kellogg," "Stephen B. Packard," "Pinckney B. S. Pinchback," and "Henry Clay Warmoth."

48. Quoted in Leon Burr Richardson, *William E. Chandler: Republican* (New York: Dodd, Mead, 1940), p. 126. Hahn, *A Nation under Our Feet*, chap. 6, offers an excellent overview.

49. See Sheldon Hackney, "Southern Violence," *American Historical Review* 74 (February 1969): 906–925; Barry Crouch, "A Spirit of Lawlessness: White Violence; Texas Blacks, 1865–1868," *Journal of Social History* 18 (Winter 1985): 217–232; Richard Valelly, "Party, Coercion, and Inclusion: The Two Reconstructions of Southern Electoral Politics," *Politics and Society* 21 (March 1993): 37–67.

50. See Jack Hurst, *Nathan Bedford Forrest: A Biography* (New York: Vintage 1993), pt. 4 (an apologetic study of the Klan's most famous leader that is factually useful); Taylor, *Louisiana Reconstructed*, pp. 161–164; Allen W. Trelease, *White Terror: The Ku Klux Klan Conspiracy and Southern Reconstruction* (New York: Harper and Row, 1971). The basic primary source is U.S. Congress, Joint Select Committee to Inquire into the Condition of Affairs in the Late Insurrectionary States, *Testimony Taken by the Joint Select Committee to Inquire into the Condition of Affairs in the Late Insurrectionary States* (Washington, D.C.: Government Printing Office, 1872). See also Williams, *Ku Klux Klan Trials*.

51. On *labor conflict*, see Crouch, "Spirit of Lawlessness"; J. C. A. Stagg, "The Problem of Klan Violence: The South Carolina Up-Country, 1868–1871," *Journal of American Studies* 8:3 (1974): 303–318. On *partisan utility*, see Moneyhon, *Republicanism in Reconstruction Texas*, pp. 93–96, 191–192; Wiggins, *Scalawag in Alabama Politics*, pp. 68–69; Paul Escott, "White

Republicanism and Ku Klux Klan Terror: The North Carolina Piedmont during Reconstruction," in *Race, Class, and Politics in Southern History: Essays in Honor of Robert F. Durden,* ed. Jeffrey J. Crow, Paul D. Escott, and Charles L. Flynn, pp. 3–34 (Baton Rouge: Louisiana State University Press, 1989); Richard Zuczek, *State of Rebellion: Reconstruction in South Carolina* (Columbia: University of South Carolina Press, 1996); David Garson and Gail O'Brien, "Collective Violence in the Reconstruction South," in *Violence in America: Historical and Comparative Perspectives,* rev. ed., ed. Hugh Davis Graham and Ted Robert Gurr (Beverly Hills: Sage, 1979), pp. 243–260.

52. On the assassination of a U.S. congressman, see Graves, *Town and Country,* p. 37. On how violence disturbed Republican campaigning, see Current, *Those Terrible Carpetbaggers,* pp. 163–165, describing the Eutaw, Alabama, riot of October 25, 1870.

53. For example, Summers, *Press Gang,* pp. 218–221, 224.

54. See Melinda M. Hennessey, "Reconstruction Politics and the Military: The Eufala Riot of 1874," *Alabama Historical Quarterly* 38 (Summer 1976): 112–125. See also Richard N. Current, "President Grant and the Continuing Civil War," in *Ulysses S. Grant: Essays and Documents,* ed. David L. Wilson and John Y. Simon, pp. 1–8 (Carbondale: Southern Illinois University Press for the Ulysses S. Grant Association, 1981), esp. p. 5.

55. Valelly, "Party, Coercion, and Inclusion."

56. Mifflin W. Gibbs, *Shadow and Light: An Autobiography* (1902, reprint: New York: Arno Press and the New York Times, 1968), pp. 141–143.

57. I arrived at the estimate of voters by taking the total size of the registered electorate for ten states in 1868 (Tennessee not included, since it "self-reconstructed" under Parson Brownlow)—1,363,640 (Du Bois, *Black Reconstruction,* p. 371)—adding the number of voters in the 1872 presidential election in Tennessee (179,046), dividing it by 930, and arriving at about 1,466—and then correcting upwards to bias the results in a slightly more conservative direction. On the pacifying impact of federal forces, see James E. Sefton, *The United States Army and Reconstruction, 1865–1879* (Baton Rouge: Louisiana State University Press, 1967), p. viii and chaps. 10–11. See Vincent P. De Santis, *Republicans Face the Southern Question—The New Departure Years, 1877–1897* (Baltimore: Johns Hopkins University Press, 1959), p. 191, for a tabulation of the number of southern counties in 1876, 1880, 1884, and 1888.

58. On the Louisiana Returning Board, authorized to throw out any votes at all, see Tunnell, *Crucible of Reconstruction,* pp. 160–161; Vandal, *Rethinking Southern Violence,* p. 180. On the term "redemption" see Stowell, *Rebuilding Zion,* p. 155.

59. See King, "Hayes Truly Won," p. 10, which quotes from U.S. House of Representatives, *Recent Election in South Carolina,* Report 175, and the accompanying testimony, Miscellaneous Document 31, 44th Cong., 2d sess., 1877.

60. Moneyhon, *Republicanism in Reconstruction Texas,* esp. pp. 191–192.

61. See Everette Swinney, *Suppressing the Ku Klux Klan: The Enforcement of the Reconstruction Amendments, 1870–1877* (New York: Garland, 1987), chaps. 7–10; Swinney, "Enforcing the Fifteenth Amendment, 1870–1877," *Journal of Southern History* 28 (May 1962): 202–218.

62. On the electoral cycle in enforcement see John Robert Kirkland, "Federal Troops in the South Atlantic States during Reconstruction, 1865–1877," Ph.D. diss., University of North Carolina, Chapel Hill, 1967, pp. 257–261.

63. Congress may have counted on a self-help remedy to white-on-black violence via the Second Amendment right to bear arms. Although eccentric, see nonetheless Stephen P. Halbrook, *Freedmen, the Fourteenth Amendment, and the Right to Bear Arms, 1866–1876* (Westport, Conn.: Praeger, 1998).

64. On *black militias,* see Wilbert L. Jenkins, *Seizing the New Day: African-Americans in Post–Civil War Charleston* (Bloomington: Indiana University Press, 1998), chap. 7; Evans, *Ballots*

and Fence Rails, pp. 137–142, discussing Wilmington, North Carolina; Fitzgerald, "Republican Factionalism and Black Empowerment," p. 487, discussing the "National Guard" movements of Montgomery and Mobile, Alabama; Rebecca J. Scott, "'Stubborn and Disposed to Stand Their Ground': Black Militia, Sugar Workers, and the Dynamics of Collective Action in the Louisiana Sugar Bowl, 1863–87," *Slavery and Abolition* 20 (April 1999): 103–126, discussing the black militia movement in Grant Parish, Louisiana; Current, *Those Terrible Carpetbaggers,* p. 323; Harris, *Day of the Carpetbagger,* pp. 640–641; Hine, "Frustration, Factionalism, and Failure," p. 432; Miller, *Gullah Statesman,* pp. 57, 63, 67, 122; Singletary, *Negro Militia.* On *state militias,* see Trelease, *White Terror,* p. 148 and chap. 10; Taylor, *Louisiana Reconstructed,* pp. 176–181; Tunnell, *Crucible of Reconstruction,* pp. 157–159; Zuczek, *State of Rebellion,* pp. 74–91, passim, and 93, 106, 140, 148; William C. Harris, *William Woods Holden: Firebrand of North Carolina Politics* (Baton Rouge: Louisiana State University Press, 1987), chaps. 10–14.

65. Zuczek, *State of Rebellion,* pp. 74, 140; *Congressional Quarterly's Guide to U.S. Elections,* 2d ed. (Washington, D.C.: Congressional Quarterly, Inc., 1985), p. 526.

66. Quoted in John David Smith, *Black Voices from Reconstruction, 1865–1877* (Gainesville: University Press of Florida, 1997), from United States Congress, *Senate Reports,* "Affairs in Insurrectionary States: Report and Minority Views, Alabama," 42nd Cong., 2d sess., vol. 2, pt. 9, no. 1 (Washington, D.C.: Government Printing Office, 1872), pp. 1000, 1003–1004.

67. Vandal, *Rethinking Southern Violence,* p. 87.

68. Although a total of fourteen black men served in Congress during Reconstruction (see Foner, *Freedom's Lawmakers,* p. xv, table 4), the maximum at any one time was seven, in the House, during the Forty-third Congress (James Rapier of Alabama, Josiah Walls of Florida, John Lynch of Mississippi, and Joseph Rainey, Alonzo Ransier, Robert Elliott, and Richard Cain of South Carolina) for a percentage of just under 2 percent (given a smaller Congress). A similar *percentage* was not reached again until 1969; see David Lublin, *The Paradox of Representation: Racial Gerrymandering and Minority Interests in Congress* (Princeton: Princeton University Press, 1997), p. 22.

Chapter Five

1. *South Carolina v. Katzenbach,* 383 U.S. 301, 310 (1966).

2. See Ross A. Webb, *Benjamin Helm Bristow: Border State Politician* (Lexington: University Press of Kentucky, 1969); William S. McFeely, "Amos T. Akerman: The Lawyer and Racial Justice," in *Region, Race, and Reconstruction: Essays in Honor of C. Vann Woodward,* ed. J. Morgan Kousser and James M. McPherson, pp. 395–416 (New York: Oxford University Press, 1982).

3. On Lamar, see Allen W. Trelease, *White Terror: The Ku Klux Klan Conspiracy and Southern Reconstruction* (New York: Harper and Row, 1971), p. 400. On Black, see Chauncey F. Black, *Essays and Speeches of Jeremiah S. Black, with a Biographical Sketch* (New York: D. Appleton, 1886), pp. 25–28, 510–556; and Robert J. Kaczorowski, *The Politics of Judicial Interpretation: The Federal Courts, the Department of Justice, and Civil Rights, 1866–1876,* New York University School of Law Linden Studies in Legal History (New York: Oceana, 1985), pp. 135–143. Also, Hans L. Trefousse, comp., *Historical Dictionary of Reconstruction* (Westport: Greenwood, 1991), s.v. "Reverdy Johnson," "Henry Stanbery." On Campbell, see Robert Saunders Jr., *John Archibald Campbell, Southern Moderate, 1811–1889* (Tuscaloosa: University of Alabama Press, 1997), chaps. 8, 11–12.

4. On the Fifteenth Amendment, see William Gillette, *The Right to Vote: Politics and the Passage of the Fifteenth Amendment* (Baltimore: Johns Hopkins University Press, 1969). See also

Michael Les Benedict, *A Compromise of Principle: Congressional Republicans and Reconstruction, 1863–1869* (New York: Norton, 1974), pp. 325–338; Earl Maltz, *Civil Rights, the Constitution, and Congress, 1863–1869* (Lawrence: University Press of Kansas, 1990), chaps. 8–9; Xi Wang, *The Trial of Democracy: Black Suffrage and Northern Republicans, 1860–1910* (Athens: University of Georgia Press, 1997), pp. 1–53.

5. On Ulysses S. Grant's role in the Fifteenth Amendment, see George Rothwell Brown, *Reminiscences of Senator William M. Stewart of Nevada* (New York: Neale, 1908), chap. 25.

6. My view of the enforcement section comes from Harold M. Hyman and William M. Wiecek, *Equal Justice under Law: Constitutional Development, 1835–1875,* New American Nation Series (New York: Harper Torchbooks, 1982), chap. 11, and Everette Swinney, *Suppressing the Ku Klux Klan: The Enforcement of the Reconstruction Amendments, 1870–1877* (New York: Garland, 1987), pp. 24–25, 85.

7. George S. Boutwell, *Reminiscences of Sixty Years in Public Affairs* (New York: McClure, Phillips, 1902), pp. 43–54; Brown, *Reminiscences of Senator William M. Stewart*, chap. 25. On the source weaknesses, see Gillette, *Right to Vote*, p. 191. They are also evident in the scholarly book-length biographies of the two men, Thomas H. Brown, *George Sewall Boutwell: Human Rights Advocate* (Groton, Mass.: Groton Historical Society, 1989), and Russell R. Elliott, *Servant of Power: A Political Biography of Senator William M. Stewart* (Reno: University of Nevada Press, 1983).

8. Quoted in Bernard Schwartz, ed., *Statutory History of the United States—Civil Rights Part I* (New York: Chelsea House, in association with McGraw-Hill, 1969), pp. 498–499, emphasis added.

9. On the lack of congressional debate about section 2 and the framers' ambiguous intentions with regard to it, see Gillette, *Right to Vote*, pp. 72–73. See also the digest of the congressional debate in *The American Annual Cyclopedia and Register of Important Events of the Year 1869* (New York: D. Appleton, 1870), s.v. "Congress," pp. 120–170, which shows no mention at all of section 2. The lack of debate may be due to the fact that no amendments to the wording of section 2 were proposed. See Edward McPherson, *The Political History of the United States of America during the Period of Reconstruction, April 15, 1865–July 15, 1870* (New York: Da Capo, 1972), pp. 399–406. On debate on section 2 during the ratification process, see Gillette, *Right to Vote*, p. 91. On Boutwell's support for enforcement, see William S. McFeely, *Grant: A Biography* (New York: Norton, 1981), p. 369. On Stewart, see Wang, *Trial of Democracy*, p. 63; Swinney, *Suppressing the Ku Klux Klan*, pp. 65–66. Note that it was only much later (between 1891 and 1894) that Stewart repudiated his Reconstruction accomplishments; see Wang, *Trial of Democracy*, pp. 248–249, p. 258.

10. Compare Michael Les Benedict, "Preserving the Constitution: The Conservative Basis of Radical Reconstruction," *Journal of American History* 61 (June 1974): 65–90; Pamela Brandwein, "Slavery as an Interpretive Issue in the Reconstruction Congresses," *Law and Society Review* 34: 2 (2000): 315–366.

11. Compare Jean Edward Smith, *Grant* (New York: Simon and Schuster, 2001), p. 571; Benedict, "Preserving the Constitution"; Alfred H. Kelly, "Comment on Harold M. Hyman's Paper," in *New Frontiers of the American Reconstruction,* ed. Harold M. Hyman, pp. 40–58 (Urbana: University of Illinois Press, 1966).

12. On the 1850 Fugitive Slave Act and the Supreme Court case declaring it constitutional, *Ableman v. Booth,* 62 U.S. 506 (1859), see Hyman and Wiecek, *Equal Justice under Law*, pp. 105–110, 146–159, 198–201; Harold M. Hyman, *The Reconstruction Justice of Salmon P. Chase: In Re Turner and Texas v. White* (Lawrence: University Press of Kansas, 1997), pp. 5, 114.

13. Heather Cox Richardson, *The Greatest Nation of the Earth: Republican Economic Policies during the Civil War* (Cambridge: Harvard University Press, 1997); Theda Skocpol, *Protecting Soldiers and Mothers: The Political Origins of Social Policy in the United States* (Cambridge: Harvard University Press, Belknap Press, 1992), pt. 1. On the loyalty oaths, see Rogers M. Smith, *Civic Ideals: Conflicting Visions of Citizenship in U.S. History* (New Haven: Yale University Press, 1997), pp. 273–277.

14. Edward A. Purcell Jr., *Litigation and Inequality: Federal Diversity Jurisdiction in Industrial America, 1870–1958* (New York: Oxford University Press, 1992), pp. 14–15.

15. On its origins see Hyman and Wiecek, *Equality under the Law,* pp. 234–235; Hyman, *More Perfect Union,* pp. 45–47, 59–60 and chap. 8. Essential background can be found in Michael Vorenberg, *Final Freedom: The Civil War, the Abolition of Slavery, and the Thirteenth Amendment* (New York: Cambridge University Press, 2001). See also Hyman, "Reconstruction and Political Constitutions: The Popular Expression," in *New Frontiers of the American Reconstruction,* ed. Harold M. Hyman, pp. 1–39 (Urbana: University of Illinois Press, 1966). A helpful study is S. G. F. Spackman, "American Federalism and the Civil Rights Act of 1875," *Journal of American Studies* 10.3 (December 1976): 313–328. See also Robert J. Kaczorowski, "Revolutionary Constitutionalism in the Era of the Civil War and Reconstruction," *New York University Law Review* 61 (November 1986): 863–940; Herman Belz, "The Consitution and Reconstruction," in *The Facts of Reconstruction: Essays in Honor of John Hope Franklin,* ed. Eric Anderson and Alfred A. Moss Jr., pp. 189–218 (Baton Rouge: Louisiana State University Press, 1991).

16. In this connection, consider the wartime habeas corpus and legal tender debates: James M. McPherson, *Battle Cry of Freedom: The Civil War Era* (New York: Oxford University Press, 1988), pp. 287–289, 444–446.

17. A useful introduction is Janice E. Christensen, "The Constitutional Problems of National Control of the Suffrage in the United States," Ph.D. diss., University of Minnesota, 1952, pp. 9–111.

18. Carl M. Brauer, *John F. Kennedy and the Second Reconstruction* (New York: Columbia University Press, 1977), chaps. 4, 6. On the role of the U.S. Marshals in Reconstruction and during the Kennedy administration, see Frederick S. Calhoun, *The Lawmen: United States Marshals and Their Deputies, 1789–1989* (Washington, D.C.: Smithsonian Institution Press, 1990), chaps. 5, 11.

19. See Wang, *Trial of Democracy,* chap. 2; Swinney, *Suppressing the Ku Klux Klan,* chap. 3.

20. On Chinese American civil rights, see Charles J. McClain, *In Search of Equality: The Chinese Struggle against Discrimination in Nineteenth Century America* (Berkeley: University of California Press, 1994), pp. 36–40; Smith, *Civic Ideals,* p. 593n142, discussing *In re Ah Fong.* The text of the statute is reproduced in Wang, *Trial of Democracy,* pp. 267–274.

21. Schwartz, *Statutory History,* 1:444–445, 485. Note that Schwartz considers this an "extreme" position, yet no Republican seems to have called it an extreme position at the time. One might instead regard Pool's view as dispositive, since he was a southerner and the legislation was directed at conditions in the South. Also, how is it that someone espousing an "extreme" position was able to write major provisions of the act?

22. Swinney, *Suppressing the Ku Klux Klan,* chaps. 5–6 and pp. 144–147. On the rise and significance of investigative committees during the Civil War see Hyman, *More Perfect Union,* pp. 181–187; on the Ku Klux Committee itself see Trelease, *White Terror,* chap. 24.

23. The text of the act available in Wang, *Trial of Democracy,* pp. 288–291.

24. Schwartz, *Statutory History,* 1:619.

25. Ibid, 1:619–620.

26. Ibid, 1:640 (for Trumbull), 1:644–645, 647 (for Edmunds), emphasis added.

27. Benedict, "Preserving the Constitution," esp. nn 5, 8, 28, 34, 38. On equity, see Peter Charles Hoffer, *The Law's Conscience: Equitable Constitutionalism in America,* Thornton H. Brooks Series in American Law and Society (Chapel Hill: University of North Carolina Press, 1990), pp. 123–134; Vandal, *Rethinking Southern Violence,* pp. 10, 281–283.

28. Robert W. Coakley, *The Role of Federal Military Forces in Domestic Disorder, 1789–1878,* Army Historical Series (Washington, D.C.: Center of Military History, United States Army, 1988), pp. 300–301, 307–313, and chap. 16; Stephen Cresswell, *Mormons and Cowboys, Moonshiners and Klansmen: Federal Law Enforcement in the South and West, 1870–1893* (Tuscaloosa: University of Alabama Press, 1991), chaps. 1–2; Ward E. Y. Elliott, *The Rise of Guardian Democracy: The Supreme Court's Role in Voting Rights Disputes, 1845–1969* (Cambridge: Harvard University Press, 1974), p. 320n52; Foner, *Reconstruction,* pp. 457–459; Robert Goldman, "'A Free Ballot and a Fair Count': The Department of Justice and the Enforcement of Voting Rights in the South, 1877–1893," Ph.D. diss., Michigan State University, 1976, chap. 1; Kermit L. Hall, "Political Power and Constitutional Legitimacy: The South Carolina Ku Klux Klan Trials, 1871–1872," *Emory Law Journal* 33 (1984): 921–951; Kaczorowski, *Politics of Judicial Interpretation,* chs. 3–5.

29. Initial scholarly assessment emphasized how dangerous and new the federal involvement was. The long-dominant interpretation that "[t]here is considerable similarity between the arbitrary orders and mailed fist in the South during the seventies and the past oppression of Ireland by England, of Bohemia and Italy by Austria, of Finland and Poland by Russia, of Alsace and Lorraine by Germany" can be found in William Watson David, "The Federal Enforcement Acts," in *Studies in Southern History and Politics* (1914; reprint, Port Washington, N.Y.: Kennikat, 1964), pp. 205–228; for the quotation see p. 205. This probably represents how leading white southerners felt. On Grant, see *Reminiscences of an Active Life: The Autobiography of John Roy Lynch,* ed. and intro. John Hope Franklin (Chicago: University of Chicago Press, 1970), p. 176, quoting from a personal interview with President Grant. See also Smith, *Grant,* chap. 18.

30. See Webb, *Benjamin Helm Bristow*; McFeely, "Amos T. Akerman"; McFeely, *Grant,* pp. 359–367 (for the background to Akerman's appointment), 367–374 (for a brief sketch of Akerman's career as attorney general that should be read in conjunction with the article on Akerman).

31. See Swinney, *Suppressing the Ku Klux Klan,* chs. 7–9 and p. 195 for docket statistics. A more confusing treatment of docket statistics can be found in Kaczorowski, *Politics of Judicial Interpretation,* pp. 87–89. Calculation of percentage increase in judicial expenditures is based on figures Swinney reports at pp. 184–185. I included the million-dollar special appropriation of 1872 in my calculations.

32. Swinney, *Suppressing the Ku Klux Klan,* chs. 7–8 and pp. 235, 263 for conviction rates.

33. Compare William Gillette, *Retreat from Reconstruction, 1869–1879* (Baton Rouge: Louisiana State University Press, 1979), chap. 2. For the counter to this position, see Smith, *Grant,* chap. 18. See Trelease, *White Terror,* chap. 25, for further description of impact and of Grant's keen interest in and concern about southern violence.

34. For conflicting accounts of the case, see Lou Falkner Williams, *The Great South Carolina Ku Klux Klan Trials, 1871–1872* (Athens: University of Georgia Press, 1996), pp. 61–74; Kaczorowski, *Politics of Judicial Interpretation,* pp. 123–129. See, however, Smith, *Civic Ideals,* pp. 588–589n114. For the trial record, see United States Congress, Joint Select Committee on the Condition of Affairs in the Late Insurrectionary States, *Testimony Taken by the Joint Select Committee to Inquire into the Condition of Affairs in the Late Insurrectionary States—*

South Carolina (Washington, D.C.: Government Printing Office, 1872), 3:1615–1645; quotations are on 3:1641.

35. *Testimony Taken by the Joint Select Committe,* 3:1644; see 3:1643–1645 for the opinion of the court.

36. Two technical legal issues stand out in the secondary literature and in several of the relevant judicial opinions of the period, one having to do with indictments and the other with criminal sentencing. Kaczorowski, Swinney, and Williams all stress how deeply puzzled the attorney general and the U.S. attorneys in the South were about how to draft criminal indictments and the ensuing experimentation in the drafting of indictments. Federal judges and the Supreme Court also focused regularly on the supposedly defective nature of the federal indictments, for instance, in *United States v. Crosby* (discussed above) and *United States v. Cruikshank* (discussed below.) See Kaczorowski, *Politics of Judicial Interpretation,* pp. 118–129, 176–177; Swinney, *Suppressing the Ku Klux Klan,* pp. 262–263; Williams, *Great South Carolina Ku Klux Klan Trials,* pp. 62–66, 69–71, 74–75. Also, the enforcement statutes did not enact a criminal code—but what then were the appropriate sentences for crimes specified by the enforcement statutes? Apparently, the schedule of punishments prescribed in any particular state seemed to be the answer. But how could the particular punishment for, say, assault be meted out for infraction of civil and political rights via conspiracy if there was no proper conviction for assault and only a conviction for conspiracy? And should proper conviction occur in a federal or a state court? These were indeed serious weaknesses in the enforcement statutes. See Kaczorowski, *Politics of Judicial Interpretation,* pp. 118–122.

37. Justice Joseph Bradley to the Hon. William B. Woods, 30 January 1871, Joseph Bradley Papers, Manuscript Group 26, box 3, folder labeled "Correspondence 1870–1874," New Jersey Historical Society, Newark, N.J.

38. Although the story of the *Slaughterhouse Cases* in the Supreme Court is well known and told often, its story in the Fifth Circuit is not. See Kaczorowski, *Politics of Judicial Interpretation,* pp. 143–149; Ruth Whiteside, "Justice Joseph Bradley and the Reconstruction Amendments," Ph.D. diss., Rice University, 1981, pp. 147–172.

39. Whiteside, "Justice Joseph Bradley," p. 167; see pp. 172–182 and Kaczorowski, *Politics of Judicial Interpretation,* pp. 14–17, discussing the remarkable holding in *United States v. Hall,* 26 Fed. Cases 79 (1871).

40. This is an oft-told story. Recent stimulating treatments are Ronald M. Labbé and Jonathan Lurie, *The Slaughterhouse Cases: Regulation, Reconstruction, and the Fourteenth Amendment* (Lawrence: University Press of Kansas, 2003), and Michael A. Ross, *Justice of Shattered Dreams: Samuel Freeman Miller and the Supreme Court during the Civil War Era* (Baton Rouge: Louisiana State University Press, 2003), chap. 8.

41. The "critical moment" view was first clearly suggested to me by J. Morgan Kousser, "The Voting Rights Act and the Two Reconstructions," in *Controversies in Minority Voting: The Voting Rights Act in Perspective,* ed. Bernard Grofman and Chandler Davidson, pp. 135–176 (Washington, D.C.: Brookings Institution, 1992).

42. In later years, the author of the opinion, Justice Samuel Miller, came—with no small degree of self-satisfaction—to see the *Slaughterhouse Cases* as the single most important decision of the Reconstruction era. See "An Address Delivered before the Alumni of the Law Department of the University of Michigan, on the Supreme Court of the United States, at the Semi-centennial Celebration of the University, June 29th, 1887," in *The Constitution and the Supreme Court of the United States of America: Addresses by the Hon. Samuel F. Miller* (New York: D. Appleton, n.d.), pp. 62–65. For texts of the opinions see 83 U.S. (16. Wall.) 36 (1873). I used *United States Supreme Court Reports Vols. 82, 83, 84, 85 [Embracing All Opinions in 15, 16, 17*

and 18 Wallace, With Others,] Cases Argued and Decided in the Supreme Court of the United States in the December Term, 1872, and October Term, 1873, ed. Stephen K. Williams (Newark, N.Y.: Lawyer's Cooperative, 1884).

43. For valuable background, see Kelly, "Comment on Harold M. Hyman's Paper," pp. 42–47. On Miller's jurisprudence more generally, see Charles Fairman, *Mr. Justice Miller and the Supreme Court, 1862–1890* (Cambridge: Harvard University Press, 1939), esp. chaps. 6, 8.

44. For criticism, see Richard L. Aynes, "Constricting the Law of Freedom: Justice Miller, the Fourteenth Amendment, and the *Slaughter-House Cases," Chicago-Kent Law Review* (Symposium on the Law of Freedom: Part I) 70:2 (1994): 627–688.

45. The best brief discussion is Robert M. Goldman, *Reconstruction and Suffrage: Losing the Vote in Reese and Cruikshank* (Lawrence: University Press of Kansas, 2001), pp. 42–51. See also Joe Gray Taylor, *Louisiana Reconstructed, 1863–1877* (Baton Rouge: Louisiana State University Press, 1974), pp. 267–277; Ted Tunnell, *Crucible of Reconstruction: War, Radicalism, and Race in Louisiana, 1862–1877* (Baton Rouge: Louisiana State University Press, 1984), pp. 189–193. For background to the black militia movement in Grant Parish, see Rebecca J. Scott, "'Stubborn and Disposed to Stand Their Ground': Black Militia, Sugar Workers, and the Dynamics of Collective Action in the Louisiana Sugar Bowl, 1863–87," *Slavery and Abolition* 20 (April 1999): 103–126.

46. See Kaczorowski, *Politics of Judicial Interpretation,* pp. 175–179; Whiteside, "Justice Joseph Bradley," pp. 204–223.

47. Whiteside, "Justice Joseph Bradley," p. 217. See Michael Les Benedict, "Preserving Federalism: Reconstruction and the Waite Court," *Supreme Court Review* (1978): 39–80, esp. pp. 68–72; Kaczorowski, *Politics of Judicial Interpretation,* pp. 179–184; Whiteside, "Justice Joseph Bradley," pp. 211–223.

48. Entries for July 3 and July 4, 1874, 1874 Diary, box 2, folder 8, Joseph Bradley Papers, New Jersey Historical Society, Newark, N.J.

49. Smith, *Civic Ideals,* pp. 334–335.

50. Kaczorowski, *Politics of Judicial Interpretation,* p. 184.

51. On Martin Delany, see Nell Irvin Painter, "Martin R. Delany: Elitism and Black Nationalism," in *Black Leaders in the Nineteenth Century,* ed. Leon Litwack and August Meier, 149–172 (Urbana: University of Illinois Press, 1988).

52. On Louisiana, see Taylor, *Louisiana Reconstructed,* pp. 274–302. On Mississippi, see Current, *Those Terrible Carpetbaggers,* chap. 15; Harris, *Day of the Carpetbagger,* chaps. 19–21; McFeely, *Grant,* pp. 418–425; Mark W. Summers, *The Press Gang: Newspapers and Politics, 1865–1878* (Chapel Hill: University of North Carolina Press, 1994), chap. 11. On South Carolina, see Current, *Those Terrible Carpetbaggers,* chap. 16 and pp. 349–355; William C. Hine, "Frustration, Factionalism, and Failure: Black Political Leadership and the Republican Party in Reconstruction Charleston, 1865–1877," Ph.D. diss., Kent State University, 1979, chap. 12; Williams, *Great South Carolina Ku Klux Klan Trials,* pp. 125–130. See also Perman, *Road to Redemption,* chap. 7; Otis A. Singletary, *Negro Militia and Reconstruction* (Austin: University of Texas Press, 1957), chap. 9. A well-executed overview adding several new details and emphasizing the scope and intensity of violence is Rable, *But There Was No Peace,* chs. 8–10.

53. Taylor, *Louisiana Reconstructed,* pp. 291–310, 480–489. See also Lawrence N. Powell, "Reinventing Tradition: Liberty Place, Historical Memory, and Silk-Stocking Vigilantism in New Orleans Politics," *Slavery and Abolition* 20 (April 1999): 127–149.

54. See Kaczorowski, *Politics of Judicial Interpretation,* pp. 188–193, for high-level judicial paralysis. On Attorney General George Williams, who succeeded the very able Amos Akerman,

see Kaczorowski, chap. 5; Swinney, *Suppressing the Ku Klux Klan*, pp. 182–183; Sidney Teiser, "Life of George H. Williams: Almost Chief Justice [Part Two]," *Oregon Historical Quarterly* 47 (December 1946): 417–470.

55. Richard N. Current, "President Grant and the Continuing Civil War," in *Ulysses S. Grant: Essays and Documents,* ed. David L. Wilson and John Y. Simon, pp. 1–8 (Carbondale: Southern Illinois University Press for the Ulysses S. Grant Association, 1981). For a first-hand account, see A. T. Morgan, *Yazoo; Or, On the Picket Line of Freedom in the South* (Washington, D.C.: A. T. Morgan, 1884), chaps. 66–69.

56. See William Gillette, "Anatomy of a Failure: Federal Enforcement of the Right to Vote in the Border States during Reconstruction," in *Radicalism, Racism, and Party Realignment: The Border States during Reconstruction,* ed. Richard O. Curry, pp. 265–304 (Baltimore: Johns Hopkins University Press, 1969), esp. pp. 286–289.

57. See *United States v. Hiram Reese and Matthew Foushee,* 92 U.S. 214 (1876). I used *United States Supreme Court Reports Vols. 90, 91, 92, 93 (Embracing all Opinions in 23 Wallace and 1, 2, and 3 Otto, With Others), Cases Argued and Decided in the Supreme Court of the United States in the October Terms, 1874, 1875, 1876,* ed. Stephen K. Williams (Newark, N.Y.: Lawyers' Cooperative, 1885), pp. 563–579; for Justice Waite's emphasis on the section 2 phrase "appropriate legislation," see pp. 564–565. See also C. Peter Magrath, *Morrison R. Waite: The Triumph of Character* (New York: Macmillan, 1963), chap. 7, for background and discussion of *Reese* and *Cruikshank.*

58. *Cruikshank,* 92 U.S. 542, 556 (1876).

59. *Reese,* 92 U.S. 214, 217–218 (1876) (emphasis added). Note, though, that the passage begins, "The Fifteenth Amendment does not confer the right of suffrage upon any one."

60. James Lowell Underwood, *The Constitution of South Carolina,* vol. 4: *The Struggle for Political Equality* (Columbia: University of South Carolina Press, 1994), p. 72. See also Benedict, "Preserving Federalism," pp. 72–75. Finally, note that in his veto message of April 29, 1879, returning a bill that a Democratic-controlled Forty-sixth Congress had passed that altered the enforcement legislation, Hayes wrote, "The Supreme Court has held that this amendment [the Fifteenth] invests the citizens of the United States with a new constitutional right which is within the protecting power of Congress. That right the court declares to be exemption from discrimination in the exercise of the elective franchise on account of race, color, or previous condition of servitude. The power of Congress to protect this right by appropriate legislation *is expressly affirmed by the court*" (emphasis added). Quoted in James D. Richardson, comp., *A Compilation of the Messages and Papers of the Presidents, 1789–1897* (n.p: Published by Authority of Congress, 1899), 7:527.

61. *Slaughterhouse Cases,* 83 U.S. 36, 123, 124 (1873) (Bradley, J., dissenting). See also Robert J. Kaczorowski, "The Chase Court and Fundamental Rights: A Watershed in American Constitutionalism," *Northern Kentucky Law Review* 21 (Fall 1993): 151–191.

62. On troop deployment, see Current, *Those Terrible Carpetbaggers,* p. 355; Taylor, *Louisiana Reconstructed,* p. 485; and John Robert Kirkland, "Federal Troops in the South Atlantic States during Reconstruction, 1865–1877," Ph.D. diss., University of North Carolina, Chapel Hill, 1967, pp. 261–271. On the deployment of marshals, see Keith Ian Polakoff, *The Politics of Inertia: The Election of 1876 and the End of Reconstruction* (Baton Rouge: Louisiana State University Press, 1973), pp. 197–198. See also Ari Hoogenboom, *The Presidency of Rutherford B. Hayes,* American Presidency Series (Lawrence: University Press of Kansas, 1988), pp. 25–69. Deployment of marshals was done pursuant to the terms of the Second Enforcement Act of February 28, 1871 and facilitated by a controversial ruling by the attorney general that the act permitted the hiring and deployment of *general* deputy marshals, in contrast to its specific dis-

allowance of *special* deputy marshals. I thank Scott James for pointing this out to me. The quotation from Attorney General Taft's circular is in Robert Anderson Horn, "National Control of Congressional Elections," Ph.D. diss., Princeton University, 1942, p. 203, emphasis in original.

63. Frederick Douglass, "Looking the Republican Party Squarely in the Face: An Address Delivered in Cincinnati, Ohio on 14 June 1876," in *The Frederick Douglass Papers,* ser. 1, Speeches, Debates, and Interviews, vol. 4, *1864–80,* ed. John W. Blassingame and John R. McKivigan, pp. 440–442 (New Haven: Yale University Press, 1991).

Chapter Six

1. Sarah A. Binder and Steven S. Smith, *Politics or Principle? Filibustering in the United States Senate* (Washington, D.C.: Brookings Institution Press, 1997), pp. 129–135; Robert Anderson Horn, "National Control of Congressional Elections," Ph.D. diss., Princeton University, 1942, pp. 254–281.

2. A very fine new analysis is Michael Perman, *Struggle for Mastery: Disfranchisement in the South, 1888–1908* (Chapel Hill: University of North Carolina Press, 2001).

3. Delaware's program, begun in the early 1870s, was actually the first of the post–Civil War legal disenfranchisements. See Amy Hiller, "The Disfranchisement of Delaware Negroes in the Late Nineteenth Century," *Delaware History* 13 (October 1968): 124–154. On Oklahoma, see *Lane v. Wilson,* 307 U.S. 268 (1939); Jimmie Lewis Franklin, *Journey Toward Hope: A History of Blacks in Oklahoma* (Norman: University of Oklahoma Press, 1982).

4. Quoted in James Lowell Underwood, *The Constitution of South Carolina,* vol. 4, *The Struggle for Political Equality* (Columbia: University of South Carolina Press, 1994), p. 85.

5. David E. Kyvig, *Explicit and Authentic Acts: Amending the U.S. Constitution, 1776–1995* (Lawrence: University Press of Kansas, 1996), pp. 178–182; Mary J. Farmer and Donald G. Nieman, "Race, Class, Gender, and the Unintended Consequences of the Fifteenth Amendment," in *Unintended Consequences of Constitutional Amendment,* ed. David E. Kyvig, pp. 141–163 (Athens: University of Georgia Press, 2000), esp. pp. 142–145.

6. See Jack L. Walker, "The Diffusion of Innovations among the American States," *American Political Science Review* 63 (September 1969): 880–899. For details, see C. Vann Woodward, *The Origins of the New South, 1877–1913,* A History of the South, vol. 9 (1951; reprint, Baton Rouge: Louisiana State University Press and the Littlefield Fund for Southern History, The University of Texas, 1971), pp. 332–335; J. Morgan Kousser, *The Shaping of Southern Politics: Suffrage Restriction and the Establishment of the One-Party South, 1880–1910* (New Haven: Yale University Press, 1974), p. 132, describing Black Belt Democrats in Alabama debating whether to adopt the Tennessee route or the Mississippi route, and p. 67, describing testimony of a Mississippi expert at the Louisiana disenfranchising constitutional convention; Underwood, *Constitution of South Carolina,* p. 68, describing attention in South Carolina to the Mississippi plan; Craig Martin Thurtell, "The Fusion Insurgency in North Carolina: Origins to Ascendancy, 1876–1896," Ph.D. diss., Columbia University, 1998, p. 322, regarding the trip to Louisiana by Josephus Daniels to study its system of black disenfranchisement; and Helen G. Edmonds, *The Negro and Fusion Politics in North Carolina, 1894–1901* (Chapel Hill: University of North Carolina Press, 1951), p. 200, on the electoral campaign uses of Daniels's glowing report of the supposedly positive effects of disenfranchisement in Louisiana.

7. See Margaret Law Callcott, *The Negro in Maryland Politics, 1870–1912* (Baltimore: Johns Hopkins University Press, 1969), chaps. 4–5.

8. Peter D. Klingman, *Neither Dies Nor Surrenders: A History of the Republican Party in Florida, 1867–1970* (Gainesville: University Presses of Florida; University of Florida Press,

1984), pp. 95–99; H. D. Price, *The Negro and Southern Politics: A Chapter of Florida History* (New York: New York University Press, 1957), pp. 13–15. But see Perman, *Struggle for Mastery*, pp. 67–68, claiming Florida was not typical.

9. See Robert Higgs, *Competition and Coercion: Blacks in the American Economy, 1865–1914*, Hoover Institution Publication P 163 (Cambridge: Cambridge University Press, 1977), p. 64, table 4.2, calculation based on the unweighted average for the region and the Border States for ordinary labor for black workers listed in that table. The day rate, $.74, is multiplied by 260 (52 weeks/year × 5) to arrive at about $192 annual income; $1 as a percentage of $192 is .5 percent. The $135 estimate is the average of two calculations available from Samuel H. Williamson, "What Is the Relative Value?" Economic History Series, April 23 2002, http://www.eh.net/hmit/compare/—one for a dollar translated into unskilled wage in 2001 and another translated into GDP per capita. See also United States Bureau of the Census, Current Population Reports, P60-209, *Money Income in the United States: 1999* (Washington, D.C.: Government Printing Office, 2000), pp. vii–viii, and Kousser, *Shaping of Southern Politics*, pp. 64–65 for similar estimates.

10. See Woodward, *Origins of the New South*, pp. 333–334, discussing debates about just this issue.

11. See Norman Ornstein, "The Risky Rise of Absentee Voting," *Washington Post*, 26 November 2000, Sunday Outlook sec.; L. E. Fredman, *The Australian Ballot: The Story of an American Reform* (n.p.: Michigan State University Press, 1968). See also Alan Ware, "Anti-Partism and Party Control of Political Reform in the United States: The Case of the Australian Ballot," *British Journal of Political Science* 30 (January 2000): 1–30.

12. Party-strip balloting is well discussed in Arnaldo Testi, "The Construction and Deconstruction of the U.S. Electorate in the Age of Manhood Suffrage, 1830s–1920s," in *How Did They Become Voters? The History of Franchise in Modern European Representation*, ed. Raffaele Romanelli, pp. 387–414, at p. 404 (The Hague: Kluwer Law International, 1998).

13. Richard L. Niswonger, *Arkansas Democratic Politics, 1896–1920* (Fayetteville: University of Arkansas Press, 1990), p. 18. See also Joseph H. Cartwright, *The Triumph of Jim Crow: Tennessee Race Relations in the 1880s* (Knoxville: University of Tennessee Press, 1976), pp. 217–218.

14. The formalization-of-defeat thesis was first articulated by V. O. Key Jr. in *Southern Politics in State and Nation* (1949; reprint, Knoxville: University of Tennessee Press, 1984), chap. 25. In response to what Key called his "fait accompli" view, the independent role of rules changes was stressed by Kousser, *Shaping of Southern Politics*, and Jerrold G. Rusk and John J. Stucker, "The Effect of the Southern System of Election Laws on Voting Participation: A Reply to V. O. Key, Jr.," in *The History of American Electoral Behavior*, ed. Joel H. Silbey, Allan G. Bogue, and William H. Flanigan, pp. 198–250 (Princeton: Princeton University Press, 1978).

15. Kent Redding and David R. James, "Estimating Levels and Modeling Determinants of Black and White Voter Turnout in the South: 1880 to 1912," *Historical Methods* 34.4 (2001): 141–158.

16. Kent Redding, *Making Race, Making Power: North Carolina's Road to Disfranchisement* (Urbana: University of Illinois Press, 2003), chap. 1.

17. Underwood, *Constitution of South Carolina*, pp. 40–41, quoting Judge Goff in *Mills v. Green* (1894); Joseph P. Harris, *Registration of Voters in the United States* (Washington, D.C.: Brookings Institution, 1929), p. 157n24. The Mississippi convention delegate is quoted in Edward L. Ayers, *The Promise of the New South: Life after Reconstruction* (New York: Oxford University Press, 1992), p. 149.

18. Kousser discusses the relative efficiency of the new rules in *Shaping of Southern Politics*. Also, on the inefficacy of white-on-black violence, see J. Morgan Kousser, *Colorblind Injustice: Minority Voting Rights and the Undoing of the Second Reconstruction* (Chapel Hill: University of North Carolina Press, 1999), pp. 23–25.

19. House Rep. No. 18, 53d Cong., 1st sess., 1893, "Repeal of Federal Election Laws," at p. 7 (in C.I.S. Serial Set 3157), also quoted by Justice Douglass in his dissent to the opinion for the court in *United States v. Classic*, 313 U.S. 299, 335 (1941); Xi Wang, *The Trial of Democracy: Black Suffrage and Northern Republicans, 1860–1910* (Athens: University of Georgia Press, 1997), pp. 294–299.

20. The considerable literature on North Carolina includes Redding, *Making Race, Making Power*; Thurtell, "Fusion Insurgency in North Carolina"; H. Leon Prather Sr., *We Have Taken a City: Wilmington Racial Massacre and Coup of 1898* (Rutherford, N.J.: Farleigh Dickinson University Press, 1984); Jeffrey J. Crow and Robert F. Durden, *Maverick Republican in the Old North State: A Political Biography of Daniel L. Russell* (Baton Rouge: Lousiana State University Press, 1977), esp. pp. 134–135; Edmonds, *The Negro and Fusion Politics in North Carolina*; and Glenda Elizabeth Gilmore, *Gender and Jim Crow: Women and the Politics of White Supremacy in North Carolina, 1896–1920* (Chapel Hill: University of North Carolina Press, 1996), chap. 4. On White, Butler, and Pritchard, see Richard B. Sherman, *The Republican Party and Black America: From McKinley to Hoover, 1896–1933* (Charlottesville: University Press of Virginia, 1973), pp. 16–17.

21. On McKinley, see Lewis L. Gould, *The Presidency of William McKinley* (Lawrence: Regents Press of Kansas, 1980), pp. 28–29, 153–160; Sherman, *Republican Party*, pp. 3–19. On Roosevelt, see Lewis L. Gould, *The Presidency of Theodore Roosevelt* (Lawrence: University Press of Kansas, 1991), pp. 22–23, 118–122, 236–244; and Sherman, ibid., chaps. 2–3, esp. pp. 77, 81; Horace Samuel Merrill and Marion Galbraith Merrill, *The Republican Command, 1897–1913* (Lexington: University Press of Kentucky, 1971), pp. 177–178, 183, 236, 239–241. On Taft, see Merrill and Merrill, ibid., pp. 275, 314–315; and Sherman, ibid, chap. 4 and pp. 84, 88.

22. United States Congress, *Congressional Record*, 57th Cong., 2d sess., vol. 34, pp. 517, 553, 3182–3183; and, Sherman, *Republican Party*, p. 75.

23. Merrill and Merrill, *Republican Command*, p. 177 (see also p. 176). See Sherman, *Republican Party*, pp. 49, 75–77.

24. The speech can be found at www.yale.edu/lawweb/avalon/presiden/inaug/taft.htm. The emphasis is mine.

25. Kyvig, *Explicit and Authentic Acts*, pp. 208–212; Claudius O. Johnson, *Borah of Idaho* (New York: Longmans, Green, 1936), pp. 124–128; C. H. Hoebeke, *The Road to Mass Democracy: Original Intent and the Seventeenth Amendment* (New Brunswick, N.J.: Transaction, 1995), pp. 161–164.

26. Kyvig, *Explicit and Authentic Acts*, pp. 212–213.

27. House Rep. No. 18, 53d Cong., 1st sess., 1893, "Repeal of Federal Election Laws," p. 7 (in C.I.S. Serial Set 3157), also quoted by Justice Douglass in his dissent to the opinion for the court in *United States v. Classic*, 313 U.S. 299, 335 (1941); J. W. Anderson, *Eisenhower, Brownell, and the Congress: The Tangled Origins of the Civil Rights Bill of 1956–1957* (University: University of Alabama Press, for the Inter-University Case Program, 1964), p. 7, discussing the 1909 codification; Wang, *Trial of Democracy*, pp. 294–299.

28. Calculations are my own; the assumption for Senate was that a 50–50 split was adequate for control given the tie-breaking power of the vice president.

29. Richard Valelly, "National Parties and Racial Disenfranchisement," in *Classifying by Race*, ed. Paul E. Peterson, pp. 188–216 (Princeton: Princeton University Press, 1995), 207.

30. For a brief sketch of the background and of the actual events, see Howard Roberts Lamar, *The Far Southwest, 1846–1912,* rev. ed. (1966; reprint, Albuquerque: University of New Mexico Press, 2000), introduction, esp. pp. 10–13. See also Charles Stewart III and Barry R. Weingast, "Stacking the Senate, Changing the Nation: Republican Rotten Boroughs, Statehood Politics, and American Political Development," *Studies in American Political Development* 6 (Fall 1992): 223–271.

31. Because of his position on the Committee on Territories, I read the papers of Senator Oliver Platt at the Connecticut Historical Society but found literally nothing in them about territorial policy. *Congressional Quarterly's Guide to U.S. Elections,* 2d ed. (Washington, D.C.: Congressional Quarterly, Inc., 1985), pp. 579–606, 838–867.

32. "President Chester A. Arthur," Address by William E. Chandler at Fairfield, Vermont on August 19, 1903, on the Occasion of the Completion by the State of Vermont of a Monument and Tablet to Mark the Birthplace of President Chester A. Arthur (Concord, N.H.: Rumford Printing Co., 1903), pp. 35–37. On Chandler's knowledge of and involvement in southern politics, see Leon Burr Richardson, *William E. Chandler Republican* (New York: Dodd, Mead, 1940), pp. 76–82, 113–115, 158–160, 168–173. On Chandler's experience in presidential campaigns, see Keith Ian Polakoff, *Politics of Inertia: The Election of 1876 and the End of Reconstruction* (Baton Rouge: Louisiana State University Press, 1973), pp. 97–98, 100, 139, 157–158; Richardson, ibid., chaps. 5 and 7 and pp. 180–183. On Chandler's role in 1877, see Polakoff, ibid., pp. 201–210, 215–216.

33. *Mills v. Green,* 159 U.S. 651 (1895).

34. *Williams v. Mississippi,* 170 U.S. 213 (1898). See Kousser, *Colorblind Injustice,* pp. 319–323.

35. *Giles v. Harris,* 189 U.S. 475, 488 (1903).

36. *James v. Bowman,* 190 U.S. 127 (1903).

37. *Giles v. Teasley,* 193 U.S. 146 (1904). On Giles and his efforts, see Louis R. Harlan, *Booker T. Washington: The Wizard of Tuskegee, 1901–1915* (New York: Oxford University Press, 1983), pp. 245–247. Giles eventually lost his job with the postal service for his pains.

38. *Jones v. Montague,* 194 U.S. 147 (1904). For the background to this case, see Andrew Buni, *The Negro in Virginia Politics, 1902–1965* (Charlottesville: University Press of Virginia, 1967), chap. 3.

39. Quoted in *Guinn and Beal v. United States,* 238 U.S. 347, 357 (1915).

40. Ibid. The case began during the Taft administration, when the United States arrested "two Oklahoma elections officials for refusing to allow a group of blacks to vote in the congressional elections of 1910," and was prosecuted during the Wilson administration. William H. Harbaugh, *Lawyer's Lawyer: The Life of John W. Davis* (New York: Oxford University Press, 1973), pp. 93–96; the quotation is on p. 94. For the broader impact, see Jerrold G. Rusk, *A Statistical History of the American Electorate* (Washington: Congressional Quarterly, 2001), p. 35, table 2-18.

41. These facts are laid out in *Lane v. Wilson,* 307 U.S. 268 (1939).

42. Quoted in Buni, *Negro in Virginia Politics,* p. 47.

43. See Benjamin Quarles, "Frederick Douglass and the Woman's Rights Movement," *Journal of Negro History* 25 (January 1940): 35–44. Also see Jean H. Baker, "Defining Postwar Republicanism: Congressional Republicans and the Boundaries of Citizenship," in *The Birth of the Grand Old Party: The Republicans' First Generation,* ed. Robert F. Engs and Randall M. Miller, pp. 128–147 (Philadelphia: University of Pennsylvania Press, Published in Cooperation with the Library Company of Philadelphia, 2002).

44. Marjorie Julian Spruill, "Race, Reform, and Reaction at the Turn of the Century: Southern Suffragists, the NAWSA, and the 'Southern Strategy' in Context," in *Votes for Women: The Struggle for Suffrage Revisited,* ed. Jean H. Baker, pp. 102–117 (New York: Oxford University Press, 2002), p. 104.

45. Rosalyn Terborg-Penn, "Discontented Black Feminists: Prelude and Postscript to the Passage of the Nineteenth Amendment," in *Decades of Discontent: The Women's Movement, 1920–1940,* ed. Lois Scharf and Joan M. Jensen, pp. 261–278, Contributions in Women's Studies, no. 28 (Westport: Greenwood, 1983); Terborg-Penn, "Discrimination against Afro-American Women in the Woman's Movement, 1830–1920," in *The Afro-American Woman: Struggles and Images,* ed. Sharon Harley and Rosalyn Terborg-Penn, pp. 17–27 (1978; reprint, Baltimore: Black Classic Press, 1997). See also Darlene Clark Hine and Christie Anne Farnham, "Black Women's Culture of Resistance and the Right to Vote," in *Women of the American South: A Multicultural Reader,* ed. Christie Anne Farnham, pp. 204–219 (New York: New York University Press, 1997). On the 1926 incident in Birmingham, see Robin D. G. Kelley, *Hammer and Hoe: Alabama Communists during the Great Depression,* Fred W. Morrison Series in Southern Studies (Chapel Hill: University of North Carolina Press, 1990), p. 9.

46. See Kousser, *Shaping of Southern Politics*; Key, *Southern Politics;* and Earl Black and Merle Black, *Politics and Society in the South* (Cambridge: Harvard University Press, 1987), for consequences for ordinary whites' participation.

47. For recent scholarship, see W. Fitzhugh Brundage, ed., *Under Sentence of Death: Lynching in the South* (Chapel Hill: University of North Carolina Press, 1997). Ida Wells-Barnett is quoted in Harold F. Gosnell, *Negro Politicians: The Rise of Negro Politics in Chicago* (Chicago: University of Chicago Press, 1935), p. 26 (from her pamphlet "How Enfranchisement Stops Lynching").

48. See Thomas G. Dyer, *Theodore Roosevelt and the Idea of Race* (Baton Rouge: Louisiana State University Press, 1980), pp. 113–114.

49. E. M. Beck and Stewart E. Tolnay, "When Race Didn't Matter: Black and White Mob Violence against Their Own Color," in *Under Sentence of Death: Lynching in the South,* ed. W. Fitzhugh Brundage, pp. 132–154 (Chapel Hill: University of North Carolina Press, 1997), figure 1-A, p. 134. On how lynching literally became mass entertainment, fed by telephone, railroads, and mass-circulation newspapers, see Grace Elizabeth Hale, *Making Whiteness: The Culture of Segregation in the South, 1890–1940* (New York: Pantheon, 1998), chap. 5. Also essential (and profoundly shocking) is James Allen, Hilton Als, John Lewis, and Leon F. Litwack, *Without Sanctuary: Lynching Photography in America* (Santa Fe: Twin Palms, 2000), especially the essay by Litwack, "Hellhounds," pp. 8–37.

50. On the underlying logic of labor segregation see Edna Bonacich, "A Theory of Ethnic Antagonism: The Split Labor Market," *American Sociological Review* 37 (October 1972): 547–559.

51. Michael Jones-Correa, "The Origins and Diffusion of Racial Restrictive Covenanting," *Political Science Quarterly* 115 (Winter 2000–2001): 541–568.

52. For an introduction to the terms of congressional debate about segregation, see Howard W. Allen, Aage R. Clausen, and Jerome M. Clubb, "Political Reform and Negro Rights in the Senate, 1909–1915," *Journal of Southern History* 37 (May 1971): 191–212. For a complete survey of legal practices, see Pauli Murray, comp. and ed., *States' Laws on Race and Color* (1951; reprint, Athens: University of Georgia Press, 1997).

53. See Hale, *Making Whiteness,* pp. 128–138.

54. See Gordon Canfield Lee, *The Struggle for Federal Aid, First Phase: A History of the Attempts to Obtain Federal Aid for the Common Schools, 1870–1890* (New York: Bureau of

Publications, Teachers College, Columbia University, 1949). On amendment of the Morrill Act, see Edward McPherson, *Hand-Book of Politics IV: 1890–1894* (1890; reprint, New York: Da Capo, 1972), pp. 194–195.

55. See Robert A. Margo, *Race and Schooling in the South, 1880–1950: An Economic History* (Chicago: University of Chicago Press, 1990); J. Morgan Kousser, "Progressivism—for Middle-Class Whites Only," *Journal of Southern History* 46 (1980): 169–194.

56. William Ivy Hair, *Bourbonism and Agrarian Protest—Louisiana Politics, 1877–1900* (Baton Rouge: Louisiana State University Press, 1969), p. 127.

57. Desmond King, *Separate and Unequal: Black Americans and the US Federal Government* (New York: Oxford University Press, 1995), chaps. 1–2. See also Kathleen L. Wolgemuth, "Woodrow Wilson and Federal Segregation," *Journal of Negro History* 44 (April 1959): 158–173.

58. See Elaine K. Swift, Brian D. Humes, Richard Valelly, Kenneth Finegold, and Evelyn C. Fink, "The Overrepresentation of the South in Congress: Measuring the Impact of the Three-Fifths Clause and the Fourteenth Amendment," at http://mccubbins.ucsd.edu/mcbrady.pdf.

59. Quoted in Douglas Price, "Careers and Committees in the American Congress: The Problem of Structural Change," in *The History of Parliamentary Behavior*, ed. William O. Aydelotte, pp. 39–40 (Princeton: Princeton University Press for the Center for Advanced Study in the Behavioral Sciences, Stanford, Calif., 1977). See also David R. Mayhew, *America's Congress: Actions in the Public Sphere, James Madison through Newt Gingrich* (New Haven: Yale University Press, 2000), pp. 181–183, on the southern "action bonus."

60. Compare Gareth Davies and Martha Derthick, "Race and Social WelfarePolicy: The Social Security Act of 1935," *Political Science Quarterly* 112 (Summer 1997): 217–235. See also Michael J. Klarman, "The Puzzling Resistance to Political Process Theory," *Virginia Law Review* 77 (May 1991): 747–832.

61. Gunnar Myrdal, *An American Dilemma: The Negro Problem and Modern Democracy* (New York: Harper and Brothers, 1944).

Chapter Seven

1. An instructive parallel might be Chester Arthur's southern strategy. He too wanted a second term. For that matter, Andrew Johnson provides useful contrast—though in his case he sought black demobilization rather than mobilization. Vice presidents thrust into office have, in short, been critical agents in the politics of black voting rights.

2. Here I have relied on Hanes Walton Jr., *Black Political Parties: A Historical and Political Analysis* (New York: Free Press, 1972), pp. 80–82.

3. Stewart E. Tolnay and E. M. Beck, "Rethinking the Role of Racial Violence in the Great Migration," in *Black Exodus: The Great Migration from the American South*, ed. Alferdteen Harrison, pp. 20–35, at p. 20 (Jackson: University Press of Mississippi, 1991); Doug McAdam, *Political Process and the Development of Black Insurgency, 1930–1970* (Chicago: University of Chicago Press, 1982), p. 78, table 5.2. McAdam's figures are higher than those offered by Tolnay and Beck, probably because they are not adjusted to reflect *net* out-migration. See also William Cohen, *At Freedom's Edge: Black Mobility and the Southern White Quest for Racial Control, 1861–1915* (Baton Rouge: Louisiana State University Press, 1991), preface.

4. Lester C. Lamon, "Document: W.T. Andrews Explains the Causes of Black Migration from the South," *Journal of Negro History* 63 (Fall 1978): 365–372, at 366–367. See also Neil R. McMillen, *Dark Journey: Black Mississippians in the Age of Jim Crow* (Urbana: University of Illinois Press, 1989).

5. A. Philip Randolph: "As the Negro migrates North and West he secures political power to help himself in his new abode and at the same time to strike a blow for his less favored brothers in wicked 'old Dixie.' " "Migration and Political Power," editorial, *The Messenger*, July 1919, reprinted in *Civil Rights since 1787: A Reader on the Black Struggle*, ed. Jonathan Birnbaum and Clarence Taylor (New York: New York University Press, 2000), p. 267. Also see Ira Katznelson, *Black Men, White Cities: Race, Politics, and Migration in the United States, 1900–30, and Britain, 1948–68* (1973; reprint, Chicago: University of Chicago Press, 1976), chap. 6.

6. Harold F. Gosnell, *Negro Politicians: The Rise of Negro Politics in Chicago* (Chicago: University of Chicago Press, 1935), p. 19.

7. Ibid., pp. 193, 195.

8. See Scott C. James, *Presidents, Parties, and the State: A Party System Perspective on Democratic Regulatory Choice, 1884–1936* (New York: Cambridge University Press, 2000).

9. Nancy J. Weiss, *Farewell to the Party of Lincoln: Black Politics in the Age of FDR* (Princeton: Princeton University Press, 1983), pp. 36, 251.

10. Gunnar Myrdal, *An American Dilemma: The Negro Problem and Modern Democracy* (New York: Harper, 1944), pp. 256–259; Gavin Wright, *Old South, New South: Revolutions in the Southern Economy since the Civil War* (New York: Basic, 1986), pp. 226–229. (See, however, pp. 230–232 on the evolution of federal farm programs after the early implementation of the Agricultural Adjustment Act.) On housing, see Michael Jones-Correa, "The Origins and Diffusion of Racial Restrictive Covenanting," *Political Science Quarterly* 115 (Winter 2000–2001): 565–566.

11. Karen Ferguson, *Black Politics in New Deal Atlanta* (Chapel Hill: University of North Carolina Press, 2002), chap. 7.

12. See Kristi Andersen, *The Creation of a Democratic Majority, 1928–1936* (Chicago: University of Chicago Press, 1979), pp. 103–106; Andrew Buni, *Robert L. Vann of the Pittsburgh Courier* (Pittsburgh: University of Pittsburgh Press, 1974), pp. 193–194.

13. Weiss, *Farewell to the Party of Lincoln*, pp. 228–229 and chap. 10; Rita Werner Gordon, "The Change in the Political Alignment of Chicago's Negroes during the New Deal," *Journal of American History* 56 (December 1969): 584–603.

14. Ferguson, *Black Politics in New Deal Atlanta*; Hortense Powdermaker, *After Freedom: A Cultural Study in the Deep South* (1939; reprint, Madison: University of Wisconsin Press, 1993), pp. 51, 137–139; Ralph J. Bunche, *The Political Status of the Negro in the Age of FDR*, ed. and intro. Dewey W. Grantham, pp. 427–429, at p. 429 (Chicago: University of Chicago Press, 1973). I have somewhat standardized the quotation.

15. The best overall discussion is John Brueggeman, "Racial Considerations and Social Policy in the 1930s: Economic Change and Political Opportunities," *Social Science History* 26 (Spring 2002): 139–178. On political outreach, see Weiss, *Farewell to the Party of Lincoln*, chap. 9; Thomas T. Spencer, "The Good Neighbor League Colored Committee and the 1936 Democratic Presidential Campaign," *Journal of Negro History* 63 (Fall 1978): 307–316; Donald R. McCoy, "The Good Neighbor League and the Presidential Campaign of 1936," *Western Political Quarterly* 13 (December 1960): 1011–1021.

16. Richard L. Niswonger, *Arkansas Democratic Politics, 1896–1920* (Fayetteville: University of Arkansas Press, 1990), pp. 90–94.

17. Harold W. Stanley, "Runoff Primaries and Black Political Influence," in *Blacks in Southern Politics*, ed. Laurence W. Moreland, Robert P. Steed, and Tod A. Baker, pp. 259–276 (New York: Praeger, 1987), table 14.3, at p. 270.

18. It could, of course, be sealed using the tried-and-true informal means of repression and intimidation. But during the disenfranchisement process southern Democrats discussed how much they preferred legal barriers that could pass constitutional muster. Illegal and unconstitutional repression inevitably signaled that they were not masters of their situation. See Frederic D. Ogden, *The Poll Tax in the South* (University: University of Alabama Press, 1958), pp. 7–10.

19. *Newberry v. United States,* 256 U.S. 232 (1921). See O. Douglas Weeks, "The White Primary," *Mississippi Law Journal* 8 (December 1935): 135–153.

20. *Breedlove v. Suttles,* 302 U.S. 27 (1937).

21. My calculations are based on data in *Congressional Quarterly's Guide to U.S. Elections,* 2d ed. (Washington, D.C.: Congressional Quarterly, Inc., 1986).

22. See Samuel Issacharoff and Richard H. Pildes, "Politics as Markets: Partisan Lockups of the Democratic Process," *Stanford Law Review* 50 (February 1998): 643–718, esp. pp. 652–668.

23. The best single discussion of the white primary cases and their impact is Michael J. Klarman, "The White Primary Rulings: A Case Study in the Consequences of Supreme Court Decisionmaking," *Florida State University Law Review* 29 (Fall 2001): 55–107. Also very useful is James Lowell Underwood, *The Constitution of South Carolina,* vol. 4, *The Struggle for Political Equality* (Columbia: University of South Carolina Press, 1994), chap. 3.

24. *Smith v. Allwright,* 321 U.S. 649 (1944).

25. *Grovey v. Townsend,* 295 U.S. 45 (1935); H. D. Price, *The Negro and Southern Politics: A Chapter of Florida History* (New York: New York University Press, 1957), p. 26.

26. *United States v. Carolene Products Company,* 304 U.S. 144, 152 (1938); *Nixon v. Herndon,* 273 U.S. 536 (1927); *Nixon v. Condon,* 286 U.S. 73 (1932); G. Edward White, *The Constitution and the New Deal* (Cambridge: Harvard University Press, 2000), esp. chap. 5 and pp. 130–132 and 160–162. Because White assumes reader familiarity with the general view of the case's importance, see also, among others, William A. Wiecek, *Liberty under Law: The Supreme Court in American Life* (Baltimore: Johns Hopkins University Press, 1988), pp. 156–157, and Henry J. Abraham, *Freedom and the Court: Civil Rights and Liberties in the United States,* 4th ed. (New York: Oxford University Press, 1982), pp. 15–21.

27. Richard Claude, *The Supreme Court and the Electoral Process* (Baltimore: Johns Hopkins University Press, 1970), pp. 68–69; Darlene Clark Hine, *Black Victory: The Rise and Fall of the White Primary in Texas,* KTO Studies in American History (Millwood, N.Y.: KTO, 1979), chaps. 7–8.

28. White, *Constitution and the New Deal,* pp. 1–2, 315, nn. 2–3; Robert K. Carr, *Federal Protection of Civil Rights: Quest for a Sword* (Ithaca: Cornell University Press, 1947), p. 26: "The Murphy order must be viewed against a background of gradually increasing interest and activity in the civil liberties field, during the preceding decade, by agencies of the national government. First of all was the increased interest of the Supreme Court in fostering civil liberties, beginning in 1931 with the case of *Near v. Minnesota.*"

29. Carr, *Federal Protection of Civil Rights,* pp. 24–25.

30. *United States v. Classic,* 313 U.S. 299 (1941).

31. The chief justice, Charles Evans Hughes, did not participate because he had been one of the lawyers who argued *Newberry* before the Court when he was in private practice after he resigned his position as associate justice (after his first stint on the Court, 1910–1916). In any case, he soon planned to resign again. There was also a vacancy left by Justice McReynolds's resignation. Hence the 4–3 vote, Stone, Roberts, Reed, and Frankfurter, in order of seniority, versus Black, Douglas, and, ironically, Murphy. Helpful discussions are Carr,

Federal Protection of Civil Rights, pp. 85–94, and Claude, *Supreme Court and Electoral Process*, pp. 31–36.

32. Francis Biddle, *In Brief Authority* (Garden City: Doubleday, 1962), pp. 159, 187, which mistakenly asserts that *Classic* regained the right to vote for African Americans and says nothing about *Smith v. Allwright*.

33. Ibid, p. 160; see also p. 187.

34. *Smith v. Allwright,* 321 U.S. 649, 666 (1994). An excellent discussion of the case is Kevin J. McMahon, *Reconsidering Roosevelt on Race: How the Presidency Paved the Road to* Brown (Chicago: University of Chicago Press, 2004), pp. 150–155. For useful details concerning the memorandum phase of Justice Reed's opinion, see John D. Fassett, *New Deal Justice: The Life of Stanley Reed of Kentucky* (New York: Vantage, 1994), pp. 361–364.

35. Price, *Negro and Southern Politics*, pp. 27–28; Claude, *Supreme Court and the Electoral Process*, pp. 71–72; Charles D. Farris, "The Re-Enfranchisement of Negroes in Florida," *Journal of Negro History* 39 (October 1954): 259–283 (the number of statutes repealed in South Carolina is noted at p. 273).

36. William D. Barnard, *Dixiecrats and Democrats: Alabama Politics, 1942–1950* (University: University of Alabama Press, 1974), p. 64 (for Alabama); J. Morgan Kousser, *Colorblind Injustice: Minority Voting Rights and the Undoing of the Second Reconstruction* (Chapel Hill: University of North Carolina Press, 1999), p. 200 (for Georgia).

37. *Lane v. Wilson*, 307 U.S. 268 (1939); Klarman, "White Primary Rulings," pp. 66–69, 84–88; Adam Fairclough, *Race and Democracy: The Civil Rights Struggle in Louisiana, 1915–1972* (Athens: University of Georgia Press, 1995), pp. 104–105; *Terry v. Adams*, 345 U.S. 461 (1953).

38. Klarman, "White Primary Rulings," p. 88; Jack Irby Hayes Jr., *South Carolina and the New Deal* (Columbia: University of South Carolina Press, 2001), p. 180, quoting John McCray.

39. What Wallace would do if he ascended to the presidency was clear enough. He told the Chicago convention that "[t]the future belongs to those who go down the line unswervingly for . . . liberal democracy and economic democracy regardless of race, color, or religion. The poll tax must go. Equal education opportunities must come. The future must bring equal wages for equal work." Robert A. Garson, *The Democratic Party and the Politics of Sectionalism, 1941–1948* (Baton Rouge: Louisiana State University Press, 1974), p. 121.

40. Paula F. Pfeffer, *A. Philip Randolph, Pioneer of the Civil Rights Movement* (Baton Rouge: Louisiana State University Press, 1990), chaps. 2–3.

41. Steven F. Lawson, *Black Ballots: Voting Rights in the South, 1944–1969* (New York: Columbia University Press, 1976), chap. 3, Garson, *Democratic Party*, p. 45; see also pp. 42–52.

42. William C. Berman, *The Politics of Civil Rights in the Truman Administration* (Columbus: Ohio State University Press, 1970), pp. 79–82; Richard M. Dalfiume, *Desegregation of the U.S. Armed Forces—Fighting on Two Fronts, 1939–1953* (Columbia: University of Missouri Press, 1969), pp. 145–147; Gary A. Donaldson, *Truman Defeats Dewey* (Lexington: University Press of Kentucky, 1999), esp. chap. 1–2, 7–8, 13–15.

43. *To Secure These Rights: The Report of the President's Committee on Civil Rights* (New York: Simon and Schuster, 1947), p. vii.

44. McAdam, *Political Process*, pp. 103–104; Alexander Heard, *A Two-Party South?* (Chapel Hill: University of North Carolina Press, 1952), pp. 183–184; Klarman, "White Primary Rulings," pp. 76–77.

45. Garth E. Pauley, *The Modern Presidency and Civil Rights: Rhetoric on Race from Roosevelt to Nixon* (College Station: Texas A&M University Press, 2001), p. 42; Harry S. Truman,

"Address Before the National Association for the Advancement of Colored People. June 29, 1947." *Public Papers of the Presidents of the United States—Harry S. Truman—Containing the Public Messages, Speeches, and Statements of the President January 1 to December 31, 1947* (Washington, D.C.: Government Printing Office, 1963), pp. 311–313.

46. Pauley, *Modern Presidency and Civil Rights*, pp. 52–54. See also Donald R. Matthews and James W. Prothro, *Negroes and the New Southern Politics* (New York: Harcourt, Brace, and World, 1966), pp. 258–260.

47. Donaldson, *Truman Defeats Dewey*, pp. 26–27.

48. Robert A. Caro, "Annals of Politics: The Orator of the Dawn," *New Yorker*, 4 March 2002, pp. 46–63, at p. 50.

49. The States' Rights platform read, "We affirm that a political party is an instrumentality for effectuating the principles upon which the party is founded" and "that to act contrary to these principles is a breach of faith. . . . We direct attention to the fact that the first platform of the Democratic party, adopted in 1840, resolved that 'Congress has no power under the Constitution to interfere with or control the domestic institutions of the several states.' . . . Such pronouncement is the cornerstone of the Democratic Party. A long train of abuses and usurpations of power by unfaithful leaders who are alien to the Democratic parties of the states here represented has become intolerable." Donald Bruce Johnson and Kirk H. Porter, comps., *National Party Platforms, 1840–1972,* 5th ed. (Urbana: University of Illinois Press, 1973), pp. 466–467.

50. Kari Frederickson, *The Dixiecrat Revolt and the End of the Solid South, 1932–1968* (Chapel Hill: University of North Carolina Press, 2001), p. 140.

51. The Progressive platform charged the Truman administration with planning a third world war and with the abridgment of domestic civil liberties and accused "the old parties" of seeking to "impose a universal policy of Jim Crow and enforce it with every weapon of terror" and of treating the "move to outlaw the Communist Party as a decisive step in their assault on the democratic rights of labor, of national, racial, and political minorities, and of all those who oppose their drive to war." The flavor of this mindset, which was for a time an important part of U.S. race relations politics, is well captured in Patricia Sullivan's sensitive treatment, *Days of Hope: Race and Democracy in the New Deal Era* (Chapel Hill: University of North Carolina Press, 1996), chap. 8.

52. Robert J. Donovan, *Conflict and Crisis: The Presidency of Harry S. Truman, 1945–1948* (New York: Norton, 1977), p. 411; Dalfiume, *Desegregation of the U.S. Armed Forces*, pp. 170–174.

53. Frederickson, *Dixiecrat Revolt*, p. 182, citing a memorandum of August 17, 1948, in the Clark Clifford Papers, Harry S. Truman Presidential Library.

54. Oscar Glantz, "The Negro Voter in Northern Industrial Cities," *Western Political Quarterly* 13 (December 1960): 999–1010. The quotations are from p. 999, the figures from table I and p. 1000n8.

55. Sherman, *Republican Party and Black America*, chaps. 2–4, 6–9; Hanes Walton Jr., *Black Republicans: The Politics of the Black and Tans* (Metuchen, N.J.: Scarecrow, 1975), chap. 4 and appendix; Glenda Elizabeth Gilmore, "False Friends and Avowed Enemies: Southern African Americans and Party Allegiances in the 1920s," in *Jumpin' Jim Crow—Southern Politics from Civil War to Civil Rights,* ed. Jane Dailey, Glenda Elizabeth Gilmore, and Bryant Simon, pp. 222–223 (Princeton: Princeton University Press, 2000), subtly discusses black-and-tan conventions and delegate selection in North Carolina between 1900 and 1920. Minor federal patronage permitted economic security for leaders; see, e.g., Fairclough, *Race and Democracy*, p. 66. Likewise, service in the black diplomatic corps prepared men for major leadership roles; see Eugene Levy, "James Weldon Johnson and the Development of the NAACP," in *Black Leaders of the Twentieth Century,* ed. John Hope Franklin and August Meier, pp. 85–104, at pp. 86–88 (Urbana:

University of Illinois Press, 1982). See also McMillen, *Dark Journey*, pp. 57–71. The failure of the antilynching bill during the Harding administration is typically taken as evidence for the opposite inference, i.e., that the historic alliance was a failure. But a plot of the lynching statistics can be suggestive. See Stewart E. Tolnay and E. M. Beck, *A Festival of Violence: An Analysis of Southern Lynchings, 1882–1930* (Urbana: University of Illinois Press, 1995), fig. 6-1, p. 184; Sherman, *Republican Party and Black America*, chap. 7 and pp. 198–199.

56. Louis T. Harlan, *Booker T. Washington: The Wizard of Tuskegee, 1901–1915* (New York: Oxford Univerity Press, 1983); David Strong, Pamela Barnhouse Walters, Brian Driscoll, and Scott Rosenberg, "Leveraging the State: Private Money and the Development of Public Education for Blacks," *American Sociological Review* 65 (October 2000): 658–681. These authors hardly credit Washington, but their own evidence speaks volumes.

57. David Levering Lewis, *W.E.B. Du Bois—Biography of a Race, 1868–1919* (New York: Henry Holt and Company, 1993), chaps. 9, 12, 14–15; Lewis, *W.E.B. Du Bois—The Fight for Equality and the American Century* (New York: Henry Holt and Company, 2000), chap. 2; Mary Gambrell Robinson, "The Universal Negro Improvement Association in Georgia—Southern Strongholds of Garveyism," in *Georgia in Black and White: Explorations in the Race Relations of a Southern State, 1865–1950,* ed. John C. Inscoe (Athens: University of Georgia Press, 1994), pp. 202–224; and Robin Kelley, *Hammer and Hoe: Alabama Communists during the Great Depression* (Chapel Hill: University of North Carolina Press, 1990), esp. pp. 8–9 on the UNIA and the NAACP during the interwar period.

58. McAdam, *Political Process,* pp. 103–104; Heard, *Two-Party South?* pp. 183–184; Klarman, "White Primary Rulings," pp. 76–77.

59. Kenneth Robert Janken, *Rayford W. Logan and the Dilemma of the African-American Intellectual* (Amherst: University of Massachusetts Press, 1993), pp. 99–106. I thank Fred Harris for bringing this facet of the history to my attention. See also Robert J. Norrell, *Reaping the Whirlwind: The Civil Rights Movement in Tuskegee* (1985; reprint, Chapel Hill: University of North Carolina Press, 1998), pp. 38–39; William A. Muraskin, *Middle-Class Blacks in a White Society: Prince Hall Freemasonry in America* (Berkeley: University of California Press, 1975), chap. 10. On veterans, see Charles M. Payne, *I've Got the Light of Freedom: The Organizing Tradition and the Mississippi Freedom Sruggle* (Berkeley: University of California Press, 1995), pp. 24–25.

60. Charles D. Hadley, "The Transformation of the Role of Black Ministers and Black Political Organizations in Louisiana Politics," in *Blacks in Southern Politics,* ed. Laurence W. Moreland, Robert P. Steed, and Tod A. Baker, pp. 133–148, at pp. 133–134 (New York: Praeger, 1987).

61. Heard, *Two-Party South?* p. 185; Merline Pitre, *In Struggle against Jim Crow: Lulu B. White and the NAACP, 1900–1957* (College Station: Texas A&M University Press, 1999), pp. 44–45; Manfred Berg, *The Ticket to Freedom: Die NAACP und das Wahlrecht der Afro-Amerikaner* (Frankfurt: Campus Verlag, 2000), pp. 260–274.

62. Heard, *Two-Party South?* p. 186. See also Ronald H. Baylor, *Race and the Shaping of Twentieth-Century Atlanta,* Fred W. Morrison Series in Southern Studies (Chapel Hill: University of North Carolina Press, 1996), pp. 22–24; Ben Green, *Before His Time: The Untold Story of Harry T. Moore, America's First Civil Rights Martyr* (New York: Free Press, 1999), pp. 62–66, 71–76.

63. More specifically, because black voter registration had nowhere to go but up, it had a propensity, once it started doing so, to go up very fast in a short period of time until it plateaued in the middle of the *S* that would be executed by the joint observations of calendar year and black voter registration in a *Y-X* plot of black voter registration in the South against time. Given the numerically large size of the voting-age black population, increasing numerical

values quickly register over a short initial time period. On the difference made by black political organizations, see the suggestive treatment of Matthews and Prothro, *Negroes and the New
Southern Politics,* chap. 8.

64. Baylor, *Race and the Shaping of Twentieth Century Atlanta,* pp. 25–26; Heard, *Two-Party
South?* p. 218.

65. Matthews and Prothro, *Negroes and the New Southern Politics,* pp. 228–230.

66. David Waldner, *State-Building and Late Development* (Ithaca: Cornell University Press,
1999), p. 29.

67. See Margaret Price, *The Negro Voter in the South* (Atlanta: Southern Regional Council,
n.d. [September 1957?]), p. 1. In 1946, the drop-off from registration to actual primary voting
was as follows: Alabama., –20 percent; Arkansas, –89 percent; Florida, –49 percent; Georgia,
–28 percent; Louisiana, –75 percent; Mississippi, –50 percent; North Carolina, –47 percent;
South Carolina, n.a.; Tennessee, –62 percent; Texas, –25 percent; Virginia, –69 percent. Heard,
Two-Party South? p. 302, nn. 1–2, and my calculations.

68. Matthews and Prothro, *Negroes and the New Southern Politics,* p. 163. See also William
E. Wright, *Memphis Politics: A Study in Racial Bloc Voting* (Rutgers, N.J.: Eagleton Institute of
Politics Studies in Practical Politics, 1962), pp. 4–5; Harry Holloway, "The Negro and the Vote:
The Case of Texas," *Journal of Politics* 23 (August 1961): pp. 526–556 (though this source must
be treated with care); Fairclough, *Race and Democracy,* pp. 179–186; Greta De Jong, *A Different
Day: African-American Struggles for Justice in Rural Louisiana, 1900–1970* (Chapel Hill: University
of North Carolina Press, 2002), pp. 163–164; Klarman, "White Primary Rulings," pp. 96–98.

Chapter Eight

1. After 1948, Dixiecrats and Democratic liberals focused on resolving conflicts concerning staffing of party organizations, on ticket-balancing in presidential campaigns, and on devis-
ing mutually acceptable presidential platforms. Congressional procedures and committee
positions that protected southern Democrats were left in place. Appointments to the federal
bench were routinized. See Donald R. McCoy and Richard T. Ruetten, *Quest and Response:
Minority Rights and the Truman Administration* (Lawrence: University Press of Kansas, 1973),
pp. 171–172, 190, 192, 284, 316, 321, 324–325, 338–340; Steven M. Gillon, *Politics and
Vision: The ADA and American Liberalism, 1947–1985* (New York: Oxford University Press,
1987), chap. 4; John Frederick Martin, *Civil Rights and the Crisis of Liberalism: The Democratic
Party, 1947–1976* (Boulder: Westview, 1979), chaps. 6–8; Timothy N. Thurber, *The Politics of
Equality: Hubert H. Humphrey and the African American Freedom Struggle* (New York: Columbia
University Press, 1999), chap. 4. On regional rollback, see Margaret Price, *The Negro Voter in the
South* (Atlanta: Southern Regional Council, n.d. [1957?]); Joseph L. Bernd and Lynwood M.
Holland, "Recent Restrictions upon Negro Suffrage: The Case of Georgia," *Journal of Politics* 21
(August 1959): 487–513; Stephen G. N. Tuck, *Beyond Atlanta: The Struggle for Racial Equality in
Georgia, 1940–1980* (Athens: University of Georgia Press, 2001), chap. 3.

2. Robert Dallek, *Flawed Giant: Lyndon Johnson and His Times, 1961–1973* (New York:
Oxford University Press, 1998), p. 219; David J. Garrow, *Bearing the Cross: Martin Luther King,
Jr., and the Southern Christian Leadership Conference* (New York: William Morrow, 1986), p. 409;
Garth E. Pauley, *The Modern Presidency and Civil Rights: Rhetoric on Race from Roosevelt to Nixon*
(College Station: Texas A&M University Press, 2001), pp. 179–186.

3. Doug McAdam, *Political Process and the Development of Black Insurgency, 1930–1970*
(Chicago: University of Chicago Press, 1982), p. 163, for survey data; Tuck, *Beyond Atlanta,*
photograph section between pp. 106 and 107, for a "swim-in"; Carolyn Jones, *Volma . . . My
Journey: One Man's Impact on the Civil Rights Movement in Austin, Texas* (Austin: Eakin, 1998),

chap. 1, for a "read-in." See also Dennis Chong, *Collective Action and the Civil Rights Movement* (Chicago: University of Chicago Press, 1991).

4. Charles M. Payne, *I've Got the Light of Freedom: The Organizing Tradition and the Mississippi Freedom Struggle* (Berkeley: University of California Press, 1995), pp. 256 (newspaper), 264 (Baker), 268–277 (Clark). Payne's book is a brilliant, powerful discussion of the gritty, ground-level hard work of the civil rights era.

5. Ibid., pp. 271–272 (emphasis added).

6. Aldon D. Morris, *The Origins of the Civil Rights Movement: Black Communities Organizing for Change* (New York: Free Press, 1984), p. 84. An essential background essay is August Meier and Elliot Rudwick, "The Origins of Nonviolent Direct Action in Afro-American Protest: A Note on Historical Discontinuities," in *We Shall Overcome: The Civil Rights Movement in the United States in the 1950's and 1960's,* ed. David J. Garrow (Brooklyn, N.Y.: Carlson, 1989), 3:833–930, reprinted from Meier and Rudwick, *Along the Color Line: Explorations in the Black Experience* (Urbana: University of Illinois Press, 1976). An accessible statement is Martin Luther King Jr.'s "Letter from Birmingham City Jail," addressed to "Fellow Clergymen," in James M. Washington, *A Testament of Hope: The Essential Writings and Speeches of Martin Luther King, Jr.* ed. James M. Washington (New York: HarperCollins, 1986), pp. 289–302.

7. Frederick C. Harris, *Something Within: Religion in African-American Political Activism* (New York: Oxford University Press, 1999), chap. 4.

8. See Morris, *Origins of the Civil Rights Movement*; Tuck, *Beyond Atlanta*; Adam Fairclough, *Race and Democracy: The Civil Rights Struggle in Louisiana, 1915–1972* (Athens: University of Georgia Press, 1995).

9. On Moore, see Ben Green, *Before His Time: The Untold Story of Harry T. Moore, America's First Civil Rights Martyr* (New York: Free Press, 1999); on Evers, see Aaron Henry, with Constance Curry, *Aaron Henry—The Fire Ever Burning,* intro. John Dittmer (Jackson: University Press of Mississippi, 2000), pp. 146–151.

10. This is a fundamental finding (among others) of Morris, *Origins of the Civil Rights Movement.*

11. See, e.g., Andrew Buni, *The Negro in Virginia Politics, 1902–1965* (Charlottesville: University Press of Virginia, 1967), p. 177.

12. John H. Scott with Cleo Scott Brown, *Witness to the Truth: My Struggle for Human Rights in Louisiana* (Columbia: University of South Carolina Press, 2003), p. 141.

13. Harry Kalven Jr., *The Negro and the First Amendment* (Chicago: University of Chicago Press, Phoenix Books, 1965), p. 71, for a succinct legal history, see pp. 65–122. Rebuilding the NAACP was not easy. See Fairclough, *Race and Democracy,* p. 273.

14. On the Supreme Court's handling of the NAACP cases see Lucas A. Powe Jr., *The Warren Court and American Politics* (Cambridge: Harvard University Press, Belknap Press, 2000), chap. 6, pp. 165–171, 218–221.

15. A useful companion piece to Morris's analysis of the rise of the SCLC in *Origins of the Civil Rights Movement*, chaps. 4–6, one written with different emphases than Morris's, is Adam Fairclough, "The Preachers and the People: The Origins and Early Years of the Southern Christian Leadership Conference, 1955–1959," *Journal of Southern History* 52 (August 1986): 403–440.

16. Clayborne Carson, *In Struggle: SNCC and the Black Awakening of the 1960s* (Cambridge: Harvard University Press, 1981), pp. 9–12; McAdam, *Political Process*, pp. 138–140 and fig. 6.4, p. 140; Michael Walzer, "A Cup of Coffee and a Seat," *Dissent,* Summer 1960, pp. 111–120; Fairclough, *Race and Democracy,* pp. 278–279.

17. See, among other acounts, Joanne Grant, *Ella Baker—Freedom Bound* (New York: Wiley, 1998), chap. 7.

18. Joseph Luders, "Countermovements, the State, and the Intensity of Racial Contention in the American South," in *States, Parties, and Social Movements,* ed. Jack A. Goldstone (New York: Cambridge University Press, 2003), pp. 27–44.

19. Pat Watters and Reese Cleghorn, *Climbing Jacob's Ladder: The Arrival of Negroes in Southern Politics* (New York: Harcourt, Brace and World for the Southern Regional Council, 1967), p. 74 n16; Michael J. Klarman, "How *Brown* Changed Race Relations: The Backlash Thesis," *Journal of American History* 81 (June 1994): 81–118.

20. See, among others, Neil R. McMillen, *The Citizens' Council: Organized Resistance to the Second Reconstruction, 1954–64* (Urbana: University of Illinois Press, 1971); Francis M. Wilhoit, *The Politics of Massive Resistance* (New York: George Braziller, 1973).

21. McAdam, *Political Process,* p. 267n1. See John T. Woolley, "Using Media-Based Data in Studies of Politics," *American Journal of Political Science* 44 (January 2000): 156–173.

22. Woolley, "Using Media-Based Data in Studies of Politics," pp. 163n15, 159; Grant, *Ella Baker,* p. 133; Fairclough, *Race and Democracy,* p. 277; Watters and Cleghorn, *Climbing Jacob's Ladder,* pp. 129–131; Taylor Branch, *Pillar of Fire—America in the King Years, 1963–1965* (New York: Simon and Schuster, 1998), p. 553; John Lewis with Michael D'Orso, *Walking with the Wind: A Memoir of the Movement* (New York: Simon and Schuster, 1998), pp. 235–237, 127–128.

23. Thomas Borstelmann, *The Cold War and the Color Line: American Race Relations in the Global Arena* (Cambridge: Harvard University Press, 2001), chap. 4.

24. Deborah Bulkeley [Associated Press], "Freedom Riders Plan a Reunion in Mississippi," *Philadelphia Inquirer,* 16 July 2001, p. A3, referring to a compilation of the names of 416 Freedom Riders based on a search of Jackson, Mississippi, police records and the *Jackson Clarion-Ledger.*

25. Burke Marshall, *Federalism and Civil Rights,* foreword by Robert F. Kennedy (New York: Columbia University Press, 1964), pp. 66–67.

26. Mary Dudziak, *Cold War Civil Rights: Equality as Cold War Policy, 1946–1968* (Princeton: Princeton University Press, 2000), pp. 158–159. See also Carl M. Brauer, *John F. Kennedy and the Second Reconstruction* (New York: Columbia University Press, 1977), pp. 106–107.

27. Brauer, *John F. Kennedy,* pp. 112–113, discussing motivations within the Kennedy administration; see also August Meier and Elliott Rudwick, *CORE: A Study in the Civil Rights Movement, 1942–1968* (New York: Oxford University Press, 1973), pp. 173–176, discussing VEP's origins. The VEP's official history is Watters and Cleghorn, *Climbing Jacob's Ladder.*

28. Harris Wofford, *Of Kennedys and Kings: Making Sense of the Sixties* (New York: Farrar, Straus, Giroux, 1980), p. 158.

29. Stewart Burns, "Overview," in *Daybreak of Freedom: The Montgomery Bus Boycott* (Chapel Hill: University of North Carolina Press, 1997), p. 32; Morris, *Origins of the Civil Rights Movement,* chap. 5. For King's first national speech, "Give Us the Ballot!," see Washington, *Testament of Hope,* pp. 197–200. On the NAACP effort, see Watters and Cleghorn, *Climbing Jacob's Ladder,* p. 49. On the pact, see Payne, *I've Got the Light of Freedom,* pp. 108–111.

30. W. J. Rorabaugh, *Kennedy and the Promise of the Sixties* (New York: Cambridge University Press, 2002), p. 95. The equivalency estimate is based on an average of four deflators: the GDP deflator, the CPI deflator, GDP per capita, and unskilled wage equivalency. These come from Samuel H. Williamson, "What Is the Relative Value?" Economic History Series,

accessed 4 January 2003, http://www.eh.net/hmit/compare/. Equivalency was set on the
Web site's automatic calculator to 1963 to capture the value of the funds as they began to be
disbursed.

31. Frederick M. Wirt, *Politics of Southern Equality: Law and Social Change in a Mississippi
County* (Chicago: Aldine for the Institute of Governmental Studies, University of California at
Berkeley, 1970), p. 73. The specific statutory foundations are well discussed in Ira Michael
Heyman, "Federal Remedies for Voteless Negroes," *California Law Review* 48 (May 1961):
190–215, at pp. 201–207.

32. Meier and Rudwick, *CORE*, p. 260, and, more generally, chap. 9; David J. Garrow,
Protest at Selma: Martin Luther King, Jr., and the Voting Rights Act of 1965 (New Haven: Yale
University Press, 1978), p. 251n58.

33. The only study of their behavior is Donald S. Strong's useful *Registration of Voters in
Alabama* (University: Bureau of Public Administration, University of Alabama, 1956).

34. Berl I. Bernhard, "The Federal Fact-Finding Experience—A Guide to Negro
Enfranchisement," *Law and Contemporary Problems* 27 (Summer 1962): 468–480.

35. Marshall, *Federalism and Civil Rights* p. 25.

36. Ibid., pp. 30–31; Robert F. Burk, *The Eisenhower Administration and Black Civil Rights*
(Knoxville: University of Tennessee Press, 1984), p. 239.

37. Garrow, *Protest at Selma*, p. 24.

38. Marshall, *Federalism and Civil Rights*, p. 30.

39. Burk, *Eisenhower Administrations*, p. 243; Heyman, "Federal Remedies," p. 207 and
n86. Horace Busby, one of LBJ's closest advisors, argued fearfully in early 1965 that direct fed-
eral registration would "represent a return to Reconstruction." Horace Busby to Bill Moyers and
Lee White, Memorandum, The White House, 27 February 1965, reproduced in Michal R.
Belknap, ed., *Civil Rights, the White House, and the Justice Department, 1945–1968* (New York:
Garland, 1991), 14:3. Quote from Marshall, *Federalism and Civil Rights*, p. 31.

40. Marshall, *Federalism and Civil Rights*, p. 54.

41. Ibid., p. 76; Wirt, *Politics of Southern Equality*, pp. 81–82.

42. Marshall, *Federalism and Civil Rights*, p. 4. For the origins of the friction see Meier and
Rudwick, *CORE*, 174n; Payne, *I've Got the Light of Freedom*, pp. 109–110. See also Earl Ofari
Hutchinson, *Betrayed: A History of Presidential Failure to Protect Black Lives* (Boulder: Westview,
1996), p. 107; Brauer, *John F. Kennedy*, p. 219.

43. Meier and Rudwick, *CORE*, p. 265.

44. Timothy B. Tyson, *Radio Free Dixie: Robert F. Williams and the Roots of Black Power*
(Chapel Hill: University of North Carolina Press, 1999), pp. 274–275; John Dittmer, *Local
People: The Struggle for Civil Rights in Mississippi* (Urbana: University of Illinois Press, 1994),
pp. 221, 227–228.

45. Marshall, *Federalism and Civil Rights*, pp. 44–49.

46. See Morton Stavis, "A Century of Struggle for Black Enfranchisement in Mississippi:
From the Civil War to the Congressional Challenge of 1965—and Beyond," *Mississippi Law
Journal* 57 (1987): 591–676, at pp. 648–656.

47. Dittmer, *Local People*, chap. 10; Michal R. Belknap, *Federal Law and Southern Order:
Racial Violence and Constitutional Conflict in the Post-Brown South,* Studies in the Legal History of
the South (Athens: University of Georgia Press, 1995), chap. 6.

48. "What Is COFO? Mississippi: Structure of the Movement and Present Operations"
COFO Publication no. 6 (n.d., n.p.), and "Council of Federated Organizations, Freedom
School Data" (mimeo), both in the Robert Lentz Papers, Peace Collection, Swarthmore College.

49. "McComb Incident Summary June–September 1964," Lentz Papers.

50. "Attempts to Obtain an Investigation of the Schwerner Case" (mimeo), Lentz Papers; Dan T. Carter, *The Politics of Rage: George Wallace, the Origins of the New Conservatism, and the Transformation of American Politics* (New York: Simon and Schuster, 1995), pp. 222–223, offers the best short account. See also Susan Harding, "Reconstructing Order through Action: Jim Crow and the Southern Civil Rights Movement," in *Statemaking and Social Movements: Essays in History and Theory,* ed. Charles Bright and Susan Harding, pp. 378–402, at pp. 387–397 (Ann Arbor: University of Michigan Press, 1984).

51. Frank R. Parker, "Protest, Politics, and Litigation: Political and Social Change in Mississippi, 1965 to Present," *Mississippi Law Journal* 57 (1987): 677–704, at 704.

52. Alex Poinsett, *Walking with Presidents: Louis Martin and the Rise of Black Political Power* (Lanham, Md.: Madison Books for the Joint Center for Political and Economic Studies, 1997), p. 171.

53. King is quoted in Dallek, *Flawed Giant,* p. 213; see Carter, *Politics of Rage,* p. 240 for voter registration in Selma.

54. Carter, *Politics of Rage,* p. 248; Branch, *Pillar of Fire,* pp. 575–583, 586–588, 591–594, 598–600; Dallek, *Flawed Giant,* pp. 214–215; Charles E. Fager, *Selma 1965* (New York: Charles Scribner's Sons, 1974), pp. 72–75, 80–81, 91–98; Lewis, *Walking with the Wind,* pp. 323–332; David Riley, "Who Is Jimmie Lee Jackson?" *New Republic,* 3 April 1965, pp. 8–9.

55. Quoted in Dallek, *Flawed Giant,* p. 219. See also Carson, *In Struggle,* p. 59; Dittmer, *Local People,* p. 229; Garrow, *Bearing the Cross,* p. 409.

56. Quoted in Garrow, *Bearing the Cross,* p. 368. See also Pauley, *Modern Presidency and Civil Rights,* pp. 172–175 (offering discussion of the Johnson administration).

57. See Robert Mann, *The Walls of Jericho: Lyndon Johnson, Hubert Humphrey, Richard Russell, and the Struggle for Civil Rights* (New York: Harcourt, Brace, 1996), pp. 460–462, for the joint session and for "long hours"; Nan Robertson, "President to Sign Voting Rights Bill Today," *New York Times,* 6 August 1965, p. 12, for "President's Room"; Mark Stern, *Calculating Visions: Kennedy, Johnson, and Civil Rights* (New Brunswick: Rutgers University Press, 1992), p. 228, for "monumental" law.

58. Belknap, *Federal Law and Southern Order,* p. 136; Steven E. Barkan, "Legal Control of the Southern Civil Rights Movement," *American Sociological Review* 49 (August 1984): 552–565.

59. Glenn T. Eskew, *But for Birmingham: The Local and National Movements in the Civil Rights Struggle* (Chapel Hill: University of North Carolina Press, 1997), chap. 1 and pp. 208–210, 212–214, 226–228, 273, 312, 314–316; Powe, *Warren Court,* pp. 221–226; Garrow, *Protest at Selma,* pp. 212–236. But see Morris, *Origins of the Civil Rights Movement,* chap. 10, and Morris, "Birmingham Confrontation Reconsidered: An Analysis of the Dynamics and Tactics of Mobilization," *American Sociological Review* 58 (October 1993): 621–636, for an argument that the actual strategy was to create a disciplined, nearly implacable mass of people able to force elites to bargain.

60. On local repression in Selma, see Lewis, *Walking with the Wind,* pp. 301–306; Fager, *Selma,* pp. 4–6, 8, 16–20 . On the climate at the state level, see Carter's shocking research findings, *Politics of Rage,* pp. 226–235. On Lingo's role in Birmingham violence, see Eskew, *But for Birmingham,* pp. 300–302, 390n2. A photograph of Lingo can be seen in *Politics of Rage* between pp. 320 and 321.

61. Garrow, *Protest at Selma,* chaps. 4–5.

62. Brauer, *John F. Kennedy,* chap. 9; Dallek, *Flawed Giant,* p. 112.

63. Stern, *Calculating Visions,* pp. 160–161; Dallek, *Flawed Giant,* p. 114.

64. Stern, *Calculating Visions,* p. 223; see also pp. 210–223, a discussion based on interviews, correspondence with protagonists, and in-depth primary research in Johnson administration papers by Stern.

65. Ibid., pp. 227–228. Also, Nina M. Moore, *Governing Race: Policy, Process, and the Politics of Race* (Westport: Praeger, 2000), pp. 162–167. Calculations from Norman J. Ornstein, Thomas E. Mann, Michael J. Malbin, *Vital Statistics on Congress, 1989–1990* (Washington: Congressional Quarterly Inc., for the American Enterprise Institute, 1990), pp. 11–16 and 49. To detect changes in racial liberalism Amelia Hoover, a research assistant, and I used the NOMINATE scores then available. Average "second dimension" scores for all Democratic "leavers" from the House were significantly more conservative, we found, than for their replacements. Our exact figures are mooted by the new release, but our finding should stand given the tight correlation between the two releases. On the underlying spatial model, see Keith T. Poole and Howard Rosenthal, *Congress: A Political-Economic History of Roll Call Voting* (New York: Oxford University Press, 1997). For data, navigate to http://voteview.uh.edu or http://www.princeton.edu/~voteview/.

66. Gilbert C. Fite, *Richard B. Russell, Jr., Senator from Georgia,* Fred W. Morrison Series in Southern Studies (Chapel Hill: University of North Carolina Press, 1991), pp. 426–428. See chapter 15 for Russell's skill at civil rights obstruction. The new release NOMINATE scores should show that Senate *Democratic* leavers and replacements are very close or identical on their "second dimension" but that *all* replacements are more racially liberal. For vote to invoke cloture and end debate, see Voteview Roll Call #67 (for Senate).

67. Michael Beschloss, ed., *Reaching for Glory: Lyndon Johnson's Secret White House Tapes, 1964–1965* (New York: Simon and Schuster, 2001), p. 162.

Chapter Nine

1. David A. Bositis, *Black Elected Officials: A Statistical Summary, 2000* (Washington, D.C.: Joint Center for Political and Economic Studies, 2002), p. 5; Michael A. Fitts and Robert P. Inman, "The Voting Rights Act and Southern State Budgets: Did VRA 65 Make a Difference?" University of Pennsylvania Law School and Wharton School, 1995.

2. On the Court, see Tinsley E. Yarbrough, *Race and Redistricting: The Shaw-Cromartie Cases* (Lawrence: University Press of Kansas, 2002); J. Morgan Kousser, *Colorblind Injustice: Minority Voting Rights and the Undoing of the Second Reconstruction* (Chapel Hill: University of North Carolina Press, 1999), chap. 8. An introduction to felony disenfranchisement is The Sentencing Project, *Losing the Vote: The Impact of Felony Disenfranchisement Laws in the United States* (Washington: The Sentencing Project, October 1998); see also Advancement Project, *America's Modern Poll Tax: How Structural Disenfranchisement Erodes Democracy* (n.p.: n.p., November 7, 2001); Stephen Knack and Martha Kropf, "Who Uses Inferior Voting Technology?" *PS: Political Science & Politics* 35 (September 2002): 541–548; Dean E. Murphy, "California's Vote Delayed by Court over Punch Cards," *New York Times,* 16 September 2003, pp. A1, A20.

3. Claudine Gay, "Spirals of Trust? The Effect of Descriptive Representation on the Relationship between Citizens and Their Government," *American Journal of Political Science* 46 (October 2002): 717–732; Kerry L. Haynie, *African-American Legislators in the American States* (New York: Columbia University Press, 2001), chap. 5; Ralph Blumenthal, "Texas Democrats Look at New Map and Point out Victims," *New York Times,* 14 October 2003, p. A14.

4. John Lewis and Archie E. Allen, "Black Voter Registration Efforts in the South," *Notre Dame Lawyer* 48 (October 1972): 105–132, at p. 120; Drew S. Days III and Lani Guinier, "Enforcement of Section 5 of the Voting Rights Act," in *Minority Vote Dilution*, ed. Chandler Davidson, pp. 167–180, at pp. 169–170 (Washington, D.C.: Howard University Press for the Joint Center for Political Studies, 1984); Charles M. Payne, *I've Got the Light of Freedom: The Organizing Tradition and the Mississippi Freedom Struggle* (Berkeley: University of California Press, 1995), pp. 396–398; United States Department of Justice, "Statement by J. Stanley Pottinger, Assistant Attorney General, Civil Rights Division, Before the Subcommittee on Civil Rights & Constitutional Rights of the House Judiciary Committee on the Extension of the Voting Rights Act," March 5, 1975, p. 25, typescript provided to the author by Peyton McCrary. See also David C. Colby, "White Violence and the Civil Rights Movement," in *Blacks in Southern Politics*, ed. Laurence W. Moreland, Robert P. Steed, and Tod A. Baker, pp. 31–48 (New York: Praeger, 1987), esp. p. 31; Jack E. Davis, *Race against Time: Culture and Separation in Natchez since 1930* (Baton Rouge: Louisiana State University Press, 2001), chap. 6.

5. Chandler Davidson defines vote dilution as "a process whereby election laws or practices, either singly or in concert, combine with systematic bloc voting among an identifiable group to diminish the voting strength of at least one other group. Ethnic or racial minority vote dilution is a special case, in which the voting strength of an ethnic or racial minority group is diminished or canceled out by the *bloc vote* of the majority": "Minority Vote Dilution: An Overview," in *Minority Vote Dilution*, ed. Chandler Davidson, pp. 1–26, at p. 4 (Washington, D.C.: Howard University Press for the Joint Center for Political Studies, 1984), emphasis in original. On the concept's emergence in the federal courts before the 1965 Voting Rights Act, see Peyton McCrary, "Bringing Equality to Power: How the Federal Courts Transformed the Electoral Structure of Southern Politics, 1960–1990," *University of Pennsylvania Journal of Constitutional Law* 5 (May 2003): 665–708, at pp. 681–685.

6. Morton Stavis, "A Century of Struggle for Black Enfranchisement in Mississippi: From the Civil War to the Congressional Challenge of 1965—and Beyond," *Mississippi Law Journal* 57 (1987): 591–673, p. 661, n. 294.

7. Ibid.; Samuel Issacharoff, Pamela S. Karlan, and Richard H. Pildes, *The Law of Democracy: Legal Structure of the Political Process* (Westbury, N.Y.: Foundation, 1998), p. 274, describing the "core" of the VRA.

8. Del Dickson, ed., *The Supreme Court in Conference (1940–1985)—The Private Discussions behind Nearly 300 Supreme Court Decisions* (New York: Oxford University Press, 2001), p. 832; see pp. 829–832.

9. James E. Alt, "The Impact of the Voting Rights Act on Black and White Voter Registration in the South," in *Quiet Revolution in the South: The Impact of the Voting Rights Act, 1965–1990,* ed. Chandler Davidson and Bernard Grofman, p. 356 (Princeton: Princeton University Press, 1994); Donald R. Matthews and James W. Prothro, *Negroes and the New Southern Politics* (New York: Harcourt, Brace, and World, 1966), p. 138; David J. Garrow, *Protest at Selma: Martin Luther King, Jr., and the Voting Rights Act of 1965* (New Haven: Yale University Press, 1978), pp. 187, 301n26.

10. *South Carolina v. Katzenbach,* 383 U.S. 301, 308–309, 327 (1966).

11. Steven F. Lawson, *In Pursuit of Power: Southern Blacks and Electoral Politics, 1965–1982* (New York: Columbia University Press, 1985), chap. 5; Dean J. Kotlowski, *Nixon's Civil Rights: Politics, Principle, and Policy* (Cambridge: Harvard University Press, 2001), chap. 3.

12. Lawson, *In Pursuit of Power,* chap. 8; Jerome J. Hanus, Paul Downing, and Donovan Gay, "The Voting Rights Act of 1965, as Amended: History, Effects, and Alternatives," Report No. 75–243 GGR (Washington, D.C.: Congressional Research Service, Library of Congress,

June 17, 1975) (rev. November 19, 1975); United States Department of Justice, "Statement by J. Stanley Pottinger." On the impact on Hispanic American electoral incorporation, see Amy Bridges, *Morning Glories: Municipal Reform in the Southwest* (Princeton: Princeton University Press, 1997); Rodolfo O. de la Garza and Louis DeSipio, "Save the Baby, Change the Bathwater, and Scrub the Tub: Latino Electoral Participation after Twenty Years of Voting Rights Act Coverage," in *Pursuing Power: Latinos and the Political System,* ed. F. Chris Garcia, pp. 72–126 (Notre Dame: University of Notre Dame Press, 1997).

13. Steven J. Rosenstone and John Mark Hansen, *Mobilization, Participation, and Democracy in America,* Longman Classics in Political Science (1993; reprint, New York: Longman, 2002), p. 201.

14. Pottinger, "Statement on the Extension of the Voting Rights Act," p. 22; Rosenstone and Hansen, *Mobilization,* p. 201n70.

15. John Lewis with Michael D'Orso, *Walking with the Wind: A Memoir of the Movement* (New York: Simon and Schuster, 1998), pp. 346 (emphasis in the original), 413. See also Lewis and Allen, "Black Voter Registration Efforts in the South."

16. Vernon E. Jordan Jr., with Annette Gordon-Reed, *Vernon Can Read! A Memoir* (New York: 2001, Public Affairs), pp. 175–179, 181–185; Lewis, *Walking with the Wind,* pp. 434–435 (emphasis in the original).

17. Thomas F. Eamon, "From Pool Hall to Parish House in North Carolina," in *Strategies for Mobilizing Black Voters: Four Case Studies,* ed. Thomas E. Cavanaugh, pp. 101–136, at p. 111 (Washington, D.C.: Joint Center for Political Studies, 1987).

18. Daniel Vincent Dowd, "Understanding Partisan Change and Stability in the Late Twentieth Century," Ph.D. diss., Yale University, 1999, chap. 2; Michael Beschloss, ed., *Reaching for Glory: Lyndon Johnson's Secret White House Tapes, 1964–1965* (New York: Simon and Schuster, 2001), p. 162.

19. *Proceedings of the State Democratic Executive Committee of Alabama* (n.p., January 20, 1962); typescript reproduction of "Rigid Race Rule Is Set—Dems Keep Governing Body 'White,' " *Huntsville Times,* 21 January 1962, pp. 1, 2 (photocopies of both documents were provided to me courtesy of Peyton McCrary); James M. Crain, "The Application of Constitutional Provisions to Political Parties," *Tennessee Law Review* 40 (Winter 1973): 217–234, pp. 226–227.

20. Julian Bond, *Black Candidates: Southern Campaign Experiences* (Atlanta: Voter Education Project, Southern Regional Council, Inc., n.d. [1968?]), p. 12.

21. William J. Crotty, *Decision for the Democrats: Reforming the Party Structure* (Baltimore: Johns Hopkins University Press, 1978), pp. 44, 73–74.

22. Hanes Walton Jr., *Black Political Parties: A Historical and Political Analysis* (New York: Free Press, 1972), pp. 80–81; see also pp. 69–77; Patricia Sullivan, *Days of Hope: Race and Democracy in the New Deal Era* (Chapel Hill: University of North Carolina Press, 1996), pp. 170–171, 189–191; Alexander Heard and Donald S. Strong, comps., *Southern Primaries and Elections, 1920–1949* (University: University of Alabama Press, 1950), p. 111; "To: All Friends of the MFDP; From: The Mississippi Freedom Democratic Party," mimeo, Robert Lentz Papers, Peace Collection, Swarthmore College; Stavis, "Century of Struggle"; Aaron Henry, with Constance Curry, *Aaron Henry—The Fire Ever Burning,* intro. John Dittmer (Jackson: University Press of Mississippi, 2000), pp. 156–198.

23. Hardy T. Frye, *Black Parties and Political Power: A Case Study* (Boston: Hall, 1980), appendix I and chap. 5.

24. Walton, *Black Political Parties,* pp. 77–79.

25. *Congressional Quarterly Weekly Report*, 7 June 1968, Convention Guide (Part 1 of 2), "Text of Hughes Letter," pp. 1343–1344.

26. Commission on the Democratic Selection of Presidential Nominees, *The Democratic Choice* (n.p.: n.p., 1968), p. 55.

27. See Henry, *Aaron Henry*, pp. 219–222, indirectly suggesting why Humphrey caved.

28. John R. Schmidt and Wayne W. Whalen, "Credentials Contests at the 1968—and 1972—Democratic National Conventions," *Harvard Law Review* 82 (May 1969): 1438–1470, at 1450–1454.

29. Byron Shafer, *Quiet Revolution: The Struggle for the Democratic Party and the Shaping of Post-Reform Politics* (New York: Russell Sage Foundation, 1983), pp. 161–168, 541.

30. Crotty, *Decision for the Democrats*, pp. 105–109; Shafer, *Quiet Revolution*, p. 595n1; Crain, "Application of Constitutional Provisions," pp. 228–233; *Georgia v. National Democratic Party*, 447 F.2d 1271 (D.C. Cir.), *cert. denied*, 404 U.S. 858 (1971).

31. Calculations are based on Crotty, *Decision for the Democrats*, p. 143.

32. Laurence W. Moreland et al., "Black Party Activists: A Profile," in *Blacks in Southern Politics*, ed. Laurence W. Moreland, Robert P. Steed, and Tod A. Baker, pp. 112–132 (New York: Praeger, 1987).

33. J. Morgan Kousser, pers. comm., 29 June 1999, citing a figure of 72 for 1965 from "Black Elected Officials in the Southern States," a 1969 typescript of the VEP of the Southern Regional Council, available from the library of the University of California at San Diego. The universe of 36,000 I calculated as follows: (1) I used figures for 1974 for total local elected officials in the seven states covered by the VRA from Richard Valelly, "Net Gains: The Voting Rights Act and Southern Local Government," in *Dilemmas of Scale in America's Federal Democracy*, ed. Martha Derthick (Washington, D.C.: Woodrow Wilson Center Press and Cambridge University Press, 1999), pp. 298–321, table 10.2, thus arriving at a figure of 26,970; (2) for the uncovered states I imputed figures that roughly matched rounded down figures for total local elected officials (LEOs) found in table 10.2 for VRA-covered states of comparable population and size, arriving at 2,000 each for NC, TN, FL, and AR, for a total of 8,000 in these states; (3) for state legislatures I used table 2 in Bernard Grofman and Lisa Handley, "The Impact of the Voting Rights Act on Black Representation in Southern State Legislatures," *Legislative Studies Quarterly* 16 (February 1991): 111–128, arriving at an estimate of 1,057 state legislators in all eleven former Confederate states; (4) for the members of the U.S. House from these states I counted 106 using Kenneth C. Martis and Gregory A. Elmes, *The Historical Atlas of State Power in Congress, 1790–1990* (Washington, D.C.: Congressional Quarterly, Inc., 1993), p. 100; (5) I added 22 for the U.S. Senate; and (6) I added 11 for the governors. I then rounded down to 36,000 from 36,166, which was spuriously precise. Left out of the figure of 36,000 are elected judges and such statewide offices as lieutenant governor, attorney general, and railroad commissioner, but leaving them out corrects for any inflation from using figures for the 1970s for LEOs and state legislatures.

34. Of two particularly full studies, the more recent, a study of massive resistance in Georgia by Laughlin McDonald, director of the Southern Regional Office of the ACLU (Laughlin McDonald, *A Voting Rights Odyssey: Black Enfranchisement in Georgia* [New York: Cambridge University Press, 2003]), is very eye-opening because Georgia is typically seen as more "modern" and less Southern Gothic than Mississippi. On Mississippi, see Frank R. Parker's pioneering *Black Votes Count: Political Empowerment in Mississippi after 1965* (Chapel Hill: University of North Carolina Press, 1990). For a thorough overview of all of the states, see Chandler Davidson and Bernard Grofman, eds., *Quiet Revolution in the South: The Impact of the Voting Rights Act, 1965–1990* (Princeton: Princeton University Press, 1994); McCrary, "Bringing Equality to Power."

35. McDonald, *Voting Rights Odyssey*, chap. 9.

36. Ibid., chap. 10.

37. McCrary, "Bringing Equality to Power," pp. 681–682; Bond, *Black Candidates,* p. 33.

38. See Peyton McCrary and J. Gerald Hebert, "Keeping the Courts Honest: The Role of Historians as Expert Witnesses in Southern Voting Rights Cases," *Southern University Law Review* 16 (Spring 1980): 101–128, for general background. On Virginia, see Peyton McCrary, "Yes, But What Have They Done to Black People Lately? The Role of Historical Evidence in the Virginia School Board Case," *Chicago-Kent Law Review* (Symposium on the Law of Freedom Part 2) 70.3 (1995): 1275–1305.

39. Earl Black and Merle Black, *The Rise of Southern Republicans* (Cambridge: Harvard University Press, Belknap Press, 2002), chaps. 2–6; Keith Reeves, *Voting Hopes or Fears? White Voters, Black Candidates, and Racial Politics in America* (New York: Oxford University Press, 1997).

40. *Allen v. State Board of Elections,* 393 U.S. 544, 565 (1969).

41. My calculations are based on Stanislaus Anthony Halpin Jr., "The Anti-Gerrymander: The Impact of Section 5 of the Voting Rights Act of 1965 upon Louisiana Parish Redistricting," Ph.D. diss., George Washington University, 1978, p. 116, table 4; Days and Guinier, "Section 5 Enforcement and the Department of Justice," pp. 56–57.

42. See Kousser, *Colorblind Injustice,* chap. 7; Davidson, "Minority Vote Dilution," pp. 1–26, at p. 17; Peyton McCrary, "History in the Courts: The Significance of *Bolden v. City of Mobile*," in *Minority Vote Dilution*, ed. Chandler Davidson, pp. 47–64 (Washington, D.C.: Howard University Press for the Joint Center for Political Studies, 1984), esp. pp. 49–57.

43. *White v. Regester,* 412 U.S. 755 (1973).

44. *Zimmer v. McKeithen,* 485 F.2d 1297 (5th Cir. 1973).

45. James Blacksher and Larry Menefee, "At-Large Elections and One Person, One Vote: The Search for the Meaning of Racial Vote Dilution," in *Minority Vote Dilution*, ed. Chandler Davidson, pp. 203–248, at pp. 216–217 (Washington, D.C.: Howard University Press for the Joint Center for Political Studies, 1984).

46. McCrary and Hebert, "Keeping the Courts Honest," pp. 106–108.

47. *City of Mobile v. Bolden,* 446 U.S. 65, 65 (1980); Thomas M. Boyd and Stephen J. Markman, "The 1982 Amendments to the Voting Rights Act: A Legislative History," *Washington and Lee Law Review* 40 (1983): 1347–1428, at pp. 1348–1356.

48. 42 U.S.C. § 1973(b).

49. Armand Derfner, "Vote Dilution and the Voting Rights Act Amendments of 1982," in *Minority Vote Dilution*, ed. Chandler Davidson, pp. 145–163 (Washington, D.C.: Howard University Press for the Joint Center for Political Studies, 1984); Boyd and Markman, "1982 Amendments to the Voting Rights Act"; Issacharoff, Karlan, and Pildes, *Law of Democracy,* chap. 6.

50. Section 4 was amended further to condition "bail-out" from preclearance on a showing that a jurisdiction has "eliminated voting procedures and methods of election which inhibit or *dilute* equal access to the electoral process." Derfner, "Vote Dilution," p. 146 (emphasis added).

51. *Rogers v. Lodge,* 458 U.S. 613 (1982); Stephen G. N. Tuck, *Beyond Atlanta: The Struggle for Racial Equality in Georgia, 1940–1980* (Athens: University of Georgia Press, 2001), pp. 240–242.

52. *Thornburg v. Gingles,* 478 U.S. 30 (1986).

53. Issacharoff, Karlan, and Pildes, *Law of Democracy*, pp. 443–499, esp. pp. 465, 499.

54. 42 U.S.C. § 1973l(e). See also Mary Frances Derfner and Arthur D. Wolf, *Court Awarded Attorney Fees,* rev. prepared by Kevin Shirey (Lexis Publishing: December 2000), chap. 34, p. 3:5.

55. Bernard Grofman and Lisa Handley, "The Impact of the Voting Rights Act on Black Representation in Southern State Legislatures," *Legislative Studies Quarterly* 16 (February 1991): 111–128; Richard Claude, *The Supreme Court and the Electoral Process* (Baltimore: Johns Hopkins University Press, 1970), pp. 185–188; Parker, *Black Votes Count,* chap. 4; Mary DeLorse Coleman, *Legislators, Law, and Public Policy: Political Change in Mississippi and the South* (Westport: Greenwood, 1983).

56. David Bositis, *Black State Legislators: A Survey and Analysis of Black Leadership in State Capitals* (Washington, D.C.: Joint Center for Political and Economic Studies, 1992), p. 25.

57. Kenny J. Whitby, *The Color of Representation: Congressional Behavior and Black Interests* (Ann Arbor: University of Michigan Press, 1997), pp. 88–89; Kousser, *Colorblind Injustice,* chaps. 5–6 and 8.

58. Whitby, *Color of Representation,* pp. 88–90.

59. Haynie, *African-American Legislators in the American States,* chap. 4.

Chapter Ten

1. Thus *Federalist* 51 concludes: "In the extended republic of the United States, and among the great variety of interests, parties, and sects which it embraces, a coalition of a majority of the whole society could seldom take place on any other principles than those of justice and the general good." Alexander Hamilton, John Jay, and James Madison, *The Federalist: A Commentary on the Constitution of the United States,* pp. 335–341 (New York: Modern Library College Editions, published by Random House, n.d.), pp. 340–341.

2. John H. Aldrich, *Why Parties? The Origin and Transformation of Party Politics in America* (Chicago: University of Chicago Press, 1995), pp. 33–36.

3. Eric Schickler, *Disjointed Pluralism: Institutional Innovation and the Development of the U.S. Congress* (Princeton University Press, 2001).

4. See Jon Elster, *Nuts and Bolts for the Social Sciences* (Cambridge: Cambridge University Press, 1989), pp. 13–21.

5. My concept of the "parties and courts" matrix is similar to (and indebted to) Stephen Skowronek's idea of the "state of courts and parties." See Skowronek, *Building a New American State: The Expansion of National Administrative Capacities, 1877–1920* (New York: Cambridge University Press, 1982). It also builds on Kousser's suggestive discussion of parties and courts in *Colorblind Injustice: Minority Voting Rights and the Undoing of the Second Reconstruction* (Chapel Hill: University of North Carolina Press, 1999), chap. 1.

6. Daniel W. Crofts, "Politics in the Antebellum South," in *A Companion to the American South,* ed. John B. Boles, pp. 176–190, Blackwell Companions to American History (Malden, Mass.: Blackwell, 2002), esp. pp. 181–185; James M. McPherson, *Battle Cry of Freedom: The Civil War Era* (New York: Oxford University Press, 1988), pp. 689–692; Peyton McCrary, Clark Miller, and Dale Baum, "Class and Party in the Secession Crisis: Voting Behavior in the Deep South, 1856–1861," *Journal of Interdisciplinary History* 8 (Winter 1978): 429–457.

7. Carl M. Brauer, *John F. Kennedy and the Second Reconstruction* (New York: Columbia University Press, 1977), pp. 112–113.

8. Thomas R. Rochon and Ikuo Kabashima, "Movement and Aftermath: Mobilization of the African-American Electorate, 1952–1992," in *Politicians and Party Politics,* ed. John Geer, pp. 102–124 (Baltimore: Johns Hopkins University Press, 1998); Harold W. Stanley, *Voter Mobilization and the Politics of Race: The South and Universal Suffrage, 1952–1984* (New York: Praeger, 1987).

9. Kousser, *Colorblind Injustice,* chap. 1. On debate and division within the Democratic Party amid the formation of the new Republican coalition of 1867–1868, see Edward L. Gambill, *Conservative Ordeal: Northern Democrats and Reconstruction, 1865–1868* (Ames: Iowa State University Press, 1981).

10. See Michael J. Klarman, "The Plessy Era," in *1998: The Supreme Court Review,* ed. Dennis J. Hutchinson, David A. Strauss, and Geoffrey R. Stone, pp. 303–414 (Chicago: University of Chicago Press, 1999), esp. p. 311.

11. Writing on October 2, 1882, to James G. Blaine, William E. Chandler presented himself as eager to secure the House. The Republican Party would not, however, be able to "carry as many seats in the North as two years ago," Chandler pointed out. How best, then, to secure the House? "We must increase our Southern representation. . . . That depends upon Republican support of the Democratic revolt in the South and the overthrow of the Bourbons there. . . . Every independent Democrat in the South pledges himself to a free vote, an honest count, the obliteration of race distinctions and popular education by the common school system. Shall we fail to follow our principles. . . ?" In the bargain white voters would be brought into coalition with black voters. For Chandler's letter, see Leon Burr Richardson, *William E. Chandler, Republican* (New York: Dodd, Mead, 1940), p. 346. (On Chandler's extensive involvement in and attention to southern affairs during Reconstruction, see pp. 76–82, 113–115, 158–160, 168–173.) The best treatment of this critical piece of oft-quoted evidence is in Vincent P. De Santis, *Republicans Face the Southern Question: The New Departure Years, 1877–1897* (Baltimore: Johns Hopkins University Press, 1959), pp. 156–158.

12. Jody Carlson, *George C. Wallace and the Politics of Powerlessness: The Wallace Campaigns for the Presidency, 1964–1976* (New Brunswick: Transaction, 1981), chap. 7.

13. Ibid., chap. 10; L. Sandy Maisel and Charles Bassett, eds., *Political Parties and Elections in the United States: An Encyclopedia* (New York: Garland, 1991), s.v. "American Independent Party."

14. Earl Black and Merle Black, *The Rise of Southern Republicans* (Cambridge: Harvard University Press, Belknap Press, 2002), pp. 246–248.

15. Herbert Brownell, with John P. Burke, *Advising Ike: The Memoirs of Attorney General Herbert Brownell* (Lawrence: University Press of Kansas, 1993), pp. 216–226; Carlson, *George C. Wallace,* ch. 10.

16. Dan T. Carter, *The Politics of Rage: George Wallace, the Origins of the New Conservatism, and the Transformation of American Politics* (New York: Simon and Schuster, 1995), pp. 354–364, quote at p. 364.

17. Steven F. Lawson, *In Pursuit of Power: Southern Blacks and Electoral Politics, 1965–1982* (New York: Columbia University Press, 1985), chap. 5; Dean J. Kotlowski, *Nixon's Civil Rights: Politics, Principle, and Policy* (Cambridge: Harvard University Press, 2001), chap. 3.

18. Lawson, *In Pursuit of Power,* chap. 8; Raymond Wolters, *Right Turn: William Bradford Reynolds, the Reagan Administration, and Black Civil Rights* (New Brunswick: Transaction, 1996), chap. 3 and p. 65.

19. On Reagan, see Black and Black, *Rise of Southern Republicans*, chap. 7; Nelson W. Polsby, *How Congress Evolves: Social Bases of Institutional Change* (New York: Oxford University Press, 2004), chap. 3; Donald Green, Bradley Palmquist, and Eric Schickler, *Partisan Hearts and Minds: Political Parties and the Social Identities of Voters* (New Haven: Yale University Press, 2002), chap. 6.

20. Byron E. Shafer and Richard G. C. Johnston, "The Transformation of Southern Politics Revisited: The House of Representatives as a Window," *British Journal of Political Science* 31 (October 2001): 601–626; Black and Black, *Rise of Southern Republicans*, chaps. 7–10.

21. Alexander P. Lamis, "The Two-Party South: From the 1960s to the 1990s," in *Southern Politics in the 1990s*, ed. Alexander P. Lamis, pp. 1–49, at p. 6 (Baton Rouge: Louisiana State University Press, 1999), quoting a South Carolina GOP official.

22. Donald R. Kinder and Lynn M. Sanders, *Divided by Color: Racial Politics and Democratic Ideals* (Chicago: University of Chicago Press, 1996), chap. 9; Tali Mendelberg, *The Race Card: Campaign Strategy, Implicit Messages, and the Norm of Equality* (Princeton: Princeton University Press, 2001), chaps. 5–6.

23. Black and Black, *Rise of Southern Republicans*, p. 108.

24. The basic source for this is still Michael Kelly, "Segregation Anxiety," *New Yorker*, 20 November 1995, pp. 43–54.

25. Carol M. Swain, *Black Faces, Black Interests* (Cambridge: Harvard University Press, 1995), and Swain, "The Future of Black Representation," *American Prospect*, Fall 1995, pp. 78–83; David Lublin, *The Paradox of Representation: Racial Gerrymandering and Minority Interests in Congress* (Princeton: Princeton University Press, 1997), pp. 104–114; David Lublin and D. Stephen Voss, "Racial Redistricting and Realignment in Southern State Legislatures," *American Journal of Political Science* 44 (October 2000): 792–810. See also Pamela S. Karlan, "Loss and Redemption: Voting Rights at the Turn of the Century," *Vanderbilt Law Review* 50 (March 1997): 291–326, at p. 303n35 and cites therein.

26. *Shaw v. Reno,* 509 U.S. 630 (1993). Quoted in Daniel Hays Lowenstein, *Election Law: Cases and Materials* (Durham: Carolina Academic Press, 1995), p. 235.

27. Kousser, *Colorblind Injustice*, chap. 8, David T. Canon, *Race, Redistricting, and Representation: The Unintended Consequences of Black Majority Districts* (Chicago: University of Chicago Press, 1999), chap. 2.

28. Quoted in Richard Valelly, "Voting Rights in Jeopardy," *American Prospect*, September–October 1999, pp. 43–49. See also Kousser, *Colorblind Injustice*, chap. 8. The phrase " 'wrongful districting' claim" is not mine and as far as I know belongs to Pamela S. Karlan.

29. Harold W. Stanley and Richard G. Niemi, *Vital Statistics on American Politics*, 5th ed. (Washington, D.C.: CQ, 1995), pp. 276–277.

30. *Miller v. Johnson,* 515 U.S. 900 (1995).

31. *Reno v. Bossier Parish School Board,* 528 U.S. 320, 341 (2000). Also disturbing is *Georgia v. Ashcroft,* 539 U.S. 461 (2003), whose significance I grasped too late for inclusion in the text.

32. See Keith J. Bybee, *Mistaken Identity: The Supreme Court and the Politics of Minority Representation* (Princeton: Princeton University Press, 1999), pp. 82–88.

33. *South Carolina v. Katzenbach,* 383 U.S. 301 (1966) (emphasis added); *Katzenbach v. Morgan,* 384 U.S. 641 (1966).

34. *Allen v. State Board of Elections,* 393 U.S. 544, 565, 566 (1969).

35. Lawson, *In Pursuit of Power*, chap. 8; Jerome J. Hanus, Paul Downing, and Donovan Gay, "The Voting Rights Act of 1965, as Amended: History, Effects, and Alternatives," Report No. 75-243 GGR (Washington, D.C.: Congressional Research Service, Library of Congress, June 17, 1975) (rev. November 19, 1975); "Statement by J. Stanley Pottinger, Assistant Attorney General, Civil Rights Division, Before the Subcommittee on Civil Rights & Constitutional Rights of the House Judiciary Committee on the Extension of the Voting Rights Act," 10:00 A.M., March 5, 1975, typescript in possession of the author. On the impact on Hispanic American electoral incorporation, see Amy Bridges, *Morning Glories: Municipal Reform in the Southwest* (Princeton: Princeton University Press, 1997); Rodolfo O. de la Garza and Louis DeSipio, "Save the Baby, Change the Bathwater, and Scrub the Tub: Latino Electoral Participation after Twenty Years of Voting Rights Act Coverage," in *Pursuing Power: Latinos and the Political System,* ed. F. Chris Garcia, pp. 72–126 (Notre Dame: University of Notre Dame Press, 1997).

36. *City of Mobile v. Bolden,* 446 U.S. 65, 65 (1980).

37. *Rogers v. Lodge* 458 U.S. 613 (1982); *Thornburg v. Gingles* 478 U.S. 30 (1986); Stephen G. N. Tuck, *Beyond Atlanta: The Struggle for Racial Equality in Georgia, 1940–1980* (Athens: University of Georgia Press, 2001), pp. 240–242; Richard H. Pildes, "The Politics of Race," review of *Quiet Revolution in the South,* ed. Chandler Davidson and Bernard Grofman, *Harvard Law Review* 108 (April 1995): 1359–1392; Peyton McCrary, "Bringing Equality to Power: How the Federal Courts Transformed the Electoral Structure of Southern Politics, 1960–1990," *University of Pennsylvania Journal of Constitutional Law* 5 (May 2003): 665–708, p. 699 and n. 186.

38. Pildes, "Politics of Race," pp. 1364, 1373; Samuel Issacharoff, Pamela S. Karlan, and Richard H. Pildes, *The Law of Democracy: Legal Structure of the Political Process* (Westbury, N.Y.: Foundation, 1998), pp. 443–499, esp. pp. 465, 499.

39. Ann Garity Connell, "The Lawyers' Committee for Civil Rights under Law: The Making of a Public Interest Law Group," Ph.D. diss., University of Maryland, 1997, chap. 3 and pp. 210–217, 223–225, 237–243, and appendix A.

40. 42 U.S.C. § 1973l(e) (emphasis added). See Mary Frances Derfner and Arthur D. Wolf, *Court Awarded Attorney Fees,* rev. prepared by Kevin Shirey (Lexis Publishing: December 2000), 3:5; United States Congress, Subcommittee on Constitutional Rights of the Committee on the Judiciary of the United States Senate, *Civil Rights Attorney's Fees Awards Act of 1976 (Public Law 94-559, S. 2278)—Source Book: Legislative History, Texts, and Other Documents,* 94th Cong., 2d sess. (Washington, D.C.: Government Printing Office, 1976).

41. Charles R. Epp, *The Rights Revolution: Lawyers, Activists, and Supreme Courts in Comparative Perspective* (Chicago: University of Chicago Press, 1998), esp. chaps. 2–4 and p. 3; Gregory A. Caldeira, "Litigation, Lobbying, and the Voting Rights Law," in *Controversies in Minority Voting: The Voting Rights Act in Perspective,* ed. Bernard Grofman and Chandler Davidson, pp. 230–260 (Washington, D.C.: Brookings Institution, 1992); McCrary, "Bringing Equality to Power," p. 697, providing a group portrait.

42. Caldeira, "Litigation, Lobbying, and the Voting Rights Law," p. 241.

43. Issacharoff, Karlan, and Pildes, *Law of Democracy,* pp. 443–499, esp. pp. 465, 499.

44. Kousser, *Colorblind Injustice,* p. 52.

45. Robert J. Kaczorowski, "The Chase Court and Fundamental Rights: A Watershed in American Constitutionalism," *Northern Kentucky University Law Review* 21 (Fall 1993): 151–191.

46. Lou Falkner Williams, *The Great South Carolina Ku Klux Klan Trials 1871–1872* (Athens: University of Georgia Press, 1996), pp. 101–102; Harold M. Hyman and William M. Wiecek, *Equal Justice under Law: Constitutional Development, 1835–1875* (New York: Harper

Torchbooks, 1982), pp. 467–468; Xi Wang, *The Trial of Democracy: Black Suffrage and Northern Republicans, 1860–1910* (Athens: University of Georgia Press, 1997), pp. 132–133, 207–208, 346–347, nn. 163–165.

47. Wang, *Trial of Democracy,* pp. 207–208.

48. *United States v. Harris,* 102 U.S. 629 (1883). For background, see Sidney Ratner, "Was the Supreme Court Packed by President Grant?" *Political Science Quarterly* 50 (September 1935): 343–358; C. Peter Magrath, *Morrison R.Waite: The Triumph of Character* (New York: Macmillan, 1963), chap. 1.

49. Scott L. James and Brian L. Lawson, "The Political Economy of Voting Rights Enforcement in America's Gilded Age: Electoral College Competition, Partisan Commitment, and the Federal Electon Law," *American Political Science Review* 93 (March 1999): 115–132.

50. Woodrow Wilson, *Congressional Government: A Study in American Politics,* 2d ed. (Boston: Houghton, Mifflin, 1885), p. 27. Martha Derthick first called my attention to this passage. See Wang, *Trial of Democracy,* chaps. 5–6; Robert Anderson Horn, "National Control of Congressional Elections," Ph.D. diss., Princeton University, 1942, chaps. 4–6.

51. *Ex parte Siebold,* 100 U.S. 371 (1879); *Ex parte Clarke,* 100 U.S. 399 (1879); *Ex parte Yarbrough* 100 U.S. 651 (1884). See Albie Burke, "Federal Regulation of Congressional Elections in Northern Cities, 1871–1894," Ph.D. diss., University of Chicago, 1968.

52. *Ex parte Siebold,* 100 U.S. 371, 396, 399 (1879).

53. *Ex parte Yarbrough,* 110 U.S. 651, 665 (1884).

54. Stanley B. Parsons, William W. Beach, and Michael J. Dubin, *United States Congressional Districts and Data, 1843 to 1883* (Westport: Greenwood, 1986), pp. 146–223.

55. Charles H. Stewart III, "Lessons from the Post–Civil War Era," in *The Politics of Divided Government,* ed. Gary W. Cox and Samuel Kernell, pp. 203–238, at p. 209 (Boulder: Westview, 1991).

56. Kirk H. Porter and Donald Bruce Johnson, comps., *National Party Platforms, 1840–1956* (Urbana: University of Illinois Press, 1956), p. 80.

57. Executive Committee of the Afro-American League to the Committee on Privileges and Elections of the Senate and House of Representatives, 22 January 1890, George Frisbie Hoar Papers, carton 44, folder titled January 20–23 1890, and carton 44, folder titled Petitions to Congress February—March 1890, Massachusetts Historical Society, Boston.

58. John R. Lynch to Hon. George F. Hoar, 22 August 1890, carton 46, folder titled August 19–22, 1890, George Frisbie Hoar Papers; Jacqueline M. Moore, *Leading the Race: The Transformation of the Black Elite in the Nation's Capital, 1880–1920* (Charlottesville: University Press of Virginia, 1999), pp. 7, 12, 134, 149. On Chalmers and Chandler, see Daniel Wallace Crofts, "The Blair Bill and the Elections Bill: The Congressional Aftermath to Reconstruction," Ph.D. diss., Yale University, 1968, p. 230.

59. Typescript copies of state party platforms provided to me by Richard Bensel and copied by him from contemporary sources; see Richard Franklin Bensel, *The Political Economy of American Industrialization, 1877–1900* (New York: Cambridge University Press, 2001), chap. 3, esp. pp. 102–117, 168–172. It is worth noting that Bensel and I might differ regarding what the platforms really say about intensity of interest in the Federal Elections Bill.

60. Crofts, "Blair Bill and Elections Bill," pp. 261–262; quote in Wang, *Trial of Democracy,* p. 237. On Spooner and Hoar's collaboration in bill drafting, see Richard E. Welch Jr., *George Frisbie Hoar and the Half-Breed Republicans* (Cambridge: Harvard University Press, 1971), p. 146.

61. Sarah A. Binder and Steven S. Smith, *Politics or Principle? Filibustering in the United States Senate* (Washington, D.C.: Brookings Institution Press, 1997), pp. 129–135.

62. In this connection, see Robert A. Margo, *Race and Schooling in the South, 1880–1950: An Economic History* (Chicago: University of Chicago Press, 1990), which underscores the relation between disenfranchisement and the sharp drop in state and local educational expenditures on African Americans in the South.

63. See, among others, Michael Jones-Correa, "The Origins and Diffusion of Racial Restrictive Covenanting," *Political Science Quarterly* 115 (Winter 2000–2001): 541–568; Gareth Davies and Martha Derthick, "Race and Social Welfare Policy: The Social Security Act of 1935," *Political Science Quarterly* 112 (Summer 1997): 217–235; Michael Klarman, "The Puzzling Resistance to Political Process Theory," *Virginia Law Review* 77 (May 1991): 747–832; Dona Cooper Hamilton and Charles V. Hamilton, *The Dual Agenda: The African-American Struggle for Civil and Economic Equality* (New York: Columbia University Press, 1997).

64. Jennifer L. Hochschild, "You Win Some, You Lose Some: Explaining the Pattern of Success and Failure in the Second Reconstruction," in *Taking Stock: American Government in the Twentieth Century,* ed. R. Shep Melnick and Morton Keller (New York: Cambridge University Press for the Woodrow Wilson Center, 1999), pp. 219–246, esp. p. 238.

65. W. E. B. Du Bois, "The Color Line Belts the World," in *W.E.B. Du Bois—A Reader,* ed. David Levering Lewis (New York: Holt, 1995), pp. 42–43.

66. John Gabriel Hunt, ed., *The Essential Abraham Lincoln* (Avenel, N.J.: Portland House, 1993), pp. 330–331.

Index